Rachael,

for your Confirmation
May 23rd, 1985

with much love
from
your Godmother, Maeve.

THE BOOK OF
BIBLE
KNOWLEDGE

Times change more than people.

The events of the Bible took place
almost 2000 years ago but it tells of people
who are really very like us.

As we explore their world, the Bible comes
alive to us in a new way.

Scripture Union

130 City Road, London EC1V 2NJ

THE BOOK OF
BIBLE
KNOWLEDGE

Contents

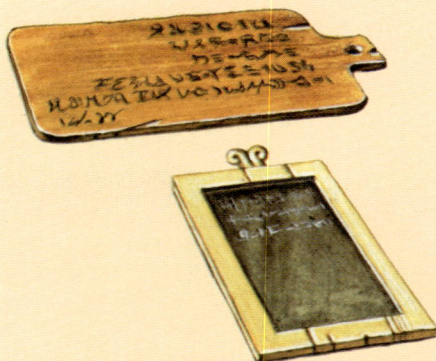

Consulting editors

F. F. Bruce MA, DD, PhD, Emeritus Professor, University of Manchester

Arthur Cundall BA, BD, Principal, Bible College of Victoria, Australia

Rosemary Mellor BEd, Teacher

Arthur Rowe MA, Lecturer in Religious Studies, Avery Hill College

Editors
Elrose Hunter BA
Paul Marsh BD

Picture research
Su Box
Elrose Hunter

Design
Tony Cantale

Illustrations & maps
Fred Apps
Simon Bull
Tony Cantale
Gary Chalk
Richard Deverell
Terry Gabbey
Paul Jones
Vic Mitchell

Index
Chris Pipe BA, A LA

© Scripture Union 1982

ISBN 0 86201 121 3

Printed in Italy by
New Interlitho S.p.A. Milan

Contributors

Arnold Anderson MA, BD. Senior Lecturer in Old Testament Studies, University of Manchester: *The Family*

John Balchin BD, MTh, Lecturer in Theology, London Bible College: *Religion*

The Rev. Michael Beaumont BA, BA (Theol): *Farming and Fishing*

John Bimson BA, PhD, Department of Biblical Studies, University of Sheffield: *Archaeology of the Bible*

F.F. Bruce MA, DD, FBA, Emeritus Professor, University of Manchester: *Translating the Bible*

George Cansdale BA, BSc, FLS, MIWES, Biological Consultant: *Animal Life*

George Cowling BSc, Dip Ed, BD, PhD, Senior Lecturer in Ancient History, Macquarie University, Australia: *Business and Trade*

The Rev. John Dunn: *Warfare*

Sheila Eastman BSc, Dip Th: former RE teacher: *The Story of the Bible*

Rachel Green Dip Th: *Clothes, Jewellery and Cosmetics*

R.K. Harrison PhD, DD, Professor of Old Testament, Wycliffe College, University of Toronto: *Health and Sanitation*

Colin Hemer MA, PhD, Librarian, Tyndale House, Cambridge: *Travel and Communication*

Nigel Hepper, BSc, FI Biol, Assistant Keeper, The Herbarium, Royal Botanic Gardens, Kew: *Plant Life*

The Rev. John Holdsworth BA, BD, MTh: *The Home*

E.A. Judge MA, Professor of History, Macquarie University, Australia: *Government and Administration*

Martin Nunn BA, Head of Geography, Caterham School: *Geography of the Bible lands*

David Payne BA, MA, Senior Lecturer and Head of Department of Semitic Studies, Queen's University, Belfast: *Contents of the Bible*

Rhona Pipe BD, teacher: *Sport and Leisure*

Arthur Rowe MA, Lecturer in Religious Studies, Avery Hill College: *Education and Training*

FOREWORD

The message of the Bible is as vitally relevant to the life of people today as ever it was — and not least to the life of young people.

But the Bible was written in different languages from ours; it tells of events that happened many centuries ago; the changing cultures which it reflects are not the changing cultures of the present day. If the message of the Bible is to be properly understood, then it is important to know something about the world in which it took shape, as well as to know the actual contents of the Bible. Who wrote the Bible? Why is it divided into two 'Testaments'? How did the people of Bible days live? What did they wear? What did they eat? How did they get about? How were they governed? How did they worship God? How has the Bible come down to us from those early days? Who translated it?

It is to provide answers to these and similar questions that this book has been published. The answers are given in words and pictures. The writers have made a special study of the subjects with which they deal, and many of them are experienced in communicating knowledge of this kind to young people. While the work has been produced with young people in mind, it will be surprising if older people do not also find much to interest and help them in its pages. It is a pleasure to introduce it, with the hope that it will be widely circulated and eagerly read.

F.F. BRUCE

Abbreviations

Books of the Bible

Names of Bible books are given in full the first time they appear in each article. Subsequently, the following abbreviations are used:

Gen.	Genesis	Mic.	Micah
Exod.	Exodus	Nah.	Nahum
Lev.	Leviticus	Hab.	Habbakuk
Num.	Numbers	Zeph.	Zephaniah
Deut.	Deuteronomy	Hag.	Haggai
Josh.	Joshua	Zech.	Zechariah
Judg.	Judges	Mal.	Malachi
Ruth	Ruth		
Sam.	Samuel	Matt.	Matthew
Kg.	Kings	Mark	Mark
Chron.	Chronicles	Luke	Luke
Ezra	Ezra	John	John
Neh.	Nehemiah	Acts	Acts
Esther	Esther	Rom.	Romans
Job	Job	Cor.	Corinthians
Ps.	Psalms	Gal.	Galatians
Prov.	Proverbs	Eph.	Ephesians
Eccl.	Ecclesiastes	Phil.	Philippians
Song of Sol.	Song of Solomon	Col.	Colossians
		Thess.	Thessalonians
Isa.	Isaiah	Tim.	Timothy
Jer.	Jeremiah	Titus	Titus
Lam.	Lamentations	Philm.	Philemon
Ezek.	Ezekiel	Heb.	Hebrews
Dan.	Daniel	Jas.	James
Hos.	Hosea	Pet.	Peter
Joel	Joel	John	John
Amos	Amos	Jude	Jude
Obad.	Obadiah	Rev.	Revelation
Jon.	Jonah		

Versions of the Bible

The following are referred to:

AV	Authorised Version
JB	Jerusalem Bible
NEB	New English Bible
NIV	New International Version
RSV	Revised Standard Version

THE STORY OF THE BIBLE

Have you ever thought how many different kinds of books there are on the shelves of a library? Story books, picture books, text books and dictionaries; books on nearly every subject you can imagine. But the Bible is a library in itself! It has sixty-six different books: some exciting stories, books of history and law, letters and love poems and books that look into the future. It is an ancient book which people all over the world have been reading for centuries, and which still speaks to people today.

The purpose of the Bible is to show us what God is like. A lot of ancient writings say nothing to us today, though they may be interesting as history. But the Bible is right up to date. First, because God does not change; the things we need to know about him are the same today as when the Bible was written. Second, though Bible people lived in a very different world, they felt sad and glad, frightened and excited just as we do. So we can learn from their writings how to trust God and obey him.

Light is an important theme in the Bible. Jesus called himself 'The Light of the World'; the Word of God is compared to light, showing the way.

The writers of the Bible

Most books that we read have the name of the author on the cover, though some special books like dictionaries and encyclopedias have a list inside of those who have contributed.

The Bible was written by over 35 different people; the first of them lived hundreds of years before Christ was born. There is no list of writers; some we know, others we do not.

The writers, though different, had one thing in common, they believed in God and listened to him. He is the 'Author' because the Bible brings his message. The writers wrote down the message God gave them and each book has the personal style of its writer.

The Bible is divided into the Old Testament and the New Testament. The Old Testament, which is about Jewish history and religion, contains thirty-nine books. Some of these writings are very old and we do not know when they were written or who wrote them.

A Hebrew scroll of the Torah (Old Testament law) in a hinged silver filigree case.

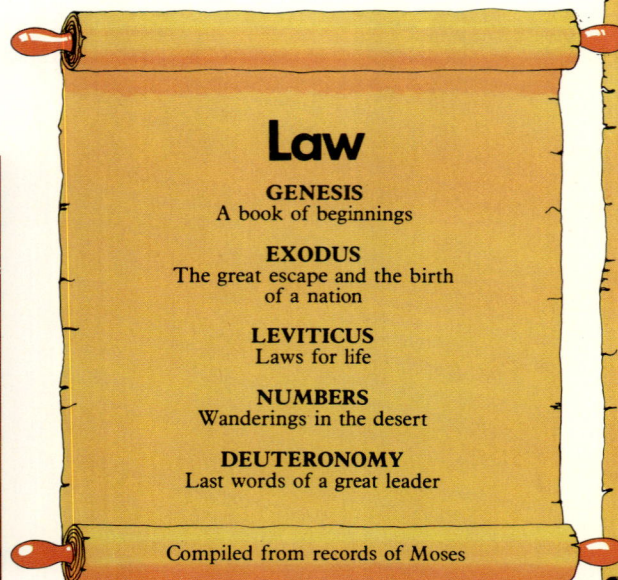

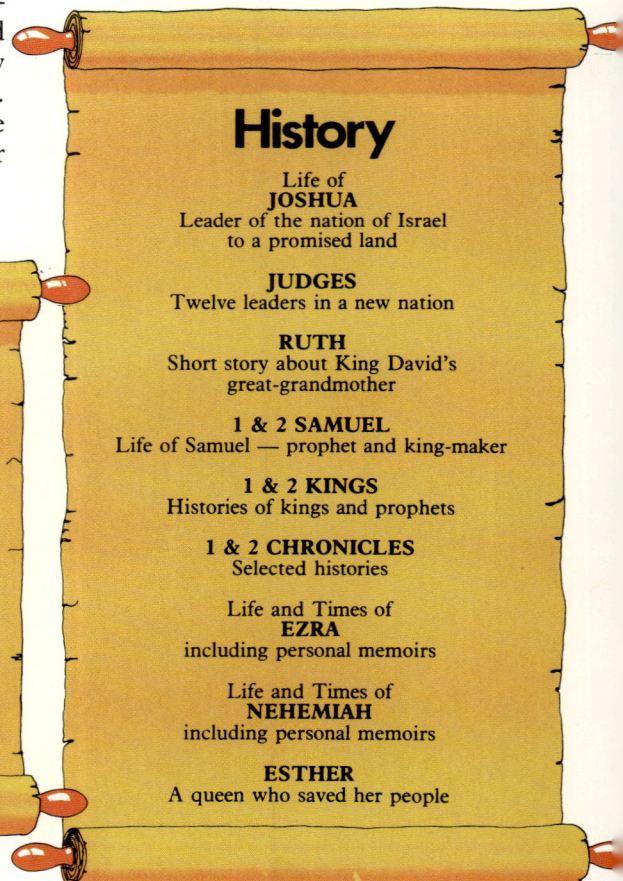

THE OLD TESTAMENT

The first five books are collections of writings. Moses received from God the laws for life and worship, and details for building their movable place of worship, the Tabernacle, or tent. All of Moses' writings were put together with ancient accounts of the creation and flood.

The books of Joshua, Judges, Ruth, Samuel and Kings are all histories. Records were kept of important events. There were court records of the lives of David and Solomon and other kings of Israel and Judah, as well as writings about the prophets Elijah and Elisha. These were put together by editors to show God's purposes through the history of his people. Some important kings in the ancient world, like Omri, who built the capital city of Samaria, got very little mention. Others like Josiah, who repaired the Temple and led his people away from idol worship back to the worship of God, were outstanding in God's view of history.

Incidents covered by the books of

Law

GENESIS
A book of beginnings

EXODUS
The great escape and the birth of a nation

LEVITICUS
Laws for life

NUMBERS
Wanderings in the desert

DEUTERONOMY
Last words of a great leader

Compiled from records of Moses

History

Life of
JOSHUA
Leader of the nation of Israel to a promised land

JUDGES
Twelve leaders in a new nation

RUTH
Short story about King David's great-grandmother

1 & 2 SAMUEL
Life of Samuel — prophet and king-maker

1 & 2 KINGS
Histories of kings and prophets

1 & 2 CHRONICLES
Selected histories

Life and Times of
EZRA
including personal memoirs

Life and Times of
NEHEMIAH
including personal memoirs

ESTHER
A queen who saved her people

Samuel and Kings are picked out and retold in the two books of Chronicles. It is possible that the same chronicler, or historian, may have written Ezra and Nehemiah as well. Personal records of Ezra and Nehemiah are included in these books.

The next group of books from Job to Songs include poetry and wise sayings. King David's name is connected with seventy-three of the psalms, sometimes as author, sometimes as collector. Like other ancient peoples, the Hebrews had a book of wise sayings, the book of Proverbs. King Solomon, who was known for his wisdom, added his wise words to this collection. 'The Preacher' of Ecclesiastes may also have been Solomon. The love poem, about the love between a beautiful girl and her prince, is sometimes called Solomon's Song.

The other sixteen books in the Old Testament are prophecies. The prophets sometimes wrote down their messages or dictated them, but mostly they spoke them to the people.

Their books are collections of their writings and teaching, and accounts of important events in their lives. Isaiah, Jeremiah and Ezekiel are called the major prophets.

The others are the minor prophets. Some of them preached and taught for as long as the major prophets, but we have only a few of their messages recorded.

Prophecy

Messages to Judah from
ISAIAH
with glimpses of the
coming Messiah

JEREMIAH
A collection of messages, poems
and acted parables

LAMENTATIONS
Poems about the fall of Jerusalem

EZEKIEL
Visions and messages for Hebrews
at home and in exile

DANIEL
Court Life in Babylon.
Accounts of miraculous escapes
from death, with records of dreams
and visions

HOSEA
Messages to Israel

JOEL
A poem about Judah

AMOS
Messages to Israel

OBADIAH
A poem about Edom

JONAH
A message for Nineveh

MICAH
Messages for Samaria and Judah

NAHUM
A poem about Nineveh

HABAKKUK
Warnings to cruel oppressors

ZEPHANIAH
Messages for Judah and
other nations

HAGGAI
A call to rebuild the Temple

ZECHARIAH
A message about rebuilding
Jerusalem

MALACHI
A call to return to God

Poetry

JOB
A man who faced life's problems

PSALMS
A collection of poems

PROVERBS
A collection of wise sayings

ECCLESIASTES
A look at life

SONG OF SOLOMON
A love poem

4

THE NEW TESTAMENT

The New Testament contains writings about Jesus' life, accounts of how the church started and grew, and letters from Paul and others.

From very early days Matthew, Mark, Luke and John were thought to have written the first five books of the New Testament. Matthew was the tax-collector who became a special friend of Jesus. Mark was a young man who went with Paul on his first missionary journey. He probably heard from Peter all about Jesus. Luke was a doctor who went with Paul on some of his missionary journeys. John was also one of Jesus' special friends who later became one of the leaders in the church at Jerusalem.

A Collection of Letters

Many of the letters in the New Testament are meant for groups of people, the churches in different cities. Just a few are addressed to individuals. The writers had something they wanted to say; sometimes to teach more about God and the good news, or to explain about living as a Christian, and at other times to answer questions and sort out problems. Thirteen of the letters were written by Paul. Some he wrote while on his journeys, others while he was in prison for preaching about Jesus Christ.

Peter wrote two letters; and John, the writer of the fourth Gospel, wrote three. James and Jude were probably the brothers of Jesus; they wrote their letters when they were old men. That leaves one letter, Hebrews. No one knows who wrote it and it is not addressed to a special place, though it is clearly meant for Jewish Christians. The last book, Revelation, has seven short letters in it, but most of it is about visions. The writer calls himself John. This was almost certainly John, the special friend of Jesus, who wrote a Gospel and the three short letters.

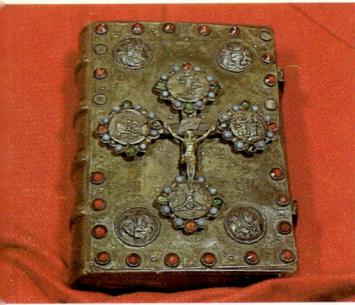

The cover of an old Armenian Bible, richly ornamented with jewels.

History

MATTHEW
Good news about Jesus

MARK
Good news about Jesus

LUKE
First book for Theophilus.
Jesus' life and teaching

JOHN
Good news about Jesus

THE ACTS
Second book for Theophilus.
How the church grew

Letters

PAUL'S LETTERS

ROMANS
For Christians in Rome

1 & 2 CORINTHIANS
For the church at Corinth

GALATIANS
For the churches in the area
of Galatia

EPHESIANS
Circular for churches at
Ephesus and around

PHILIPPIANS
For the church at Philippi.
Written in prison

COLOSSIANS
For the church at Colossae.
Written in prison

1 & 2 THESSALONIANS
For the church at Thessalonica

1 & 2 TIMOTHY
To his helper Timothy

TITUS
To his helper Titus

PHILEMON
To Philemon about his
slave Onesimus

OTHER LETTERS

HEBREWS
A letter to make faith strong.
For a group of Christian Jews

JAMES
Everyday advice to all
God's people

1 & 2 PETER
Circular letters to Christians
in trouble

1, 2 & 3 JOHN
Letters with one main message,
'Love one Another'

JUDE
Keep on believing in Jesus

Prophecy

REVELATION
Seven letters and visions
of heaven

The time-span of the Bible

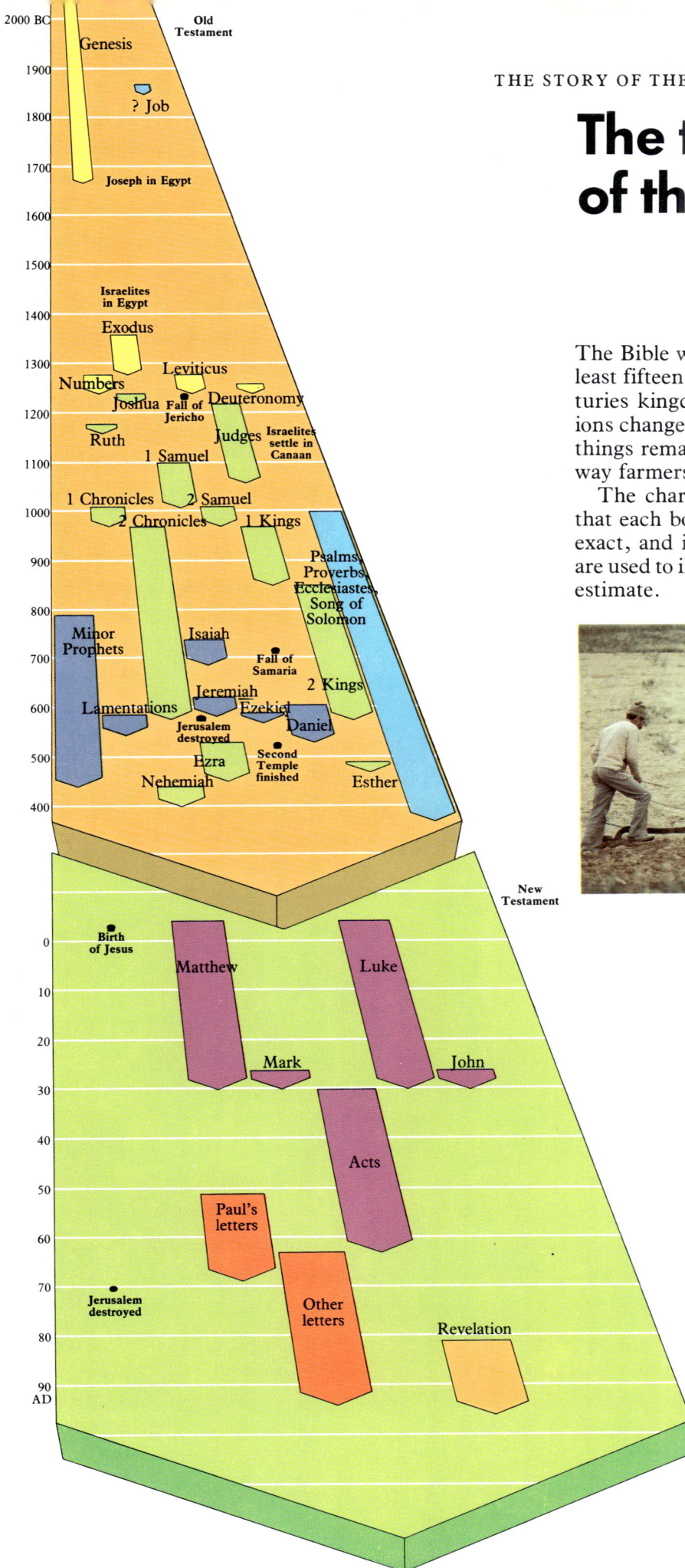

The Bible was written over a period of at least fifteen hundred years. Over the centuries kingdoms rose and fell, and fashions changed just as they do today. Other things remained much the same, like the way farmers did their work.

The chart helps us to see the periods that each book covers. The dates are not exact, and in some cases question marks are used to indicate that we are able only to estimate.

In the hilly country of Samaria farmers still use simple ploughshares drawn by a horse or donkey, as they did in Bible times.

Chart labels

2000 BC
1900
1800
1700
1600
1500
1400
1300
1200
1100
1000
900
800
700
600
500
400

Old Testament

Genesis
? Job
Joseph in Egypt
Israelites in Egypt
Exodus
Leviticus
Numbers
Deuteronomy
Joshua
Fall of Jericho
Ruth
Judges
Israelites settle in Canaan
1 Samuel
1 Chronicles
2 Samuel
2 Chronicles
1 Kings
Psalms, Proverbs, Ecclesiastes, Song of Solomon
Minor Prophets
Isaiah
Fall of Samaria
2 Kings
Lamentations
Jeremiah
Ezekiel
Jerusalem destroyed
Daniel
Ezra
Second Temple finished
Nehemiah
Esther

New Testament

0
10
20
30
40
50
60
70
80
90 AD

Birth of Jesus
Matthew
Luke
Mark
John
Acts
Paul's letters
Jerusalem destroyed
Other letters
Revelation

The different styles of writing

A poem, a newspaper report and a letter are three examples of different kinds of writing. The Bible has books just as varied as that. They are mostly grouped together, so we will look at the style in each group.

The Law

Not many of us have read a book of law, though we recognise notices that tell us what the law forbids, like road signs. The first five books were called The Law because they contained God's laws for life. The Jews call them the Torah, which means 'law' in Hebrew. Sometimes these books are given the Greek name, Pentateuch, meaning 'five scrolls'. God's laws were given to his people especially through Moses. God explained to them about worship and how they should carry out their religious ceremonies. The best known laws are summed up in the ten commandments (Exodus 20:1–17).

History

The history of God's people covering eight hundred years is in the next twelve books.

Whoever wrote these books collected together writings from many sources; there are official records of the kings, sayings of the prophets, prayers and accounts of important events like battles and coronations.

The story begins with Joshua leading the people in their conquest of the promised land of Canaan. The early rulers, the judges, were followed by the long line of kings. The nation split into two parts – Israel and Judah. The overthrow of first the northern kingdom of Israel by the Assyrians and then the southern kingdom of Judah by invading Babylonian forces led to forced exile. This part of the history is in the books of Joshua to Kings. Chronicles repeats part of the history.

David played the harp and wrote many psalms. His music soothed King Saul in fits of madness. This mosaic of David the harpist is from the floor of a synagogue in Gaza from the 5th century BC.

Esther tells of incidents in exile and Ezra and Nehemiah tell of the eventual return of God's people to their promised land.

Poetry and wisdom

The psalms are a collection of poems, songs and prayers which were used by the Israelites in their worship. A great range of thought and feeling is expressed. There are hymns of wonder and praise to God, as well as poems telling God about the wrong things in life; they are for sad and glad occasions. The books of wisdom, Proverbs, Job, and Ecclesiastes contain many everyday sayings and proverbs, but they also talk about difficult and important problems like suffering and the meaning of life. These books describe life that is 'wise' because it follows God's rules. The Song of Solomon is a collection of poems about the love of a man and a woman.

Prophecy

Prophets were men called by God to take his message to people. They spoke out strongly against all that was evil. People were warned that if they did not put their ways right and turn back to God they would be punished by invading armies. When their countries were destroyed and the people taken away to live in foreign lands the prophets encouraged them, and

reminded them that God still loved them.

Some messages were given to the prophets by dreams and visions, like Ezekiel who had a vision of a valley full of dry bones which came together and became a great army as God's Spirit breathed into them. This showed how God would restore the nation of Israel (Ezekiel 37:1–14).

Other messages were given direct from God. To make people pay attention sometimes the prophet acted a parable, like Jeremiah who took a pot and smashed it to show how God would break up and destroy Judah because of all the wrong that had been done (Jeremiah 19:1–13). People often ignored the prophets or ill-treated them.

Biography and history

Four pictures are given of the life of Jesus in the Gospels. They were written so that people could know about him: who he was, what he did and said, and how and why he died. Mark wrote his Gospel first and it is the shortest. He was interested in all that Jesus did, and it may be that he heard directly from Peter about him.

Matthew wrote his Gospel for Jewish readers. When describing the birth of Jesus he was careful to show that Jesus was a descendant of David. He recorded much of Jesus' teaching; he wanted to show that Jesus was the Messiah, the special leader the Jews were waiting for.

As a doctor Luke included many of Jesus' healing miracles in his account. He was also very interested in the poor and Jesus' concern for them. He addressed his Gospel to a Gentile called Theophilus, so he explained Jewish religious customs.

John's Gospel was the last and was very

The prophet Jeremiah compared the local potter working with his clay to God dealing with his people Israel.

different from the others. There is more of Jesus' teaching in John than the others. John assumed that people knew the facts about Jesus' life, so he picked out special events and miracles. He explained the importance of these 'signs' as he called them.

The Acts is the history book of the early church, covering about thirty years. It starts with the adventures of Peter and Paul as they took the good news about Jesus from Jerusalem to other cities in the Roman empire, and it ends with Paul in prison in Rome.

Letters

We all know how a letter begins today. Letters in New Testament times started with the name of the sender, then the name of the person who would receive it. Paul began many of his letters like this, for example, 'Paul an apostle of Jesus Christ . . . to Timothy . . .'. Sometimes the letters were addressed to a group of churches, or groups of Christians. Most of the letters were from Paul, though Peter, James and Jude wrote others. Only the letter to the Hebrews has no name of the sender.

Prophecy

The last book of the Bible, Revelation, was written by John to encourage Christians who were being persecuted. Like the Old Testament prophets, John saw visions which he described in vivid picture-language. These were of things that would happen on earth and in heaven, ending with a wonderful picture of a new heaven and a new earth. It is a difficult book to understand as we are not used to this kind of writing.

Left: Christ healing the blind. An illustration from a 17th century manuscript of the Gospels.

Right: The seven-branched lampstand (the Menorah) is still used in Jewish worship. In the book of Revelation it is a symbol of seven churches. This large Menorah stands outside the Parliament in Jerusalem.

Writing

When we think of writing we immediately think of paper and pen. But there are other materials and things with which we can write. Chalk is used on a blackboard, or carving on wood and stone, or engraving on metal. Ancient peoples used different methods as well. The very first picture signs were carved or drawn on stone, in caves, on rocks and on tablets – flat rectangular stones. Later, clay tablets were used, as the surface could be made smoother and it was easier to cut the marks. One of the reasons why cuneiform letters changed to wedge-shaped marks was because it was difficult to carve the curves of the earlier picture-letters on stone. Victories and other special occasions were recorded on monuments of stone which varied in shape and size.

Writing materials

Writing boards were in use before 1500BC. They were rather like the old-fashioned slate that was used in schools in the earlier part of this century. These boards were made of wood or ivory, and could have a hollow which would be filled up with wax. This made an easy surface for marking which could be replaced by putting in fresh wax. Sometimes the writing was done directly on the wood.

When we want to write a note we use a scrap of paper. People centuries ago wrote their notes, not on scraps of paper, but on pieces of broken pottery. A broken jug or bowl was no more use, but the pieces provided cheap writing material. Lots of these pieces of pottery have been found with bills, letters and notes written on them, and they tell us details about everyday life.

After the time of Christ a new way was found of putting together sheets of papyrus, leather or parchment. Instead of joining them lengthways into scrolls, a number of sheets were folded and fastened at one edge, just like our books. This was called a codex. It seems that the early Christians used this method as they collected together the Gospels and letters of the New Testament.

Writing tools

The earliest tool for writing must have been some sort of chisel which could cut stone or rock. A sharp pointed instrument called a stylus may have been used for cutting the softer surface of wax on a writing board, but no special type of stylus has been found, so probably anything with a sharp point was used. Writing on papyrus or parchment was done with a reed pen. The end of the reed was cut so that it was more like a brush. This was just right for drawing the picture letters. Gradually this reed brush was replaced by a quill pen. Ink was made from carbon (charcoal) mixed with gum or oil.

This obelisk to Queen Hatshepsut is the tallest obelisk still standing in Egypt. It is over 30 metres high and is covered with inscriptions about the greatness of the queen.

Ancient writing materials (clockwise from top left): official records were often inscribed on stone tablets and clay prisms; wooden hinged writing boards and an ivory writing board with a hollow for wax; on some writing boards the writing was done directly on the wood.

A clay stamp for impressing inscriptions on bricks, used in Mesopotamia in 2280 BC.

A seal of Darius, King of Persia, from the 5th century BC. The cylinder was made of soft stone and was rolled over clay or wax, leaving an impression.

'Papyrus'

Thousands of years ago the Egyptians discovered that they could make a type of paper from the papyrus reeds that grew in the swampy areas around the river Nile. It is a very large reed, growing to between three and six metres in height. The pith was taken out of the strong stems and cut into strips. These were laid in a row overlapping each other; then another layer of strips were laid across them. The two layers were then beaten into a flat sheet very like paper. These sheets were joined together length-ways to make a long piece which could be rolled up into a scroll. Scrolls were also made of leather and parchment, a specially prepared thin skin from sheep.

Papyrus reeds growing in a swamp.

This modern papyrus, showing papyrus reeds being cut, is a copy of a wall painting on an Egyptian tomb from 2600 BC.

An Egyptian tomb painting from 1400 BC showing a man with his wife and daughter hunting wild fowl in papyrus marshes.

Languages

Most of us learned how to read and write when we were quite young, so now we do it without thinking about it. We only begin to realise that it is not easy when we learn another language; especially if that language uses letters different from our alphabet, like Greek and Russian. We would find it even harder if we had to learn to read and write from right to left, like Persian writing, or from the top of the page to the bottom, like Chinese writing.

Hieroglyphs

The oldest known writing dates back to 3100BC in Babylon. It had about eight hundred simple pictures. The Egyptians made up their own picture symbols, called hieroglyphs. This was a difficult form of writing which they continued to use on monuments until the fifth century AD, although simpler types of handwriting were worked out by this time. For many centuries hieroglyphic writing was a mystery. No one could read it. Then a stone was found with a decree by Ptolemy V (about 196BC) written in three scripts: hieroglyphics, the simpler Egyptian handwriting and Greek. This made it possible to work out what the hieroglyphs stood for.

Cuneiform writing

In Babylon the pictures gradually began to stand for syllables, that is, parts of words. For example, the drawing of a bee followed by the drawing of a leaf could stand for the word 'belief', because the word sounds like that when it is said. These pictures were then simplified still further into patterns of wedge-shaped marks; this is known as cuneiform writing. This type of writing was used in a number of different languages until about the first century AD, just as today the Roman letters are used in English, French, Italian and other languages.

Hebrew

Hieroglyphic and cuneiform writing were difficult to learn, so only a few educated men, called scribes, could read and write. Other people who wanted to write their wills, or send a letter, or keep a note of an account, had to go to a scribe. If they wanted anything read they had to use the services of a scribe again. In Canaan around 1500BC an alphabet of 20 to 30 letters was worked out. Each symbol in the alphabet stood for a different sound. In this way a word could be made up by selecting the right letters from the alphabet. It was now possible for many more people to learn to read and write because it was much simpler, though scribes still did much of the writing and

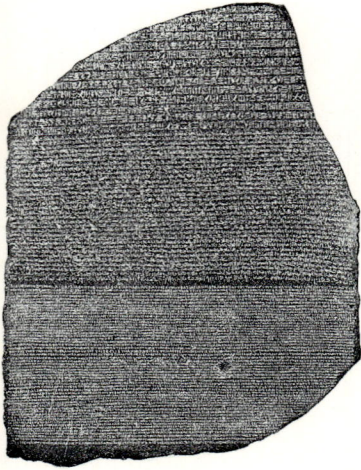

The Rosetta Stone, discovered in Egypt in 1799, was inscribed with a decree in three parallel scripts – Greek, Egyptian and hieroglyphic. It gave translators the vital key to the meaning of the hieroglyphs.

Right: The walls of the tombs in the Valley of the Kings, Egypt, were covered with murals and hieroglyphic texts in praise of the gods worshipped by the Pharaohs.

Far right: The sandstone pillars in the magnificent hall of columns at the Temple of Amūn, Egypt, are ornamented with reliefs and royal titles. Each of the pillars is about 3 metres in diameter and 17 metres tall.

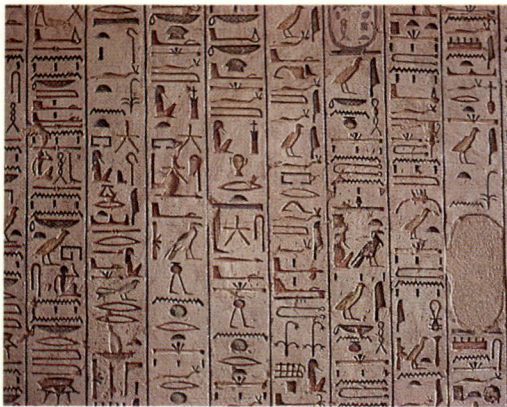

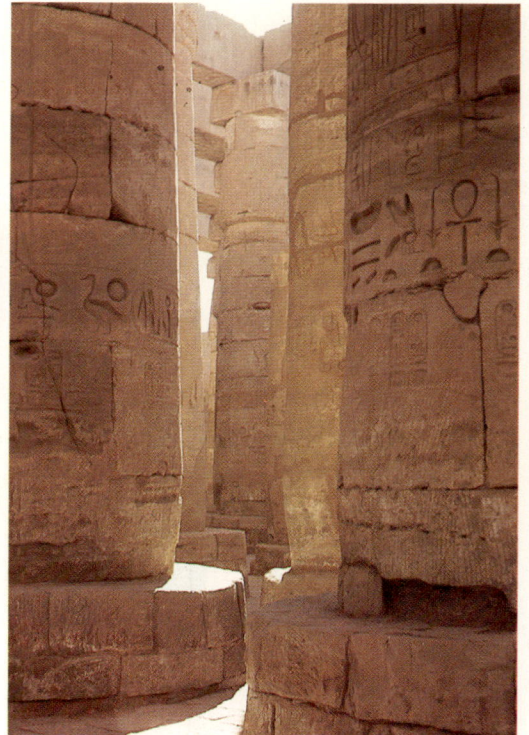

copying. Hebrew was one of the languages that used an alphabet. It had just twenty-two letters for the consonants, but no vowels. Unlike our language, Hebrew is written from right to left. It was in the Hebrew language that most of the Old Testament was written.

Greek

The Greeks learned the alphabet and made changes to suit their language. They were the first to have letters for the vowels as well as the consonants. The first two letters in the Greek alphabet, alpha and beta, have been joined to form our one word 'alphabet'. Greek became a language that was known and used over a wide area because of Alexander the Great's victories. So the New Testament was written in the 'common Greek' that was known by people in many of the Mediterranean countries.

A Hebrew scroll on parchment of part of the book of Esther.

Greek writing on The Rock of Inscription, Sinai, where camel caravans camped. It reads, 'The wife of Stephanus, the Katerina Monastery architect, was going to visit her husband with her little daughter, who hasn't seen her father for many years'.

Left: Jews reading from the Torah at a Bar-Mitzvah ceremony at the Western Wall in Jerusalem.

Below: Greek mosaic in the Church of the Loaves and Fishes beside the Sea of Galilee.

12

Collection into the Old Testament and the New Testament

There are thirty-nine books in our Old Testament. We do not know when they were first collected together. The Jews say that Ezra the scribe, who wrote one of the books in the Old Testament, first collected and arranged the books. This is not certain; but we do know which books were in the Bible at the time of Jesus. Most of the books in our Old Testament are quoted somewhere in the New Testament, so Jesus and his disciples took these thirty-nine books as their Scriptures. Also

Below: In the first century AD the Christians in Rome used to meet secretly underground in the Catacombs because they were persecuted by the Roman authorities. Letters from Paul and the other apostles were read aloud. The same letters in our Bible today are still read aloud when Christians meet for worship (below right).

the scrolls found near the Dead Sea contained parts of all our Old Testament books except Esther; in the first century BC these thirty-eight books were obviously considered important. The Greek translation included a few other books which we call the Apocrypha. These books are not accepted as part of the Scriptures by many Christians.

We are more certain about how the New Testament came together. It was important to have a record of the life, death and resurrection of Jesus which would remain when the first disciples who were witnesses of these things, died. So the Gospels, accounts of Jesus' life and teaching, were of great importance to the early Christians, and were read whenever they met for worship. The letters, written by Paul, Peter and others, were shared because they gave general advice about the Christian life. Luke's book of Acts explained how the Church started and spread into Europe. Some books like Hebrews and Revelation were not used and read much until the third century AD. The twenty-seven books which we have in our New Testament gradually came to be accepted by the early Church and recognized as inspired by God. Other books written about Jesus' life were not considered of the same value, and were rejected.

How the Bible text was preserved

As we have seen, men have been able to write for thousands of years. Moses wrote down the rules that God gave him for the people of Israel. He told them clearly, 'Do not add to what I command you, and do not subtract from it.' (Deuteronomy 4:2) These laws with the historical records and the writings of the prophets were carefully copied by trained scribes.

The Scribes
Scribes were men who had learned to read and write; they were considered very important. The king had his own scribes, and amongst the priests and prophets there were scribes whose special job was to copy the laws of Moses and the writings of the prophets. Ezra was both a priest and a scribe. Later on, by the second century BC most scribes were priests. From this time and into New Testament times the

scribes began to explain the Old Testament writings and to apply them to everyday life. In the New Testament we read about the scribes, or lawyers, who taught the law and added many extra rules for every good Jew to keep.

Josephus, a Jewish historian, said, '. . . no one has ventured either to add, or to remove or alter a syllable (of the scriptures) . . . every Jew . . . regards them as the decrees of God.' So the scribes carefully checked their manuscripts, their hand-written work; they even counted the number of lines to be sure nothing was missed out. They wrote down which manuscript they were copying, and whether there was any damage to the text. Sometimes a second scribe went through the work. When the new manuscript was completed and checked, the old one was destroyed. Later, groups of scribes would write while a head scribe dictated, so producing several copies of one manuscript. But to produce one copy of any manuscript took a long time, so they were very valuable.

The Massoretes
About five hundred years after Christ the work of the scribes was taken over by the Massoretes (which means transmitters)

A Rabbi of Jesus' time reading from a scroll like those used in a synagogue.

Assyrian scribes recording booty after a battle. Part of a wall frieze at Nineveh from the 7th century BC.

Fragments of a Coptic translation of St John's Gospel, written on papyrus.

Right: A team of Japanese translators at work on a Bible translation.

Below: Work on the preservation of the Dead Sea Scrolls in an Israel museum laboratory.

who saw their job as passing on the Old Testament just as they had received it. They took even greater care than the scribes. They counted every word and noted the middle word of what they had copied; and they even counted every letter.

For many years the very oldest copy of the Hebrew Old Testament available was one by the Massoretes in the ninth century AD. Because old manuscripts were destroyed it seemed unlikely that anything older would be found. Then in 1947 a shepherd boy discovered some very ancient scrolls in a cave near the Dead Sea. In the first century there had been a 'monastery' at Qumran by the Dead Sea. When the Romans threatened invasion, the library from the monastery was hidden in the Qumran caves. Because these caves were dry the scrolls lay there undisturbed for over two thousand years.

Following the shepherd boy's discovery, the caves were thoroughly searched and parts of all the Old Testament books were found. Amazingly, there was very little difference between these manuscripts and the ninth-century Massoretic ones, which were a thousand years later. Obviously, the scribes had obeyed Moses' command and had been very careful in their copying.

The Septuagint

Two hundred and fifty years before Christ came the Old Testament was translated into Greek. It is said that seventy men worked on the translation, which is therefore called the Septuagint – meaning 'The Seventy' in Latin – and is often referred to by the Roman number 'LXX'. Later there were other translations into Greek as well as Latin, Syriac and Coptic (an old Egyptian language).

If we look at the time-chart on page 5 we can see that all the New Testament was written by AD100. The earliest papyrus fragment of the Gospels dates from AD100–150. There are many ancient manuscripts of the New Testament which can be used to help us produce reliable translations. By the third century AD, the New Testament had also been translated into Latin, Syriac and Coptic for Christians who did not speak Greek.

THE CONTENTS OF THE BIBLE

The Bible is the story of what God has done for the world and for all the people who live in it. There are 66 different books in the Bible, written by all sorts of different people, but there is really only one story – a long story, of course, covering several thousand years.

The earth seen from space with the continent of Africa clearly visible.

The Old Testament

Adam and Eve

The book of **Genesis** begins the story. First it tells how God made everything and everybody (Genesis 1, 2). In seven days he made the whole universe: the sky with the sun, moon and stars, the world with all the trees and plants, and then all the animals, birds and fishes. Last of all he made human beings. The first man and woman were called Adam and Eve, and God prepared a lovely home for them, called the Garden of Eden (Gen. 3). They had everything they could wish for, but very soon they disobeyed God, when they ate the fruit of a tree which God had forbidden them to touch. God punished them for this: he would not let them stay in Eden, and when they left it, their troubles began.

A drawing of Adam and Eve with the Tree of Knowledge from a 13th century Bible and prayer book.

They now had to work very hard as farmers to grow the food they needed. They began to suffer aches and pains. When they began to have children, serious quarrels started, and their eldest son Cain hated his brother Abel, and eventually killed him (Gen. 4).

Noah and the Flood

Adam and Eve had other children, and they in turn had many children and grandchildren, and after many years there were many people living in the part of the world which we call the Near East. Very few of them were good people; most of them were very wicked in all their behaviour. Presently the day came when God decided that he would punish them all. Only one man pleased God by his behaviour: he was called Noah, and God made sure that Noah, his wife and his family would not be hurt. God's plan was to send a terrible flood, which would be so deep that all human beings and animals would be drowned (Gen. 6).

Long before the flood came, God warned Noah about what was going to happen, and told him how to build a special boat, called the ark. It had to be big enough to carry not only Noah and his family but also many animals and birds. God planned that a few animals and birds of every kind should be kept alive; otherwise there would have been no creatures left alive after the Flood.

All this work took a long time, but the day came when Noah and his family, and all the creatures he had collected, went into the ark. Then the waters came: it began to rain heavily, and the rain did not stop until even the highest mountains had been covered, so everybody was drowned. No people escaped except Noah and his family, and no animals escaped except those in the ark (Gen. 7, 8).

So the world had a new beginning, with one family of human beings, and one family each of all the creatures. They all had children, however, and presently there were once again many people and many creatures in the world. Genesis chapter 10 gives a list of ancient nations after the Flood. Once again, many people were disobedient to God, but there were some good men and women too.

God gave Noah the exact dimensions for the ark. It was 133 metres long, 22 metres wide and 13 metres high. The boat was coated on both sides with bitumen to make the wood waterproof.

Abraham

After many years, there lived a man called Abraham with his wife Sarah. At first their home was in a city called Ur, in a country now called Iraq. God had special plans for him. God planned that there should be one special nation in the world, one nation that would serve him in a special way. God chose Abraham and Sarah to be the parents of that future nation. He had also chosen the land he wanted that nation to live in – the land of Israel (often called Palestine). So God called Abraham (Gen. 12) and told him he must travel all the way to the land which would one day be called Israel. Abraham quickly obeyed, and left his old home behind. When he reached the land promised to him, he made his home there, although he moved about to different parts of the country, because he had great flocks and herds. He had a son called Isaac (Gen. 21), and Isaac had a son called Jacob (Gen. 25).

Joseph

Abraham, Isaac and Jacob sometimes did wrong, but they all loved God and did their best to please him. God looked after them too, and they became rich. Jacob had twelve sons, who are very important, because each one was the father of a big 'family' or tribe in the nation of Israel (Gen. 35:22–26). In fact, one son was the father of *two* tribes. His name was Joseph,

and his story is told in the last chapters of Genesis. God promised Joseph that he would be more important than his older brothers, and this made them very jealous. Their father Jacob tried to protect him, but when they got the chance they seized him, and sold him to some traders as a slave. The traders took him from his own country into the neighbouring land, Egypt, and there he lived for the rest of his life (Gen. 37). At first he was a slave, and

Joseph organised the grain stores of Egypt during the seven years of famine. This Egyptian tomb painting shows the measuring and recording of the grain crop.

ABRAHAM

At God's command Abraham and his family left Mesopotamia and travelled over 1000 miles to Canaan. God promised to give Canaan to Abraham and his descendants.

Abraham led a semi-nomadic life in Canaan, living in tents and moving his large flocks and herds in search of pasture.

Abraham and Sarah grew old and still they had no children. One day three men arrived at their tent and announced that Sarah would have a son.

Some time later God tested Abraham's obedience by telling him to offer up his son Isaac as a sacrifice.

When God saw that Abraham trusted him, he stopped him at the last moment. Abraham is regarded as the founder of the Jewish nation.

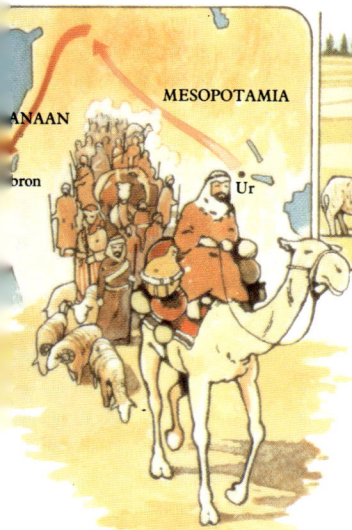

When the Israelites left Egypt they asked the Egyptians for gold and silver jewellery. These Egyptian gold earrings are from the same period.

Far right: The original Passover meal consisted of roast lamb, unleavened bread and bitter herbs. The people were dressed ready to leave and ate standing up, their staffs in their hands.

he was even put in prison for a time; but God looked after him, and eventually he was able to help the king of Egypt (Pharaoh). As a result the king raised him to a very high position in the land. Joseph became the chief government minister in charge of food supplies (Gen. 41). Food was in very short supply for seven years, both in Egypt and in neighbouring lands, and so Joseph invited his father and his brothers to come to Egypt where they could get food from the stores which Joseph had arranged.

In this way the whole family of Jacob moved to Egypt (Gen. 46), and they all stayed there for many, many years, long after Jacob and Joseph had died.

Moses
The book of **Exodus** tells the story of how Jacob's descendants left Egypt to return to Canaan, the land which God had promised to Abraham. An Egyptian king had made

MOSES
Moses was born in Egypt at a time when the Pharaoh decreed that all Hebrew boy babies should be killed at birth. His mother hid him in a reed basket by the river where he was found and adopted by Pharaoh's daughter.

When Moses had grown up he tried to help the Hebrew slaves but had to flee from Egypt because he killed an Egyptian. God spoke to him out of a burning bush in the desert and told him to go back and lead his people out of Egypt.

Moses and his brother Aaron went to Pharaoh and asked him to release the Israelites to hold a feast to God in the desert. Pharaoh refused and God sent ten plagues on Egypt before Pharaoh relented.

Moses led the Israelite nation out of Egypt. They rebelled against God and had to wander in the desert for 40 years. During this time God gave Moses the Ten Commandments. Moses died before the Israelites reached Canaan.

the Israelites his slaves, and ill-treated them cruelly. Among other things, he killed all baby Israelite boys. One baby boy escaped, because his mother hid him. His name was Moses. A princess found him, and he was brought up in the king's palace (Exodus 2). When he grew up, he was called by God to rescue the Israelites from slavery, and lead them back home to their own land. At first the Egyptian king would not let them go, so God punished him and his people with ten disasters (called 'plagues'). Even then the Egyptian army chased after the Israelite people, but God saved them by a miracle: he parted the waters of the sea and let them walk across on dry land – but the Egyptian soldiers were drowned (Exod. 14). The Israelites held a special festival to celebrate their escape from Egypt; it is called the Passover (Exod. 12).

The Covenant and the Law
Moses led the Israelites into the desert, to a mountain called Sinai (Exod. 19). There God made a special agreement with Israel: he promised to be their God and to look after all their needs, and they promised to obey him in every way. This special agreement was called 'the covenant'. God told them what laws he wanted them to obey. The most important of these laws are known as the Ten Commandments (Exod. 20). God also gave instructions to Moses about matters of worship. The Israelites were told to make a 'tabernacle', a large tent which could be folded up and carried through the desert. This tent was the place where the Israelites worshipped,

offering animals as sacrifices to God. Moses' brother Aaron became the first priest in charge of this holy tent.

Reaching the promised land

The Israelites spent 40 years wandering in the deserts between Egypt and Canaan, the land promised to them. The books of **Leviticus, Numbers** and **Deuteronomy** tell about these wanderings. Moses died just before his people marched into Canaan, and Joshua became their leader. It was Joshua who led the Israelites into Canaan. First they had to cross the river Jordan, and then they had to capture the city of Jericho. This city had huge walls all round it, and the Israelites could not break them down; but God was on their side, and, by a miracle, the walls suddenly fell down flat, and the Israelite soldiers were able to march in and take the city (Joshua 6).

They went on to capture other big cities, and made Canaan their own land at last. Afterwards the whole country was divided up, so that every tribe could have its own part of Canaan to live in.

Below: Sunrise across the Sinai mountains from the peak of Mt. Moses. God gave Moses the Ten Commandments on Sinai.

Bottom: Bedouin tents by the Jericho road.

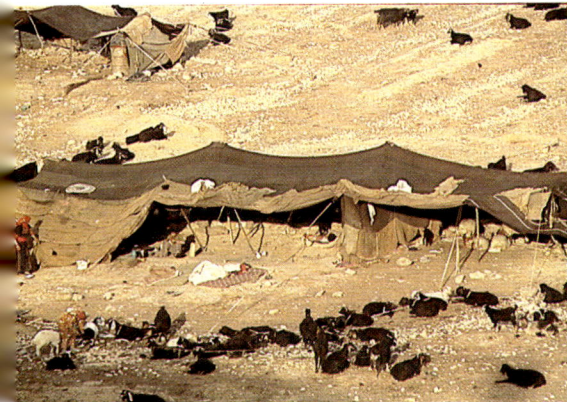

The judges

Although they now lived in their own land, the Israelites had many problems and many enemies. Often they began to forget God, and went to the temples of other gods instead. God was angry when they did this, and after a time he punished them by allowing a foreign enemy to attack them. At last the Israelites turned back to their own God, and begged him to help them get rid of the enemy. Then God chose a man to lead them in battle, and the result was that the enemy was defeated and driven away. The man chosen by God to lead the Israelites was called a 'judge' in those days, but we should probably call him a general.

But after some years the Israelites forgot what had happened, and once more they turned away from God; once more he allowed an enemy to invade their country, and once more they turned back to God and he found another leader or judge for them. This kept on happening for many, many years.

One famous judge was Gideon, who defeated a large foreign army, even though his own little army had only 300 men in it (Judges 7). Another judge was Samson, a very strong man who helped his people against the Philistines, one of

A Canaanite jar from Jericho dating back to the 15th century BC. The Israelites invaded a country where crafts and trading were advanced but where primitive worship of idols involved human sacrifice and other cruel customs. The ivory below from Calah in Assyria shows the pagan fertility goddess Ishtar. It dates from the 9th century BC and may have been a house shrine.

An Egyptian relief showing captives from Palestine. The central figure is a Philistine; the others are Israelites.

Solomon's Temple was looted and sacked by Babylonian invaders in 587 BC. This model is a reconstruction of his temple.

Israel's worst enemies. Samson had never cut his hair, because he knew that if he did, he would lose all his strength; but one day his wife tricked him and cut his hair off when he was asleep. Then the Philistines were able to capture him (Judg. 16).

The first kings

After this the Philistines became stronger and stronger. The last judge was called Samuel, and he led his people against the Philistine soldiers, and won a victory (1 Samuel 7). But the Israelites became frightened of the Philistines, and they told Samuel that what they really needed was a king to lead them into battle. God gave them permission, and the first man chosen to be king over Israel was Saul (1 Sam. 9). At once the Philistines attacked Israel again, but Saul was able to win several battles against them. He was a clever soldier, and so was his son Jonathan; but Saul disobeyed God's instructions so badly that God decided to choose another king, and he sent Samuel to pick the right man. A young shepherd boy called David was chosen (1 Sam. 16). Soon afterwards David visited his brothers, who were soldiers fighting against the Philistines, and he found that a Philistine giant called Goliath was terrifying the Israelites. David bravely marched forward to fight the giant and was able to kill him by using a sling, which was a sort of catapult (1 Sam. 17).

David came to the palace afterwards, and became a great friend of Jonathan. King Saul was friendly to him at first, but really he hated David and before long he tried to kill him. In the end David had to run away for his life.

Saul and Jonathan were both killed in battle (1 Sam. 31), and the Philistines seemed to have won the war. But now God's promise to David came true, and he became king. His first job was to defeat the Philistines, and to drive their army right out of the land. He also managed to defeat other enemies, and he captured several countries around Israel, so that his kingdom became big and strong. The most important city which he captured was Jerusalem, which he made the capital of his kingdom.

The books of **Samuel** tell the story of the first two kings of Israel, Saul and David, and the books of **Kings** and **Chronicles** tell about all the other kings. David's son Solomon became king after his father, and in his reign Israel remained strong, and was very rich. Solomon built a wonderful temple in Jerusalem, to replace the tent which Moses had made long ago as a place of worship (1 Kings 6–8).

David was a musician as well as a king, and wrote many songs, called psalms. The book of **Psalms** in the Old Testament contains many of his psalms. His son King Solomon was famous for his wisdom and many of his wise sayings are written in the books of **Proverbs** and **Ecclesiastes**.

The two kingdoms

After Solomon died, his son Rehoboam became king, but he was not a wise man like his father. Many people in the north-

DAVID

David was a shepherd boy when he was secretly anointed king of Israel by the prophet Samuel.

His skill in using a sling and his trust in God enabled him to kill the Philistine giant Goliath. The Israelite army routed the Philistines.

David played the harp and wrote many psalms. He played to King Saul to soothe him in his fits of madness.

David reigned as king for 33 years. He was a brave and skilful commander and his army conquered many surrounding hostile nations.

David led the nation in the worship of God. He brought the Covenant Box, which was a symbol of God's presence, to Jerusalem. David led the procession with dancing and singing.

ern part of the kingdom thought they were being treated unfairly; but when they complained, Rehoboam threatened to make things worse! As a result, his kingdom split up into two parts. Rehoboam still ruled the southern part, called the kingdom of Judah, and he kept the city of Jerusalem as his capital (1 Kings 12). But the northern part of the country refused to obey Rehoboam, and set themselves up as a new kingdom, with their own kings. (They kept the name 'Israel' for their kingdom). From now on the nation was divided into two, and both kingdoms were small and weak. Several great foreign nations attacked them, invading their land and taking away a great deal of money and other treasures.

Eventually the kingdom of Israel came to an end, when the powerful armies of a country called Assyria invaded it. The Assyrians killed many Israelites, and took many others far away from their own land (2 Kings 17); the kingdom of Israel never had kings again.

The small kingdom of Judah lasted longer, but the time came when another powerful nation, the Babylonians, invaded it. Jerusalem was destroyed, and so was the Temple. Many of the people (known as 'Jews' because they came from 'Judah') were taken as prisoners to far-away Babylon; the last Jewish king was one of the prisoners (2 Kings 25). For about 70 years these Jews remained in Babylon, forbidden to return to their own land; this period is known as 'the Babylonian Exile'.

Ezra, Nehemiah and Esther

The books of **Ezra** and **Nehemiah** tell us about some of the things that happened after the Exile. The Exile ended when a Persian king called Cyrus conquered the Babylonians, and allowed the Jews in Babylon to return home. So many Jews went home, where they soon rebuilt the Temple. They gradually built houses in Jerusalem, and later on they were able to repair the city walls.

The book of **Esther** tells a story about some Jews who had not returned to Jerusalem, but who still lived far away to the East. Both in Jerusalem and elsewhere, the Jews were unable to help themselves against strong nations like the Persians; but they knew that they could trust God to look after them.

The Prophets

The last books of the Old Testament

Part of an 8th century BC frieze from Nimrud in Assyria, showing the capture of a town. During this period Assyria was building up a mighty empire and its army invaded Israel, carrying away many captives.

ELIJAH

Elijah's first assignment as prophet was to tell King Ahab that God was sending three years of drought. Elijah went into hiding on God's orders.

After three years Elijah summoned Ahab and the prophets of Baal, a heathen god, to a public challenge to show which God was true and real.

Baal's followers failed to make their god send fire from heaven. When Elijah prayed, God sent fire and the Israelites were convinced of his power.

Ahab's wife, Jezebel, planned to kill Elijah and he fled for his life to the mountains. There God spoke to him and assured him of his protection.

God told Elijah to appoint Elisha to succeed him as prophet. One day when they were walking together, horses and a chariot of fire came between them and Elijah was taken up to heaven in a whirlwind.

During the 5th century BC many Jewish exiles were allowed to leave Babylon and return to their homeland. Under the leadership of Nehemiah they rebuilt the walls of Jerusalem which had been destroyed by the Babylonians. The builders were threatened by hostile governors of neighbouring provinces but they kept on working, with weapon in one hand and tool in the other.

Ruth worked in the fields of Bethlehem as a gleaner during the barley harvest.

(from **Isaiah** to **Malachi**) are the books of the 'prophets'. From the time of Samuel and David, there had been many men in Israel who heard God calling to them. God sent these prophets to speak to kings and to preach in the open air to the people. He gave them all sorts of different messages, which were written down in these Bible books. Sometimes the prophets accused the people of disobedience to God's laws; but often they promised wonderful things, because God had wonderful plans for his people. The most important promise of all was that one day God would send them another king, from the family of David. This king, the prophets said, would be the greatest king Israel would ever have. He would make the country rich and peaceful, and he would not allow any wicked men to ill-treat other people in any way. This king would defeat Israel's enemies and become king over all the world. (See especially Isaiah 9:2–7).

Other books

There are three other Old Testament books. The book of **Ruth** tells the story of a foreign girl who came to live in the land of Israel, at Bethlehem. She became famous because King David was her great-grandson.

The book of **Job** tells of a rich man who lost everything he owned and became very ill (Job 1). He was very angry with God, so three of his friends came along to argue with him, and tried to change his mind. Most of the book tells about their conversations. Eventually God Himself spoke to Job, and the story ends happily (Job 42).

The **Song of Solomon** is a long poem, made up of a conversation between two lovers, telling each other about their love.

Between the Testaments

For several hundred years after the exile in Babylon, the Jewish people were ruled by foreigners. After the Persians the Greeks were their rulers. One Greek king, called Antiochus, attacked the Jews and tried to stop them from worshipping God. Before long, the Jews decided to fight back, and they defeated several Greek armies (the story is told in the Books of Maccabees, in the Apocrypha). The Jewish leader was called Judas Maccabaeus.

For nearly 100 years afterwards the Jews had their own kings once again, but

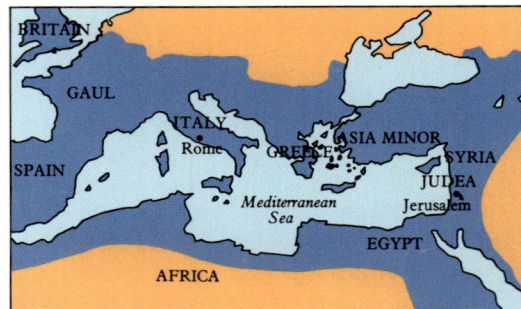

The Roman Empire at the time of Christ (in blue).

The Jews were ruled by Greek kings during the 2nd century BC and used their currency. These coins show (left) Antiochus VI, 144 BC and (right) Tryphon who seized the throne and murdered him.

Below right: A typical large synagogue showing: 1 – the shrine where the sacred Torah scrolls were kept, 2 – pulpit, 3 – gallery for the women and children, 4 – extension containing school rooms and guest rooms for pilgrims.

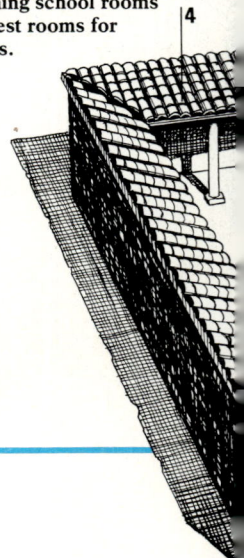

then the Romans came along and conquered all the lands of the Eastern Mediterranean, including the Jews' land (now called Judea). The Romans ruled Judea, but sometimes they set a Jewish king over the Jews, although he had to obey the Romans, of course. One such king was Herod, who was reigning in Jerusalem when Jesus was born (Matthew 2:1).

During all these years, many Jews had obeyed God's laws and worshipped him, both in the Temple and in local places of worship called 'synagogues'. They did not like their foreign rulers, nor did they like evil men like Herod; all the time they longed for the day when God's promises would come true, especially His promise to send His chosen king, who would be of David's family. They waited hopefully for this king, whom they called 'the Messiah' (or 'the Christ'). The New Testament tells how God's promises came true.

Above: Excavations of the remains of a synagogue in Capernaum from the 2nd century AD. The pillars supported the balcony for women.

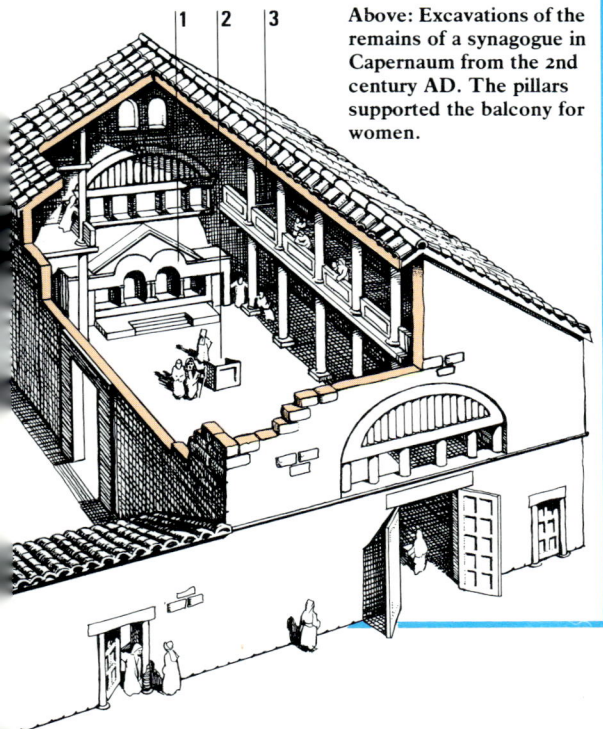

The New Testament

The first four books of the New Testament tell how God's promises came true. These four books are called the Gospels of **Matthew, Mark, Luke** and **John**. They all tell the story of the life and death of Jesus Christ.

The birth of Jesus

The story begins with his birth (Matt. 1, 2; Luke 2). His mother's name was Mary. She was married to a man called Joseph, and they had to travel together from their home in Nazareth to Bethlehem, and there, in a stable, the baby boy was born. Joseph was not really his father, because Jesus was the Son of God himself. Some wise men knew this, and they travelled many miles from the East to see the royal baby. Angels also told some shepherds near Bethlehem about the baby, and they too came and bowed down to the baby Jesus. But one man wanted to kill the baby. His name was Herod, the king in Jerusalem, and he sent soldiers to Bethlehem to kill all baby boys; but Mary and Joseph had already escaped to the land of Egypt. They stayed there till Herod died, and then returned to their own land. They made their home in Nazareth again, a town near the Lake of Galilee, many miles to the north of Jerusalem and Bethlehem.

A view over modern Nazareth – the town where Jesus grew up.

The work of Jesus

When he grew up, Jesus left home and began to do two remarkable things. First, he helped many sick people, curing them of blindness and deafness and all sorts of diseases. Second, he preached to the crowds, teaching them what God wanted them to do and how he wanted them to live. His most famous teachings are in the Sermon on the Mount (Matt. 5–7). Often he told interesting stories called parables as a way of explaining what God wanted. One well-known parable is called 'The Good Samaritan' (Luke 10:30–37). Jesus told a story about a Jewish man travelling on a lonely road who was attacked by robbers. He was badly beaten, and left helpless on the roadside. Two other Jewish men came along, but they did nothing to help him. Then a foreigner (a Samaritan) came along, and he felt very sorry for

Jesus chose the lonely road from Jerusalem to Jericho as the setting for his parable about The Good Samaritan.

Galilee fishermen. Jesus' disciples, Peter, James, John and Andrew were fishermen from this area.

An illustration from a 14th century French prayer book showing Jesus feeding the multitude.

the wounded man, and spent a lot of time, trouble and money to help him. Jesus told this story, and then said to the people who were listening that they ought to behave just like the Samaritan. Jesus often taught lessons in this way.

Wherever he went, crowds followed him, and he needed helpers, so he chose twelve men to be his companions. They travelled with him everywhere, helping him in many ways. They are called the disciples or apostles (Matt. 10:1–4). The apostles gradually realized that Jesus was more than just a wonderful man. Three of them – Peter, James and John – were with him once when something very strange happened, known as the Transfiguration. On a high mountain one day he suddenly became shining bright (like an angel), and then two prophets from long ago, Moses and Elijah, suddenly appeared, talking with Jesus. Then they heard God himself speak, saying that Jesus was his own Son (Matt. 17). Of course, the disciples were very frightened at the time, but afterwards they became more and more sure that Jesus really was the Son of God.

The teaching of Jesus about himself

Jesus also told his followers many things about himself. They often called him 'Teacher', but he wanted them to understand that he had come to do much more than teach. He often used special names or titles for himself which they would easily remember, such as 'the Son of God', 'the Son of Man', 'the Good Shepherd' and 'the True Vine'. All of these titles helped the disciples understand who Jesus was and what he had come to earth to do.

In John 10 Jesus explains the title 'Good Shepherd' in full detail. Because he was the Good Shepherd, Jesus had come to meet the needs of ordinary people – just as a real shepherd looks after his sheep. Jesus would provide everything they needed, and he was willing to die to prevent anyone hurting them. In this way Jesus taught that he had come to bring good things to all those people who believed him and followed him; that he was going to die for them; and that one day he would return to earth to put the world right. Then wicked men would be punished, but Jesus' own people would be wonderfully happy, because Jesus would be always with them, and everything that is wrong with the world would be removed.

Jesus is put to death

But Jesus had enemies too, especially among the religious leaders in Jerusalem. An important religious society called the Pharisees disagreed with many of his teachings, and they began to challenge him and to argue with him in public. Gradually they began to hate him, and so they made plots to kill him. Their chance finally came when Jesus arrived in Jerusalem at the time of the Passover festival. One evening Jesus and his disciples had a special meal together (Matt. 26:17–30). Jesus knew it was their last meal together, and he gave his disciples bread and wine, telling them 'This is my body' and 'This is my blood'. After the meal they went to a quiet garden (called Gethsemane), just outside the city, and there Jewish soldiers were able to arrest him, because one of his own disciples, Judas Iscariot, turned traitor and told his enemies where to find him.

The Jewish leaders questioned Jesus and decided that he deserved to be executed. But they had no king now, and first they had to persuade the Roman governor, called Pilate, that Jesus must be killed. So Pilate also asked him many questions. He thought Jesus ought to be set free, but he was rather afraid of the Jewish leaders, so in the end he agreed to their wishes. Jesus was whipped and then crucified on a wooden cross (Matt. 27).

The Resurrection

After his death, the body of Jesus was put in a tomb. But that was not the end of the story, because two days later Jesus came back to life and left the tomb (this is called the Resurrection). He showed himself at different times to several of his friends and especially to the disciples, both in Jerusalem and on the shores of Lake Galilee. He told the disciples that they must continue to teach all the things he had taught them, not only in Judea but throughout the whole world (Matt. 28:16–20). After that he left them; they saw him going up into the sky (Luke 24:51). This is known as the Ascension.

An Eastern shepherd with his flock on the Golan Heights. Jesus called himself The Good Shepherd.

Pentecost

The book of **Acts** tells us what the followers of Jesus did afterwards. These men (the apostles) waited quietly in Jerusalem for about 6 weeks, till the next Jewish festival, called Pentecost (Acts 2). Then something wonderful happened to them: a violent wind blew in their house, and people could see what looked like tongues of fire coming to rest on top of them. This meant that the Holy Spirit of God had filled them. At once they became brave, strong men, able to heal sick people and to preach like Jesus. So they began preaching immediately, telling the crowds in Jerusalem all about Jesus. Many people believed what they said, and joined them; these were the first Christians. Before long there were groups of Christians not only in Jerusalem but in every part of Palestine, as the apostles and other Christians went everywhere telling the story of Jesus; and in a few years the Christian message was being told in many countries.

The apostles

In Jerusalem, however, the Jewish leaders were very angry about what was happening, and they did their best to stop it. They put Peter and John (two of the apostles) in prison for a time (Acts 5); and presently they killed a young Christian preacher called Stephen (Acts 7:54–60). After his death many Christians in Jerusalem were attacked. One Jew who hated Christians was called Saul (but we usually call him by his other name, Paul). But he too became a Christian; one day he was on a journey, when suddenly he saw a bright light and heard a voice from the sky. The voice was

Bottom: A rock tomb in Carmel with a rolling stone. It dates from the time of Christ.

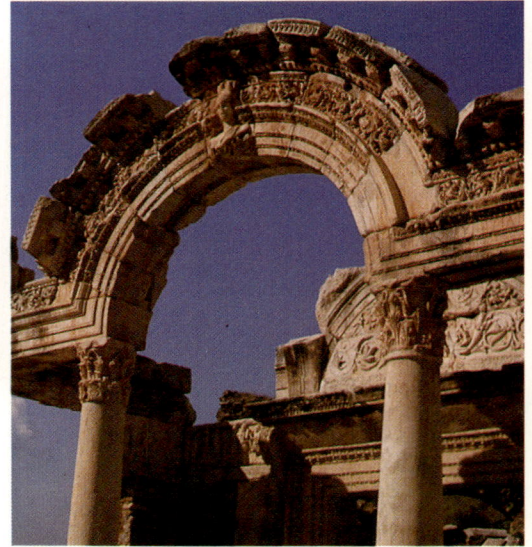

that of Jesus, and Paul became a follower of Jesus from that very moment (Acts 9:1–18).

The life of Paul

A year or two later Paul became one of the greatest Christian preachers, and one of the first missionaries. He left his home and began to travel to several nearby countries, telling the story of Jesus and persuading many people to become Christians. So wherever he went, he left behind little groups of Christians. The book of Acts tells the story of several of his missionary journeys (Acts 11–21). In many places, however, Jewish leaders argued with him and plotted against him. Finally he returned to Jerusalem (Acts 21), and his enemies seized their chance to capture him. They nearly killed him, but Roman soldiers rescued him. He was put in prison, however, and his enemies tried to persuade the judges to execute him as a criminal. In the end he was taken by ship to Rome, and was kept in prison there, but nothing could stop him preaching (Acts 28:30–31). (The Roman king, or emperor, at last gave orders that he should be executed, but the Bible does not tell us how this happened.)

The New Testament Letters

Paul spent many months as a prisoner, then, and was not free to go where he liked; but he was free to write letters, and the New Testament contains many of his letters (called **Epistles**). Sometimes he wrote to friends; one was **Timothy**, another was **Titus**, and yet another was **Philemon**. Most of his letters are to groups of Christians in different cities – such as Rome and Corinth and Ephesus. The Christians in all these places had many problems and questions, so Paul in his letters tried to help them, and to teach them, and to remind them of how Jesus

PAUL

Paul hated the followers of Jesus and had many arrested. One day God spoke to him in a blinding flash of light and he was converted.

Paul became a missionary, telling people about Jesus in many parts of Asia and Europe, including Athens, and founding many churches.

Several times he was attacked by hostile crowds and imprisoned. Eventually he was arrested and sent for trial before the Roman governor.

Some of the letters which Paul wrote to the groups of Christians he had visited are in the New Testament. Several were written from prison. It is believed that Paul was put to death by the Roman Emperor Nero.

wanted them to live.

Paul was not the only Christian missionary who used letters as a way of teaching. In the New Testament you will also find letters by **Peter**, **James**, **John** and **Jude**; there is also a long letter, to 'the **Hebrews**'. Nobody knows for certain who wrote it, but like all the New Testament letters, it contains some very important Christian teaching, useful for all Christian people.

The book of Revelation

The last book of the Bible is not a letter, although it contains seven short letters to Christian groups (Revelation 2, 3). It is called 'the **Revelation**', because it tells us what God 'revealed' to a man called John. It is a difficult book to understand, because many of the things in it are 'signs'; for instance, lampstands represent churches, we are told (Rev. 1:20). But it is easy to see that Revelation tells us that although many disasters will happen in the world (such as wars and famines), Jesus is really the king of the whole world. One day he will defeat all his enemies, and then there will be a wonderful 'new heaven and a new earth' (Rev. 21:1). So Christians need never be afraid, because Jesus himself tells us he is coming back again to be with his people (Rev. 22:20).

A 13th century illustration of the angels at the winepress, described in Revelation 14:17–20.

A view over the island of Patmos. The apostle John was a prisoner here when he had the visions described in the book of Revelation.

TRANSLATING THE BIBLE

The Bible which we have today is the result of many translations down the centuries since it was first written. The Old Testament was originally written for the most part in Hebrew; the New Testament was written entirely in Greek. People who speak other languages need to have the Bible translated into their languages. Today there are parts of the Bible in over sixteen hundred languages.

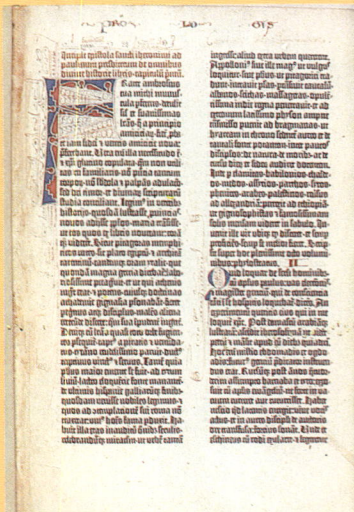

A 16th century woodcut showing an early printing press, similar to that on which the Gutenberg Bible, shown below, would have been printed.

Part of a decorated 'carpet' page from the 8th century Lindisfarne Gospels.

Before the Norman Conquest

The Bible was first known in Great Britain and Ireland in a Latin translation. This was the form in which it was known in Roman Britain; it is also the form in which it was used by the great missionaries who evangelised these islands after the Romans left – St. Patrick in Ireland, St. Columba in Scotland and St Augustine in England.

But when the English-speaking people had accepted the Christian faith, it was desirable that they should have access to the Bible in their own language. Many centuries passed before they had the whole Bible in English, but at quite an early date they had considerable parts of it.

In an age when few people were able to read, the Bible story was turned into verse and set to music so that they could sing it and memorize it. Of the men who turned it into verse the most famous is Caedmon, a cowherd attached to the abbey of Whitby, on the Yorkshire coast, who lived around AD660. Caedmon received the gift of song quite suddenly one night in a dream, in which an angel commanded him to sing and gave him the ability to do so. In due course he sang the whole Bible story, from the creation to the last judgment, and taught many others to sing it, too.

One book of the Bible which from the first was intended to be sung was the book of Psalms. This was translated into English by Aldhelm, first bishop of Sherborne in Dorset, shortly after AD700.

A very different person from the unlearned Caedmon was Bede, a learned monk of Jarrow in Northumbria, who was the greatest scholar in Western Europe at that time. His learned works, like his *Ecclesiastical History of the English Nation,* were written in Latin. But he had a concern for his less well-educated fellow-Englishmen, and translated parts of the Bible into their language. One of his pupils has left us a moving account of Bede's last night on earth, Ascension Eve in AD735, when he kept on dictating an English translation of the Gospel of John so long as he had any breath left.

Alfred the Great, King of the West Saxons from AD871 to 899, encouraged the Christian education of his subjects and undertook some translation himself. A law-code which he issued began with an English translation of the Ten Commandments and some other texts of Scripture.

From the 10th century we have a complete English version of the first seven books of the Old Testament by Aelfric, abbot of Eynsham (near Oxford) and a complete English version of the four Gospels, called the Wessex Gospels.

Other English translations of the Gos-

Augustine preaching to Ethelbert, King of Kent in AD 597. He and many of his subjects became Christians.

An artist's impression of the death of Bede whilst translating the Gospel of John into English.

pels from the same period are written between the lines of the Latin text of some famous manuscripts, like the Lindisfarne Gospels in the British Museum, London, and the Rushworth Gospels in the Bodleian Library, Oxford. These manuscripts, with some letters decorated in gold, silver and bright colours are called illuminated manuscripts.

After the Norman Conquest

All these versions are written in various dialects of Old English or Anglo-Saxon. To us that is practically a foreign language. In the three centuries following the Norman Conquest of 1066 the English language changed greatly, partly under the influence of the conquerors' Norman French. As a result, when we read the works of Geoffrey Chaucer, who wrote about 1360, we feel that his language (Middle English), though old-fashioned, is our own, but we do not feel that about works written in Old English.

From about the year 1200 we have in the Bodleian Library, Oxford, one copy of a work called the *Ormulum*, a poetical English version of the Gospels and the Acts of the Apostles, together with a commentary, by a monk named Ormin. About 1250 there appeared versions of

Genesis and Exodus, and of the book of Psalms in Middle English verse. Two versions of the Psalms in Middle English prose survive from the early 14th century. One of these is by Richard Rolle, a hermit of Hampole, near Doncaster. It was included in a verse-by-verse commentary on the Psalms which, to judge from its rather wide circulation, seems to have been quite a popular work.

Later in the 14th century there was produced an English version of the New Testament letters, made especially for the devotional use of monks and nuns.

But all such translations of small parts of the Bible were far surpassed by the work of John Wycliffe and his associates, in the last twenty years of the 14th century.

John Wycliffe

The first English translation of the complete Bible is associated with the name of John Wycliffe (1330–1384). Wycliffe was Master of Balliol College, Oxford, and one of the most distinguished English scholars of his day. But he was not interested only in scholarly matters; he was very much concerned about the state of society at that time, and thought that a completely new system was necessary. The basis for this new system, he thought, should be the law of God – that is, the Bible. But it was most desirable that the law of God should be widely known. The only language in which the whole Bible was available in England was Latin; Wycliffe therefore decided to translate the whole Bible from Latin into English. This was an immense undertaking for a busy man, and Wycliffe had the help of some of his pupils and other friends, including Nicholas of Hereford, who translated most of the Old Testament. The whole work was completed shortly before Wycliffe's death in 1384.

After his death it was thoroughly revised and improved by his secretary John Purvey, a man who had a very sound understanding of what a translator's task involved. Purvey completed the second edition of Wycliffe's Bible about 1395.

Two things have to be remembered about Wycliffe's Bible. First, it was not a translation from the original languages

A monk illuminating a manuscript. The art of decorating manuscripts with highly intricate designs, like that shown opposite, was widely practised in the Middle Ages in Britain and Europe. The art lapsed with the invention of printing in the 15th century.

Below: An illuminated drawing from the 14th century Ormesby Psalter, showing Jonah being swallowed by the fish.

Right: An illuminated drawing of St Luke from the opening page of his Gospel in the 11th century St Margaret's Gospels.

(Hebrew and Greek) but from the Latin Bible, which was itself a translation from the original languages. Second, it was a manuscript Bible: every copy of it had to be written out separately by hand. It was therefore very costly. Even so, there was a steady demand for it, especially in Purvey's edition.

But its circulation was not encouraged by leaders in church and state. Wycliffe's views of the necessary reform of society were regarded as revolutionary. Some of his followers, the travelling preachers called Lollards, were suspected of being involved in the Peasants' Revolt of 1381, led by Wat Tyler. A decree of 1408 forbade anyone to translate or possess a copy of the Bible in English except by permission of the church authorities.

William Tyndale

The next Bible translation in English was different from Wycliffe's work in two important respects.

First, whereas Wycliffe's Bible was a translation (English) from a translation (Latin), this one was made direct from the Hebrew of the Old Testament and the Greek of the New Testament. The knowledge of Greek in particular was very rare in Western Europe in Wycliffe's day. By 1500, however, there was a great renewal of interest in ancient Greek language and literature, especially as a result of the Turkish conquest of Constantinople (Istanbul) in 1453. Until 1453 Constantinople had been a Greek-speaking city; when it fell, many scholars left it and made their way to the west. One scholar who made his way to England was a man called Emmanuel, who found employment with the Archbishop of York about 1468. To this day there is in the city library of Leicester an important manuscript of the New Testament in Greek which Emmanuel copied out from another manuscript, about 1000 years older.

Second, the version of the English Bible at which we are now about to look was *printed*, not written out by hand. The invention of printing in Western Europe is dated about 1450. The credit for the invention is usually given to Johann Gutenberg of the German city of Mainz. The great advantage of printing is that an edition of several hundred, or even thousand, copies can be produced in one operation, whereas with the manuscript process each copy had to be produced separately. Gutenberg's greatest achievement was a magnificent printed edition of

One of the pages of Wycliffe's handwritten New Testament.

Right: A richly ornamented page from the 9th century Macregol Gospels.

Below: A drawing of the building of the Tower of Babel from 14th century French illustrations for the book of Genesis.

The first printed copies of the New Testament in English were smuggled into England in bales of cloth.

A drawing of the martyrdom of William Tyndale from Fox's 'Book of Martyrs'.

the Latin Bible, published in 1456. There are not more than half a dozen copies of this edition known to be in existence now; one of them is in the John Rylands University Library, Manchester. The Hebrew Bible was first printed in 1488, the Greek New Testament in 1514.

The English Bible could have been printed at any time after 1483, when William Caxton set up his printing press in Westminster. But the restrictions on the production and circulation of the Bible in English were still in force. It was necessary, therefore, to print it on the continent of Europe. The man responsible for doing so was William Tyndale (1494-1536).

Tyndale was a native of Gloucestershire, a graduate of both Oxford and Cambridge. At Cambridge he seized the opportunity of studying Greek. Tyndale, along with others known as the Reformers, believed that it was necessary to have the whole Bible available to everybody, so he decided to produce a faithful English translation of the Bible from the original languages. The authorities in church and state opposed this and insisted that no one should translate, or even read a copy of the Bible in English without their permission. When Tyndale found no means of doing his translation in England, he crossed to the continent and set himself to translate the New Testament from Greek into English. When this translation was finished, it was printed at Worms, in West Germany in 1526. Copies began to find their way into England two or three months later, but they had to be smuggled in, wrapped in bales of cloth and other merchandise, because it was against the law to import them. Only two copies of this first printed edition of the English New Testament are known to exist, one in Bristol and the other in London. A photographic facsimile was published in 1976, to mark its 450th anniversary.

Having translated the New Testament, Tyndale (among other concerns which occupied his time) started to translate the Old Testament. He published his translation of the first five books (the books of Moses) in 1530, and Jonah in 1531. He also translated the books from Joshua to 2 Chronicles, but his translation of these books was not published in his lifetime. He realized that his English New Testament was capable of improvement, and produced a revised edition of it in 1534, and yet another in 1535.

In May 1535 Tyndale was kidnapped in Antwerp, where he was then living, and taken into adjoining territory which was under the control of a ruler hostile to the Reformers. There, after nearly seventeen months in captivity, he was put to death on 6 October, 1536. It is said that his last words were: 'Lord, open the king of England's eyes' – meaning, 'Let him permit the free circulation of the English Bible'. Because of his long imprisonment, he could not know that in that sense the eyes of King Henry VIII had already been opened, for by the end of 1535 a printed edition of the complete English Bible was circulating in England with the king's consent.

Tyndale's name should always be held in honour as the greatest in the history of the English Bible. No other English translator paid so dearly for his work as he did. The principal English translations which have appeared after his, right down to the Revised Standard Version of 1952, are to a large extent revisions and updatings of Tyndale's version, so thoroughly and skilfully did he carry out his work.

Coverdale and 'Matthew'

The translation which began to circulate in England with the king's consent late in 1535 was edited by Myles Coverdale, a friend of Tyndale's who shared the same Reformation attitude to the Bible. Coverdale was not the scholar that Tyndale was, but relied on the work of other men. For the New Testament and for the first five books of the Old Testament he relied on the work of Tyndale. For the rest of the Old Testament he relied on the work of Latin and German translators. Coverdale's Bible was the first *complete* printed English Bible.

Two new editions of Coverdale's Bible appeared in 1537, and the second of these had the royal permission printed on the title-page. Another edition of the English Bible printed in 1537, also with the royal permission shown on the title-page, bears the pen-name 'Thomas Matthew'. The editor was really John Rogers, another of Tyndale's close associates, who later had the sad distinction of being the first Protestant martyr to be burned at the stake in the reign of Mary Tudor (1555). John Rogers wished to take no credit to himself for his edition, since it was the work of others. He reproduced Tyndale's whole Bible so far as Tyndale had translated, including his translation of the books from Joshua to 2 Chronicles, which had never been printed before. For the rest of the Old Testament he simply revised Coverdale's first edition.

The Great Bible

A further step forward was the king's command in September 1538, providing that 'one book of the whole Bible of the largest volume in English' should be set up in every parish church in England, so that every parishioner who wished could read it. At this very time a new edition of the English Bible was being printed in Paris and, being a large edition, it was well designed to meet the terms of King Henry's order. The work of printing it was interrupted by the French inquisitor-general at the end of 1538, but the printers, paper and type were transported to England, and it was published in London in April 1539.

From its size this edition was popularly called 'The Great Bible'. So far as its contents were concerned, it was a revision of the Bible of 'Thomas Matthew', carried out by Coverdale. This was the final achievement in Bible translation and publication in the reign of Henry VIII (1509-1547). Henry's reign had indeed brought changes in this whole business which would have been thought incredible less than twenty years before. Instead of the common people being strictly forbidden to read the Bible in their own tongue, without special permission, they

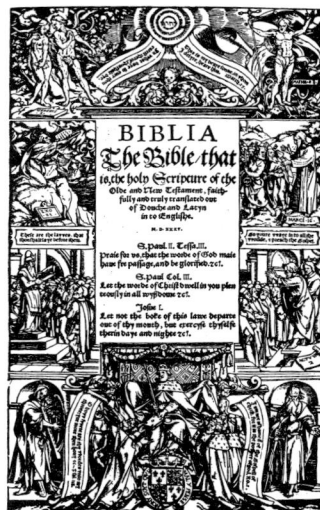

The title page of the first edition of Coverdale's Bible. This was the first complete printed English Bible.

were now being actively encouraged to read it, by the authority of the king himself.

Even the Great Bible left much to be desired, and within a generation it had been replaced by other translations. But one part of it is still in use. The version of the Psalms still most commonly sung in Anglican churches all over the world is the version which was first printed in the Great Bible.

King Henry VIII decreed that a Bible should be placed in every parish church in England. The Bible was chained to the lectern to prevent it being stolen.

The Elizabethan Bible

In the reign of Elizabeth I (1558-1603) two further English translations of the Bible appeared.

One of these, first issued in 1560, is called the Geneva Bible because it was produced in Geneva by a group of English Protestant scholars who found refuge in that city during Mary Tudor's reign. Geneva at that time was a centre of Protestant study, and the translators had ample resources for their work. The Geneva Bible was the most scholarly Bible translation of the 16th century. It was also the first English Bible in which *all* the Old Testament was translated direct from Hebrew. Tyndale had not lived long enough to complete this work, and none of his immediate associates and followers was capable of doing it.

This monument to the leading figures of the Reformation stands in Geneva, Switzerland. The city became an important centre of Protestant theological study in the 16th century.

The Geneva Bible, which bore a dedication to Queen Elizabeth, was imported freely into England and was widely used. It was the Bible known and used by Shakespeare. The Reformed religion was established in Scotland in 1560, the year of the Geneva Bible's first publication, and the Geneva Bible was promptly adopted by the Scots.

The Geneva Bible has often been called the 'Breeches Bible', from the statement in Genesis 3:7 that Adam and Eve 'sewed figtree leaves together, and made themselves breeches' – where the Authorised Version says 'aprons'.

For all its merits, the Geneva Bible was not officially authorised in England, probably because its outspoken notes were felt by the religious leaders to be too strongly Protestant. A scheme was launched a few years later to produce another version which would be more acceptable. This version was published in 1568. It is called the Bishops' Bible, because all its translators were either bishops when they did the work, or else became bishops soon afterwards; and the Archbishop of Canterbury, Matthew Parker, was chief editor. This was a very good translation: it would, indeed, have been the best translation ever to have appeared in English, if the Geneva Bible had not appeared before it. Although it was produced by bishops of the Church of England, it was never officially authorised. Perhaps Queen Elizabeth recognised that it was not such a good translation as the Geneva Bible and decided that, if she could not authorise the better version, she would not authorise the worse one.

Authorised Version

At the end of Queen Elizabeth's reign, then, there were two English Bibles in general use – the Geneva Bible, which was specially popular with the Puritans (but not only with them), and the Bishops' Bible, which appealed more to those who liked the way in which affairs were ordered in the Church of England under her reign.

When James I succeeded her in 1603, he called a conference at Hampton Court to regulate affairs in the Church of England. The only decision of importance taken at this conference was that a new edition of the English Bible should be prepared, which would – it was hoped – take the place of both the Geneva Bible and the Bishops' Bible.

This project had the king's warm approval, and it is because of the encouragement he gave it that the version which appeared as a result is sometimes called the King James Version. About fifty scholars were appointed to carry the work through; they were divided into three groups, meeting in Oxford, Cambridge and Westminster. They were instructed to revise the Bishops' Bible. But in fact the version which they produced combined the virtues of the Geneva Bible and of the Bishops' Bible, and added several of its own; so well did they do their work.

When their version was published in

1611, it was authorised by the Privy Council – so far, at least, as we can tell (the records of the Privy Council for that period were accidentally burned). It is therefore known in Britain as the Authorised Version. For 300 years and more the Authorised Version came to be recognised as The Bible above all others throughout the English-speaking world. It was superior to all versions that had gone before it, and in some respects it remains the best. The beauty of its style and the rhythm of its prose have ensured that it is still the most suitable version of the English Bible for reading aloud in public.

All this reflects great credit on the men who produced it. But the man on whom it reflects greatest credit is William Tyndale, who had died 75 years before. For in those parts of the Bible which Tyndale had translated, much of his wording was taken over in the Authorised Version; it has been calculated that nine-tenths of the Authorised New Testament is still Tyndale's.

The Catholic Bible

Relations between English Roman Catholics and Protestants in the reigns of Elizabeth I and James I were such that the idea of a Bible translation which could be used by both sides was out of the question. So, during Elizabeth's reign, a group of Catholic exiles prepared a Catholic version at Douai and Rheims, in the north of France, where a college was set up to train men for the Catholic ministry. This is called the Douai version. The actual translator was an Oxford scholar named Gregory Martin. He is said to have worked very systematically, at the rate of two chapters a day. As he completed each stint, two of his colleagues checked it through. The New Testament was published in 1582, the Old Testament (in two volumes) in 1609 and 1610. The whole work was revised very thoroughly by Bishop Richard Challoner between 1749 and 1772.

In the 20th century there have been

A 12th century illustrated Bible codex at St Catherine's Monastery, Sinai.

several new Catholic versions in more up-to-date English. The best known of these are Ronald Knox's version (1945-1955), the Jerusalem Bible (1966) and the New American Bible (1970). But the time is now happily past when it was thought necessary to have separate versions of the Bible for Protestants and Roman Catholics.

Revised Version

If the Authorised Version was such an excellent work, why should anyone think of improving on it? There are two main reasons.

One reason is that languages in regular use do not stand still. The only languages that do stand still are 'dead' languages. Words change their meanings; old words die; new words come into use. No one today would refer to a bow and arrows as 'artillery', as the Authorised Version does in 1 Samuel 20:40, and we do not say 'we took up our carriages' when we mean 'we picked up our bags', as the same version does in Acts 21:15. There is a need to translate the Bible into a more modern form of language which uses words in the sense which they have today.

Another reason is that much more is known nowadays about the Hebrew and Greek languages in which the Old and New Testaments were written, so that the original meaning can be conveyed more accurately. In addition, the Authorised Version of the New Testament was translated from printed Greek texts of the 16th and 17th centuries which were not as correct as they might have been. More and more Greek New Testament manuscripts of early date have come to light in the interval between 1611 and the present day

which make it possible to establish a more accurate Greek text on which to base translations.

A major revision of the Authorised Version was undertaken from 1870 onwards. The revisers were British scholars who worked closely with a body of American scholars. The British revisers produced the Revised New Testament in 1881 and the Revised Version of the complete Bible in 1885. Their American associates produced what is called the American Standard Version in 1901. The British Revised Version and the American Standard Version were much more accurate than the Authorised Version, and therefore were widely used by students. The English style, however, was felt to be rather ungainly, especially in the New Testament, and the two versions never won great acceptance with the general Bible-reading public.

Revised Standard Version

Much more successful was the Revised Standard Version, the work of a team of North American scholars. It was designed to be a revision both of the Authorised Version (1611) and of the American Standard Version (1901). The New Testament first appeared in 1946, the complete Bible in 1952, and slightly revised editions were published in 1962 and 1971. The edition of 1971 is acceptable to Roman Catholics and Protestants alike, so it is sometimes printed with the title *The Common Bible*. One obvious difference between it and the older versions is that 'thou', 'thee', 'thy' and 'thine' are not used except when divine beings are addressed. Other old-fashioned forms, characteristic of the older versions, have been replaced by those now generally in use; thus 'saith' has given place to 'says' and 'giveth' to 'gives'. Although the Revised Standard Version was produced by United States and Canadian scholars, its language is standard English as spoken also in Britain, and it quickly proved to be as acceptable in the rest of the English-speaking world as in North America.

New English Bible

If the Revised Standard Version was a North American production, the New

Some modern versions of the Bible.

English Bible was made in Britain. Careful consideration was given in Britain to the possibility of revising existing versions of the Bible, but it was decided that the best scheme would be a completely new translation from the Hebrew and Greek texts, independent of all previous versions. A joint committee of the principal denominations in Great Britain and Ireland (apart from the Roman Catholic Church) and the leading Bible Societies was set up in 1947 to take responsibility for this enterprise. The committee established panels of translators and a panel of literary experts to check the English style of the translation. The New Testament translators' panel finished its work in time for the New Testament to be published in March 1961. The other panels completed their work in the next nine years, and the entire New English Bible was published in March 1970.

This version was an instant success. In the first year after the publication of the New Testament, 4 million copies had been bought, and by the time the complete Bible appeared this figure had grown to 9 million.

The style of the New English Bible is modern but dignified. As in the Revised Standard Version, 'thou', 'thee', etc. are used only when divine persons are being spoken to. Also as in the Revised Standard Version, inverted commas or quotation marks are used to indicate words and passages in direct speech; the older versions did not use them.

Several features of the New English Bible, both in translation and in style, have been criticised. Some of these criticisms are well founded. But a committee remains in being to take note of criticisms and to keep the work under review. It will probably issue a slightly improved edition before long.

Good News Bible

An English translation of the New Testament was published in 1966 under the title *Today's English Version* or *Good News for Modern Man*. It was sponsored by the American Bible Society with the cooperation of similar societies elsewhere in the English-speaking world. The translator was Dr. Robert G. Bratcher, and the text was illustrated with line drawings by Mlle. Annie Vallotton. The language is simple and to a large extent conversational. Unusual words have been avoided. Great care, however, has been taken to

The roots of our modern English Bible stretch back almost four thousand years.

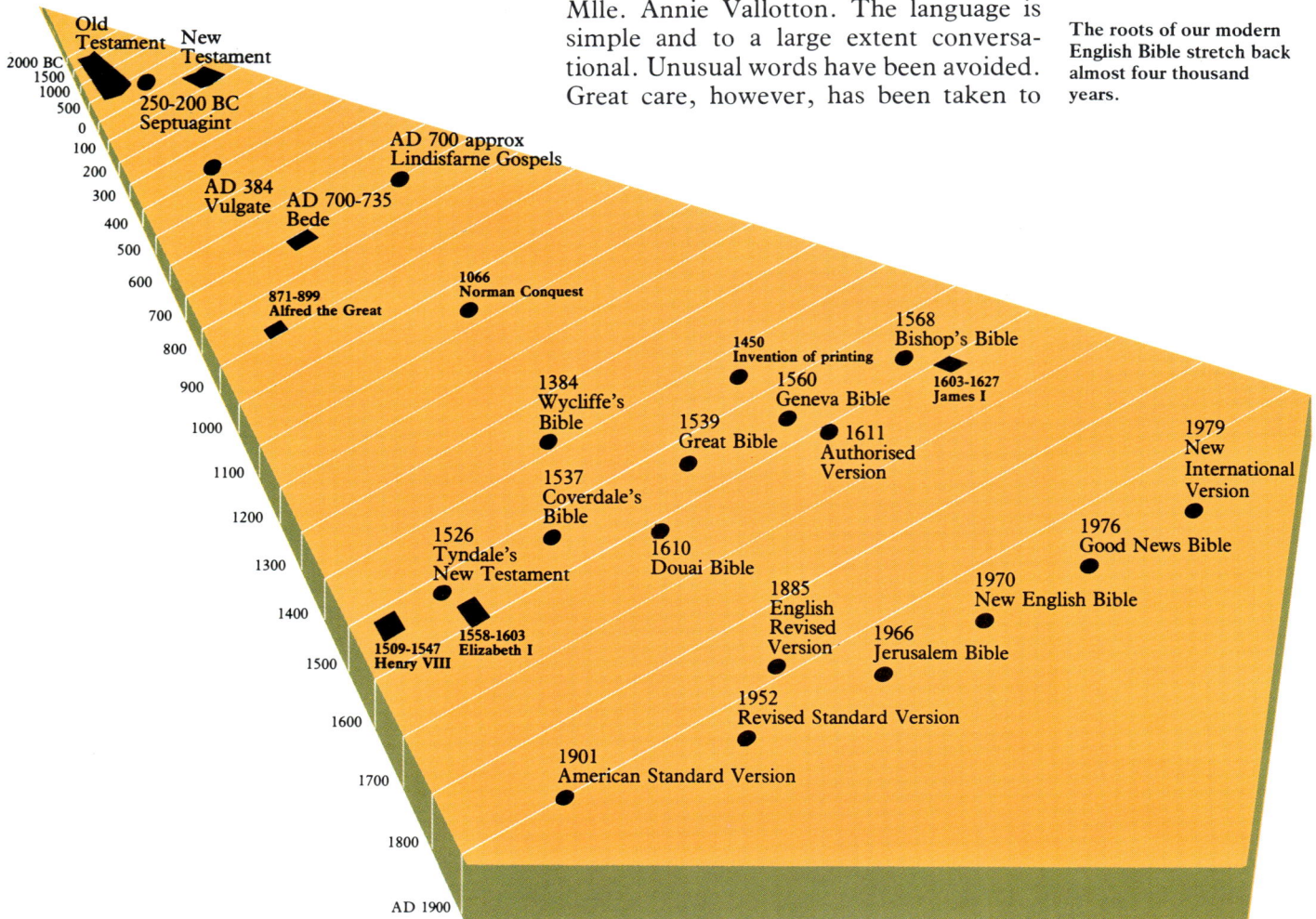

38

Roman soldiers could force civilians to carry their pack.

A drawing by Annie Vallotton in the style of those used in the Good News Bible.

Canon J. B. Phillips, whose paraphrases of Bible books have been very popular.

express the original meaning as clearly as possible.

When the New Testament had been published in this version, work was continued on the Old Testament, and the result was the appearance of the *Good News Bible* in 1976. Separate American and British editions were produced, with spellings and other features characteristic of the two forms of English. In the British edition weights and measures have been metricated, so we now have kilograms instead of pounds and kilometres instead of miles. The passage in the Sermon on the Mount where Jesus tells the disciples to go a second mile with the soldier who compels them to go one mile with him is rendered: 'If one of the occupation troops forces you to carry his pack one kilometre, carry it two kilometres' (Matthew 5.41). One kilometre is much less than one mile, but the point is not the distance travelled, but the willingness to go twice as far as one is compelled to go.

The separate New Testament volume in paperback presented as pleasing and readable an appearance as any paperback could do. To get the whole Bible into one volume of convenient size it was necessary to use smaller print and compress the text somewhat; even so, the *Good News Bible* is an attractive book, pleasant to handle and easy to read. Mlle. Vallotton has provided the same kind of illustrations for the rest of the Bible as she did for the New Testament.

New International Version
The most recent English translation of the Bible is the New International Version, published in America in 1978 and in Britain in 1979. This work was sponsored by the New York International Bible Society and was entrusted to a band of scholars drawn from many of the English-speaking countries and from a wide range of different denominations. All of them were committed to a firm belief in the authority of the Bible as the written Word of God.

The New Testament in this version was published in 1973. Even earlier, in 1969, a sample version of the Gospel of John was published. At that time the version was called simply *A Contemporary Translation*.

Like the New English Bible, the New International Version is a completely new translation, not a revision of any existing version. In one respect it is more modern than the New English Bible: even God is addressed throughout as 'you', not 'thou'. He is also addressed as 'you' in the *Good News Bible*, but then the style of the *Good News Bible* is conversational, whereas the English of the New International Version, while modern, is more literary and dignified. If comparisons were made, then the version to which the New International Version bears closest resemblance is the Revised Standard Version. The translators have all been diligent Bible students for many years, and while they set themselves to produce an entirely independent version, it would have been unreasonable to expect them to forget the phraseology of the older versions with which they were familiar. Indeed, it is a strength, not a weakness, of the New International Version that it so often recalls the phraseology of the older versions. The translators have discharged their task with the seriousness of men who knew that they were handling the Word of God, and they have been outstandingly successful in their aim to express faithfully in modern terms what the writers of the Bible meant.

Modern paraphrases
There are two well-known Bible versions which are called paraphrases rather than translations. It is not easy to explain the difference between paraphrase and translation, but in a paraphrase greater variation or addition of words is permitted so that the sense may be brought out more fully. Some parts of the Bible lend themselves specially well to paraphrasing – the letters of Paul, for example, because Paul tends to write in a rather brief way which invites the translator to fill it out with words of his own.

During World War II there was a London clergyman named J. B. Phillips, who was concerned because so many of his young people found the New Testament letters very difficult to follow in the older versions. He used the hours of duty as a firewatcher for fires started by bombs, to paraphrase the letters in modern speech.

The result, entitled *Letters to Young Churches*, was a best-seller when it was published in 1947. It was followed by similar paraphrases of other books until at last *The New Testament in Modern English* appeared in 1958. A completely revised edition was published in 1973.

In 1963 Dr Phillips produced a paraphrase of *Four Prophets* (Amos, Hosea, Isaiah 1-39, Micah), but tackled no more of the Old Testament.

It was a similar awareness of the difficulty felt by young people in understanding Paul's letters that moved Dr. Kenneth N. Taylor to produce a paraphrase of them. The young people for whom he was primarily concerned were his own children, who complained that they could not follow the family Bible reading. So he turned the New Testament letters into language that they could follow, and published *Living Letters* in 1962. Then he went on to paraphrase the rest of the Bible, section by section, until at last he published *The Living Bible* in 1971. *The Living Bible* has proved immensely popular, especially with young people – which is not surprising, in view of its origin. Similar paraphrases along the same lines are being produced in a number of other languages.

Bible Societies and similar agencies

The translation and circulation of the Bible have been greatly promoted in the 19th and 20th centuries by the Bible Societies of many lands. The earliest of these, the British and Foreign Bible Society, was founded in 1804. The American Bible Society was formed in 1816, the National Bible Society of Scotland in 1826, and the Trinitarian Bible Society, based in London, in 1831. Most of the Bible Societies have been linked since 1946 in the United Bible Societies. The Bible Societies publish the Bible, in whole or in part, in about 1500 languages.

The Wycliffe Bible Translators are an international body, officially organised in 1942, dedicated to translating the Bible into languages in which no version at present exists. They reckon that there are about 2000 of these languages. Many of them are spoken by small numbers of people, but all these people have the right to hear or read the Word of God in their mother-tongue. The Wycliffe Translators have set up the Summer Institute of Linguistics to train translators in the most up-to-date scientific techniques for learning and recording new languages and translating the Bible into them. This is a very different procedure from the hit-

Local people help the Wycliffe Bible translators to put parts of the Bible into their mother tongue.

and-miss methods which translators of earlier days were often compelled to use, because nothing better was available.

The Scripture Gift Mission distributes the Bible, or portions of the Bible, all over the world. It is specially well known for its attractively produced booklets of carefully selected Bible texts on various important subjects and for various outstanding occasions, suitable for presentation to all age groups.

The Gideons International are an association of Christian business and professional men, best known for their activity in placing Bibles in hotel bedrooms and other public places, distributing them in schools, hospitals and so forth. At one time they used only the Authorised Version, but now they use the New International Version also.

When the Bible has been translated it needs to be read in such a way as to get the greatest possible benefit from it. It was for this purpose that Scripture Union was founded in 1879, and has grown into the largest Bible reading organisation in the world.

THE ARCHAEOLOGY OF THE BIBLE

Archaeologists have to work carefully when excavating a site because of the risk of damaging buried objects. Everything that is uncovered has to be recorded and kept for study later.

Archaeology is a way of recovering knowledge of ancient times, by discovering and studying the remains which people of those times have left behind. Today, archaeology is not just one science, but many. Every object an archaeologist discovers is studied in detail, and the study of pieces of bone, stone, metal, pottery, wood and many other items will involve many different sciences. Very often, the work will also include the translating of ancient writings, and the study of an ancient city's art and architecture.

These detailed studies are carried out in museums and laboratories, but to recover all the material in the first place, the archaeologist has to excavate an ancient city very carefully. To understand how this is done, we have to know how the ruined cities of the Ancient Near East have been formed.

Methods of archaeology

Ancient cities and their remains

In the lands of the Bible, houses and other buildings were usually of bricks and stone. The bricks were made from mud or clay dried in the sun. Buildings made of these bricks, or of bricks on stone foundations, were easily destroyed by fires, floods, earthquakes or attacking armies. Often, whole towns were destroyed, not just a few buildings. When the people began rebuilding their town, they would simply make the ruins of their old brick houses level, and build new ones on top. This made the new buildings slightly higher than the old ones.

Over a period of thousands of years, towns would be rebuilt very many times. In this way, the sites of the ancient towns became large mounds (seventy feet high or more), with their houses on top. A town built on a mound was, of course, easier to defend against an attacking army. The sites of these towns in the Ancient Near East are called *tells* (the Arabic word 'tell' means 'mound').

When a team of archaeologists excavates a *tell*, they are therefore cutting into a mound which has many layers. As they dig down from the top, they uncover more and more of these layers, and each layer (called a stratum – several together are called strata) will be *older* than the one above it. The lowest stratum will be the

Lachish was an important city in Judah in the 8th century BC. This relief from the walls of Sennacherib's palace in Nineveh shows the siege of the town in 701 BC. On the left is a battering ram and archers are seen shooting over the walls into the city. The *tell* which is the site of Lachish was excavated in the 1930's and evidence of the siege was found.

Below: A cross-section through a typical *tell* showing methods of excavation and the various time levels archaeologists might expect to find.

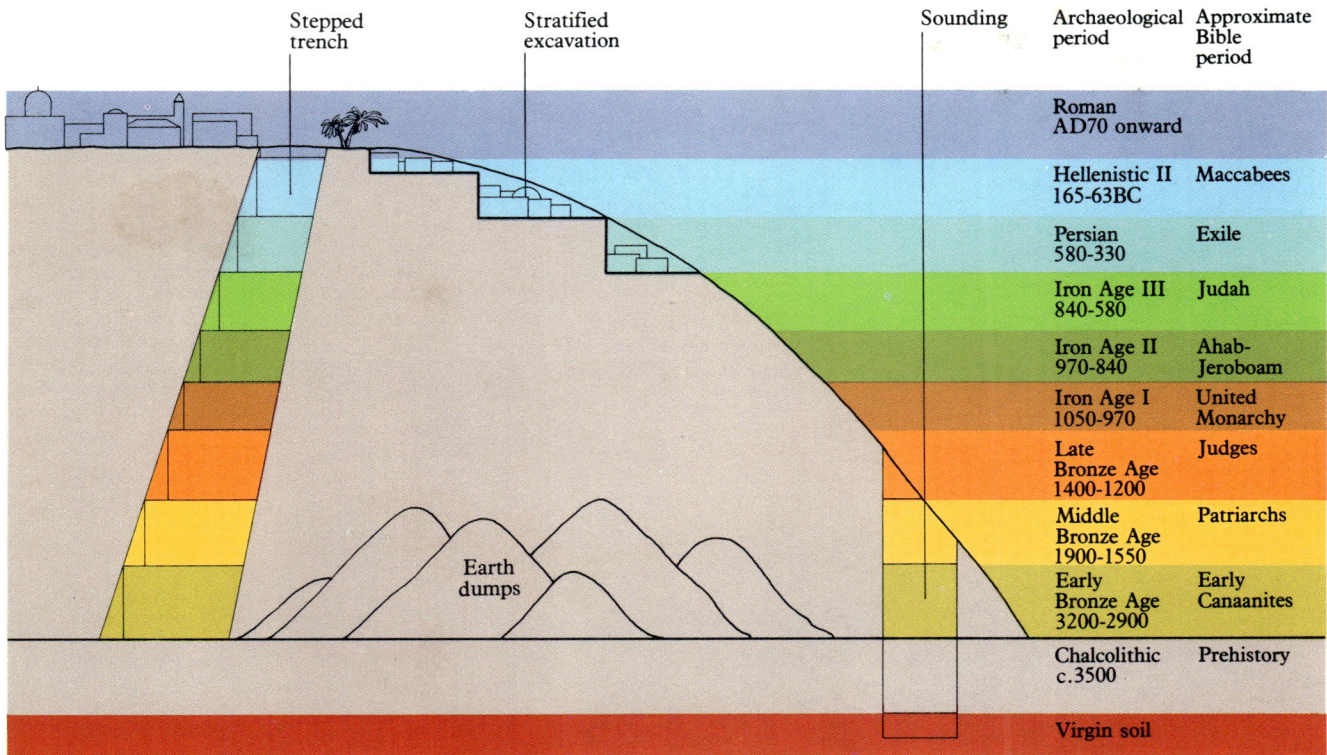

			Archaeological period	Approximate Bible period
Stepped trench	Stratified excavation	Sounding	Roman AD70 onward	
			Hellenistic II 165-63BC	Maccabees
			Persian 580-330	Exile
			Iron Age III 840-580	Judah
			Iron Age II 970-840	Ahab-Jeroboam
			Iron Age I 1050-970	United Monarchy
			Late Bronze Age 1400-1200	Judges
Earth dumps			Middle Bronze Age 1900-1550	Patriarchs
			Early Bronze Age 3200-2900	Early Canaanites
			Chalcolithic c.3500	Prehistory
			Virgin soil	

oldest of all, dating from the time when people first came to live on that spot.

Each stratum will contain not only the remains of buildings (floors of hard earth, the foundations of walls, and perhaps a layer of debris from a destruction), but also many of the objects used every day by the people who lived at that time. These objects will include weapons, tools, small statues, and ornaments such as necklaces. But the most common thing will be pottery. This is often found broken in pieces, but many pottery vessels can be pieced together again.

Everything found has to be carefully recorded, and kept for detailed study later on. Only a small part of each stratum can be excavated, but even if only a little is known about each of the many strata, this is usually enough to give some idea of the history of the *tell*.

From his record of everything found, an archaeologist can easily see how many times in its history a town has been des-

troyed and rebuilt. But he will want to know much more than this! He will want to know the *date* of the town which each stratum represents, how long it lasted, and why it was destroyed. Only when the date of each stratum is known can the complete history of the site be worked out and put in its proper place in the history of the Ancient Near East.

The archaeologist's work

How does an archaeologist interested in the cities of the Bible know *which* ancient city he is excavating? Sometimes a city keeps its ancient name into modern times. Damascus, for example, has had the same name for about 3500 years or more. If a site has been abandoned for many centuries, an old tradition will sometimes preserve a memory of which ancient city of the Bible lies buried there. Or sometimes the Bible itself gives clear enough details of where a city was, in relation to a mountain or river, or to another city, for

A wall of mud and straw bricks enclosing a courtyard in front of a small Eastern house.

How pottery provides the dates

The pottery which an archaeologist finds is often his best guide to the date of each stratum. Pottery styles were always changing, sometimes quickly, sometimes slowly, so that the pottery from one time is different from that of another. If different styles of pottery can be dated, they can be used to date the strata in which they are found. The history of Egypt is the best guide to the dates of different pottery styles. The dates of Egypt's pharaohs are well known for most of

its long history, and if a certain type of pottery turns up in Egypt, it can usually be dated from the Egyptian remains found with it. Or an archaeologist may find some objects from Egypt in one stratum of a *tell* he is excavating, and these will help him to date that stratum and the pottery found in it. If a type of pottery can be dated at *one* site, it can be used to date the strata in which it is found at *other* sites.

In this way, a set of dates for different types of pottery has been worked out, and names given to the periods when different types were common. The names of the main divisions are shown in the table. The names 'Bronze Age' and 'Iron Age' can be misleading; they do *not* mean that iron was never used until the Iron Age, or that bronze was used only in the Bronze Age! They are simply the labels which archaeologists have used for a very long time to describe the main periods, and especially to classify pottery styles. They are the names you will find in most books on archaeology.

This chart shows how pottery jars changed in style over a period of 4500 years.

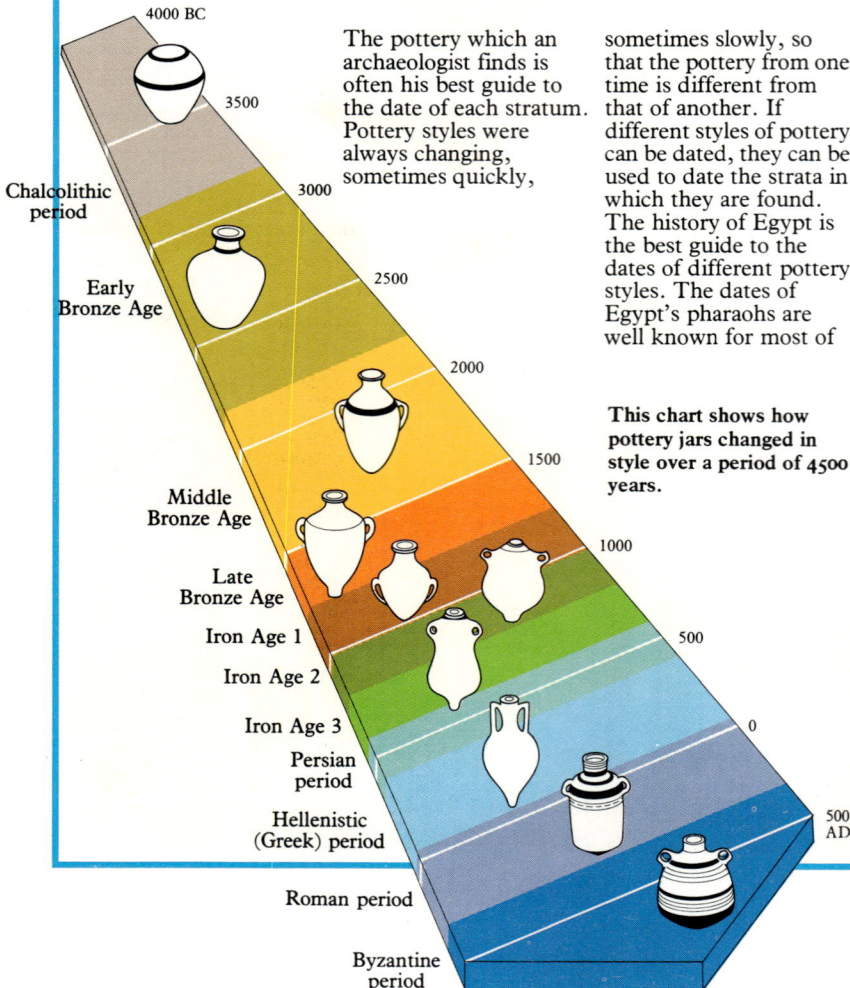

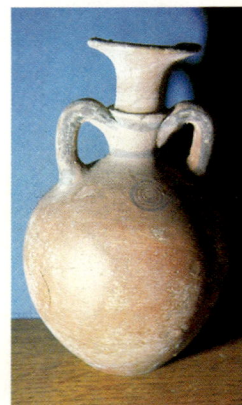
A pottery jar found in excavations in Egypt.

us to know which ancient mound conceals its ruins. But the archaeologist always has to be careful – the city he is excavating may not always be the one he *thinks* it is!

The excavation will begin at several small areas of the site, after a small 'sounding' has given some idea of the number of strata and their ages. It is more important to excavate small areas in detail than to

Archaeology and the Bible

An ivory comb from the 9th century BC, found at Megiddo.

A clay tablet from Lagash in Mesopotamia dating from around 2400 BC. It is a contract for the purchase of a slave.

excavate a large area poorly. The excavator will hope to find the most important parts of the ancient city – its royal or administrative buildings, its gateway and part of the city walls, and the homes of the ordinary people. He will also hope to find the city's cemetery, since household objects were often buried with people in ancient times, and these can tell us a great deal about the everyday lives of those people.

There will often be many seasons of excavations over a period of several years. But the excavation of the city's remains is only the beginning. The work then moves into museums and laboratories for the detailed study of everything found, and a report has to be published to make all the information available to other archaeologists and scholars. If this were not done, the discoveries made would never be added to our general knowledge of the world of the Bible.

Below: 1 and 2. A Roman style oil lamp and metal figurines found recently by local people near Jerusalem and photographed on site before cleaning.
3. A pestle and mortar and a millstone of black basalt found at Capernaum.
4. Fragments of pottery can be pieced together to show what the original was like.
5. A simple Judean oil lamp. The wick was placed in the lip and floated in the oil.

During the last century, when the archaeology of the Bible lands was still only just beginning, the excavators were usually hoping to make discoveries which would confirm the main events of Bible history. Today, the aims of the archaeologists are rather different. It is now understood that many things cannot be proved by archaeology in a straightforward way. Instead of providing proof of particular events, archaeology is used to increase our knowledge of the everyday life, the history and the customs, of the people who appear in the Bible's long story – the Egyptians, the Phoenicians, the Philistines, the Moabites, the Assyrians, the Babylonians and others, as well as the Hebrews themselves.

For example, discoveries of ancient texts on clay tablets, in many languages, show us what the various peoples of the Ancient Near East thought about the world, the kind of gods they worshipped and the kind of laws they lived by. Ancient texts also tell us of alliances, trade and wars between the great cities and nations of the past. In this way, they help us to write the history of the lands surrounding the people of Israel.

Archaeological discoveries therefore paint in the background to the Bible, and help to explain and illustrate many of its stories. We will look now at some of the ways in which they have done this.

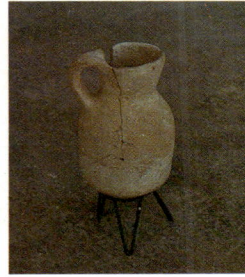

1 2 3 4 5

Right: The Standard of Ur, a wooden box covered with mosaic pictures illustrating aspects of Sumerian life in the 3rd millenium BC. It is thought that the standard was carried in processions.

Right: The Standard of Ur, a wooden box covered with mosaic pictures illustrating aspects of Sumerian life in the 3rd millenium BC. It is thought that the standard was carried in processions.

Women's jewellery from the Royal Tombs of Ur, arranged as on the body in the tomb.

From Abraham to the Exodus

Thanks to archaeology, we now know that in the time of Abraham (about 2000BC), there were already many great and prosperous cities in the Ancient Near East. Civilisation was already over a thousand years old in Egypt and in the region around the Tigris and Euphrates Rivers. It was from a city on the River Euphrates, called Ur, that Abraham (then called Abram) began the journey which eventually brought him to the land of Canaan (Gen. 11:31). Ur was excavated early this century by Sir Leonard Woolley, and some of the discoveries were spectacular. The Royal Tombs, dating from about 2500BC, contained many beautiful objects made with gold, silver and precious stones. The Ur which Abraham's family left a few centuries later was a rich city with many skilled craftsmen and merchants.

New discoveries of this kind are being made all the time. Recently, archaeologists excavating the ancient city of Ebla, in Syria, have found the remains of roughly fifteen thousand clay tablets over 4000 years old. When all these have been translated (a job which will take many years), they will tell us a great deal about the ancient world at the time of Abraham and earlier.

Archaeology cannot be expected to prove the existence of Abraham himself, and the same applies to other individuals in the Old Testament story, such as Joseph and Moses. However, written evidence from Egypt does show that people of Semitic race (like the Israelites) were to be found in Egypt at certain periods, and some, like Joseph, held important jobs and were given Egyptian names. Others, however, like the Israelite tribes after Joseph's death, were slaves of low status. So there is no reason to doubt the Old Testament's story of a long period of slavery in Egypt for the people of Israel, and an eventual Exodus under the leadership of Moses.

The conquest of Canaan

After the Exodus and forty years in the wilderness, the Israelites were led by Joshua in a war of conquest in which, according to Joshua 1–11, most of Canaan's important cities were destroyed.

The tombs of the wealthy in ancient Egypt were often decorated with scenes associated with the life and activities of the dead person. These tomb paintings provide an interesting record of life and customs. This painting from around 1400 BC shows a garden pool surrounded by fruit trees. Fish and ducks can be seen in the water and lotus flowers float on the surface.

This event is one for which we would expect some archaeological evidence, since the destruction of a city usually leaves clear traces.

While the Book of Joshua tells of the destruction of many cities, the city of Jericho is the most famous of these, and the one about which most has been written. In the 1930's, an archaeologist called Garstang discovered evidence of an earthquake and a destruction of the city which he thought marked the end of Jericho as described in Joshua 6. Later, in the 1950's, Dame Kathleen Kenyon excavated more of Jericho's mound, and found that the walls which had fallen in the earthquake really belonged to Abraham's time, and so could not have had anything to do with Joshua 6. Dame Kenyon found no trace of a destruction, or even of a city wall, at the end of the Late Bronze Age – which is when most scholars think Joshua lived. This does not mean that the Bible's story is not true, because it is known that when an ancient city is abandoned for a long time, wind and rain can eventually remove the latest layers, washing their remains down the sides of the mound. The Bible tells us that Jericho was abandoned until the time of King Ahab after its destruction in Joshua's day (1 Kings 16:34), so the remains of that destruction could have been completely eroded during that long period.

There is, however, another way of understanding the evidence. We should perhaps connect the destruction in Joshua's day with an earlier city at Jericho – in other words, with an older stratum of the mound. It is a fact that not all biblical scholars agree over the date of the Exodus and Conquest. While many put these events in the 13th century BC, and place the Conquest at the end of the Late Bronze Age, some prefer a date almost 200 years earlier, in the 15th century BC. (We have to remember that with dates BC, the *higher* dates are the *earlier* ones!) If this earlier date is the right one, it may be that Joshua's destruction of Jericho came at the end of the *Middle* Bronze Age city. There is plenty of evidence that this earlier city was violently destroyed and burnt, as in Joshua 6:24.

Many of the other cities which Joshua destroyed, for example Hazor (see Joshua 11), have produced evidence which fits both the high and low dates for the Conquest, so whichever date we decide to follow, we have evidence which may illustrate the Old Testament story. The one city which has produced no evidence of a destruction at either date is Ai (Josh. 7, 8), but this probably has a simple explanation – the mound identified as the site of Ai may not be the right one! Several people have suggested this, and if they are right, the real site of Ai is still waiting somewhere for an archaeologist to excavate it.

King Solomon and later

Moving on some centuries from the time of Joshua, we come to the time when Israel was ruled by a monarchy. The Old Testament tells us that Israel's third king, Solomon, was a great builder. He built the Temple at Jerusalem, and also a royal palace. Unfortunately, there has been so much other building activity in the same area since Solomon's time, that no remains of Solomon's buildings at Jerusalem seem to be left – though some may still wait to be found in the future. But Solomon built at other places too. The Bible mentions in particular that Solomon rebuilt the three important cities of Hazor, Megiddo and

A reconstructed model of the city of Megiddo. In the foreground is the gateway with tower and guard chambers.

A horse trough discovered during the excavations at Megiddo.

46

Part of a frieze from Nineveh showing the Assyrians deporting prisoners.

Gezer (1 Kings 9:15).

Archaeologists have discovered the same kind of city gateway at all three of these cities, and the pottery from the same strata as these gateways is the pottery dated to Solomon's time (the 10th Century BC – Solomon reigned roughly 970–930BC). So it looks as though we have here the remains of the walls and gates built on Solomon's orders – all built from the same plan, with only slight differences. These gateways have towers at their entrances, and three guard-chambers on each side of the passage leading into the city.

At Megiddo, buildings were found which seem to be stables, and at first it was thought that these also belonged to the city of Solomon's time, especially since the Bible says that Solomon traded in horses and built 'cities for his chariots' (1 Kings 9:19). It is now known, however, that the stables at Megiddo belong to a later stratum, and were part of the city of Ahab's time (roughly 870–850BC).

The history of Israel under its later kings is a tragic one, with Assyrian armies invading in 733BC, 722BC, and 701BC, and invasions by the Babylonian armies of Nebuchadnezzar soon after 600BC. These resulted in the destruction of Jerusalem (including the Temple) and the Exile of the Jewish people in 587BC. Archaeology has shown that many Israelite and Judean cities were destroyed at these times, providing clear evidence of the violence of the Assyrian and Babylonian invasions.

Qumran and the Dead Sea Scrolls

Before we move on to the New Testament period, we must say something about the famous Dead Sea Scrolls. These were found in 1947 and the following years, rolled up in jars which had been hidden in caves near the western shore of the Dead Sea. Soon after the accidental discovery, archaeologists decided to excavate the nearby ruins – the site now known as Qumran. The buildings at Qumran belonged to the community where the scrolls had been produced. One of the buildings was a hall where the scrolls were copied. Another was a potter's workshop where jars were made, of the kind in which the scrolls were found. Other rooms included a kitchen, a bakery, and various storerooms and workshops. Coins found on the site tell us that the settlement was founded in about 135BC. It was abandoned during the Jewish war with the Romans in AD66–73.

The scrolls are the library of the people who lived at Qumran, and are our best guide to their beliefs. The people of Qumran were probably a branch of the Essenes, a religious group mentioned by some ancient writers. They were certainly a very strict sect, even stricter in their interpretation of the religious laws than the Pharisees of the New Testament. They

Jerusalem in the time of Jesus

Jerusalem in Jesus' time was largely the work of Herod the Great, who rebuilt many parts of the city. Remains of Herod's buildings still survive, and from these (with the help of some descriptions written by a first-century historian called Josephus), we have a good idea of what many areas looked like at the time of Jesus' ministry.

The huge platform of Herod's temple still survives, and so do traces of the palace which he built on the opposite side of the city. We know the site of the Pool of Bethesda (or Bethzatha), where Jesus healed the man who had been lame for 38 years (John 5), and of the Pool of Siloam, where Jesus sent the blind man to wash after he had put clay on his eyes (John 9). Some places are more difficult to identify. For example, there are three possible sites for the Praetorium (the house of the Roman governor) where Jesus was brought before Pontius Pilate (John 18:28–33).

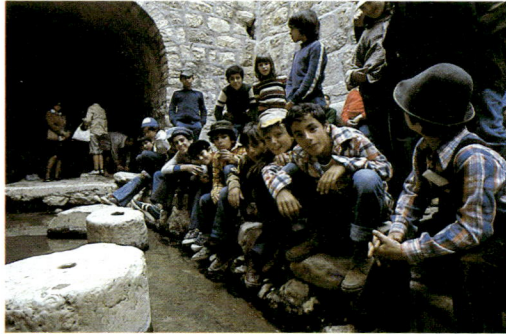

A group of schoolchildren visiting the Pool of Siloam.

There has also been disagreement over the sites of Jesus' crucifixion and burial. At the end of the 19th century, General Gordon suggested that Calvary and Jesus' tomb lay in an area just north of the Old City's present walls. A much older tradition, probably going back to before AD135, puts both sites *inside* the present-day walls. This is the area where the Church of the Holy Sepulchre now stands. We know that Jesus was crucified and buried *outside* the walls of Jerusalem (John 19:17; Hebrews 13:12). However,

expected the early coming of a new age, and believed that a king, a prophet and a priest would arise to rule in it.

As well as many of the community's own books, the scrolls include parts of several books of the Old Testament. Of about 500 documents, about 100 are books of the Old Testament, and

are some of the oldest copies we have.

Although the finds at Qumran do not relate directly to any events described in the Bible, they throw useful light on the way some people were thinking in the period between the Old and New Testaments. Some writers have suggested that John the Baptist lived for a while among the people of Qumran, before beginning his work of announcing the ministry of Jesus – but this is only a possibility, and many disagree with the idea.

1. The caves at Qumran where the scrolls were found in clay jars.
2. Many of the fragments of the scrolls are now kept in this jar-shaped building, known as The Shrine of the Book, in Jerusalem.

The black marble slab on the right contrasts with the white roof of the Shrine to symbolise the conflict between light and darkness which was basic to the beliefs of the Essenes.
3. Excavations at the site of the Essene community.

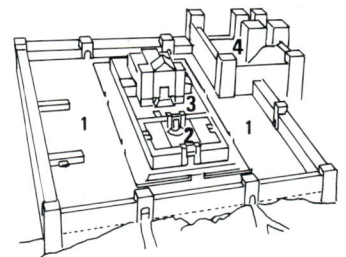

Herod's Temple was a magnificent structure in cream stone. It was finished only six years before the Romans destroyed it when they sacked Jerusalem in AD 70.

1. Court of the Gentiles.
2. Court of the Women.
3. Priests' Court.
4. Castle of Antonia.

48

excavations around the Church of the Holy Sepulchre have uncovered the remains of a tomb of the kind used in Jesus' day. This proves that the area was once a cemetery, and since the Jews never had their cemeteries inside the city, the site must have been *outside* the city walls of Jesus' time. It is therefore quite likely that the traditional site of Jesus' burial, now inside the Church of the Holy Sepulchre, really was the tomb in which His body was placed after the Crucifixion (which took place close by according to John 19:41–2) – the tomb which His disciples found empty on the first Easter morning.

Jesus would have been led up these steps to the house of the High Priest before his trial.

The limitations of archaeology

We have looked at only a few examples of how archaeology helps us to understand the Bible. A lot more could be said. However, there are certain things which archaeology cannot do. Usually, it cannot prove that a particular Bible event happened, or that a particular person existed. This is not surprising when we remember what a *small* amount of evidence archaeology can really recover. Many objects do not survive long enough for a modern archaeologist to discover them. Paper, wood and clothing will rot away very quickly unless they are buried in extremely dry conditions. Also, archaeology discovers only a very small portion of the things which *do* survive. For example, the careful and detailed excavations at Hazor between 1956 and 1970 uncovered only *a very small fraction* of the whole mound. It has been said that to excavate every area of Hazor's twenty-one strata would take 800 years!

In spite of these limits to what archaeology can do, its discoveries still give us confidence in the truth of the Bible. Archaeology has confirmed the general background of history and customs against which the Bible's stories take place, as well as painting in many new details in that background. In this way, it gives us every reason to trust the stories themselves.

An inscription mentioning the name of Pontius Pilate found on a stone at Caesarea, the main Roman port at the time of Jesus.

THE HOME

The kinds of home in which families lived in Bible times depended on two things. First, their homes had to be suited to the climate and terrain of the Bible lands; second, they had to be suited to the needs of the people at the different times in their varied history! In the very earliest times, between about 2000 and 1300BC and during the lifetimes of people like Abraham, Isaac, Jacob and Joseph, the people of Israel had no settled base. Until they became slaves in Egypt they were wandering desert shepherds. We know less about this period than the later ones, because any evidence has long since perished.

A modern Bedouin village in the hills near Bethlehem.

Cave homes

In early times some people probably lived in the caves which abound in the slopes of some of the hills, such as Mt. Carmel. These early cave homes were a protection against lions and bears as well as other fierce animals. Discoveries made on Mt. Carmel when stone was being excavated to build the new port of Haifa suggest that an average cave home would have been about 9m. wide and about 2m. high. The natural caves were enlarged and adapted for human use with the help of primitive tools. Seats were cut out of stone and there may have been some niches where lamps were put. The hearth was near the mouth of the cave for the smoke from the fire to escape; and most daily life took place in this area. It was here that the women sewed rough garments with bone needles and the men made their tools and hunting implements. In some of the caves which have been found, there are recesses and chambers which were used for storage and, possibly, for cremating the dead.

There was no furniture as such, though a rougly hewn divan bed has been found in the Caves of Ophel under the south-east brow of the plateau on which the city of Jerusalem stands.

We read of no family in the Bible who used caves as a permanent home though they were sometimes used as a temporary refuge or hide-out. When the Israelites were under threat of attack from the Midianites they 'made for themselves the dens which are in the mountains and the caves and the strong-holds' (Judges 6:2). David and Saul also used caves in similar circumstances (1 Samuel 24). But for most of the time caves were used for storage and for burial of the dead. The famous Dead Sea Scrolls – ancient manuscripts of part of the Bible discovered in 1947 – were found stored in a series of caves. Even today, the very poorest families can be found living in caves – some in the region of Bethlehem. According to one very old tradition, the manger in which Jesus was born was in such a cave.

One group of people who did make their homes in caves were bands of brigands and robbers. When Jesus cleared the money-changers out of the Temple he referred to them: 'It is written, "My house shall be called a house of prayer; but you make it a robbers' cave".'

Cave-like dwellings near Bethany.

Plan of a cave dwelling

storage chests

family living area

doorway

fireplace

lower area for animals

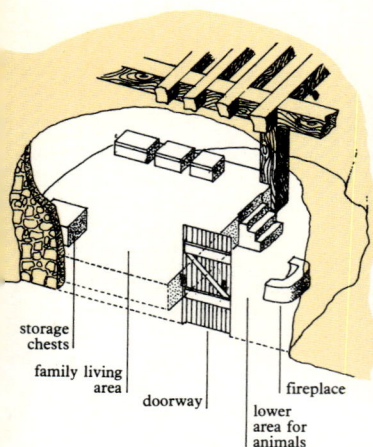

Tents

The earliest homes in which we actually see people living in the Bible are tents. The people of Israel lived in tents during the time before their slavery in Egypt and during the Exodus from Egypt to the promised land, Canaan. During these periods homes had to be mobile because the people were constantly on the move either following Moses to Canaan or following their flocks. Even after the people had settled in their new land some chose to continue living in tents, and for those who did not, the experience of having been a nomad tent-dwelling people continued to influence the way they lived. Even the way they spoke shows us this. The word in Hebrew for 'to depart' means literally 'to pull out (the tent pegs)'.

Tent-making

The earliest tents would probably have had animal skins for a covering but the more usual tents were the 'houses of hair' made from the coats of the goats. The weaving of the tent followed shearing time when this hair was plentiful. The women were responsible for the weaving on simple looms, first spinning the hairs into strands. The tent was usually black – the colour of the goats' hair – but if repairs had been carried out, the tent could have a striped effect. The fabric produced was heat- and water-resistant but would shrink taut with the rain.

In later Bible times the wool of Cilicium goats was found to be especially suitable for tent-making. This produced a material which was stiffer than the ordinary goats' wool. Of course, this meant that it was more difficult to cut and so tent-making became a specialised occupation in the district of Cilicia, around Tarsus. It was here that St. Paul grew up and he was a tent-maker by trade (Acts 18:3).

Each tent was erected in the way that tents are erected nowadays with a system of poles, pegs and guy ropes. Only late in Bible times were any fittings made of metal. For the most part wood was used. The number of poles in a tent was a status symbol – a sign of the family's standing. Usually there were at least nine, between

A goatskin churn. The churn was swung to and fro to turn the milk into butter.

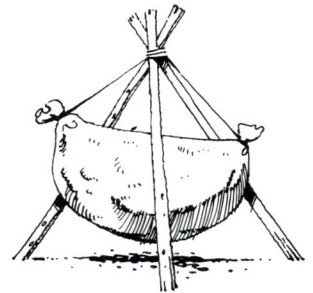

Tent furnishings

Inside the tent there were usually two rooms, the tent being divided by a hanging goat-hair curtain. The tent entrance would normally face the direction from which strangers were expected to approach. This was a precaution against attack but it was also arranged like that so that strangers could be offered hospitality. The offering of hospitality is one of the most important of Bible customs (Gen. 18:1–8). The room nearest the entrance was used for entertaining and for the men. The further, or private 'room' was for the women and children. This was also where the cooking was done. The richer families sometimes had separate tents for the women. Isaac's mother Sarah had a tent of her own, for instance. The animals would also find their way into the tents. Sometimes they had a separate entrance.

52

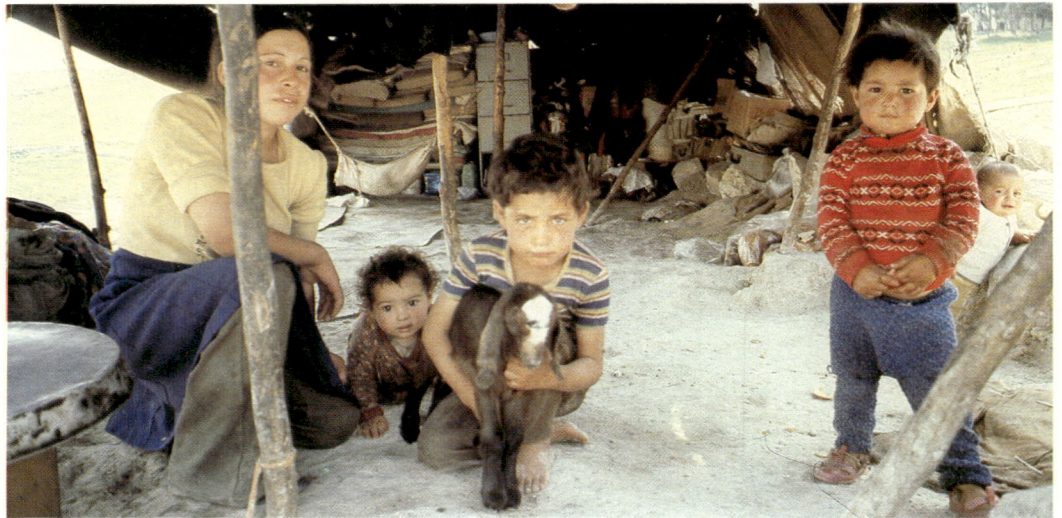

A Bedouin family in front of their tent.

A water bottle made of animal skin being filled at a desert well.

The Bedouin life style has changed little since the days of Abraham.

1.5m. and 2.5m. high, arranged to make a rectangular pattern. It was a simple home but we have to remember that the only 'building materials' available to these people were those afforded by their flocks, and the trees near to which they camped.

Life in tents was not luxurious. Materials for making equipment or furniture were very scarce, and apart from that, everything had to be portable. That is, it had to be able to be rolled or folded down and packed on the backs of asses – which meant it had to be light. So there was nothing made of stone and very little of wood or clay. There were no beds as such. Mats were used as beds and sometimes people just slept in their cloaks. The richer families may have had some cushions stuffed with animals' hair to be used mostly for guests. The 'table' was a simple circle of leather. Even this was dual purpose with rings round the edge so that it could be drawn up with a piece of cord and used as a carrying-bag. Otherwise there may have been a few baskets, and, of

course, a mallet for the tent pegs.

The water bottle was very important in the desert. This 'skin of water' as it was sometimes called, was made of a whole skin of a goat or kid carried on the back. When goats' milk was carried in such a skin it quickly became sour and this sour milk was thought most refreshing – more so than fresh milk. What was not drunk was left to churn into an oily kind of butter.

Camp sites

Tents were pitched in groups, partly for protection against attack, but mostly because the Hebrew people enjoyed being part of a community and wanted to live together. Family ties were strong and married children would usually stay with their father's group. They had to find camp-sites near water and they particularly liked spots which were near oak trees. So Abram 'moved his tent and dwelt by the oaks of Mamre'. Later, villages grew up around these sites. Shepherds continued to live in tents throughout the period of the Bible and even today very similar tents are used by bedouin tribesmen living a similar kind of life to that of Abraham and Isaac.

Booths

A different kind of tent-like building called a hut or booth was sometimes used by shepherds. It was made of branches and meant to be a temporary shelter for someone who had to be in a certain place for a while because of his job. It was particularly associated with those who picked the grapes in the vineyards, and the watchmen who kept an eye on the vineyards. The Israelites had a yearly 'Festival of Booths' to celebrate the wine-harvest. Later they also celebrated their escape from Egypt at this Festival, remembering the times when, as a nation, they lived in tents.

Houses

It took a great deal of adapting for the Israelites to settle in permanent villages and towns, and live in anything other than tents. But this is what they had to do after they entered the promised land. However, many of the traditions and customs of nomad days survived. Some people still lived in tents, forming a kind of suburb around the towns. During dry spells, the tent dwellers would be joined by the nomadic herdsmen from the semi-desert areas.

The Canaanite towns they came to occupy looked rather like castles on tops of hills. Inside the walls the houses were packed tightly together in what today we would call slum conditions. When the Israelites took over they began by patching and making do. The larger official buildings were used as hostels until proper homes were available.

Most families lived in overcrowded conditions, possibly all sharing one room with an assortment of sheep and goats. Though things gradually improved, in the beginning life was pretty dismal. In winter, since there were no chimneys, the rooms would be stuffy and ill-lit. In summer they would be infested with insects.

Canaanite towns were built on hills and were strongly fortified. The Israelites had to conquer and occupy such towns when they settled in Canaan.

A village of beehive-shaped houses in Syria.

In the old quarters of cities like Jerusalem, streets are narrow and houses packed tightly together.

When they began to build for themselves things improved. The first houses were circular – rather like big bee-hives – looking something like a permanent tent! The typical house was square, facing north to avoid the heat of the sun. There was just one floor with a small yard in front which was the scene of most activity during the day. The insides of the houses were dark, there being few windows so that the house would stay cool. Animals were usually kept in the yard. The walls of the houses were made of mud. When it was wet these walls would have leaked water. Proverbs compares the effect of an argumentative woman to the continual dripping from such a wall on a rainy day.

Roofs

The roof was always flat and made of brushwood overlaid with clay and rolled. Such a roof would have to be continually re-rolled and it was not uncommon for roofs to start sprouting vegetation. Though it was firm enough to walk on, the roof could be broken open easily as was the roof of the house in which Jesus was teaching when the paralysed man with four friends let him down through the roof so that Jesus could heal him. (Mark 2:1–12.) The roof was used as an extra room and access to it was by a staircase going up the outside of the house or in poorer cases by a ladder. The floors of the houses were simply mud. Sometimes, depending on the area, this was mixed with limestone chips and rolled or beaten hard. Villages consisting of houses like this were commonplace to Samuel, David and even the young Jesus.

In summer, a temporary second storey would sometimes be made with a shelter of branches. In later times more houses had a permanent 'upper room'. As is usual, the rich had these first. One King of Moab is described in the book of Judges as having a 'cool roof chamber' which also had a door with a lock. These roof chambers were the coolest and airiest and therefore the best rooms and were reserved for the head of the household or for guests. It was on this basis that Jesus had his last supper with his disciples in just such an upper room.

The houses of the rich

Between the tenth and eighth centuries BC, as the Israelites got used to town life and had their own kings, a big social change took place. The 'civil service' increased and business boomed. A merchant navy was built and trading ties between the Israelites and Egypt and Syria were strengthened. The old tribal ties broke down. The result was that the gap between the rich and the poor, once very narrow, became wider and this was most obvious in the kinds of house the two groups lived in – as is generally the case nowadays. The rich built bigger houses. They would not have had more floors but they covered more ground space. A typical rich merchant's house was shaped like a capital E with the middle prong cut out, built around a central courtyard. This pattern continued in Palestine well into New Testament times. In the poor village homes there was one ground-floor room split into two levels, the higher level (sometimes called a *mastaby*) possibly supported by arches. Everyday life would continue on the platforms while the cattle lived underneath. The flat roof pattern continued, and by law a wall or parapet had to be built around the outside of it so that no one would fall off and kill himself (Deut. 22:8).

The houses of the rich in New Testament times could be 15 or 20 metres high. There were still few windows. This was most basically a matter of security because a man's wealth was kept in his house. A heavy gate opened from the street on to a passage or courtyard around which the main quarters would be built. In such houses there were a number of storage rooms, including one for storing riches! The rich tended to live upstairs in summer and downstairs in winter.

Building materials

Other developments in housing between the early settled days and New Testament times were in the building materials used. Two types of bricks were used. Sun-baked mud bricks were made from a mud called *libri* and left in the sun to harden. Bricks 53 cms × 25 cms × 10 cms have been unearthed by archaeologists. These could be bound with straw as they were in Egypt when the captive Israelites had the job of gathering the straw. Fire-baked bricks were rarer but have been found, for example in the foundations of the Chaldean city of Ur from which Abraham came.

Stone houses were found where the materials were available – initially in the highlands. Built to the same design, the main feature was the importance of the cornerstone. Jesus is compared to the cornerstone in the New Testament (Ephesians 2:20). There were stone houses in the Bethlehem area and it is likely that David's father's

Inside a typical Israelite house. The family occupied the raised platform. The lower area was used for storage and the animals sheltered there at night.

One-storey houses like these were typical throughout the East in Bible times.

house was built with stone. Later, as stone could be transported, stone houses were built elsewhere. They have been found at Bethel, for instance, where they had floors made out of flagstones.

We know more about the houses of the rich because they were made out of these stronger materials, and lasted longer. We know that rich homes had sturdy wooden doors with metal hinges. But the cloth and

A fire-baked brick inscribed in cuneiform writing, found in the foundations of Ur, the city of Abraham.

leather doors have not survived. The wooden doors were locked rather like a modern fire door, with a bar on the inside.

A mosaic floor decoration in the bath house of King Herod's palace at Masada.

Roman houses

By New Testament times the rich had become a totally separate class and in their homes were some of the new ideas that had come with the arrival of foreigners to what we now call Israel. The Romans had built houses in their native style and the richer Jews copied some of their ideas. The Romans in fact re-built several towns, including Jericho, and the better houses there had libraries, picture galleries and art studios. The floors were decorated with mosaic. Whereas the Hebrew people

preferred to live in groups, it was now more common to see isolated rich mansions surrounded by shops which supplied their needs. Wallpaper was unknown but wall-painting was common. In Gentile (non-Jewish) homes there may have been a small chapel attached to the house where some pagan goddess would be worshipped. In poorer homes decorations were few.

Poorer people influenced by the Roman way of life might have lived in *insulae*, which we would call flats, let in blocks or floors. During New Testament times building regulations increased. Emperor

Nero was especially keen on these. He decreed the houses should have fire escapes and that fire-proof materials should be used for outside walls. Some scholars think that the great fire of Rome for which the Christians got the blame, and which probably led to the persecution in which Peter and Paul died, was started at Nero's command to bring his regulations into effect and clear some of the slums. However, most of the Bible tells of people who lived in homes which had not been influenced by newcomers from the West – homes which were native to Palestine.

Furniture

For the Hebrew people hospitality was everything. Under one roof, apart from the immediate family, there may have been orphans, widows, wandering travellers or 'sojourners' and servants. There was very little room, therefore, let alone money, for furniture. By and large the furnishings did not differ greatly from those of their forefathers' tents. Unlike most houses we know the hearth and fireplace were not important – indeed only the larger homes had them inside. The fireplace consisted of a hole dug in the floor where wood, thorns and dung-cakes could be burned. Most people sat and slept on mats on the floor. The whole family would sleep lying together fully clothed. This was the case in the story Jesus told of the man who would not lend to his neighbour with the excuse, 'Do not bother me . . . my children are with me in bed.' (Luke 11:7.) Sometimes a mattress took the place of a mat. These were easy to carry so it is quite easy to understand how Jesus could say to the man who had been cured of paralysis,

Food, drink and cooking

While they were a travelling people, the Israelites had to depend largely on their herds for much of their food and some of their drink, although of course they usually camped near water. Food was therefore rather dull. During the Exodus the people constantly complained that either they had nothing to eat or that what they had lacked variety (Num.

A Roman dual purpose bed, used for sleeping by night and for reclining at table by day.

Right: an attractive display of fruit and vegetables at a stall in Jerusalem.

Below: Eastern markets sell a rich variety of spices for use in cooking.

'Rise, take up your bed and go home.' (Mark 2:11.) Some sleeping families may have covered themselves with a simple coverlet.

The poorer the person, the nearer the ground he slept. Kings, such as Og, King of Bashan, had proper iron bedsteads (Deut. 3:11 NIV). Other simple wooden divans were used by the richer of the ordinary people in later times, when mattresses stuffed with rushes, wool or feathers were also more common. The beds of the rich were sometimes lavishly decorated. Babies slept in woollen cradles slung from the roof – another custom from more primitive days. Tables were rare. In New Testament times Roman influence made low tables more popular. Roman influence was also responsible for 'dual-purpose' beds. At night they would be used for sleeping and by day they would be used for reclining by the table to eat. Most of the other implements in the house were used for cooking, lighting or heating.

1 This limestone figure of a baker kneading dough comes from Egypt, about 2000BC.

2 Baking bread in a chimney oven.

3 A delivery of bread to a stall in a Jerusalem street market.

4 A millstone used for grinding grain into flour for bread.

5 Druze girl baking a pancake type of bread on a metal plate over a fire.

11:4–6). When they settled in Canaan, things became easier. Not only could crops be grown but more rare commodities such as spices could be bought in the market places which were supplied by caravans of traders.

Bread-making

Bread was the basic ingredient in every meal. In Hebrew 'to eat bread' means, 'to have a meal'. When we read that the disciples who walked with Jesus to Emmaus after the Resurrection then 'broke bread' with him, we understand that they had a meal together (Luke 24:20). Bread was

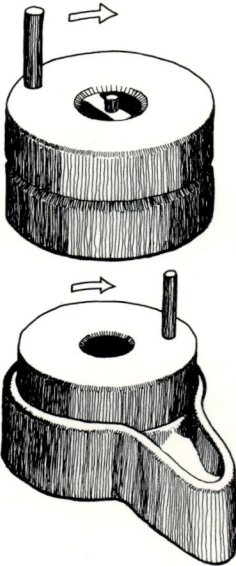

How a millstone works. The grain dropped into the centre hole is crushed between the stones and comes out as flour. Below: a quern was an earlier form of grindstone.

made from barley flour or wheat flour. Barley loaves such as those with which Jesus fed the multitude, were the commonest. Bread was baked every day.

First the ears of corn were ground into meal. This was done in early times with a pestle and mortar similar to those used in old-fashioned chemists' shops. Later, corn was ground on a stone shaped like a saddle called a *quern*. Very late in Old Testament times, the mill was introduced. This consisted of two large round stones. The bottom one remained still and the top one was turned with a wooden handle. The grain was ground between them. Two women were needed to work this: one to pour grain and the other to turn the wheel (Matt. 24:41).

The meal was then mixed with salt and water to form a dough which was kneaded in a special bowl and could then be left either to leaven in the sun, or baked unleavened. Bread was baked in a variety of ways. 'Ash cakes' such as Elijah ate when he was fleeing from Queen Jezebel (1 Kings 19:1–8), were baked on hot stones (heated by wood and dung cakes) which were covered with ashes. Other bread was baked in simple 'ovens'. An oven was a simple earthenware plate (or later, a metal sheet) placed on a fire and supported by stones – a kind of early 'hot-plate'. Such bread would resemble a dry pancake. Otherwise a fire was lit at the bottom of something resembling an earthenware chimney pot and the dough was stuck in flat cakes to the side of the 'chimney'. Variations included the popular 'parched corn' made from ears of corn lightly roasted, cakes and pastry. Sometimes the cake was made more moist by adding olive oil to the mixture and sometimes honey was added to make it sweeter.

Olives were plentiful and olive oil was the basic cooking fat. Its other household uses included medicinal uses and as a personal washing agent. The jars for storing this oil and the equipment for baking bread were the basic kitchen utensils. Bread was baked in the house (or tent), in the courtyard or on the roof.

Cooking methods

Among the fruits and vegetables which were available were grapes (including

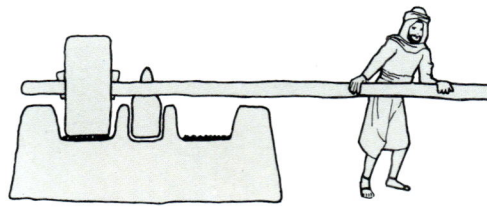

A type of olive press. The olives were placed in a circular trough. They were crushed by the heavy stone, pushed by the man walking round the trough.

Right: an olive crusher used to extract olive oil.

raisins), figs, dates, pomegranates and mulberries. The fruits were sometimes dried and pressed into cakes – the way in which we still eat them. Near to the Sea of Galilee fish was an important food – often just roasted on an open fire (John 21:9–14). Most of the food was vegetarian.

Meat was a luxury reserved for special feasts (including religious festivals) and guests. The meat was usually mutton but a calf would sometimes be specially fattened

An old jug found recently in an archaeological excavation outside Jerusalem.

Fish being unloaded at Fishing Harbour, Tiberias.

Women carrying waterpots are still a common sight in many Eastern countries.

1 Pomegranates were eaten fresh and were also used to make wine.

2 Olives are grown throughout the Mediterranean area.

3 Quail were eaten by the Israelites during their desert wanderings.

for a really special guest, as when the father welcomed home the prodigal son (Luke 15:23). There were strict rules governing how animals should be killed and meat prepared. Meat was usually boiled but the Passover lamb was always roasted. The tail of the sheep was most prized and could weigh up to fifteen pounds. The very rich ate meat more often. The court of King Solomon would get through a thousand sheep each day.

Some vegetables such as small cucumbers, were eaten raw. Others were boiled or stewed in either water or oil in deep round bowls. Lentils and some green vegetables would have been prepared in this way. Beans, onions, leeks and garlic often formed part of the menu which could even include insects. Skewered locusts were a delicacy and grasshoppers were also cooked and eaten, first having been mixed with honey to take away the bitterness. Locusts and wild honey were the main diet of John the Baptist in the wilderness.

Drinks

Unlike the Philistines, the Israelites were not great beer drinkers but wine was a popular drink. The rich mixed their wine with water. The poor mixed theirs with spices and got drunk very easily – this was the kind of drink Jesus was offered on the Cross. A wine was made from pomegranates and a popular laxative drink was made from figs. Wine, like milk and water, was kept in skins, but was sometimes decanted into long-necked bottles.

Simple kitchen utensils like these may have been in use in New Testament times.

A Greek cooking pot.

Meals

There is no mention in the Old Testament of breakfast but we read that Jesus once made breakfast for his disciples (John 21:12). The most important meals were taken at midday and evening. Ritual was important at mealtime. The seating plan showed the order of importance of guests and, particularly in the case of festival meals, the meal itself followed a set formal pattern. In New Testament times Roman custom added more colour to the existing ritual. At a typical dinner party there would be nine guests, each specially dressed in colourful robes. The guests would eat reclining on couches or mats, their sandals having first been removed and their feet washed. The hands were used for eating and they were washed between courses.

In Roman times there were a greater variety of utensils for 'kitchen' use. These included urns and metal cauldrons and even sometimes a saucepan. There might also have been found strainers, spoons, forks, knives and ladles. There were wicker baskets for holding fruit, wooden casks for storage and containers for charcoal which was the main material used in heating for cooking.

There was no special menu for babies. These were breast-fed until they were two or three years old. It is worth recalling that some foods common to us would not have been available in most Bible homes. Most important of these is the egg – unknown till New Testament times as the hen was not kept until then. Poultry as a whole was rare though partridge and quail were eaten occasionally. Fruits and vegetables which were not known include bananas, apricots, tomatoes and pumpkins.

These pottery bowls, found in excavations at Beersheba, date back to the time of the prophet Isaiah.

Essential services

Included under this heading are the household services we take for granted: water, lighting, heating, drainage and sanitation. One of the reasons why early towns were so overcrowded and slum-like was that they had to be situated near to a spring or well. Water could not be stored. Once the people found how to make a waterproof cistern lined with lime plaster they could build further away and store rain-water. The ancient town of Lachish was probably one of the first to be built away from a spring. Here archaeologists have found homes with cisterns dug out of the ground or excavated out of rock. There was also some attempt to build drains and gutters to feed these tanks but they were not very satisfactory and very unhygienic. To have a cistern of one's own was everyone's dream (2 Kings 18:31 NIV). Otherwise water had to be carried, having first been drawn from a well, in a leather bucket on a piece of rope. If, as was usual, the town was on a hill, this meant a long and tiring walk!

By New Testament times cisterns had been improved and were in common use. However, the Romans improved things greatly by organising a water supply from reservoirs through aqueducts. This water supply was state-owned and controlled by a high-ranking official who fixed a charge for it. The poor got their water from the public fountain supplied by the same source.

Lighting

The basic form of lighting was the olive oil lamp. In its basic form this was a saucer filled with oil into which was fed a wick of flax or hemp. Such a lamp would either be placed on a lampstand or suspended from the ceiling by a chain. Later, olive oil lamps were more ornate and lamps of many patterns have been found by archaeologists, but the basic working principle remained the same. Candles were made of wax or tallow with the pith of a rush for a wick. These were used by the very poor, and in funeral processions. The lamps had to be lit somehow and of course there were no matches! It was therefore most important to keep a fire going. Sometimes fire was borrowed. The initial fire was probably started with flint, steel and tinder. This fire was also used for heating.

In New Testament times a hollow depression in the floor would be filled with charcoal or uncharred wood and lit, the flames being fanned with bellows. When they had died down, a board and then a carpet would be placed on top. Alternatively a bronze or pottery brazier could be used which would be raised and

An olive oil lamp was the basic form of lighting in Jewish homes.

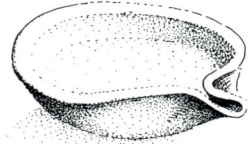

Oil lamps became more ornate later. This Roman lamp from the 1st century AD shows men treading grapes.

Steps leading down into a cistern at El Jib.

A little girl carrying a waterpot. She balances it on a pad on her head.

open, like the one around which Peter warmed himself after Jesus' arrest.

Central heating was invented in the first century AD in the form of under-floor heating. A central furnace supplied hot air or hot water by means of pipes to the various rooms. Some rich Jews may have had such a system in their houses, though such homes would have been exceptional.

Sanitation

Sanitation, until New Testament times, was very primitive but the Romans introduced toilets with running water. These drained into cesspools which were cleared by carts. The Law or Torah laid down basic regulations for personal hygiene but the quality of sanitation varied greatly even towards the end of the Biblical period. It was better in the towns – especially in the Temple area. Nothing which might be a risk to health, e.g. cemeteries, was allowed within 20 to 25 metres of a town. The Romans also introduced the domestic bath. It was only late in our period that hot baths were common. In the bigger cities there were then public baths for which a charge was made. These were rather like our Turkish baths and oil was used lavishly in the bathing process.

Ruins of the bath house at Masada, showing the underfloor area where hot steam was circulated.

Home life

The main features of home life were family loyalty and a sharing of work. Food and clothing were the main responsibilities of the mother who would start work before dawn, making bread. She would also have to keep the house tidy, look after the children, prepare the meals, help in the fields and perhaps go to town to sell produce or craftware. If she stayed at home her afternoons would be spent sewing, weaving, spinning or plaiting straw.

An Arab housewife sweeping the house.

The children helped with collecting fuel, filling and trimming the lamps and carrying the water. They might also do some spinning and baking. The men were out all day working and older sons would help – perhaps as shepherd boys, or in the fields or vineyards. Younger children would still find time to play with toys such as whistles, rattles, miniature furniture, like that found in modern dolls' houses but made of pottery, and clay animals.

Washing clothes was probably done by all the women together at the brook or other water source. Crafts were probably localised and handed on in families. The girls would learn to weave and decorate clothes. The boys might learn some more technical 'craft' as a kind of apprentice. Some villages specialised in certain crafts such as pottery ware or iron work.

A woman carrying produce to market.

A farmer threshing wheat. He is standing on a threshing board which is pulled over the wheat to separate the grain from the stalks.

The clay animal on wheels was probably a child's toy in Babylonia before the time of Abraham.

Social activities

The roof was of special importance in home life, particularly in the summer. Looking at the uses to which it was put gives us a good final view of what home life was like in Bible times. Whether it was uncovered, covered with boughs or made into a permanent upper floor, it was the pleasantest part of the house, the best place to sleep and therefore the automatic quarters of any guest.

If uncovered, the roof was a natural social centre where families gathered. News was exchanged from the roof tops, washing was dried there and some cooking could be done there. It was the place where fruits were ripened and bread was left to leaven. Feasting, music and dancing which were the main spare-time activities would be centred there with the women taking their part. Small altars could be set there and prayers were said on the roof. It was, in fact, the centre of a full and busy home life of a very industrious and adaptable people.

A view over the rooftops of the ancient city of Hebron.

THE FAMILY

In Bible times the family was a much larger group than our Western family of father, mother and children. It was more like a clan or the extended family of Eastern countries, and included grandparents, aunts, uncles and cousins. Servants were thought of as part of the family too. The father was the central authority in the home with power to divorce his wife without explanation and even to have disobedient children put to death. While it is unlikely that a father would go to such lengths, discipline was strict but family loyalty and stability were strong.

A Bedouin family inside their tent.

Birth

Children as a gift of God

In Israel children were regarded as a blessing from God (Psalm 127:3), and a large family was the Israelite ideal. There were, of course, certain practical reasons for desiring many children. A large family would make a strong team in various walks of life, and many sons, in particular, would make their father more important in the local community (Ps. 127:4–5). Also, children were, in a sense, their father's property, and if the family were very poor they could be sold as slaves in order to make some money (Exodus 21:7). Above all, however, the Israelites believed that in some way or other they continued to live in their children, especially their sons. At the least, one could say that without sons the family would come to an end for ever. The family which had only daughters was in a serious situation because girls usually married into another family, and so they became part of their husband's household. For this reason the birth of a girl was a less joyous occasion. Nevertheless, children as such were a great blessing while childlessness was a real misfortune (1 Samuel 1:5–6).

Preparing for a baby

In the ancient world there were no antenatal clinics and the mothers-to-be received no special instruction apart from listening to the sayings and stories told by the women of the family or of the village. Just as boys learned their trade and other useful knowledge from their fathers or elders so also girls received their necessary instruction and training from their mothers and from watching other people. It is possible also that children's games played some little part in this process of education for life (Matthew 11:16–17).

The amount and nature of the preparations for the arrival of the baby would largely depend on the wealth and status of the family. Most communities of the ancient world had their own ideas of what prospective mothers should or should not do. Some of these do's and don'ts were the results of common sense observations, e.g. a pregnant woman should not carry heavy burdens or do strenuous work. Other kinds of advice, however, were largely based on superstition, for example, the idea that simply by wearing small stone charms a woman could prevent miscarriage.

It is very likely that some time before the birth of the baby, the mother and her closest female relatives gathered together some of the items needed for the forthcoming birth, e.g. salt, oil, swaddling-clothes, and other useful articles.

Baby clothes

It is doubtful that there were any special baby dresses, apart from the swaddling-clothes which were strips of cloth, not necessarily new. The baby was wrapped in a sort of small sheet or blanket or a piece of old cloth, and then bandaged with the swaddling-band (Luke 2:7). The main purpose of these articles was to protect the newborn child and to make it easier to carry the infant. It was also thought that this wrapping of the baby would strengthen its back and limbs so that they would develop properly and grow straight.

Bedouin children drinking camel milk.

66

A chair used in the Jewish ceremony of circumcision.

A Greek vase depicting a child learning to walk.

Jewish children enjoyed playing pretend weddings and funerals. Jesus referred to these games and probably joined in them when he was a boy.

Baby's birth

Since there were no hospitals, births usually took place in the home, and the mother-to-be was often assisted by a midwife or female relatives or simply by her neighbours (Exod. 1:19). The midwife was probably an older local woman with some experience of childbirths. They were not always professional.

Normally the father was not present at the birth of his child but the good news would be taken to him (Jeremiah 20:15).

In ordinary circumstances, immediately after the birth, the most elementary care for the infant consisted of four essential details: the baby's navel-string was cut and tied, then the baby was washed in water, rubbed with salt, and finally wrapped in swaddling-clothes or a blanket. After this basic treatment the infant could be laid in a trough or manger, like the infant Jesus (Luke 2:7), and it would serve as a simple cradle. At some point, of course, the baby would be given its first feed.

The purpose of rubbing the baby with salt is not clear. In some cases it probably meant that the infant was washed with salt water, as in more recent times in bedouin families of the Near East. This practice may well have had a real medicinal value, however limited, but originally it probably had a religious if not superstitious significance.

The date of birth was, no doubt, remembered but it does not seem that birthdays were celebrated in Israel. They are usually mentioned in connection with foreigners, and therefore it may have been a non-Jewish custom (Matt. 14:6).

Babies were breast-fed by their mothers a good many months, perhaps even for two or three years. So the young Samuel remained with his mother until he was weaned; then he was taken to the sanctuary at Shiloh to start his training. This suggests that he must have been several years old (1 Sam. 1:24). Not infrequently a celebration was made on the occasion of weaning. For example, we are told that Abraham made a feast on the day when his son Isaac was weaned (Genesis 21:8).

After the birth the mother was regarded as ceremonially unclean for seven days if she bore a son and for fourteen days if she bore a daughter (Leviticus 12:2, 5). This time of ritual impurity was followed by an additional period of thirty-three and sixty-six days, respectively. These ideas were part of the accepted customs but the real reasons for these practices were probably forgotten. At the end of these days of ritual uncleanness, the woman had to offer a sacrifice, a year-old ram or a pair of young pigeons (Lev. 12:7–8).

Circumcision

Circumcision was a minor surgical operation (removal of the foreskin) performed on all boys. So, in accordance with the law, Jesus was circumcised on the eighth day and, at the same time, was given his name (Luke 2:21). In some Jewish circles the seven days preceding the circumcision were occasions for small nightly celebrations, and this period was known as the 'son's week'. In every Jewish home the actual day of circumcision was a festive time. The infant boy was usually circumcised by the head of the family but at a later time the rite was performed by a professional doctor.

Circumcision was regarded as the outward sign of belonging to the people of Israel, and also as a token of belonging to God. In the course of time the Early Church decided that circumcision was not necessary for non-Jewish Christians and therefore this practice is not observed in Christian churches.

Circumcision was used by many peoples of the ancient past, and therefore it is likely that its earlier significance also for the Hebrews may have been different from that given to it by the Jewish people at a later time. It could well be that at first it was an initiation rite performed on older boys to mark their growing up from boyhood to manhood.

Names

The naming of the child was done by the mother and sometimes by the father but in exceptional circumstances it could be done by some other people (1 Sam. 4:21). During the earlier part of the Old Testament period people's names usually had a special meaning and they could denote many different ideas. Some names were an expression of the parents' own attitude to God or of some other religious experience; sometimes the name (which is often in the form of a short sentence or sentence-name) could be even an implicit prayer. So for example the name Elijah means 'My God is Yahweh', Isaiah is 'Salvation of Yahweh', while Jonathan can be translated as 'Yahweh has given (the child)'. Yahweh is the particular Hebrew name for the God of Israel.

Other types of names may refer to a particular happening at the time of the child's birth. Eli's grandson was called Ichabod which means 'No glory', and the reason for the name was the fact that he was born immediately after the news of Israel's defeat by the Philistines was received in Shiloh (1 Sam. 4:19). Deborah's colleague may have been called Barak, meaning 'Thunder', because of a thunderstorm during his birth.

However, although most names have a fairly clear meaning, it is not always easy for us to see why some were chosen, such as Tamar ('palm-tree'), Caleb ('dog'), Rachel ('ewe'), Ahab ('father's brother') or Azzan ('strong'). It is possible that names of this type could describe some characteristic of the child or express some wish on the part of the parents that the child should or should not become like the object or creature denoted by the given name.

Towards the end of the Old Testament period it became the custom to give traditional names to children and the meaning of the name was no longer of any great

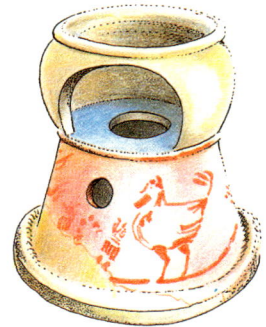

A drawing on a Greek vase, showing a baby's combined high chair and potty, enabled a reconstruction to be made from a broken chair discovered in Athens.

A Bedouin woman and her child with their flock of goats.

importance. So we read that the relatives of John (later known as John the Baptist) were surprised that his mother called him John (Luke 1:61) because there was no one in their family who had that name. Customarily, the boy would have been given the name of his grandfather, especially if the latter was dead.

During Old Testament times the baby was named soon after its birth (Gen. 35:18) but not necessarily at circumcision. There were no surnames, so children in the same family could have 'the son (or the daughter) of so-and-so', added to their name.

Right: the hippopotamus goddess Taueret, the Egyptian patron of women in childbirth.

A Roman relief showing a baby being bathed.

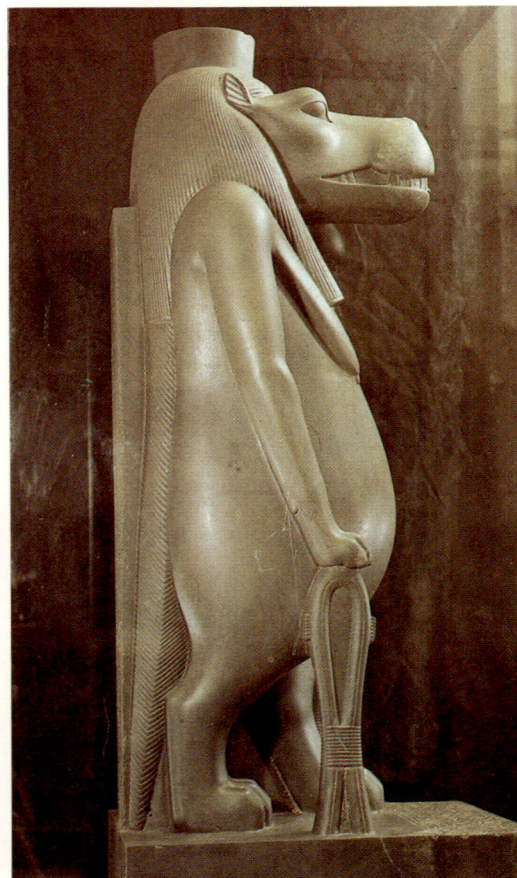

A quarter shekel Jewish coin from the 4th century BC.

Right: the Egyptian god Bes, believed to help women in childbirth.

The first-born son was believed to belong to God in a very special way (Exod. 22:29), and so at the end of the first month he had to be 'redeemed' (meaning 'bought back') (Luke 2:22) by paying five shekels (Num. 18:16). A shekel was a silver coin also used as a unit of weight – about 11.5 gms. This was roughly the economic value of a young child while the average price of a slave was around thirty shekels (Exod. 21:32). This so-called payment of the redemption money was a clear acknowledgement by the parents that they owed the child to God, and it pointed to the belief that all life belonged to God and came as a gift from him.

Marriage

The nature of marriage

In Bible times marriage was a legally binding arrangement between a man and woman to live as husband and wife, and this type of marriage we describe as monogamy or marriage to one wife or husband at a time. However, it was possible for an Israelite or Jew to marry more than one wife, and in such a case we speak of polygamy which means having more than one wife. Since the main purpose of marriage in ancient Israel was to produce a large family, it is understandable that polygamy served this aim fairly well. In practice most Israelites had only one wife, mainly because they could not afford two or more wives. Clearly there were some exceptions to the general rule. King Solomon is said to have had seven hundred wives and three hundred concubines (I Kings 11:3) but this was very unusual even for the Israelite kings.

It does not seem that during the Old Testament period polygamy was regarded as wrong in any way or that monogamy was the ideal form of marriage.

In the early Church the attitude to marriage was already different. The New Testament writers never mention polygamous marriages with approval, while monogamy is either definitely required (I Timothy 3:2) or is implied (I Corinthians 7:2).

In Biblical times marriage was primarily a business transaction rather than a love match, and it did not involve any special religious ceremonies. Love was usually the result of marriage rather than its reason. Nevertheless, occasionally we hear of people falling in love, as in the case of Jacob and Rachel (Gen. 29:18), and David and Michal (1 Sam. 18:20).

Marriage contract

Further, since most marriages, if not all, involved dealing with money, it follows that the parents normally arranged the marriages for their children and settled the terms of the marriage agreement. For financial reasons alone the young couple could not have acted on their own. The situation might be different when the groom happened to be an adult or when the circumstances were unusual; so we find Jacob arranging his own marriage (Gen. 29).

It is very likely that in the process of arranging the marriage a contract or written document would be made, or the agreement spoken out loud in front of witnesses. This latter alternative may have been normal practice during the earlier part of the Old Testament period. Such a contract, written or oral, usually stated how much money or goods each party had contributed, what would happen in the event of the death of one partner or in the case of divorce; it could also mention the prospective heirs.

A Jewish woman wore her dowry as a decoration of coins across her forehead.

Bride price

Once the terms were agreed upon, the groom's father (or whoever acted on the bridegroom's behalf) gave to the girl's family the 'bride price' and various presents. The payment of the bride price does not suggest that the bride was actually bought, like a slave, although this may have happened at some early stage. During the Old Testament period this payment was a sort of compensation to the girl's family. They had lost the services of their daughter while the other family had gained an extra worker. The bride price could be not only a payment in goods or money but also some form of service. So Jacob worked seven years for each of his two wives (Gen. 29:18, 27), while David was asked to perform a kind of military

A Jewish wedding in Bible times

1. In the evening of the wedding day the bridegroom and his friends set out in procession for the bride's home. The bridegroom wears a garland and his friends provide music on tambourines and other instruments.

2. Meanwhile, the bridesmaids have been helping the bride to put on her wedding dress and jewels. She sits with a veil covering her face awaiting the bridegroom.

3. When the bridegroom arrives, he and the bride form in procession with the bridesmaids and attendants to walk to the bridegroom's house. Torches are carried and there is singing, music and dancing.

4. The bridegroom's parents have arranged a marriage feast for the couple and their friends and relations.

5. Everyone comes dressed in their best clothes. They bless the couple and wish them well.

6. After they enter the bridal chamber the bridegroom lifts the bride's veil.

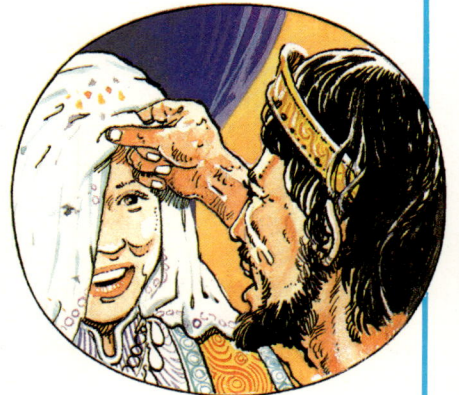

7. The wedding feast lasts for at least seven days and maybe for two weeks.

service by slaying two hundred Philistines, in order to marry Saul's daughter (1 Sam. 18:27).

The bride price may also have been a sort of primitive insurance policy for the wife. If she became a widow or if she was divorced for no fault of hers, then the bride price provided at least a temporary financial support for her. In later Jewish families this bride price was replaced by the so-called *Ketubah* or a document in which the groom promised to give to his bride a certain amount of money to be paid only at divorce, or in the event of his death. The giving of presents was still observed, and the bride usually received a dowry from her own family, which remained her own property.

Betrothal

The making of the marriage agreement, the giving of presents, and the payment of the bride price marked the beginning of the betrothal which is not to be confused with our modern engagement. These two arrangements are similar but betrothal was far more binding legally than our engagement. So, for example, the betrothed couple could be called 'man' and 'wife' (Gen. 29:21) and if the man died the bride became a widow. Furthermore, in order to end the betrothal one would have to divorce the fiancée, as in the case of the intended divorce involving Joseph and Mary (Matt. 1:19). If the betrothal was broken for some reason or other, the bride price would be lost (if the guilty party was the groom or his family) or repaid doubly (if the fault lay with the girl's family); at least, this was the practice in other neighbouring countries, and it may have existed also in Israel. However, normally the husband only was allowed to obtain divorce while the wife could not divorce her husband. In some Jewish circles a wife could be divorced for the smallest reason; if a husband saw another woman whom he liked better than his wife, this could be a sufficient cause for divorce. However, he would no doubt lose the bride price which could be a fairly substantial amount; at a later time he would have to pay the *Ketubah*.

In most cases there was hardly any real courtship before the actual marriage.

A Jewish bride from the Yemen in her traditional wedding head-dress and garland.

72

A modern Jewish wedding.

A Greek bride wearing a wedding veil and dress, depicted on a fragment of a vase from the 5th century BC.

A Roman relief showing a marriage procession. The wedding was followed by a banquet and then a torchlight procession to the bridegroom's house.

According to a later Jewish practice a betrothed couple should not spend any time together by themselves. Obviously there must have been certain exceptions, and different communities may have adopted different attitudes to courtship. Above all, we should not assume that Jewish women were prisoners in their own homes or that they were excluded from all social contact with men.

Wedding ceremonies
Some Jewish traditions suggest that the marriage ceremony followed twelve months after the betrothal although widows could be remarried after a shorter period of time. During this interval between the betrothal and the wedding, the bride prepared her wedding clothes and jewellery while the groom's family was responsible for the marriage feast and for the home of the young couple.

The actual wedding ceremonies varied from place to place, and from time to time, but basically they consisted of a joyful procession during which the bride was taken from her father's home to that of the bridegroom, and of the marriage feast. The bride was specially dressed for this happy occasion and, apparently, she wore a veil (Gen. 24:65); this would explain why Laban was able to deceive Jacob (Gen. 29:23) by giving him Leah instead of her sister, Rachel. Jacob didn't find out until after the ceremony that he had married the wrong girl!

The bridal procession took place with much singing and music, shouting and dancing, and most neighbours and friends joined in the merriment. If the procession was held in the evening, the people in the procession carried torches (Matt. 25:1-10). The bridegroom was attended by a group of his closest friends and relatives, and one of them probably acted as the 'best man' (John 3:29) and was in charge of the activities. Similarly, the bride was accompanied by a number of bridesmaids or companions. The two parties met either on the road or at the bride's home, and then both groups proceeded to the groom's home where, normally, the wedding feast took place. Usually the feast lasted seven days but the length of the celebrations might depend upon the wealth of the families involved and upon the local customs (Judges 14:12). It is possible that in later Israel, just as among some Syrian peasant communities, the groom and the bride were regarded as king and queen during the wedding festivities. If this was so, then the bridal wreaths, worn at one time by the newly-weds, would have been their 'royal crowns'.

Much of the feast was spent eating and drinking, and it is likely that men and women would sit separately. There would also be music, singing, dancing, and various other amusements and contests.

It may seem surprising that the marriage ceremonies, as far as we know, did not involve any religious ritual, apart from the blessing pronounced upon the couple (Gen. 24:60). Yet, on the other hand, it may be true to say that according to the Old Testament, or the Bible as a whole, one's whole life should be lived in a religious setting. Furthermore, if marriage itself was believed to have been instituted by God then the wedding, in all its aspects, could be seen as the fulfilment of God's plan for man and woman.

Death

Life and death

Reading the Bible it becomes quite clear that life was regarded as one of the greatest gifts of God. The writer of the Book of Ecclesiastes could say that 'a live dog is better off than a dead lion' (9:4). However, a man in great trouble or pain may prefer death to life. So Job, overwhelmed by his suffering, cursed the day of his birth (Job 3:1) and longed for death. On the whole, the Israelites were very realistic about life and death, and they fully accepted the fact that in the present world death was the inescapable lot of all human beings. However, early death was regarded as a great disaster and it could be understood as a divine punishment for some sin or other (2 Sam. 12:15), while death after a long and prosperous life was seen as the natural end or the attainment of the goal of one's earthly life. Of course, some good man could be killed in his very prime of life by evil-doers.

The average length of a man's life was reckoned to be seventy years, seldom eighty (Ps. 90:10) but not many people reached that age. There were, naturally, some exceptions; e.g. Moses is said to have died at the age of one hundred and twenty years (Deuteronomy 34:7) but normally life was hard and dangerous, and therefore the usual life span must have been much shorter. Many babies died because people did not understand very much about what causes disease. War, illness, famine, and bad sanitation caused many deaths.

Preparation for burial

When we discuss mourning rites and burial customs, we must remember that the period from Abraham to Jesus spans almost two thousand years, and changes of various kinds took place during these centuries. Therefore any description of the customs of this period as a whole may not be very accurate in all its details. For example, we know far more about life in the time of Jesus than about the way of life of Abraham, Isaac, and Jacob, but we cannot presume that the customs in Jesus' time were the same as those away back in Abraham's time.

In the event of death two main things were of special importance: the preparation of the dead person for burial and the mourning of those bereaved.

Due to the hot climate of Palestine, burials usually took place on the day of death or as soon as practically possible. It was customary to bury the dead in the family tomb, and therefore it could be said that the dead person slept with his fathers (2 Kings 14:29). The Israelites did not as a rule practise cremation. Nor did they use embalming except in very special circumstances, as in the case of Jacob and Joseph in Egypt (Gen. 50:2, 26). Coffins of any kind were not common during the Old Testament period although they came to

The Columbarium at Masada. Ashes of the deceased were placed in the wall in niches.

King Antiochus (1st century BC) tried to immortalise himself by building colossal statues on a mountain top in Turkey.

be used at a later time and they were normally made of wood or stone. A stone coffin was called a sarcophagùs. Dead infants were often placed in large pottery jars which were then placed in the family grave.

The dead person was usually anointed (sprinkled with oil or perfume), washed, and his head was bound with a napkin or a burial cloth (John 20:7); the body itself was wrapped in shrouds. In the Gospels we read that Jesus was wrapped with spices in strips of linen (John 19:40), in accordance with Jewish burial customs.

Mourning

While the dead body was prepared for its final rest, the family and friends of the dead person showed how upset and sad they were. The near relatives would tear their clothes, and these tears were not to be sewn up until after the mourning was over. During the week following the death in the family, mourning clothes were worn by the relatives, and they sprinkled their heads with dust and ashes. It is possible that most bereaved men would cut their hair and shave their beards (Isaiah 22:12). There is some evidence that, at least after the Old Testament period, the mourners did no work during the first seven days, and even the poor were forbidden to work during the first three days of mourning.

Alongside these and other expressions of grief, there was much uncontrolled crying (Mark 5:38). From our point of view this type of apparently excessive mourning may appear to be greatly overdone yet, in a way, this was no more unnatural for

the Israelites and Jews than to speak the Hebrew language. It could be, perhaps, remarked that our 'stiff upper lip' could appear to others as a total lack of feeling yet this would be equally unjustified.

In most cases mourning lasted for seven days but in special circumstances its dur-

A painted terracotta sarcophagus of an Etruscan woman from 130BC. She is shown holding a mirror and adjusting her mantle.

Entrances to rock tombs showing the stone slab in its groove rolled to one side.

The interior of a cave tomb with two chambers.

ation could vary. So the people of Israel mourned for Moses thirty days (Deut. 34:8). Some of the mourning practices could last even longer especially when the dead person was a famous man or a very close relative.

Burial

The burial ceremony began with a funeral procession. The body was carried on a bier or stretcher to the family grave or cemetery which was outside the town or city, and hardly ever on the west side of the settlement because the prevailing winds blew from that direction. The bereaved were usually assisted in their wailing by professional mourners who were paid for their services. According to a later Jewish ruling a husband was expected to provide at least one professional woman mourner and two pipers (flute players) for his wife's funeral. Furthermore, all who saw the funeral procession joined in the mourning rites. It is very likely that most funerals would also have a skilled person who would make a speech praising the character and achievement of the dead person, at some stage during the procession. It was not unusual to exaggerate the attainments of the dead. In the Old Testament we are told that David lamented over the death of Saul and Jonathan, and that he composed the well-known dirge in 2 Samuel 1. There is another shorter lament by David on the

The Egyptians wrapped a mummified body in layers of linen and buried it in a coffin shaped like a mummy. These coffins were usually made of wood or cartonnage (moulded linen and plaster) and were richly decorated.

An Egyptian funerary boat. Wooden models of this kind, representing the journey to the after-life, were placed in Egyptian tombs.

An Egyptian painting showing a mourner at a funeral. Ashes were sprinkled on the head as a sign of grief by many peoples in the ancient world.

Section through the Great Pyramid of Cheops, showing the passages leading to three burial chambers.

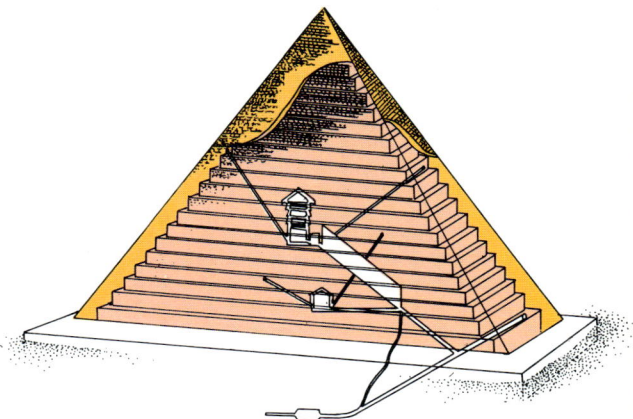

occasion of Abner's death (2 Sam. 3:33–34).

Burial places

The burial sites were mostly private but there was also a public burying ground (2 Kings 23:6) or a field for the burying of strangers (Matt. 27:7). Most tombs were natural or artificial caves outside the city walls, and the dead were simply laid on the projecting rock ledges alongside the walls of the cave or the enlarged underground chambers. A frequent alternative was to cut at right angles a number of niches or recesses into the soft limestone rock walls, and so each body could be placed in its own niche, head first. Some cave tombs consisted of a number of chambers, each having continuous ledges or rows of individual niches. The entrance to the tomb was sealed with a stone slab or heavy boulder or even a sort of large mill-stone shaped rock which could be rolled along a groove in order to close or open the entry to the tomb.

The burial place of Jesus was a similar hewn out rock-tomb with a low entrance (John 20:5). His body was laid on the projecting ledge within the chamber of the tomb, probably awaiting its final burial rites (Luke 24:1) because his death occurred shortly before the Jewish Sabbath and thus there was not enough time to do all that was necessary for the proper burial. Clearly a coffin was not used in this instance. The tomb of Jesus was sealed with a large stone or boulder (John 20:1).

After the funeral

After the funeral the mourners were comforted by friends and acquaintances from far and near. They also brought with them food and drink. The mourners who had touched the dead body or had been in the dead man's house or tomb were thought to be ritually unclean for seven days, and they had to perform certain purification rites (Num. 19:11–19). The same uncleanness affected also the house and its contents.

At least according to a later Jewish practice the tomb was visited at some stage during the first three days in order to see whether the buried man was actually dead. Since most funerals took place on the day of death, it is understandable that sometimes the supposedly dead man revived in the cool tomb. Therefore such an inspection of the tomb helped to avoid situations where a man could be mistakenly entombed alive.

Jewish graves did not normally contain any articles which had belonged to the dead man. Such things as were buried with the deceased were usually only of sentimental or symbolic value. Burials from earlier times, especially non-Israelite ones, often contained a number of articles which were believed to be useful to the dead person in the after life. Logically the Israelites had no need for such a custom because most of them accepted the view that death was a form of prolonged sleep (Job 14:12 NIV), and therefore one's final and undisturbed resting place was all that was required.

A modern Jewish burial in Brazil.

Ossuaries

A century or so before the time of our Lord, there arose a Jewish custom to collect the bones of the dead man after the body had decayed and to place them in a small box or chest, called ossuary. These boxes were usually made of limestone, and were often ornamented and inscribed with the name of the dead person. The box or ossuary was finally re-buried in the same tomb or in some other appropriate place.

A limestone ossuary from Jerusalem, dating from the 1st century AD.

CLOTHES, JEWELLERY AND COSMETICS

Although the Bible covers almost two thousand years, fashions did not change much in that time. Some Jewish styles came from the countries round about. Solomon, for example, copied Assyrian clothes.

The Israelites thought highly of clothes. Achan was tempted by them as much as gold (Joshua 7:21). Samson offered clothes to the guests who could solve his riddle (Judges 14:12).

Some Jews worried too much about what they wore. Jesus said that God clothes wild flowers beautifully, and he would be sure to clothe them, too (Matthew 6:30).

Just like today, rich people then showed off with their expensive clothes. Many of the prophets spoke out against this.

Poor people had only one set of clothes of wool or animal hair. The rich had winter and summer clothes, long and short ones, and clothes for work and leisure. They were made of fine materials like linen or silk in bright colours and with decorations. Even men followed the latest fashions.

Babies wore 'swaddling clothes' (made by winding a square of cloth tightly around the baby to stop him moving his arms and legs). Once they grew out of these, babies wore smaller sizes of exactly the same style as their parents. In some parts of the country children ran around naked.

There were certain customs connected with clothes, such as:
1. Jews had to take off their clothes in a set order before a bath.
2. The enemy's clothes could be taken by the winning side after a battle.
3. Soldiers could have the clothes of a person who had been condemned to death. They shared out Jesus' at his crucifixion (John 19:23).

An ancient Egyptian necklace. Gold, silver and semi-precious stones were used in beautiful and intricate designs from ancient times.

Headwear

Most people wore a covering on their heads, because the sun was so hot.

ISRAELITE MEN

Squares of cloth Jesus would have worn this style. It had been popular for hundreds of years, and all the village and desert people of Jesus' time used it.

The head-square was either white or coloured, and made of wool, linen, cotton or silk. Usually the cloth was folded into a triangle with the point at the back. A circle of cord, rope or plaited wool held the head-dress in place.

This was a good style as it protected a man's head, face, eyes and neck from the sun. And in a gale he could wrap the cloth round his face to keep out hail and sand.

Turbans A turban was a thick cloth, usually of linen, which men wrapped around their head. They could make a turban out of their head-square. Sometimes men wore a neck covering too. In Jesus' day rich men like Joseph of Arimathea wore turbans with fringes.

Hats and caps A few men wore hats or caps like the Persians did, but strict Jews would not wear Gentile hats. When Jesus lived, some men wore a round cap with a long cloth wound round the edge of it.

Prayer shawls The prayer shawl was called a 'large tallith'. It was made of white cotton or wool, with a black border or stripes, and a tassel hanging from each corner. Each tassel had eight threads twisted together in five knots.

The prayer shawl measured about two metres by one, and covered the head and shoulders. Some men wore a close-fitting cap, known as a skull cap under the shawl; others used just the shawl fastened with a cord.

Like all Jewish boys, Jesus would have worn this shawl from the time he was thirteen. All male Jews took it to the synagogue and wore it at the special hours of prayer.

Phylacteries Every Jewish male over the age of twelve wore phylacteries when he said the daily prayer.

A ploughman wearing a traditional head-dress.

Jewish head-dresses. Back, left to right: village and town style head-dresses and a man wearing a head-square. Centre: a fringed turban and a boy wearing phylacteries. Front: a woman's veil and a prayer shawl and skull cap.

Phylacteries or 'guards' were small boxes, usually of black leather. Inside were tiny rolls of parchment on which four parts of the Law were written in special ink. The Jew wore one box on his forehead and another on his left arm. When this arm was bent, the box was over his heart. The boxes were fastened on with leather straps.

Phylacteries were to remind people of God's commandments. Jews who thought they were very religious wore extra large phylacteries, and not just at prayer times.

ISRAELITE WOMEN

Veils Most women wore some kind of veil. This was the main difference between men's and women's clothes.

Most veils were more for decoration than for hiding the woman's face. They were of many different patterns.

Some women wore a cap with a horn on top of it, and fixed their veil to the horn. This veil was usually white, but widows wore black ones.

Rebekah's veil, which she put on before meeting Isaac, was probably a sign that she was not married (Genesis 24:65). The women of Ruth's time had thick veils made of at least two metres of material. These veils covered their head and shoulders and were used for carrying things in. Ruth carried the corn which Boaz had given her in her veil (Ruth 3:15). When women used their veil for carrying things they often covered their face with their long sleeves.

When Jesus lived, most women always kept their head covered in public. Those who did not were thought of as immoral. Ladies with fancy hair-styles would wrap their head in a large white gauze or embroidered scarf.

Women usually carried water-pots and other heavy objects on their heads. They used pads to steady these loads.

Other nations

An Egyptian dancing girl wearing a headband.

Egyptian royal head-dresses. The king's carries a cobra and the queen's a vulture.

Philistine warriors wore distinctive feather head-dresses.

Court head-dress of gold from 2000BC found in excavations at Ur.

Greek head-dresses. Front: a woman wearing a headband of gold called a *stephane*. Centre: a small hat known as a *tholia*. Back: a man's sun-hat.

An Assyrian king wearing a cone hat during a hunt.

A Roman woman wearing a veil.

80

Footwear

Palestine and the other countries of the Bible were hot and dusty with sandy tracks for roads. Most people wore sandals, as close-fitting shoes would make their hot, swollen feet sore. But wearing sandals meant that feet got very dirty, and people often had to stop and shake the dust off their feet.

ISRAELITES
The cheapest kind of sandal was just a flat cowhide sole fastened to the ankle by a leather strap from between the big and second toe. Other kinds of soles were made of wood or dried grass.

Rich people wore leather slippers, or even red leather shoes with turned-up toes. They often carried their shoes to make them last longer. In early Old Testament times some of the women wore brown half-length boots.

Children, workmen, very poor people and those in mourning went barefoot.

Customs about shoes
Some of these seem rather strange to us.
1. People always put on and took off their right shoe before the left one. This was a Roman superstition which the Jews copied.
2. People took off their shoes at a holy place. God told Moses to do this at the burning bush (Exodus 3:5). Imagine everyone doing this when going to church nowadays!
3. Before going into a house, people took their shoes off.
4. It was the job of the least important servant to remove the visitor's sandals and wash his feet. John the Baptist said he was not fit to do even this for Jesus.
5. If you put on your shoes, it showed you were ready for a journey. The Israelites ate the Passover meal with their shoes on, prepared to leave Egypt straight away (Exodus 12:11).
6. When a person sold something, he took off his shoe and gave it to the buyer. It showed his property no longer belonged to him. This happened when Boaz bought Naomi's field (Ruth 4:7, 8).

Jewish sandals.

Other nations

Egyptians
In Egypt where the Hebrews were slaves for a time some people went barefoot. Others wore decorated sandals of leaves, papyrus or leather.

Egyptian sandals made of palm leaves and papyrus.

An Assyrian sandal, from a relief found in a palace at Nineveh.

Greek sandals.

Greek scent bottles in the shape of sandalled feet, from 550BC. The soles are made of layers of leather.

Romans
The Romans mostly kept sandals and slippers for indoor wear. Outside they wore shoes or boots, often of red leather.

Roman boots.

Everyday clothes

ISRAELITES

Years ago artists did not often draw women, so we know a lot more about men's clothes than women's. They dressed nearly but not exactly alike. A law said they must not wear one another's clothes (Deuteronomy 22:5).

Women wore different headwear to men. Apart from that, the main difference was that women's clothes were longer, of finer material and more colourful and decorated.

Clothes worn only by men

The small tallith was like a shirt made of purplish-blue cotton with four tassels. It had tiny Hebrew verses from the Old Testament written on it. A new one was sold without a slit for the head. The wearer cut it to fit himself.

Every Jewish man had to wear this next to his undergarment. The small tallith was like a badge to the Jews.

Clothes worn by both men and women

Undergarment This was usually called a tunic and sometimes a shirt. It was made of leather, haircloth, wool, linen or cotton depending on how rich a person was. Many women wore blue tunics, but they could also be red, yellow, black, white or striped.

This was the first thing people put on. A few rich women wore expensive underwear, but most people did not wear underclothes like we have.

A tunic was a long piece of material folded in the middle and sewn up the sides, with openings for head and arms. There were many styles and patterns depending on people's wealth and work. It could be loose or tight-fitting, have no sleeves, short sleeves or long ones. Some were knee-length, some mid-calf and some full-length. Tunics could have fringes round the hem.

People wearing only an undergarment were thought of as naked. They did not like to be seen like this. But outdoor workmen like Peter and other fishermen wore just a tunic for their job.

Women wearing long tunics could lift up the hem and use it as a bag for carrying things in.

Belt or girdle Men and women fastened their undergarment with some kind of belt, making it look neater. Most Hebrews had girdles of leather, wool or camels' hair. They folded a long piece of material into a strip and wound it two or three times round their waist. Then it was either twisted and tucked in or knotted.

Just above the belt, people made their undergarment into a kind of pouch. In

Kinds of tunic

1. People with indoor jobs had a tunic with sleeves and a V-neck, sometimes decorated. There was a slit of about thirty centimetres on each side of the skirt so that they could move freely.

2. Rich men who went hunting had a V-shape hemline often with a gold fringe.

3. People who did not do much work had a tunic divided into two from the waist down, making a pair of baggy trousers.

4. A special woollen tunic, woven without seam, was worn by kings, prophets and other important people. It was long, loose and sleeveless. Hannah took one of these each year to the Temple as a present for Samuel (1 Samuel 2:19).

In Old Testament times and sometimes in New Testament times the undergarment was often much smaller than a tunic. A loincloth was the smallest undergarment.

A waistcloth was similar but a little bigger. A cloth, usually of leather or linen, was wrapped tightly round the body between the waist and knees. Workmen wore waistcloths.

A larger kind still was a plain sheet wound round the body with one end flung over the shoulder. This is what John Mark left behind when he ran away at Jesus' arrest (Mark 14:51, 52).

One of a group of smiths from Palestine shown on an Egyptian tomb painting. His brightly coloured clothes contrast with the Egyptians' plainer colours.

Men working in the fields sometimes wore their tunic tucked up out of the way to make movement easier. The onlookers are dressed as townsmen.

this they carried many things including coins and food. Shepherds put lambs in there.

Cloak Everyone wore some kind of cloak out of doors unless they were working. Most cloaks were long pieces of material with the sides folded in and sewn along the top. There were slits for the arms. People usually draped their cloak over their shoulders; a few hung them over one shoulder.

Women's cloaks were more ornate than men's. Some were like very long shawls.

Styles of belt

1. Fashionable ladies wore highly decorated belts. Sometimes their sashes were embroidered like Persian ones.

2. The rich people of Jesus' day had bright silk girdles about five metres long. They wound them round and round their body.

3. Some rich men had leather belts. Into these they pushed swords, daggers, knives or inkhorns. (Inkhorns were containers for ink made from animal horn.)

4. A few people had a double belt. A narrow leather strip held in place a wide leather band, often with a gold buckle.

'Girding up the loins'
The Bible often uses this odd expression. It was something that a traveller, workman or anyone who wanted to be ready for action did. It was not easy to run in long robes, so they tucked their tunic into their belt. This made the tunic much shorter. Sometimes they brought the tunic between their legs and tucked it into the front of their girdle.

Anyone who did not want to be too active tucked one end of his tunic into his belt and threw the other end over his shoulder.

Top left: a silk girdle; top right: an embroidered sash; below: belts used for carrying a dagger, a purse and inkhorns; bottom: a double belt.

Top left: Bedouins in the Sinai desert.

Above right: Bedouin women wear traditional dress of dark material with multi-coloured embroidery for everyday work.

Above: Judean women prisoners wearing long coats. They are shown on an Assyrian wall frieze depicting the capture of the city of Lachish.

In early Old Testament times cloaks were like brightly coloured calf-length woollen blankets.

In later Old Testament times women sometimes wore a large fringed woollen shawl or a short fringed cape.

When Jesus lived, the desert and village women wore full length blue cloaks with wide sleeves. The rich ones wore silk cloaks. All Jews except those who lived in towns wore cloaks of coarse material, usually full length. They were made of wool or animal skin or hair. Often they were black with brown or white stripes made by weaving first with camels' then with goats' hair.

These strong sack-like cloaks lasted poor people a lifetime. They kept out rain, heat, cold and dust. They were useful for carrying things in. When folded up they made a comfortable seat.

Most Hebrews had no nightwear. They slept on the floor with their cloak over them. Shepherds and travellers wrapped themselves in their cloak when sleeping out.

Poor people needed their cloak very much. A law said that if a cloak was borrowed it must be returned by bedtime (Exodus 22:26–27). Another law said it must never be taken as payment for a debt.

Coat Poor people could not afford coats. When Jesus lived, rich people wore a long coat over a long undergarment. It had long wide sleeves, no belt and was open at the front. The coat was often gaily striped or in check patterns. One kind of long coat was called an 'aba'. Wealthy people even wore light coats indoors too.

Other Nations

Egyptians
In Egypt, where Moses grew up, people wore little clothing. Children wore none. Men wore a loincloth, and the rich ones had a skirt and cape. The women's clothes were similar, though some wore dresses.

Persians
Esther lived in Persia. Men and women wore tunics and the women had a shawl. Important men wore trousers and a coat.

Assyrians
Jonah went to Nineveh, the capital of Assyria. The Assyrians wore tunics, and women had fringed shawls. All their clothes were very decorated with fringes and tassels and the materials were richly patterned.

Romans
Paul was a Roman citizen. The boys were expected to rough it: they had only one set of clothes, and no covering for their legs.

All Romans wore a toga wrapped round their body. Togas were of different material according to a person's rank.

Greeks
Greeks like Luke wore a full tunic, a belt, and a short cloak.

Joseph's coat

In the story of Joseph we read that his father gave him a special coat. The Bible does not call it a coat of many colours; this is only a later tradition (Gen. 37:3). It may have been of many colours, woven in bright stripes, but it is more likely it was white. This was the favourite colour for special clothes. The coat was full-length with long pointed sleeves that covered his hands. The sleeves covering his hands meant he was not going to work. Years later workmen wore coats like this. But when Joseph lived, workmen wore short sleeveless tunics. Only the head of the family and the son who would be head one day wore such a coat. Jacob had put Joseph in the place of Reuben, his eldest son, making Joseph superior to his hardworking brothers; and showing favouritism. No wonder Joseph's brothers were angry and jealous!

Clothes for special occasions

Everyone except very poor people had a set of best clothes to wear on the Sabbath (the first day of the Jewish week, which was set aside for worship and rest, and was very important to all Jews), and special occasions like feasts and parties.

The style of these clothes was not very different from everyday ones. It was the material that was different. It was more expensive and usually white. Women liked to decorate their clothes, especially with gold and silver.

After Naaman had been cured of leprosy he gave Elisha's servant two sets of best clothes (2 Kings 5:23). When Joseph's brothers went to buy corn in Egypt he gave them each a set of best clothes (Gen. 45:22). When the prodigal son went home his father gave him the best clothes in the house (Luke 15:22). These were kept for special guests.

Traditional clothes
Each village had its own traditional dress which the women wore on special occasions. The material usually was maroon, blue or apricot colour. Another colour was used for stripes which they sewed onto the skirt. A square piece of material covering the chest (called a breast-plate) of the same colour as the stripes was sewn to the bodice. This had lots of patterns and colourful embroidery on it. Every village had local embroidery patterns.

Where special clothes were kept
When Jesus lived, most families had a strong wooden chest to keep all the family's best clothes in. The mother's wedding dress would be there waiting for the day when her daughter would wear it.

The lid had to fit tightly or the silvery fish moth would get in and eat the clothes. Jesus spoke about the damage this moth could do to material (Matthew 6:19).

Wedding clothes

These were often made of silk.

The Bride
Her wedding dress was usually white and sometimes embroidered. As well as her veil, she wore lots of jewellery. Often her clothes were a present from the bridegroom.

A Jewish bride in her traditional wedding clothes and jewellery.

The Bridegroom
The bridegroom dressed as much like a king as possible. His little boy attendant was dressed exactly the same. Some bridegrooms wore a garland.

The Guests
They were expected to wear special clothes which their host sometimes gave them. In Jesus' parable a man was turned out of a wedding feast because he was not dressed in proper clothes (Matthew 22:11–13).

Colours

The Israelites loved bright colours. They often dyed wool, sometimes before weaving. Wool comes in different colours (Jacob had black, white, striped and spotted sheep in his flock), so the dyes made lots of shades.

Sources of dyes

The dyes used for thread and cloth in Bible times came from these natural sources.

1. The Purple Dye Murex shell-fish found around the shores of the Mediterranean Sea.

2. Cochineal insects yielded a bright scarlet when crushed.

3. Almonds gave a yellow dye.

4. From the rind of pomegranates blue dye was obtained.

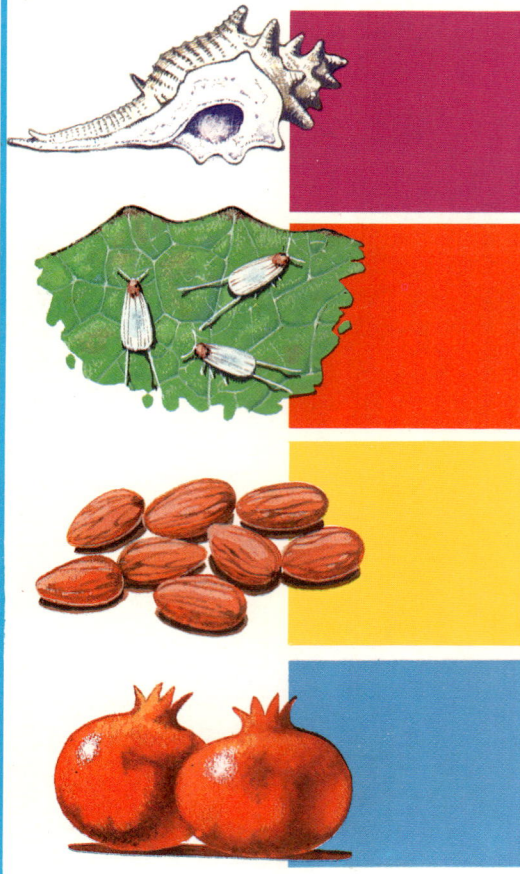

A stone dye vat of the type used in Israel in the 7th century BC.

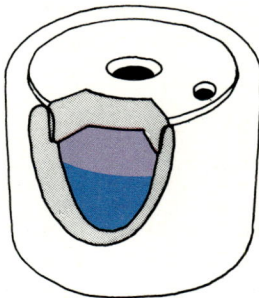

Colours the Israelites wore

There were many natural colours such as those of animal skins and hair. Apart from these, men often wore red or blue clothes, and women blue or green ones. They also wore black and white, and rich people wore purple.

Colours the Egyptians wore

When Joseph was in Egypt he would have seen most people wearing white. They often bleached their linen clothes because the sun faded them. Many other colours were worn, but not black. They did not like wearing red either; it was thought wicked and violent.

Dyes

Purple This was the most valuable dye. It came from a shell-fish in the Mediterranean Sea. Some fish gave a red-purple, others a blue-purple. 'Canaan' means 'Land of the Purple'.

Dyeing with blue and then with red gave a cheaper kind of purple. Only royal or rich people wore the best kind. When the soldiers mocked Jesus, they put a purple robe, like a king's, on him. Lydia in the Church in Philippi sold purple clothes.

Red A bright scarlet came from the stain of crushed cochineal insects found in oak trees. It was a fast dye. Isaiah talked about sins being glaring like scarlet – only God could wash them out.

The Hebrews got other shades of red from plants or the earth.

Blue Plants and pomegranate rind gave a blue colour.

Yellow The Jews had about five ways of dyeing material yellow, including using almonds or pomegranates.

Dyeing was usually done in stone 'vats', round containers made for the purpose. Potash and slaked lime were first put in the vats. After two days the dyes were added. Sometimes thread was dyed before weaving; at other times cloth was dyed. Cloth was left to soak in the dye, and if a deep colour was wanted, the material would be given several 'baths'. Shellfish, plants or whatever else was used to make the dye were crushed or ground until only the juices remained.

Types of material

Hanks of dyed wool.

Animal skins These were sometimes worn as they were and not shaped or sewn in any way, or they were made into shirts or cloaks. Only poor Israelites, shepherds and prophets wore animal skins. God clothed Adam and Eve in them. Egyptian priests wore leopard skins.

Camels' hair Hair from camels was woven into coarse cloth. It was warm, but could make lightweight coats. John the Baptist wore camel hair.

Goats' hair Goats' hair, too, was woven into coarse brown or black cloth. Heavy cloaks for shepherds who had to be out all night were made from it.

Cilicium This was a special kind of black goats' hair. It got its name from the Cilician goats who have this hair. 'Cilice' the French word for hair cloak or hair shirt comes from this material.

These goats lived on the Taurus mountains, and their hair was woven in Tarsus, Paul's home town. Cilicium was tough cloth used for clothes, sails and tents which would stand up against wind and weather. Paul worked with cilicium.

The material made the worker's hands black and rough. This was why Paul once showed his hands to prove that he had worked hard (Acts 20:34).

Sackcloth was a woven material, usually a mixture of goats' and camels' hair. Poor people wore it because it was strong and cheap. But sackcloth was rough and uncomfortable, and the Hebrews usually wore it for one of these special reasons.

1. When they were mourning for someone who had died. Jacob wore it when he saw Joseph's blood-stained coat (Genesis 37:34).

2. When they wanted to show they were turning away from their sins. The King of Nineveh put on sackcloth after

88

Cloth for sale in an Eastern market.

A tanner treating an animal hide.

hearing Jonah speak (Jonah 3:6). Prophets like Isaiah sometimes wore it to show the people they ought to leave their sins behind.

3. When something awful had happened to them. Job put it on when he got bad news (Job 16:15).

4. When a terrible thing happened (or was about to happen) to their people. Mordecai put on sackcloth when he heard that all the Jews were to be killed (Esther 4:1).

The Israelites first tore their clothes, then put on sackcloth. Sometimes they wore it next to their body all night.

Leather A tanner made leather from animal skins. After the skins had dried in the sun, he treated them with lime, plant juices, bark or leaves. Leather was shaped and sewn to make clothes and footwear.

Wool Many Hebrews were shepherds and there was plenty of wool. They were very good at weaving. Most people had woollen clothes, and they often handed them down in the family.

Linen Linen was made from the flax plant that grew in Palestine. It had blue flowers and grew to about forty-five centimetres. In Jericho Rahab hid the spies among the flax on her roof (Joshua 2:6).

In Old Testament times linen was mostly worn by special, holy people. Samuel wore linen for his work in the Temple.

In New Testament times wealthy people wore linen, and ordinary people wore it on special occasions. In Jesus' parable the rich man wore linen and Lazarus was in rags (Luke 16:19). Jesus' body was wrapped in linen for burial (John 19:40). Men gave linen as a very special present to the women they loved.

The Egyptians made 'fine linen' which was very soft and almost transparent. The Israelites probably used this for Temple clothes. Everyone in Egypt wore linen – a cool material for such a hot country. When Pharaoh made Joseph governor he gave him a robe of fine linen.

There was a strange law that Hebrews must not make a garment of two materials. If they obeyed this, they never wove wool and linen together.

Other materials

Cotton was not used much by the Jews until New Testament times.

Silk was worn by rich people, and sometimes by others on special occasions.

Sources and uses of materials

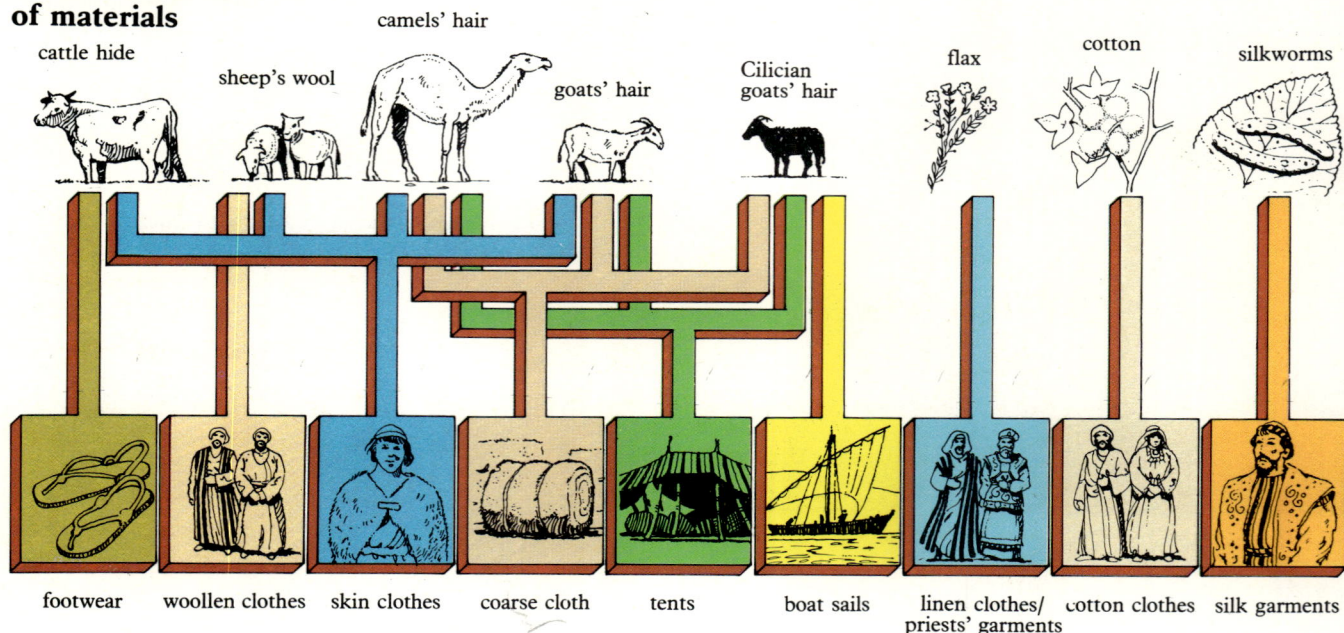

cattle hide | sheep's wool | camels' hair | goats' hair | Cilician goats' hair | flax | cotton | silkworms

footwear | woollen clothes | skin clothes | coarse cloth | tents | boat sails | linen clothes/ priests' garments | cotton clothes | silk garments

Dressmaking

Jesus had a seamless tunic for which the soldiers threw dice (John 19:23, 24).

Two pieces Most Jewish looms were only 90 centimetres wide. As cloaks were often over two metres round, two pieces of cloth were woven, then stitched together.

Three pieces If the loom was narrow, a garment was made in three pieces. These were the front skirt, the back skirt, and the bodice and sleeves.

A circle The weaver began in the middle and broadened the web a little at a time.

Decorations

The Hebrews loved to decorate their clothes with brightly coloured borders and fringes. When Jesus lived, most rich people trimmed their clothes with braid and tassels. You could tell a person's rank by the length of the fringes on his clothes.

The Israelites brightened up their clothes with weaving patterns, tapestry, embroidery and sewing materials together.

Persian material was famous for lots of designs. They even put pictures of flowers, trees and lions on their cloth.

So many patterns and pictures were used by the Assyrians that it was unusual

In Bible days there were no sewing machines, patterns or material bought by the metre. Yet nearly all clothes were hand made by the women. Their dress-making began with the wool from the sheep or the flax growing in the field. It was hard work, so it was no wonder that the Israelites thought a lot of their clothes.

Shaping clothes

Nearly every home had a loom. There were different ways of shaping clothes on looms.

One piece If the loom was wide, clothes could be woven in one piece. This was often done in Galilee. The weaver started at the sleeve edge and worked across to the other sleeve, leaving a hole for the head.

A patterned Assyrian robe with a tasselled fringe.

This ancient piece of weaving dates back to 4000BC. Stone weights keep the threads taut.

Bedouin women spinning wool.

to find a plain material. They put fringes and tassels on everything, and even painted on leather.

Embroidery

The Jews' best clothes were embroidered. The women did complicated patterns in cottons and silks. Black, red, yellow and green were their favourite colours for embroidery. Sometimes they used gold thread, made of real gold. The Egyptians liked bright embroidery on the borders of their clothes.

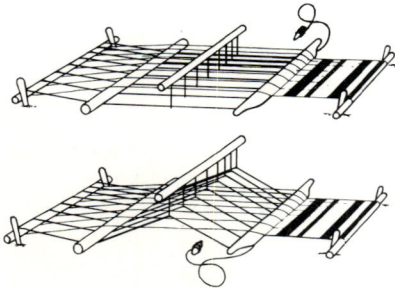

How a loom works. The shuttle which carries the thread is passed from side to side of the loom, travelling alternately over and under the warp threads.

A Bedouin woman weaving on a hand loom.

Ornaments

ISRAELITE ORNAMENTS

Women Most Israelite women had a lot of fairly cheap ornaments. Rich ladies wore so much expensive jewellery that they 'jingled' as they walked.

Ornaments were made of gold, silver, bronze or other metals, or carved ivory. They also used coloured glass, and a lot of precious stones like diamonds.

Men The Hebrew law said that only women could wear jewellery. In other countries like Persia and Assyria the men wore many ornaments.

Some Israelites broke the law, but it was unusual for men to wear as many ornaments as women. Many of them wore a ring with their personal seal on it, and had a walking stick with an ornamental top. Rich men wore a gold jewelled collar with matching bracelets.

Kinds of ornaments

The Jews had beads, pendants, crowns, bracelets, and rings for ears, fingers and nose. When the Tabernacle was made, people brought more ornaments than were needed.

Kings and other important people in

An ancient seal discovered in Israel. It is thought to have belonged to Queen Jezebel.

A gold pendant of 1650BC from the Minoan civilisation which flourished on the Mediterranean island of Crete. Minoans traded with Egypt and Mesopotamia.

the Old Testament wore an armlet. It was a metal ring on the top of their arm. King Saul had one (2 Samuel 1:10).

Ornaments and wealth

Before there were coins, ornaments were used for buying things. Even afterwards many Israelites preferred jewellery to money or goods. They found an expensive necklace easier to carry round than a heavy bag of coins or a herd of cattle.

Loot

Jewellery was taken as loot after a battle. After Gideon's battle against the Midianites and Amalekites, the Israelites captured many ornaments. These included ear-rings weighing nearly twenty kilograms.

Grave jewellery

Jewellery was even put in graves with bodies. Tombs had to be well sealed to keep out thieves.

Seals

Today most people sign their names. In Bible days many people had their own seal to mark important papers. When the seal was stamped into wax or clay it left a pattern which was like the owner's signature.

Jewellers made and engraved seals with designs and sometimes the person's name. Rich people's were made of precious stones, and poor people's of rough clay.

Seals were worn as rings, brooches or necklaces. When Haman became Prime Minister King Ahasuerus gave him his seal ring (Esther 3:10).

A bride's ornaments

Brides wore lots of jewellery, which was usually given by the bridegroom. Isaac gave Rebecca two bracelets and a nose-ring of gold. A bride loved a nose-ring. It went through a hole in her nostril and the jewel in the ring lay against her cheek.

All her life a woman treasured the string of coins worn across her forehead on her wedding day. In Jesus' parable it was very likely one of these coins that the woman searched for (Luke 15:8). If a woman lost a coin as she did, people thought her very careless or even unlucky.

Roman earrings from the 1st century AD.

Sumerian jewellery from Ur. Necklaces of gold, lapis lazuli and carnelian, dating from 2500 BC.

Gold pendants from the Gaza region of Palestine.

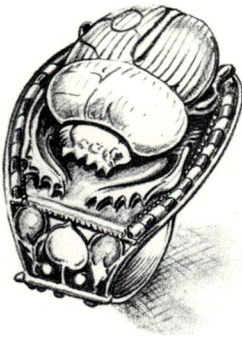

An Egyptian scarab ring.

EGYPTIAN ORNAMENTS

The Egyptians made some of the most beautiful jewellery ever seen. Blue Egyptian beads have even been found at Stonehenge in England!

When the Israelites left Egypt they took lots of Egyptian ornaments with them.

Egyptians wore wide jewelled collars. Many ornaments were really charms to keep away evil spirits.

A jewelled collar in an Egyptian tomb painting. Large collars like this, made of gold or silver with stones and beads, were commonly worn by wealthy Egyptian men.

A gold armlet with winged goats. Part of the Oxus Treasure from the 4th century BC.

Scarabs Scarabs were very popular charms. They were precious stones cut in the shape of a scarab beetle. This beetle hid its eggs in the sand where they hatched. Egyptians believed the eggs magically hatched themselves.

Cosmetics

Make-up

Eyes Many Hebrew women including Queen Jezebel used eye-paint. They made it by mixing a coloured powder with water or glue, sometimes using a tiny mortar and pestle. Eye-paint was even put on children's eyes because they believed it strengthened them.

Nearly all Egyptian women used black eye-paint on the upper lid and green on the lower. They coloured their eye-brows grey and often gave each eye a black out-

A bronze Egyptian mirror with ivory handle from 1300BC.

An Egyptian cosmetic spoon in the form of lotus flowers and buds of tinted ivory and a comb with an animal-shaped handle.

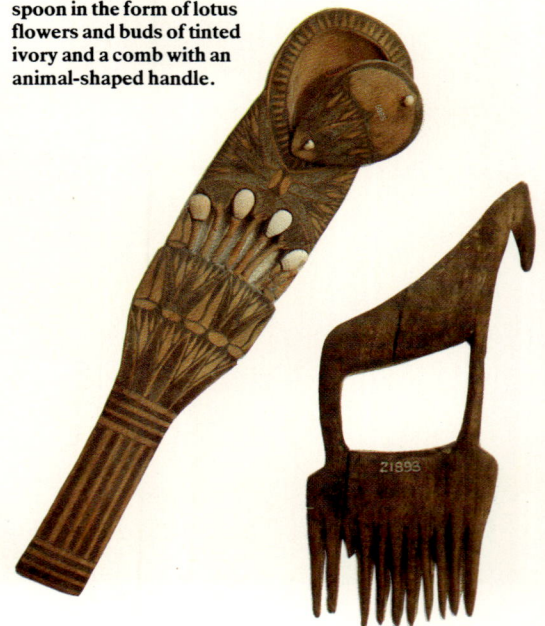

line. The princess who found baby Moses probably looked like this. Even men painted their eyelids.

Israelite women, too, tinted their eyebrows and lashes, put shadows on their eyelids and drew round their eyes. The paints may have protected them against eye infections so common in hot countries.

Ladies used their fingers, brushes, or wooden or bronze spatulas to put on their eyeshadow. They had palettes for mixing cosmetics, and decorated jars with a brush attached to the stopper for their eye-paint. Rich ladies had fancy cosmetic spoons with pictures on.

Face Some Israelite women painted their faces, often black or red. They put it on with paint sticks. Ladies had powder puffs, and they usually kept their face powder in shells. In early Old Testament times, when Sarah lived, they called their yellow face powder 'face bloom'. The lipstick women wore was made from crushed insects. They kept their cosmetics in clay, bronze or copper boxes.

Hands and feet Women painted their toe and finger nails often using yellowy-red dye from crushed leaves. Egyptians also put it on the palms of their hands and soles of their feet.

Beauty aids

Some women were fortunate enough to have mirrors. In Old Testament times they were of polished metal, often bronze. By the time of Jesus glass ones were used, too. But neither kind gave a good reflection, and many ladies had to put on their make-up without seeing the result. Ladies also had manicure sets, tweezers and combs.

An Israelite ivory cosmetic palette from Hazor, 8th century BC. The handle has a tree of life design.

An Egyptian glazed toilet box in the form of a lotus capital, from 300BC.

A Roman comb made of ivory, inscribed with the name of its owner 'Modestina'.

An Egyptian cosmetic container in the shape of a swimming girl pushing before her an ointment box. From 1250BC.

94

Oils and creams

Oils, creams and ointments were used all the time. They protected people against sunburn and insects. Although we would wash more often in hot weather, most families then used more oil than water.

Oils were rubbed on their bodies not only after a bath, like Ruth did, but at many other times, even by poor people.

A manicure set used by Roman ladies in New Testament times.

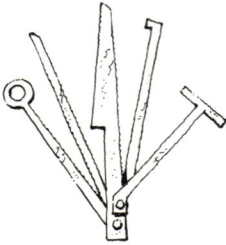

An alabaster flask bearing the inscription 'Cinnamon' in Greek.

Egyptian ladies at a party wearing perfume cones on their heads.

Hair-oils, too, were very popular. But when the Israelites were in mourning they never used oils. Esther had to use oil of myrrh and oil of balsam for a year before going in to the king (Esther 2:12).

Perfumes

The Hebrews were very fond of perfume. The best ones came from outside Palestine. Perfume was one of the Queen of Sheba's presents to Solomon (1 Kings 10:10).

People put perfume on their bodies, hair, clothes, beds, and on dead bodies and grave-clothes. Women sometimes had small bags of perfume under their dresses. Rich people used lots of perfume: it covered over their less pleasant smells.

Perfume cones At feasts small cones of perfume were put on the guests' heads. The heat slowly melted it and the perfume dripped down onto their clothes. This custom began in Egypt, but Palestine and other countries copied the idea.

Perfume containers Ointment was stored in ivory boxes, and olive oil in jars and jugs. Perfume was kept in tiny bottles of burnt clay. But the best perfume was thought to improve if put in alabaster containers. Mary used perfume in a tiny alabaster jug to anoint Jesus. She broke the jug's narrow neck and let the scent drop onto Jesus' head (Matthew 26:7).

Some perfumes and oils They had many kinds of perfume made from flowers, spices, herbs, fruit, vegetables, roots and leaves. Perfumers usually made perfume by dipping the flowers into hot fats at 65 degrees centigrade.

One of the Israelite's most popular oils was olive-oil made from crushed olive fruits.

The wise men gave Jesus frankincense. This was an expensive perfume made from gum from the bark of a tree. They also gave him myrrh which was also a gum with a sweet scent. Jesus' body was anointed with myrrh at his burial.

Nard or spikenard was a beautiful smelling oil. Jesus was anointed with half a litre of it, which would have cost nearly a year's wages for a labourer.

The Israelites had many other perfumes including cinnamon, myrtle, balm and balsam.

Hair-styles

ISRAELITES

The Israelites spent a lot of time on their hair. Most of them had straight black or dark brown hair. They liked dark hair.

Hebrews respected older people with grey hair. Herod the Great (who tried to kill the baby Jesus) dyed his hair as soon as it began to go grey.

The Jews did not like baldness. This may have been partly because lepers had to shave their heads. So when some young men called Elisha 'Baldy', they were really insulting him (2 Kings 2:23).

When people were in mourning they left their hair uncombed. When they were afraid or upset, they tore it.

Men in Old Testament times

They let their hair grow long and thick. Absalom's was so heavy that he cut it once a year, and it weighed over two kilograms (2 Samuel 14:26).

Samson was told never to cut his hair. He wore it in seven plaits as was the fashion in those days. Later plaits were no longer worn.

When the Hebrews went to war they let their hair hang loose. They believed there could be magic in plaits.

Men in New Testament times

Most men wore their hair short. They had to trim their hair in special ways. The hair at the sides by their ears was never cut.

Shaving

In Old Testament times the men were very proud of their beards which were usually pointed. David's servants were ashamed to go home until their beards had grown again (2 Samuel 10:5). Some men had moustaches. The young men may have shaved, but the older ones certainly only shaved when they were in mourning or at the end of a special vow. In times of mourning the men not only shaved their beards off, but also their hair, probably leaving a little patch on top. Job did this when he got bad news (Job 1:20). Razors were expensive, so most men went to the barber.

By New Testament times many men no longer wore beards.

Women in Old Testament times

Women usually let their hair hang down over their shoulders. In early Old Testament times some women fastened it with a white ribbon round their forehead. Fashionable ladies had little curls in front of their ears.

Women in New Testament times

Ladies did not let their hair hang loose in front of men. Mary broke this rule when she wiped Jesus' feet with her hair.

Women had curlers and hair-pins, and they plaited, curled or braided their hair. They kept their hair-styles in place with ivory combs, hair nets (sometimes of gold) or small decorated caps. They put flowers and expensive ornaments in their hair.

Many women piled their hair on top of their head. Others had about three rows of tight curls across their forehead and quite short hair at the sides.

A Canaanite woman's hairstyle, shown on a Megiddo ivory carving.

An Egyptian tomb relief showing some Semites bowing down to an Egyptian official gives us information about men's hairstyles in the land where the Israelites settled.

OTHER NATIONS

Egyptians
They dyed their hair when it began to go grey. Men shaved both their head and face. Joseph had to shave before he interpreted Pharaoh's dreams. Rich men wore wigs.

Women wore plaits, though rich ones had short hair and a fringe.

A copper razor of the scraping type with a handle in the shape of an animal's head, from 1900BC.

An Egyptian priest with a shaved head.

A Roman lady has her hair done.

Assyrians
Men had waved long bushy hair and long beards. Women had fancy plaits.

An Assyrian curled hairstyle and long beard.

Persians
Persian men had tightly curled hair and round or pointed beards.

Romans
Both men and women dyed their hair and wore wigs. Men had short hair and no beards. Some teenage boys used curling tongs!

Women had very fancy styles and wore lots of hair ornaments. Girls often wore a plait round the front of the head. When they married they changed to one of the women's styles such as curls kept in place with rows of beads and decorated with lots of fancy combs, nets and hair bands. When they grew older, women piled their hair on top of their head.

A Roman man's hairstyle.

GEOGRAPHY OF THE BIBLE LANDS

If we were to plot on one map all the hundreds of known places mentioned in the Bible, our map would have to cover a vast area, stretching from Spain in the west to India in the east, and from Italy, Greece and the lands around the Black Sea in the north to Ethiopia in the south. Yet at the heart of this area, the land of Palestine, where the great majority of the events in the Bible took place, is remarkably small, only a little larger than Wales or about the area of a small American state like Vermont. From north to south (Dan to Beersheba) it is only about 280 kilometres (150 miles), and only about half that distance across, from the Mediterranean to the mountains of Transjordan. It is possible to see all of it from an aircraft on a clear day. In Bible times the land lay near the centre of the 'Fertile Crescent', the curving belt of agricultural and well-populated land linking the great river-based civilisations of Egypt and Mesopotamia. Sandwiched between sea and desert, Palestine was indeed at the hub of the ancient world, a focal point of commerce and, all too often, of conflict. The Israelites of Old Testament times believed that God had placed them in this position, and dreamed of the time when all nations would come and worship him in Jerusalem (Micah 4:2).

The area known as the Fertile Crescent and its main products.

Key to symbols
- Wheat and barley
- Sheep
- Cattle
- Olives
- Dates

**4.
The Greek empire**
spread east as far as India under Alexander the Great in the 4th century BC. The Greek culture and language became strong influences throughout the Middle East. The New Testament was written in Greek

Asia Minor
The apostle Paul travelled throughout Asia Minor, Macedonia, Greece and as far west as Rome in the first century AD, spreading the gospel and founding many Christian churches

**5.
The Roman empire**
included all the lands around the Mediterranean from Spain in the west to Palestine in the east, at the time of the birth of Christ. Many Jews hoped Jesus would be a political Messiah who would deliver them from the Roman occupation and set up an earthly kingdom

Palestine
— the country where most of the Bible events took place. God promised the land to Abraham and his descendants who were the founders of the nation of Israel

Egypt
—the home of one of man's earliest and greatest civilisations. The Egyptian empire flourished from 3000BC onwards. The Israelite nation lived in Egypt for 400 years until their escape — the Exodus

Sinai
God gave Moses the Ten Commandments on Mt. Sinai

R Tiber
Apennine Mts
Rome
ITALY
Adriatic Sea
Mt Vesuvius
SICILY
Mt Etna
Ionian Sea
R Danube
Balkan Mts
MACEDONIA
Mt Olympus
GREECE
Aegean Sea
Corinth
Athens
Ephesus
CRETE
Mediterranean Sea
Black Sea
ASIA MINOR
Taurus Mountains
Tarsu
Anti
CYPRUS
Byblos
Sidon
Damaso
Tyre
Joppa
PALESTINE
Jeru
D S
Beersheba
LIBYA
Alexandria
Nile Delta
Memphis
Route of the Exodus
Arabah
R Nile
Western Desert
Gulf of Suez
Sinai Peninsula
Gulf of Aqaba
EGYPT
Eastern Desert
Thebes
Red Sea

Lands of the Bible
During Bible times the land of Palestine was invaded and annexed by five major world empires in turn over a period of 800 years (see red panels)

The land between the rivers

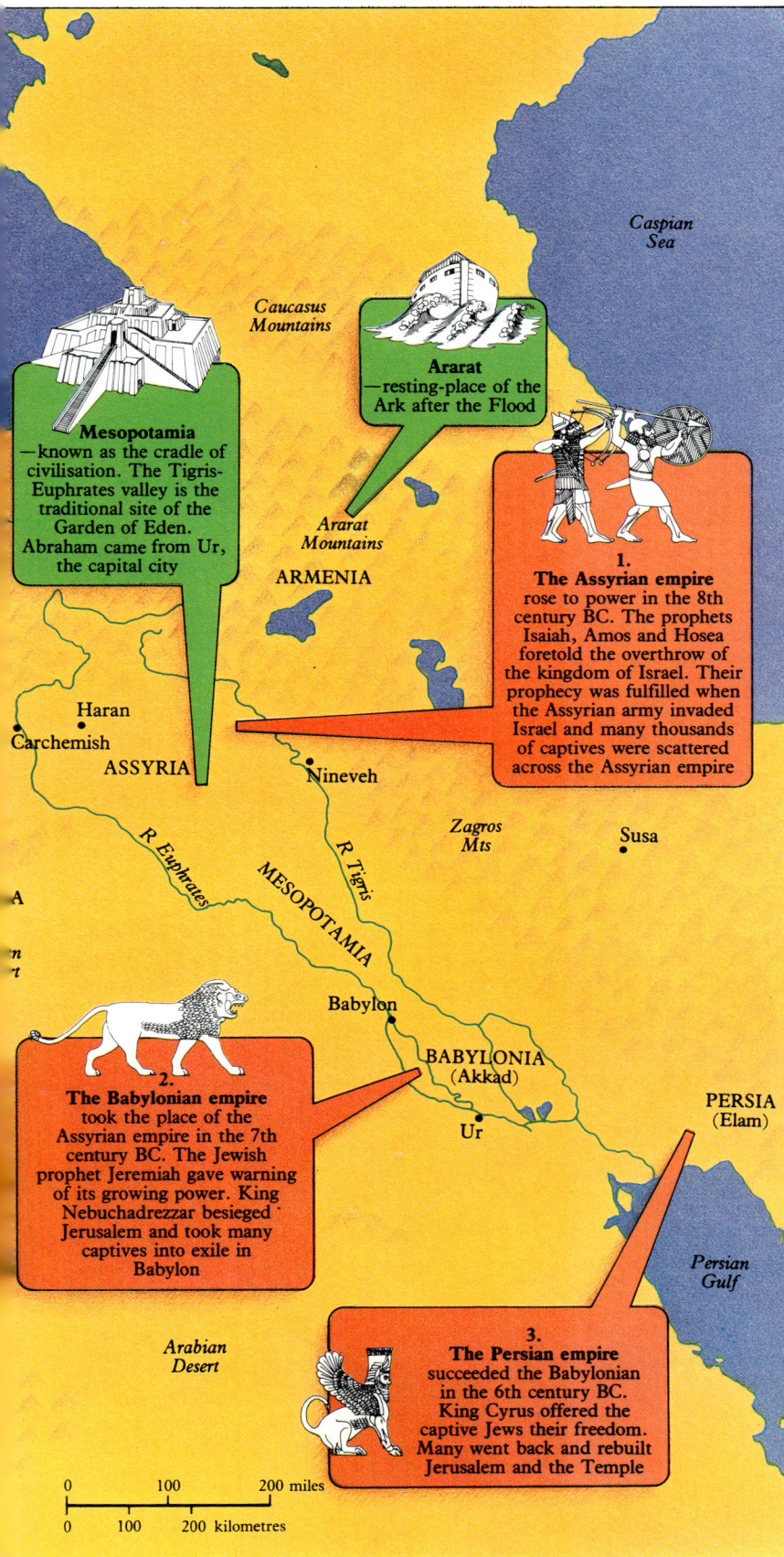

Map labels

Caspian Sea

Caucasus Mountains

Mesopotamia
—known as the cradle of civilisation. The Tigris-Euphrates valley is the traditional site of the Garden of Eden. Abraham came from Ur, the capital city

Ararat
—resting-place of the Ark after the Flood

Ararat Mountains

ARMENIA

1.
The Assyrian empire
rose to power in the 8th century BC. The prophets Isaiah, Amos and Hosea foretold the overthrow of the kingdom of Israel. Their prophecy was fulfilled when the Assyrian army invaded Israel and many thousands of captives were scattered across the Assyrian empire

Haran

Carchemish

ASSYRIA

Nineveh

Zagros Mts

Susa

R. Euphrates

MESOPOTAMIA

R. Tigris

Babylon

BABYLONIA
(Akkad)

PERSIA
(Elam)

2.
The Babylonian empire
took the place of the Assyrian empire in the 7th century BC. The Jewish prophet Jeremiah gave warning of its growing power. King Nebuchadrezzar besieged Jerusalem and took many captives into exile in Babylon

Ur

Persian Gulf

Arabian Desert

3.
The Persian empire
succeeded the Babylonian in the 6th century BC. King Cyrus offered the captive Jews their freedom. Many went back and rebuilt Jerusalem and the Temple

0   100   200 miles

0   100   200 kilometres

Mesopotamia is a Greek word meaning 'between the rivers'. It describes the fertile land between the Tigris and Euphrates, an area now mostly in northern Syria and Iraq. This region, more than twice the size of Britain, has been called the 'Cradle of Civilisation', for advanced cultures based on settled agriculture existed here before 3000BC. In the south, towards the Persian Gulf, the Sumerian civilisation grew up, where the famous city of Ur, birthplace of Abraham, lay. Later this region became known as Babylonia, after its capital city, which, like Ur, lay close to the Euphrates. Further north was Assyria, whose capital was Nineveh, beside the Tigris.

Climate

The prosperity of these agricultural countries was almost entirely due to the fertile

Date palms in the fertile land between the rivers Tigris and Euphrates.

Farmers still water their flocks at desert wells as the Patriarchs did.

over 40°C (104°F). Throughout the summer clouds are rare, and the torrid sun seems to have everything in its power. It is no accident that the Babylonians worshipped Marduk, the sun-god.

Winter in Mesopotamia, though brief, is by contrast a cloudier and more pleasant season, about as warm as late May or early June in England, though with chilly nights. Refreshing rains fall, especially towards the north, where amounts are sufficient for grain, figs, olives, grapes and other fruits and vegetables without the need for irrigation. However, the northern-most stretch of the Fertile Crescent, in present-day Syria, was mainly grazing-land; on this, semi-nomads (including at one time the Patriarchs Abraham, Isaac, Jacob and their families) kept flocks of sheep, goats and cattle, together with asses, which were their main beasts of burden. These peoples, although living in tents, did not travel long distances; we know they possessed – and jealously guarded – their own precious wells and springs. Asses restricted the distance and speed of travel to thirty or forty km a day at best, and they would need water at least once a day. When the Israelites entered the Promised Land they were 'ass nomads', and as such occupied fairly restricted areas, except when forced to move by drought; they built shrines and established burial-grounds, showing they regarded certain areas as their own territory.

silt spread every year over the flat plains by the spring flooding of the two mighty rivers. Both of these rise in the mountains of eastern Turkey, and the Euphrates flows about 3,800 km (2,400 miles) south-eastwards across the plains to end in the salt-swamps at the head of the Persian Gulf, close to Abadan. The Tigris, about half as long, joins the Euphrates about 200 km upstream, after flowing parallel to it for over 1,500 km. All the plain has a very dry climate, and much would be true desert but for the life-giving waters of the two rivers; Baghdad has a yearly average of only 175 mm (7") of rain, falling entirely in the winter months. For most of the year it is very hot, the average temperature in summer being around 35°C (95°F), almost every day recording furnace-like figures of

Sunset in a marsh village in southern Iraq, near Ur, birthplace of Abraham.

Mountains

The prophet Habakkuk spoke about the 'eternal mountains' and 'everlasting hills', highlighting the enduring character of these physical features in a world where so much was fragile and passing. 'As the mountains surround Jerusalem, so the Lord surrounds his people now and for ever,' wrote the Psalmist (Ps. 125:2). Mountains were often regarded as holy places, towering as they did towards heaven; it was on the mountain-tops that God often encountered his servants, as for example Abraham on Mt. Moriah, Moses on Mt. Sinai, Elijah on Carmel and Horeb and Jesus on the Mount of Transfiguration (which may have been Mt. Hermon). Pagan gods were often worshipped on mountains and hilltops, where idols and images were set up and sacrifices offered (see, for example, Jeremiah 3:21–24).

Fold ranges

Many geologists think that the mountains of the Middle East were formed by huge earth-movements which threw up massive fold ranges across southern Europe and virtually the whole width of Asia. To the north of the Fertile Crescent, in Turkey and Iran, these fold mountains reach heights of 5,000 metres, with intervening basins and plateaux. Away to the north-east is Great Ararat (5,165 metres), the traditional resting-place of the Ark after the Flood. This is an incredibly remote and inaccessible area, close to the border with the USSR (Armenia), and only a few expeditions have visited it.

These northern mountain ranges shut off Mesopotamia from the rest of Asia, and their melting snows and spring rains are responsible for the floods along the Tigris and Euphrates, which generally reach a peak around May or June in the lower courses. Sometimes avalanches or earth-slides occur in the mountain valleys, as a result either of sudden thaws or earthquakes (the crust here is still very unstable). These may block the narrow

Bottom left: Mt Carmel in Israel where Elijah, the prophet of God, challenged the prophets of the god Baal.

St. Catherine's Monastery nestles at the foot of the rugged Sinai range, seen below.

gorges of the tributaries, holding back the water until the natural dam bursts, releasing a surging wall of water to devastate settlements on the plain.

In the mountain basins of Asia Minor, Syria, Iraq and Iran, where there were winter rains for cereals and good pastures for goats, sheep and camels, it is thought that village life began amongst agricultural peoples, some 10,000 years ago. These village communities migrated to the plains of Mesopotamia and eventually Egypt over the next few thousand years, so that by 3200BC they had reached as far as the Sudan. Jericho, in the Jordan valley north of the Dead Sea, was one of the

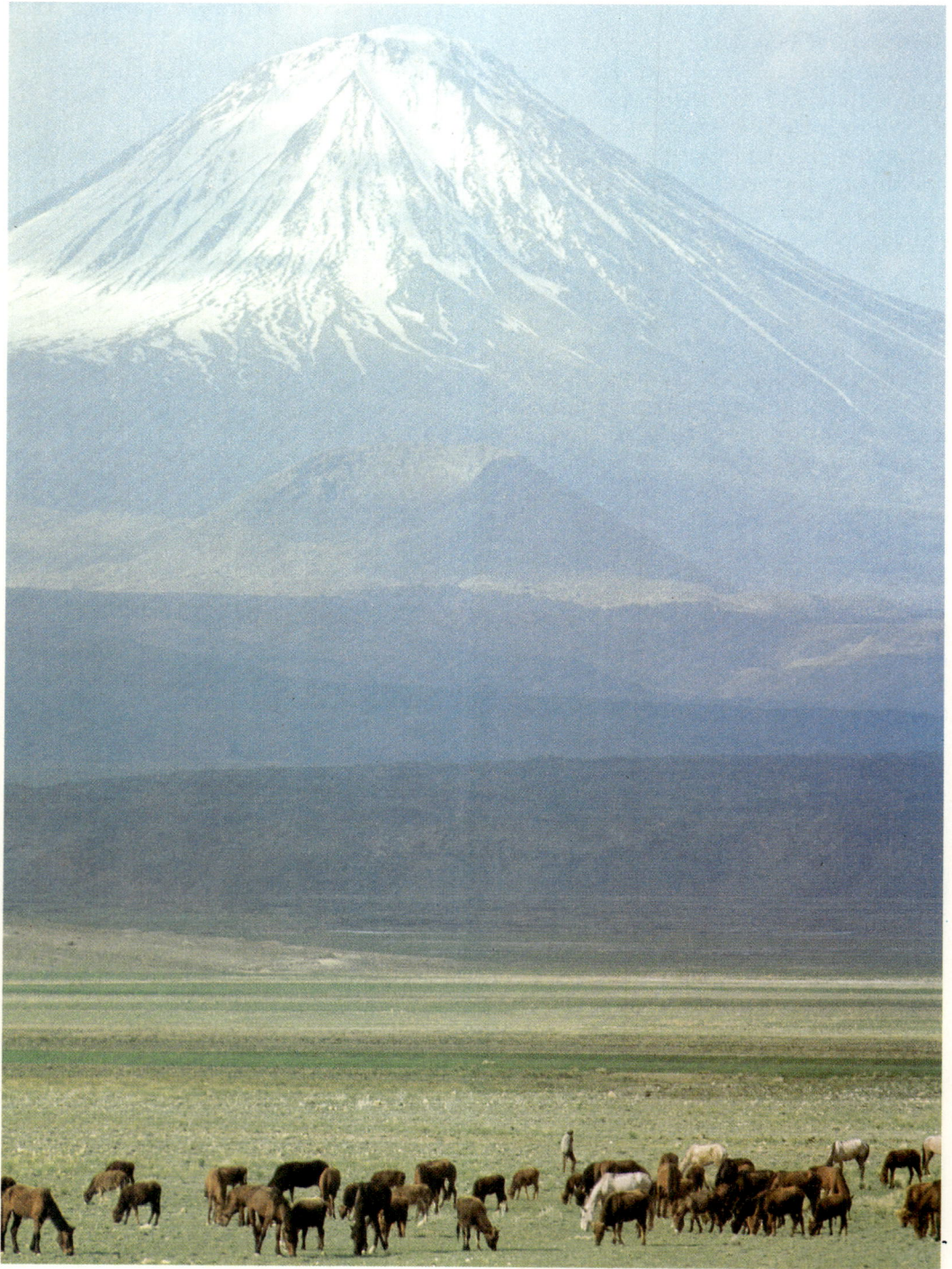

Mt Ararat in Turkey, the traditional resting place of Noah's Ark.

oldest oasis towns of the ancient world, with a continuous history of settlement and irrigated farming stretching back as far, perhaps, as 7000BC. It was several times conquered, destroyed, rebuilt and re-fortified before Joshua captured it about 1200BC.

Syria and Palestine ranges

In Syria and Palestine there are broken mountain and hill ranges which generally decrease in height southwards. The Lebanon and Anti-Lebanon ranges are 120 km long and exceed 3,000 metres high in places; Mt. Hermon on the northern border of Palestine rises to 2,814 metres, and its summit, snowcapped for much of the year, can be seen from as far away as Jerusalem. Hermon was always regarded as a source of blessing, for its 'dews' (Psalm 133:3) feed the headstreams of the Jordan.

In Palestine itself the ranges are lower, only 1,200 metres in Upper Galilee and 1,000 metres in Samaria and Judea. Far to the south, in the Sinai Peninsula, is a separate group of very old volcanic peaks, reaching over 2,600 metres. The exact location of the biblical Mt. Sinai (Mt. Horeb), where Moses received the Ten Commandments and Elijah heard God's 'still small voice', is uncertain, though many scholars favour a peak called Gebel Musa, at the foot of which stands the ancient monastery of St. Catherine. Here in 1859 was discovered the famous Codex Sinaiticus, one of the oldest-known manuscripts of the Bible in Greek; this is now in the British Museum in London.

Egypt

At the south-western end of the Fertile Crescent the great Egyptian civilisation grew up, totally dependent upon the Nile and its annual flood. Unlike the Tigris and Euphrates, however, the Nile's flood-waters are the result of summer monsoon rains, falling between May and October in Ethiopia. These surge down the Blue Nile to join the very steady flow of the White Nile at Khartoum. Nearly 2,000 km further downstream the Nile branches into its huge delta on the south coast of the Mediterranean; here the prosperous kingdom of the Pharaohs flourished throughout Old Testament times, almost unimpeded. Hardly any rain falls here – Cairo has barely 25 mm (1″) in a whole year – but the annual flood of the Nile was

The Nile valley, Egypt. The green plain where the river floods annually, contrasts sharply with the surrounding desert.

Left: Mt Hermon, snow-capped for much of the year, is one of the highest mountains in Palestine.

The farming year in the valley of the River Nile

Summer
The Nile overflows its banks and floods the surrounding land.

Autumn
Rich silt deposits are left behind. The farmers plough and sow.

Winter
The crops grow.

Spring
Harvest time. The fields are prepared for the summer floods.

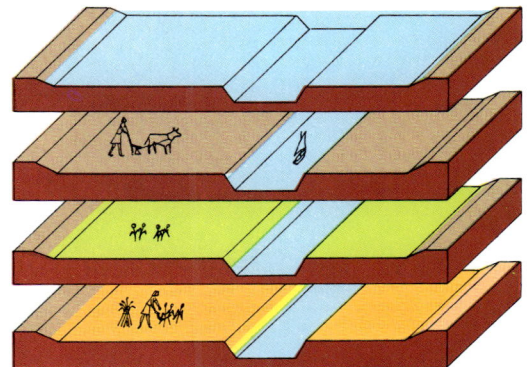

so vital that the seasons were fixed according to its annual rhythm. From mid-July to mid-November was flood-time, or 'Inundation', when the Nile overflowed into embanked fields called 'basins', spreading not only water but a precious layer of fertile silt. The next season, from mid-November to mid-March, was known as the 'Coming Forth', when grain and other crops were sown and cultivated. By the end of this season the Nile had dwindled almost to a trickle, and the period from mid-March till the flood arrived in July was called, simply, 'Drought'.

Throughout the year temperatures were very similar to those in Mesopotamia, with the same scorching summer sun; here too worship of a sun-god flourished, though in Egypt he was called Amon-Ra. For some 400 years after Joseph died, the Hebrews lived in Egypt, having been attracted originally by the reliability of its food-supply when Palestine was suffering an intense drought. The seven years of plenty and seven years of famine, foretold by Joseph, were undoubtedly times when the flood-level was first above and then below the normal.

Because the Israelites were herdsmen and not cultivators like the Egyptians, they were looked down on and were given a separate area on the east of the Nile delta, known as the Land of Goshen. On the rich irrigated pastures their flocks and herds flourished, and the numbers of the Israelites rose till their prosperity and increased population were seen as a threat to the continued dominance of the Egyptians. Eventually, after a period of repression and God's intervention through the ten great plagues, the Israelites left Egypt and crossed into Sinai by way of the Sea of Reeds, probably one of the Bitter Lakes (the Hebrew term 'yam sūp' is sometimes wrongly translated 'Red Sea').

A gourd growing by the Nile at Luxor.

Egyptians are proud of the imposing remains of their great civilisation which was dependent on the Nile and its annual flood.

Desert and wilderness

Within the semi-circle formed by the Fertile Crescent from Mesopotamia to Egypt lies one of the driest and most desolate of the world's deserts, vast stretches of which remain almost completely uninhabited. This is the great Arabian Desert, covering much of present-day Saudi Arabia, an area ten times the size of the United Kingdom. However, 'desert' is a relative term, and covers a variety of landforms and surfaces, from shifting dunes to stark rocky crags and sheets of angular pebbles almost impossible to cross by land-vehicle or beast of burden. A few parts which appear completely barren do have some wells, and dried-up watercourses suggest that in the past the climate may have been wetter than at present. However, with rainfall now almost non-existent and a lack of wells and oases many areas continue to be virtually uninhabitable.

Towards the northern and western edges rainfall increases, scrub vegetation occurs and water is obtainable in places. The Hebrews generally used the word 'midbar' for this kind of territory, which means an unenclosed, uncultivated plain, inhabited by wild animals such as wolves, hyenas, jackals, and the hyrax, which the Authorised Version of the Bible calls the coney. Sometimes 'midbar' was used for natural grazing land such as was found around the edge of many Palestinian villages. Thus the usual English translation of the word as 'wilderness' is rather misleading; the terms 'steppe' or 'semi-desert' would be more accurate most of the time.

Of the areas described in the Bible, one

Much of the Negeb in southern Palestine is steppeland where little grows.

An oasis, like that at Ein Khudra, would have been a welcome sight to the Israelites on their trek.

Desert land in the Sinai Peninsula. The Israelites travelled across country like this on their way from Egypt to the Promised Land.

of the most notable was the Wilderness of Zin, lying on the southern edge of Palestine, south-west of the Dead Sea. Here the Israelites wandered for many years after the Exodus from Egypt, lacking the faith to occupy the Promised Land although the twelve spies had reported that it was 'an exceedingly good land . . . flowing with milk and honey' – a report confirmed by alluring samples of grapes, figs and pomegranates brought from near Hebron (Deuteronomy 1:23–25).

Palestine

Palestine is the name given to the land promised by God to Abraham, and repossessed by the Israelites under Joshua after Moses had led them to its eastern border. The word 'Palestine' is derived from the Philistines, who once inhabited much of it; however, the older name 'Canaan' is more frequently used in the Bible, although originally this described the coastal strip from around Gaza northwards to Tyre and Sidon.

The land the Israelites occupied lay mostly to the west of the Jordan, but some of the tribes settled on land to the east, called by them Gilead; this had been won from the Amorite kings Sihon and Og. The area west of the Jordan settled by the other tribes extended from Dan in the north, near the headstreams of the Jordan, to the land opposite the southern end of the Dead Sea, in which Beersheba was the main town.

To the north of Palestine lived the Aramaeans, descendants of Abraham's brother Nahor, who were later to cause the Israelites much trouble (e.g. under Ben-hadad, 2 Kings 6). To the west and south-west was the territory of the Philistines, a tribal group who were a source of harassment to the Israelites for hundreds of years. Their five main cities lay close to the Mediterranean coast – Gaza, Ashkelon, Ashdod, Ekron and Gath. To the south, extending across the Arabah (the name given to the southern part of the great rift-valley linking the Dead Sea with the Gulf of Aqaba), was the region occupied by the Edomites. These were the descendants of Esau, Jacob's elder brother, but their attitude towards the Israelites was seldom brotherly, and they prevented Moses and his people from travelling through their territory to reach the Promised Land (Numbers 20:14–21).

Much later, in the tenth century BC,

Palestine

1. The Coastlands
This flat fertile plain stretches along the coastline and has been an important trade link since Bible times.

2. The Central Hill-Country
Shepherds with their flock at dusk in the hills near Bethlehem, which is visible on the sky-line.

3. The Jordan Valley
The River Jordan winds through wheatfields overlooked by steep barren hillsides.

4. The hills and plateaux of Transjordan
In the south, this hot spring at Madaba is a reminder of ancient volcanic activity in the area.

The natural regions and important towns

Sidon
Damascus
ARAM
Mt Hermon
Tyre
SIDONIA
CENTRAL HILL COUNTRY
Dan
Caesarea Philippi
UPPER GALILEE
Lake Huleh
Merom
BASHAN
Acco
Plain of Asher
Capernaum
Cana
Sea of Galilee
Sepphoris
LOWER GALILEE
Mt Carmel
Nazareth
Tiberias
Mediterranean Sea
Plain of Esdraelon
Mt Tabor
Nain Valley of Jezreel
Megiddo
Jezreel
HILLS OF TRANSJORDAN
Caesarea
Mt Gilboa
ISRAEL
JORDAN VALLEY
Dothan
Samaria
Mt Ebal
R Jabbok
Plain of Sharon
Shechem
Mt Gerizim
River Jordan
GILEAD
The Arabah
CENTRAL HILL COUNTRY
Joppa
The Ghor
COASTLANDS
Bethel
Jericho
AMMON
Aijalon
Jerusalem
Qumran
THE SHEPHELAH
Bethlehem
Ashkelon
PHILISTIA
JUDAH
Hebron
Gaza
Debir
Wilderness of Judea
Dead Sea
Beersheba
Masada
MOAB

This map covers places relevant to the entire biblical period.

o indicates places which became important only in New Testament times.

0   10   20 miles
0   10   20 kilometres

AMALEK
EDOM

There have always been important ports along the Mediterranean coast of Palestine. The northern ports of Tyre and Sidon which thrived in Bible times have long since disappeared. Haifa is a modern port further south.

Below: the 'Via Maris' or 'Way of the Sea' winds over a pass through the Carmel hills.

Bottom: the Valley of Jezreel, the area of the historic battle between the Canaanite forces under Sisera and the Israelite forces led by Deborah.

Below right: the port of Acre dates back to Old Testament times.

David conquered Edom, and Solomon established a port at Ezion-Geber on the Gulf of Aqaba, near modern Eilat. However, Israelite control over the area did not last long, for the Edomites won back their independence when they successfully rebelled against King Jehoram of Judah.

Other traditional enemies of the Israelites lived to the east of Palestine, in Transjordan – the Moabites, Ammonites and Midianites. The first two were tribes descended from sons of Lot, and because of their racial links with the Israelites Moses was commanded not to attack them, nor attempt to seize any of the land God had already given them. However, their leaders hired Balaam the seer to curse the Israelites, and thereafter they often clashed with them, although there were periods when relations were more friendly. It must be remembered that Ruth, David's great-grandmother, came from Moab. The Midianites lived further south, on the desert borders, and their forays on camel-back into Israel during the period of the Judges were eventually repelled by Gideon.

Relief and scenery

Although the area of Palestine is small, it has a surprising variety of scenery. The major relief features all have a north-south trend, forming four distinctive parallel zones: the coastlands, the central hill-country, the Jordan rift-valley, and the hills and plateaux of Transjordan.

The Coastlands Along the Mediterranean coast are a series of lowlands, small and fragmented in the north but wider and continuous in the centre and south. North of Mt. Carmel, which forms a steep headland projecting into the sea immediately south of the modern port of Haifa, is the small Plain of Asher, extending up the coast almost as far as the ancient Phoenician ports of Tyre and Sidon. Ptolemais (Acre or Acco) was the chief port here in Old Testament times. South of Carmel lies the Plain of Sharon, about 80 km from north to south and 15 km across. Near the coast a belt of sandy country was thickly wooded in biblical times, whilst inland were areas of uncolonised swamp – though all this is now fertile agricultural land, famous for its oranges. Joppa (modern Jaffa) was the only port of significance, serving Jerusalem; here Peter had his vision of a sheet full of animals (Acts 11:5–10). Further south the coastal plain widens further, and is an area of low rolling hills and fertile open valleys; in Old Testament times this was the homeland of

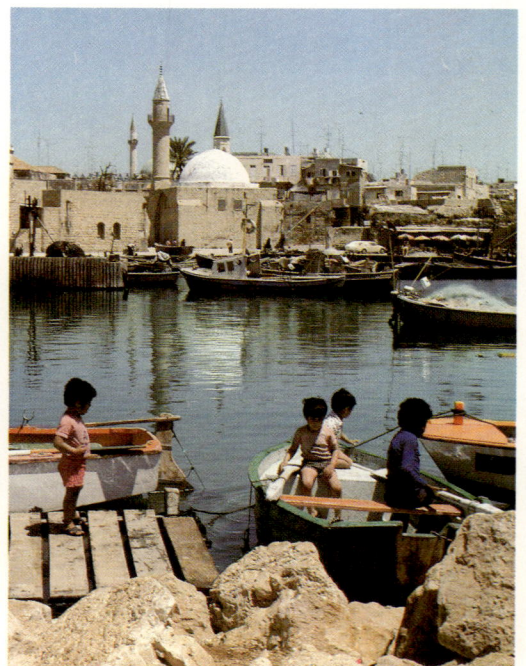

the Philistines, where much grain was produced.

Inland from this coastal plain is a belt of low hills known as the Shephelah, which acted as a military buffer-zone between the territories of the Philistines on the coast and the Israelites further inland. Fortresses such as Aijalon, Keilah and Debir were built here. Samson and later David fought battles in the area, but it was never densely populated and remained quite thickly wooded.

The coast plain was the site of an important trade route, the 'Via Maris' or 'Way of the Sea' which ran northwards from Egypt as far as Mt. Carmel, where it turned inland via Megiddo to Damascus.

The Central Hill-Country The 'backbone' of the country is an undulating ridge of limestone and chalk, which is broken into dissected blocks in the north. Along the Lebanese border is the rather remote and once heavily forested area known as Upper Galilee, which hardly figures at all in Bible history. Just to the south, however, is the lower and more open hill-country of Lower Galilee, which adjoins the Sea of Galilee to the east. This is the area where Jesus spent much of his life, for here was the village of Nazareth (now a thriving town), Cana, scene of his first miracle, and Nain, where he raised the widow's son. Mt. Tabor, a steep-sided isolated dome away to the south-east, is

Waterfalls near the source of the River Jordan.

thought by some to have been the Mount of Transfiguration, although Mt. Hermon seems more likely.

South of Nazareth, and separating the hills of Galilee from the hill-country of Samaria further south, is the triangular-shaped Plain of Esdraelon, flat and fertile, forming an easy routeway across the country from the coast to the Sea of Galilee. Its apex reaches the coast at Haifa, in the shadow of Mt. Carmel, which lies at the north-western end of a long spur of the central Palestine ridge. On this ridge, between the Plains of Sharon and Esdraelon, lay the city of Megiddo, called in the New Testament 'Armageddon' (Hill of Megiddo), scene not only of many battles in Bible times but of the prophesied last great conflict on earth (Rev. 16:16). The Plain of Esdraelon is linked to the Jordan valley by a faulted trough, the Valley of Jezreel, overlooked by Mt. Gilboa on its southern side; this area too is rich in biblical associations,

Left: the Judean hills south of Jerusalem. Jesus spent forty days fasting in this area before starting his ministry.

Below: evening over the Sea of Galilee.

such as the battle in which Saul and Jonathan were killed, and Ahab's seizure of Naboth's vineyard.

From Gilboa southwards the hill-region becomes higher, broader and more continuous. In the centre of this area lay the towns of Shechem and Samaria; the former is the first place in Palestine to be mentioned in the Bible – Abraham camped and built an altar there (Genesis 12:6, 7). Samaria became capital of the Northern Kingdom (Israel); here Ahab built a luxurious palace. Only a few kilometres to the east was Jacob's well, at the foot of Mt. Gerizim; by this well, which is still in existence today, Jesus met the woman of Samaria (John 4). Further south, beyond the town of Bethel where Jacob had his vision of a ladder set up to heaven, the broad undulating ridge continues for another fifty km through Jerusalem, Bethlehem and Hebron before its height begins to drop below about 600–800 metres, towards Beersheba. A north-south routeway, parallel to the 'Via Maris' but less important, linked most of the towns along the central ridge, many of which lay at the crossing-points of routes between the coast and the Jordan valley.

East and south-east of Jerusalem lies a desolate area of waterless gorges and glistening crags of chalk and limestone, where the central ridge slopes towards the Dead Sea. This is the Wilderness of Judea, where Jesus spent forty days fasting and being tempted before starting his ministry. The road from Jerusalem to Jericho – scene of the parable of the Good Samaritan – winds its way between menacing cliffs and boulders, descending over 1,100 metres in thirty km before suddenly opening out onto the small but richly fertile irrigated area around Jericho.

The Jordan Rift-Valley This lies at the northern end of one of the most remarkable features on the Earth's surface – a huge split in the crust which can be traced thousands of kilometres through the Red Sea and East Africa. It begins west of Mt. Hermon, near the Old Testament city of Dan and the New Testament city of Caesarea Philippi, where a number of spring-fed streams join to form the River Jordan. After meandering across the marshy floor of the small Plain of Huleh, the river falls more than 250 metres in less than twenty km before entering the fresh-water Sea of Galilee (or Lake of Gennesaret), whose surface is over 200 metres below the level of the Mediterranean. The eastern slopes of the lake are quite steep – it was here that a herd of pigs drowned when Jesus cured the man called Legion – but around the gentler western shores were, in New Testament times, several prosperous trading and fishing towns such as Tiberias, Capernaum, Bethsaida and Magdala. The lake is notorious for its sudden storms, caused by winds rushing down the narrow valleys which open onto the eastern side.

Between the Sea of Galilee and the Dead Sea, a distance of a hundred kilometres, the Jordan descends a further 190 metres as it winds its way southwards in a gradually widening valley, overlooked by rocky cliffs and steep barren hillsides. The Dead Sea is the lowest point on the Earth's surface, almost 400 metres (1,300 feet) below sea-level, but it is certain that its surface-level and size have fluctuated considerably in recent geological time. At one time it extended much further up the

Dead Sea salt is collected from deposits left when the water evaporates.

112

Jordan valley, laying down soft alluvial deposits into which the river is now cutting quite sharply. The plain in which the river is entrenched is known as the Ghor; in biblical times it was a thick jungle, inhabited by lions and wolves.

The eastern and western margins of the Dead Sea are bounded by steep cliffs and gorges, in general lying some way back from the shore. The settlement of Qumran, where the Dead Sea Scrolls were found, lay near the western shore, whilst Herod the Great's fortress of Masada was built on an impregnable crag a little further south. A few springs feed the Sea on the west, whilst on the east four wadis stretch down from the hills of Moab, but the water these and the Jordan add to the

Rocky headlands around the Gulf of Aqaba.

Dead Sea is scarcely able to maintain its level, so intense is the evaporation. It is no wonder that the water is 25 per cent salt, and that nothing can live in it. Somewhere beneath the Dead Sea lie the cities of Sodom and Gomorrah, destroyed by God for their wickedness. They may have perished in a volcanic eruption, for the crust here is very unstable, and earthquakes are frequent; lava and sulphurous gases may be released when a major fracture opens up. It is possible that God used an earthquake to block the Jordan at Adam, near Jericho, which allowed the Israelites to cross into the Promised Land (Joshua 3:16).

South of the Dead Sea the rift-valley continues into the Arabah, a wide trench 160 km long which rises gradually southwards before it again falls to the head of the Gulf of Aqaba. All the way it is bounded on both sides by steep fault-scarps up to 1,000 metres high. The whole trench from Galilee to the Red Sea is an active earthquake zone.

The hills and plateaux of Transjordan
This is the area lying immediately to the east of the Jordan valley, where limestone and sandstone strata lie almost horizontally on a platform of ancient crystalline rocks. These are generally steppe-lands, gradually changing southwards and eastwards into true desert. However, in the north the region of Bashan, with its higher rainfall and fertile volcanic soil, has long been an area of settled agriculture, and was occupied by part of the tribe of Manasseh; southwards from this, the hilly, steep area along the east bank of the Jordan, known as Gilead, afforded grain-growing land and good grazing to the tribes of Gad and Reuben. The poorest land lay well to the south, in Edom, but trade and military prowess brought a wealth to the land that its barren surface could never produce. From the head of the Gulf of Aqaba northwards through the lands of Edom, Moab and Gilead lay another important trade route known as the 'King's Highway'. This followed the more fertile and densely-populated grain-producing lands, and was a major link between Egypt, Arabia and Mesopotamia.

Climate

Most of Palestine has what may be termed a true Mediterranean climate, with hot, dry summers and mild, wet winters; however, as with the relief, there is considerable local variation. The entire land is virtually rainless from June to September inclusive, when skies are largely clear and scorching winds sometimes blow from the deserts, quickly drying up the vegetation. However, heavy dews in the uplands are sufficient, when added to the residual moisture from winter, to permit the cultivation of grapes, cucumbers and melons. Mean summer temperatures on the coast are around 25°C (77°F), slightly cooler on the interior uplands, but exceeding 30°C (86°F) in the enclosed Jordan valley, where Jericho has a mean daily maximum above 38°C (100°F) for four successive months. The winter rainy season begins in October or November with the 'former rains' (or early rains), on which farmers depend for the planting of grain crops; barley, with a shorter growing season than wheat, was normally ready for harvesting in late March or April, wheat in May or June. Grapes are gathered in September, olives from October to December.

Winters are everywhere mild enough for active plant growth, averaging 11° or 12° on the coast, though cooler on the interior hills, where snow is an occasional intruder (Jerusalem, January 8°C). Only on the heights of Hermon does snow linger for most of the year. The rainy season (though with good sunny intervals) continues throughout the winter to end with the 'latter rains' of April and early May, which tend to be rather variable and unreliable in amount. Since the winter

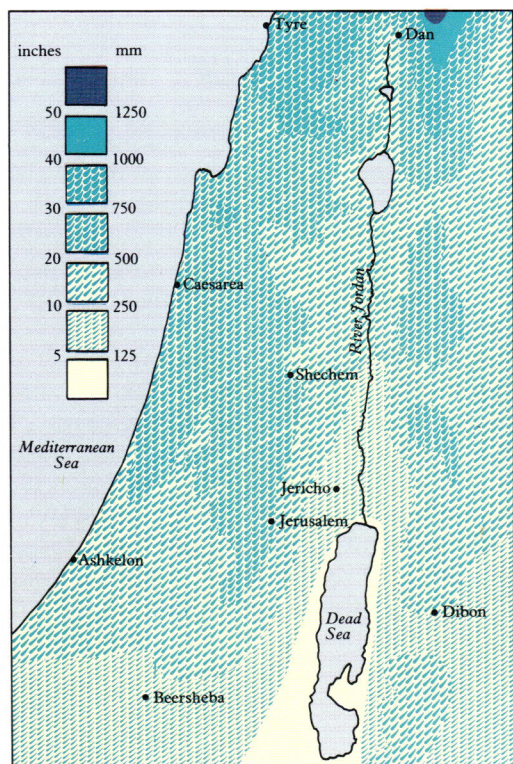

A plentiful selection of vegetables grow in the Mediterranean climate of Palestine. A customer chooses from the colourful display at a shop in Jerusalem.

Annual rainfall in Palestine.

Wild flowers – lilies of the field – in the fields of Galilee.

inches   mm
50   1250
40   1000
30   750
20   500
10   250
5   125

Tyre
Dan
Caesarea
River Jordan
Shechem
Mediterranean Sea
Jericho
Jerusalem
Ashkelon
Dead Sea
Dibon
Beersheba

rain is brought by winds off the sea, associated with areas of low pressure, slopes facing west and north-west receive most, Hermon and the higher hills of Galilee having over 1,000 mm (40″) a year, the hills of Samaria and northern Judea over 600 mm (24″), but amounts fall off sharply as the air descends into the Jordan valley, and there is only about 50 mm around the Dead Sea, one of the world's most marked rain-shadow areas. The head of the Gulf of Aqaba receives even less, some years being completely rainless, but east of the Jordan trench amounts again increase, the hills of Transjordan receiving 375–600 mm. Much of Palestine's rainfall comes in short, heavy downpours which can cause 'flash' floods, such as that which trapped Sisera's chariots on the Plain of Esdraelon, when the River Kishon overflowed (Judges 4 and 5). Jesus drew on such an occurrence in his parable of the foolish man whose house had insecure foundations (Matthew 7:26, 27). Rainfall varies widely not only from place to place, but also from year to year, making planting and harvesting much less predictable than in Egypt with its fairly reliable annual Nile flood. Drought was a quite common feature; it drove Abraham, and later Jacob, to Egypt, and in the reign of Ahab one acute drought lasted three years (1 Kings 17–18).

Soils and vegetation

With an annual drought, erratic heavy downpours, and geology dominated by porous limestone and chalk, soils over much of Palestine are rather thin, poor and stony. There has been a good deal of erosion and impoverishment over the centuries as protective vegetation has been cut down and slopes ploughed or overgrazed. The variation of soils over quite short distances is illustrated in Jesus's parable of the Sower. Some of the fertile alluvial lands, such as the Plain of Esdraelon, which are intensively cultivated today, were swampy wastes in Bible times, although others – for example, along parts of the Jordan valley and the Philistine plain – were drained and settled at an early date. In Old Testament times many of the wetter areas, such as the slopes of Hermon and the hills of Galilee and Bashan, were quite well wooded, with forests of cedars, oaks, pines and firs, and the Plain of Sharon was noted for its oak forests; other wooded areas were steadily cleared for grazing or cultivation. Much of Palestine was covered in steppe and heathy scrub, which in spring was a riot of colour as hundreds of species of wild flowers ('lilies of the field') burst into bloom. Drought-resistant trees such as acacias, tamarisks and terebinths and many types of thorny shrub were common in the drier areas, and the date-palm was widespread; Jericho was known as 'the city of palm-trees' (Deut. 34:3).

Below: barley ready for harvesting.

Below right: soils over much of Palestine are poor and stony.

Bottom: sunset over the hills of Samaria.

Rivers, springs and wells

In a land of intermittent drought, water has always been a precious commodity. Moses told the Israelites towards the end of their wilderness journey that the land they were about to enter was 'a fertile land, a land that has rivers and springs, and underground streams gushing out into the valleys . . .' (Deut. 8:7). Although the Jordan and a few of its spring-fed tributaries, together with four or five coastal streams, are the only permanent rivers, the existence of wells and springs throughout the country ensured that life could continue through the hot, dry summer. More than seventy ancient place-names in Palestine are said to include the word 'ain', meaning 'spring', and another sixty the word 'bir' (or 'beer'), meaning 'well'. Cisterns and reservoirs were constructed from early times, and several towns had a water-

supply from springs outside their walls; the best-known example of this being Jerusalem's supply, which Hezekiah constructed from the Virgin's Fountain (Gihon) through a tunnel into the Pool of Siloam.

Throughout the Bible water is seen as symbolic of life; at the well in Samaria, Jesus spoke of himself as 'living water' – water which would quench all thirst, and be a spring of eternal life to all who drink.

Such then was the land of Palestine which God gave to the people of Israel; to quote Moses' words again, '. . . a fertile land . . . that produces wheat and barley, grapes, figs, pomegranates, olives and honey . . . Its rocks have iron in them, and from its hills you can mine copper. You will have all you want to eat, and you will give thanks to the Lord your God for the fertile land he has given you.'

Irrigation channels to carry water to crops and livestock are vital in Eastern countries where there is no rain for long periods.

Hezekiah's tunnel

In the sixth century BC King Hezekiah ordered a tunnel to be dug below Jerusalem to ensure that the city's water supply would not be cut off by the invading Assyrian army. One group of workmen started digging outside the city walls at the Spring of Gihon and another group started the other end of the tunnel at the Pool of Siloam, a reservoir inside the walls. There was also an overflow from the reservoir.

This tunnel was an amazing feat of engineering because only simple hand tools were available and as the two teams of diggers got closer to each other they were guided by each other's voices. Water still flows through Hezekiah's tunnel.

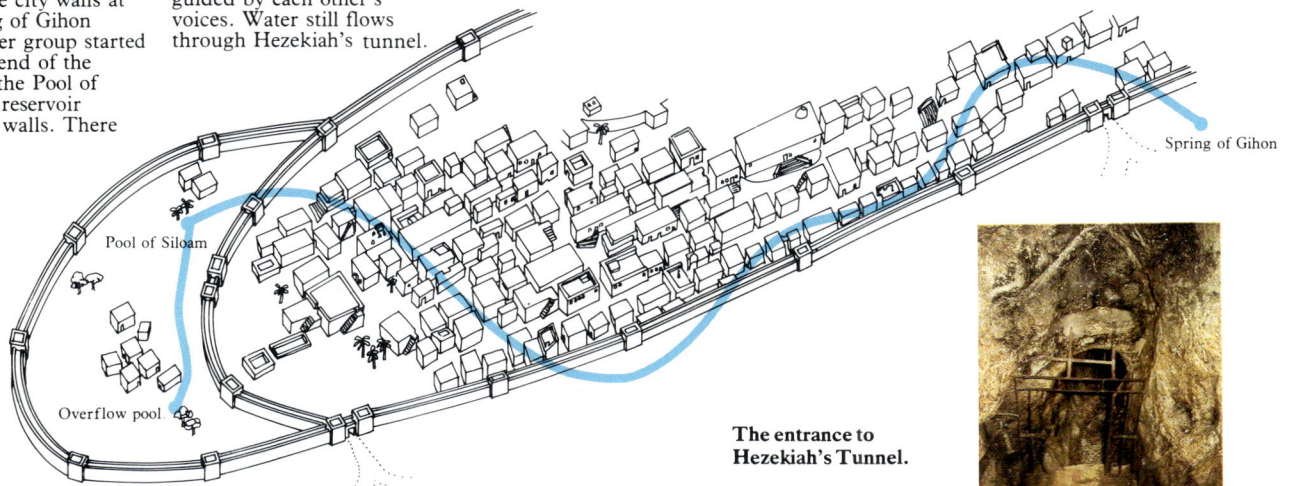

Pool of Siloam

Overflow pool

Spring of Gihon

The entrance to Hezekiah's Tunnel.

PLANT LIFE

The people we read about in the Bible lived mainly in the countryside, or in villages and small country towns. Farms, gardens, wild flowers and trees were all part of their everyday lives. They needed trees for firewood and furniture, wild plants for medicines and salads; their flocks grazed on the hillsides and most people grew their own corn for bread. Therefore it is not surprising that plants are mentioned very frequently in the Bible and it is helpful for us to understand how important they were. Because many of us today live in large cities and eat food grown in other countries, we may know little about our own countryside, and even less about the lands of the Bible. The events recorded in the Bible took place in the orient at the eastern end of the Mediterranean region where the trees and wild flowers, as well as the animals, are different from our own. The summers are hot and dry, while the winters are cool or mild and in most places quite wet. Wild flowers and crops, such as corn, grow during the winter, while there is enough moisture in the soil, and before the heat of summer dries them up.

Translators of the Hebrew script in which the Old Testament was written, and of the Greek of the New Testament, often had difficulty in knowing which plants were intended by certain Hebrew and Greek words. Therefore the various versions of the Bible may use different plant names. This book is based on Today's English Version – the Good News Bible – with reference to others.

Darnel weed growing in a wheatfield. These are the weeds Jesus mentioned in the parable of the wheat and the tares.

Development of plant life

Wherever we live, plant-life is still as important for us as it was in Bible times. We need plants for the food we eat and the air we breathe; and the animals that provide us with milk, meat and wool also depend on grass and other plants. This is a complicated food-chain, so we need to learn about ecology and how to protect the environment.

Agriculture and the cultivation of plants first started in the Bible lands where some of the most important crop plants, such as wheat, barley, flax and grape-vine grow wild. Better varieties have been developed, but their wild relatives that still grow in the region are threatened with extinction unless the land is used wisely and there is conservation of nature.

A long time ago forests and bushy places covered many of the hilly regions of the Bible lands and sometimes the plains as well. Then people cut down the trees and burnt the bushes, cultivated the land and kept goats which nibbled off the tree seedlings. The exposed soil was blown away by the wind or washed down into streams and rivers, sometimes blocking them up, as happened at Ephesus and Miletus in western Turkey, both of which used to be ports in Paul's day and are now well inland. To prevent rainwater from washing away the soil, stone walls were often built to retain terraces on the hillsides where vineyards and olives were planted.

This picture of the ruins of Ephesus shows Harbour Street which used to lead direct to the port. Now it is well inland because of silting.

Terraces on a hillside near Bethlehem. The walls prevent soil being washed away by rain, so that vineyards can be planted.

Extensive soil erosion in a wadi near the Dead Sea.

Wild flowers

There are so many wild flowers in the Bible lands that we can mention here only those referred to in the Bible itself. It is often difficult to be sure which kinds of plants are intended by the Hebrew or Greek words. Just as we group similar kinds together under one name, so did the writers of the Bible. For example, they referred to prickly plants as 'thorns' or 'thistles', but in fact there are several quite different plants and we cannot always be sure which one was intended.

There are many colourful flowers in the Holy Land and Jesus could have been looking at any of them when he said that King Solomon in his wealth and glory was not as beautiful as one of them (Matthew 6:28). They may have been the common anemone or crown daisy rather than a true lily. The names lily, crocus, asphodel and rose have been used by the translators of the Bible for some of the wild flowers of the Holy Land.

Gourds The gourds of the wild vine collected by Elisha's servant were the fruits of the poisonous colocynth (2 Kings 4:39). This is a plant that grows in hot, dry places such as the Jordan valley. It is a kind of marrow or squash, but the fruits are yellow and about the size of tennis balls. They dry up and contain lots of seeds, which are released when the gourd blows away and cracks open against a rock. The bitter and poisonous plant or the gall mentioned in the Bible (Deuteronomy 29:18, Jeremiah 23:15) is probably the colocynth. Some translators think that it was a climbing gourd that shaded Jonah (Jonah 4:6); others think it was the castor oil plant.

Hyssop There are three different plants referred to by this name in the Bible. The first is a kind of white marjoram that was used in Jewish ceremonies for cleansing (Exodus 12:22). It is fragrant like mint and grows in rocky places all over the Holy Land.

The second 'hyssop' was the kind that grew in walls (1 Kings 4:33) and was probably the prickly caper bush.

The third 'hyssop' was used to hold the sponge to Jesus' mouth when he was on the cross (John 19:29); it must have been a stick such as a reed.

Lily The lily mentioned in several places in the Bible could refer to several flowers. The one in Song of Solomon 5:13 is probably a scarlet tulip or the red anemone, as lips are mentioned. Probably

The water-lily, known as the lotus, appears in many Egyptian paintings.

A colocynth gourd. This poisonous fruit was put into a stew by mistake by Elisha's servant.

The anemone is one of the flowers described as lily in the Bible.

the yellow iris is referred to in Hosea 14:5 as it grows in water. The lily-work that was carved on the columns of King Solomon's temple was almost certainly the flowers and leaves of the water-lily famous in Egypt as the lotus (1 Kings 7:19).

Mandrake This plant grows in rough places in the Mediterranean region. It has a rosette of large leaves with purple flowers sprouting amongst them during the autumn or very early spring. The round yellow fruits are fragrant (Song of Sol. 7:13). Several superstitions have arisen about this plant which has long roots that can look like a person.

Myrtle This is a wild shrub, usually found on hillsides, with fragrant shiny evergreen leaves. Branches of myrtle were used by the Jews for the shelters they built at the Festival of Shelters (or Booths) (Nehemiah 8:15). It was also one of the choice plants that Isaiah pictured would replace the prickly plants of the desert (Isaiah 41:19).

Nettles, Thistles and Thorns On the dry hillsides, in waste places and on sandy

Colourful spring flowers growing wild in Golan.

Far left: mandrake fruit ripening on the plant.

Left: thorns grow in abundance on the dry hillsides of Palestine. Jesus told a parable of corn being choked by thorns growing up through it.

A myrtle shrub.

Incense, spices and seasoning herbs

Plants with strong perfumes or spicy taste were very much more important in Bible times than they are today. Drains were poor and personal washing was often neglected, and the dull food required seasoning to make it tasty. Leaves and roots of wild plants were also collected for medicines, although they are seldom referred to in the Bible. Some trees and other plants produce gummy resins, usually from cut stems, and these were used for medicines and incense. Many religions of those days used to burn incense as it gave a fragrance which was thought to be acceptable to God, both as a precious gift because incense was expensive, and as a sweet smell ascending to heaven like prayer.

The following such plants are mentioned in the Bible.

Aloe
The aloe mentioned in the Old Testament (Psalm 45:8) was an expensive spice obtained from the wood of an Indian tree, the eaglewood. But the aloe of the New Testament was a different plant with thick, sword-like leaves with sharp teeth, which grew in dry places in the Bible lands. It was the bitter substance from its leaves that was used at Jesus' burial (John 19:39).

Balm
This was a medicinal ointment made from resin produced by various kinds of plants (Gen. 37:25).

The flower of the balm plant.

Bitter herbs
These were eaten during the Passover celebrations (Exod. 12:8). They were usually the leaves of certain wild plants that had a bitter taste, such as dandelion and wild lettuce.

An old man selling bitter herbs in Jerusalem.

Cassia
The fragrant bark of this tree was ground up and mixed with cinnamon and sweet smelling cane in olive-oil that was used for anointing the priests (Exod. 30:24).

Cinnamon
A spice used with olive oil for anointing priests (Exod. 30:24). It was precious because it was obtained from the bark of trees that grew in Sri Lanka (Rev. 18:13).

Cinnamon leaves.

Calamus
This was the cane mentioned in Isaiah 43:24 (RSV) that was sweet smelling. It was the lower stem of a plant sometimes called sweet flag that grows in wet places.

Coriander
A small plant like parsley with small round seeds that looked like the manna of the desert the Israelites had to collect (Exod. 16:31). The seeds of coriander are fragrant and since ancient times have been used in cooking and for medicine.

Coriander

Cumin and dill
Isaiah knew that these delicate fragrant seeds would be damaged by rough treatment such as is given to wheat during threshing (Isa. 28:25–27). These plants are similar to parsley

Black cumin.

Dill.

and they have been grown for centuries as food seasoners. The Pharisees even gave a tenth of their tiny crops of cumin, dill and other garden herbs to the temple, but they neglected the more important teachings in God's law (Matt. 23:23).

Frankincense
Incense is frequently mentioned in the Bible and the most important substance in it was the resin frankincense (Lev. 6:15). The priests burnt incense on an altar as a sweet smell to the Lord, and the smoke was also thought to be like prayer going up to God (Ps. 141:2). It was also mixed with a little olive oil which was poured on the head of priests when they were anointed (Exod. 30:34).

The frankincense resin was obtained from cuts made in the branches of a desert tree growing in Southern Arabia and North East Africa. Local people collected the resin which was like tears hardening into a whitish substance. It then had to be carried by camels along the ancient spice routes where traders sold it to others who put up the price. By the time it reached cities like Jerusalem it was

very expensive, and it was along such a route that the Queen of Sheba came to bring precious spices to King Solomon (1 Kings 10:2). Frankincense was one of the gifts, together with gold and myrrh, brought to the infant Jesus by the wise men (Matt. 2:11).

Galbanum
This was a very strong-smelling resin obtained from the stem of a parsley-like plant growing on the dry mountains of Iran. It was used with frankincense and other spices which were all burnt as incense (Exod. 30:34).

The henna shrub.

Henna
A straggly shrub that grows in warm places such as Engedi by the Dead Sea where Solomon cultivated it (Song of Songs 1:14, 4:13). The henna flowers are small and white with a very sweet fragrance. Its crushed leaves provide a dye that stains skin, nails and hair a yellow colour.

Camel train carrying precious spices.

The herb mint.

Mint
This well-known garden herb was one of those tithed by the religious leaders in Jesus' day while at the same time they neglected justice and love for God (Luke 11:42). Its fragrant leaves have long been used for seasoning food.

Mustard
Jesus twice mentioned mustard: once when he spoke about its small seeds growing into a plant tall enough for birds to nest in (Matt. 13:31). The second time he said that with faith as big (or as little) as a mustard seed his followers could do anything (Matt. 17:20). Mustard has bright yellow flowers and spicy seeds.

Myrrh
Like frankincense, the myrrh resin was collected from certain shrubs and small trees growing in the deserts of North East Africa and Southern Arabia. When the branches were cut slightly the brownish coloured resin oozed out and hardened before collection. Myrrh bushes are very thorny, while frankincense trees do not have thorns.

Myrrh resin was very important in the ancient Bible lands for religious ceremonies, medicines

and cosmetics. It was mixed with other substances for the holy oil with which the priests were anointed (Exod. 30:23). The psalmist and Solomon both wrote about its fragrance (Ps. 45:8, Song of Songs 3:6). When Jesus was visited by the wise men they brought a gift of myrrh (Matt. 2:11). At the end of his earthly life Jesus was offered a drink containing it (Mark 15:23) and a large quantity of myrrh was used at his burial (John 19:39).

Rue
A strong smelling shrub 50 cm or more high with grey-green divided leaves and yellow flowers. It was another of the herbs tithed by the Jewish leaders (Luke 11:42).

The herb rue.

Saffron
This is one of the spices mentioned by King

A jar of ointment.

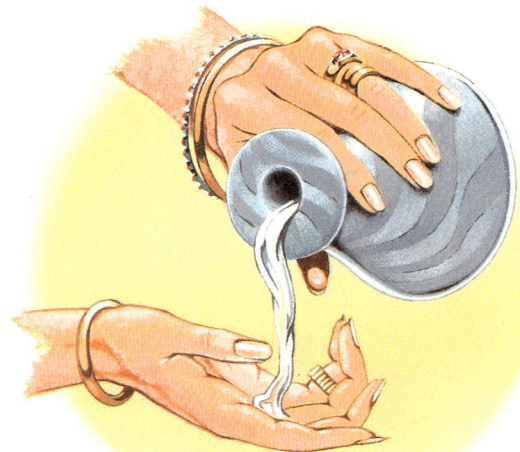

Crocus sativus from which saffron yellow is made.

Solomon (Song of Songs 4:14). It was a yellow powder made from the pistils of a kind of crocus flower; very many were needed which made it an expensive substance. Saffron was used for colouring and flavouring food, and also in medicines.

Spikenard or nard
This was a very expensive oil that was used as a perfume (Song of Songs 4:13, John 12:3). The oil was obtained either from the leaves of a grass that grows in the desert or from the roots of a small plant found in the Himalaya Mountains.

Stacte
Moses was told to make incense of sweet spices, including stacte (Exod. 30:34). This was a resin which probably came from a small bush that grows in Southern Arabia and North East Africa.

plains of the Holy Land stinging and prickly plants abound. They were a curse to Adam, as they still are to farmers (Gen. 3:18). In the fields they prevent the crops from growing properly, as Jesus knew when he told the parable of the sower in which some of the growing corn was choked by thorn bushes (Matt. 13:7). In the Bible the writers often mentioned them as troublesome plants that were fit only to be burnt (Isa. 9:18). However, the farmer could use thorn bushes as living hedges or they could be cut down and placed on top of a wall to stop animals or people crossing (Matt. 21:33). Jotham spoke of a thorn-bush (brier or bramble) in his parable of the trees (Judg. 9:14, 15). Jesus wore a crown of thorns when the soldiers mocked him before he was crucified (Matt. 27:29).

Papyrus, Reeds and Rushes These are all grass-like plants of watery places (Job 8:11–14). The papyrus plant is a tall sedge with a large mop-like head and a three-cornered stalk that was used for making papyrus paper. The English words paper and papyrus come from the Greek word for this plant. The Greeks called the pithy part of the stem that was used for the paper *biblos* and books made of papyrus were *biblia*, which gave us our word *Bible*. To make paper in the old-fashioned way, the papyrus stalks were sliced up and placed side by side with another layer across them. After the strips had been pressed together and dried, a sheet of papyrus was ready for use. Writing was done with a pen cut from a reed and with ink prepared from soot scraped off cooking pots. Much of the Bible was written and copied in this way.

Reeds of one sort or another were used for making the basket in which baby Moses was hidden (Exod. 2:3) and also for the boats used by the Egyptians (Isa. 18:2).

Wormwood This small shrub (*Artemisia*) with grey leaves grows in the desert and on dry hillsides. It has a strong smell and a bitter taste like poison, which explains why the writers of the Bible referred to it in connection with sorrow, bitter experiences and punishment (Jer. 9:15).

A section through a papyrus reed showing the pithy part of the stem used for making paper.

Flowers of the flax plant. Linen fibres are made from the stems of the plant. Embroidered linen was used for Jewish priests' robes. Around the hem hung gold bells and pomegranates.

Vegetables

Vegetables were very important for the poor peasants in Bible lands where they had little meat. They were grown in small gardens near the houses where they could be watered every day. In Egypt vegetables were easily grown on the wet soil near the River Nile. People also used the leaves of wild plants which they gathered as vegetables and salad.

Beans Several kinds of beans and peas (sometimes called pulses) were grown in the Bible lands. They were important food for the peasants who had little meat to eat, as beans provide protein. Perhaps the vegetables eaten by Daniel and his friends (Dan. 1:12–14) were beans.

Cucumber When the people of Israel wandered in the desert after leaving Egypt they longed for the cucumbers they had eaten there (Num. 11:5). The ancient Egyptian cucumber was rather different from our well-known salad vegetable as it was shorter and had lines along its sides.

Garlic It is a kind of onion that is very strongly flavoured and was popular with the ancient Egyptians. When the Israelites left Egypt they remembered the garlic and other vegetables they had eaten there (Num. 11:5).

Leeks This was another vegetable that the people of Israel missed during their wanderings in the desert (Num. 11:5). Leeks are a kind of onion that does not develop the swollen bulb and has a milder flavour.

Lentils This is one of the pulses mentioned above under 'beans'. It is a small plant of the pea family that is often cultivated in the Bible lands for its small round seeds. They make very good soup that is reddish in colour: it must have been lentil soup that Jacob gave to his brother Esau (Gen. 25:29).

Esau sold his birthright to his brother Jacob in exchange for a bowl of bean soup.

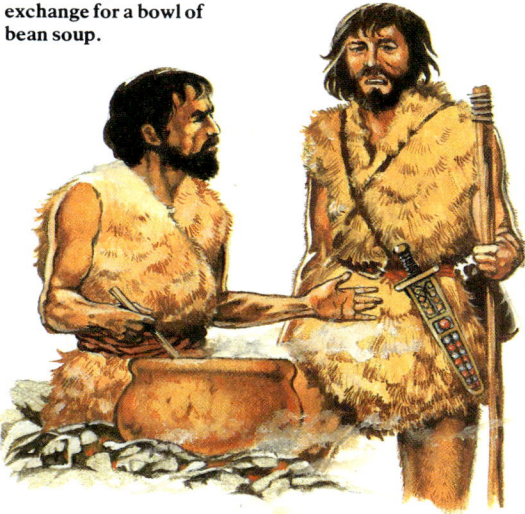

Melons The water-melons grown in Egypt were very refreshing in the heat. This is why the Israelites remembered them during their journey through the desert (Num. 11:5).

Onions A well-known vegetable with a large bulb that is rather strongly flavoured. It was popular in Egypt and missed by the Israelites after their departure (Num. 11:5).

Flax Although this is not a vegetable that was eaten, it was widely cultivated in Bible lands such as Egypt (Exod. 9:31). The flax plant is a slender annual with bright blue flowers. The plants were pulled up and dried on the flat house roofs (Josh. 2:6). The seeds were crushed to produce useful linseed oil and the stems gave linen fibres. The soft parts of the stems had to be 'retted' away leaving the fibres which were woven into cloth. Jewish priests had to wear linen clothes during the sacrifices probably because they were cooler and cleaner than wool (Lev. 6:10). After his crucifixion Jesus' body was bound in linen cloths (John 19:40). Wicks for lamps and candles were made from these fibres, too, as they were slow burning (Isa. 42:3).

Locally grown vegetables for sale in a market in the Yemen.

Cereals

Two kinds of corn are frequently mentioned in the Bible: barley and wheat. They were the most important crops as most people lived on bread. The peasants usually ate the coarser barley which was able to grow in the poor, dry ground better than wheat (Ruth 1:22). Barley was also fed to horses and brewed for beer. Barley ears have long whiskers, while wheat (at least our modern kind) is not bearded.

Wheat was grown in the better soil and it was therefore more expensive. Egypt was famous for its wheat grown in the fertile Nile valley. When Joseph was governor of Egypt he stored the corn from the good harvests and he was able to sell it during the years of famine (Gen. 41–44). Wheat takes longer to grow than barley

and it also ripens later (Exod. 9:31–32).

The cultivation of barley and wheat is described in another part of this book, but here we can mention some other points connected with cereals in the Bible.

When cereals are growing, a poisonous weed, the darnel grass, is difficult to distinguish from the corn until it begins to come into ear because the grass's leaves are similar to those of the corn. This explains the parable Jesus told about the enemy sowing weeds among the corn (Matt. 13:25, sometimes called the parable of the tares).

When the standing corn ripens it is very easily burned, as we know from Samson's revenge against the Philistines when he released foxes with burning tails into the cornfields (Judg. 15:5). In fact, the straw and chaff from the threshed grain was often burned as fuel (Isa. 47:14).

Fresh grains were often eaten roasted at harvest time (Ruth 2:14). However, both barley and wheat were usually ground to flour for bread making. Best wheat flour was used in various Jewish offerings (Exod. 29:2 etc), but barley was seldom used in this way (Num. 5:15).

Bread was made with or without yeast (sometimes called 'leaven'). This is a common kind of fungus that ferments sugar and causes the dough to rise because of the bubbles of carbon dioxide gas released in the process. In the Bible yeast is often taken as an example of sin because the fermentation reminds us of decay, so it was not to be used in certain of the Jewish offerings (Exod. 12:15, Lev. 2:4). Unleavened bread was eaten at the Jewish festival of the Passover (Exod. 12:1–27), and at the Last Supper Jesus gave his disciples bread, which was symbolic of his broken body (Matt. 26:26–30).

Egyptian grain storehouses at the time of Joseph.

Above: a field of barley on the island of Patmos in the Aegean Sea.

Right: wheat has been one of the main crops grown in Egypt and Palestine from Bible times. Far right: sheaves of wheat ready for threshing in the Yemen.

Trees

There are fewer trees now in the lands of the Bible than there were in earlier days. This is because man has cut them down for fuel and timber, and he has cleared the land for agriculture and flocks. Grazing animals, such as sheep and goats, nibble the seedlings and prevent them from growing into trees. Much of the Holy Land is too dry for dense forest, although there used to be large trees in woodland and thickets where nowadays the hillsides are bare, as the soil has been washed down into the valleys.

Even so, some forests are still to be seen in the mountains where the different kinds of trees that are mentioned in the Bible grow. Oaks, terebinths and pine tree form woodland, while the huge cedar trees grow in forests on Mount Lebanon. As each kind of tree needs a suitable place to grow, we find poplars, willows and plane trees rooting beside streams where there is always water, yet in parts of the desert the acacia tree, palm and tamarisk are able to flourish.

Acacia Flat-topped, prickly acacia trees grow along dry river beds that occur in the deserts of Sinai, and especially in the hot Arabah valley near the Dead Sea. It was in these regions that Moses wandered with the Israelites during their forty-year journey from Egypt to the Promised Land. He used acacia-wood for parts of the tabernacle tent and the covenant box (ark) (Exod. 25).

Algum, Almug A specially valuable timber is mentioned in 2 Chronicles 2:8 (RSV) and 1 Kings 10:11, but it is not known from which trees it came. It may have been a kind of juniper or a tree from a tropical country.

Balsam These were the tall poplar trees with leaves that shake and rustle in the wind; David was told by the Lord to attack the Philistines by these trees when he hears 'the sound of marching in the tree tops' (2 Sam. 5:23, 24). Poplars usually grow by water, especially in the dry Bible lands, and have a sweet scent like balsam when the leaf-buds begin to burst early in the year.

Broom trees grow in dry sandy places and are really shrubs with masses of white pea flowers in the spring. The roots are used for making charcoal for warmth (Job 30:4). Arrows with burning charcoal attached to them were shot into the enemy's town in order to set fire to the houses (Ps. 120:4).

Cypress The cypress tree usually seen growing in Mediterranean cemeteries and gardens is a tall dark green tree, with the leaves reduced to scales, and bearing small cones. Its timber is useful, so very few natural forests of it occur nowadays on hills in the Bible lands. Isaiah pictured it as one of the choice trees the Lord would plant in the desert (Isa. 41:19). It may have been the timber (gopher) used by Noah to build his ark (Gen. 6:14).

A cedar of Lebanon.

Cedar The Cedar of Lebanon is a flat-topped tree which grows to a huge size when it is old. It has needle leaves and bears large cones that break up easily to free the seeds. Its timber is fragrant and very valuable. On Mt. Lebanon, where remains of the large forest that used to grow there are still to be seen, armies of

126

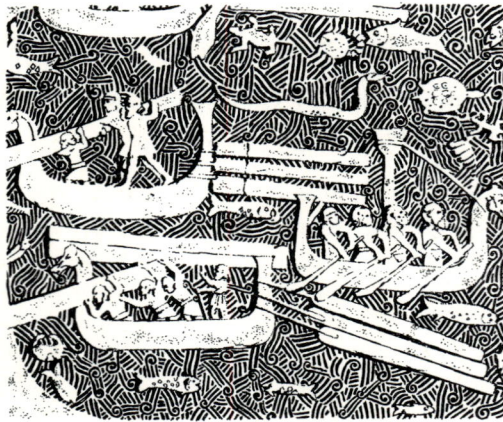

An ancient relief shows timber being unloaded from Phoenician ships. Solomon imported cedar and pine for the Temple from Phoenicia.

countries into Egypt and Palestine. Because of its value it was used for special furniture (Ezek. 27:15).

Fir This is a kind of juniper that grew in the mountains of Hermon and Lebanon and its timber was used for boat building (Ezek. 27:5) and probably also in King Solomon's temple.

Juniper A shrub or tree with prickly, evergreen scaly leaves and small berry-like fruits. Some kinds grow in the mountains of Lebanon and others in the desert hills of Sinai (Isa. 41:19). Its timber was very useful for buildings (2 Chron. 2:8, 1 Kings 10:11, in some versions referred to as algum or almug, an imported timber).

Laurels grow on the hillsides in Palestine. As they are slow growing trees with several slender trunks, the timber is hard and was used for carving heathen idols (Isa. 44:14). Their leathery evergreen leaves were plaited into a crown as a prize for athletes (2 Tim. 4:7) and for the Roman king; nowadays they are known as bay-leaves and used for seasoning food.

Oaks There are several kinds of oak trees that grow in Palestine and some of them are evergreen and shady (Hos. 4:13). They all have acorn seeds in little cups that are sometimes prickly. Arabs still bury

timber cutters were sent to fetch wood for King David's house (2 Sam. 5:11) and King Solomon's temple (1 Kings 5:6–10); his throne was also of cedar (Song of Songs 3:9 RSV).

Ebony This is a black wood that is very hard and had to be imported from tropical

A crown of laurel leaves.

Below: oak trees on Mount Carmel, Israel.

Below right: juniper branches.

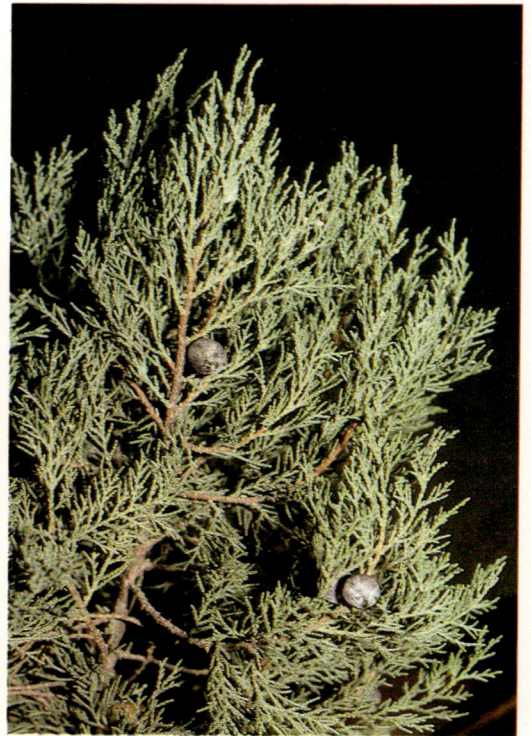

their dead under oak trees as was Deborah, Rebecca's nurse (Gen. 35:8). Oak wood is very hard and lasts a long time so it was one of the timbers used for making heathen idols (Isa. 44:14) and ships' oars (Ezek. 27:6).

Pine There are many kinds of pine trees, several of which grow in the Mediterranean area where they form forests on

the hills or as scattered trees near the coast. They have long needle-leaves and woody cones. Pine timber is soft and easily worked and it was used in King Solomon's temple (1 Kings 5:8, 10) with fir, cedar and olive wood.

Plane Twigs of the plane tree were peeled by Jacob (Gen. 30:37–43) together with those of poplar and almond. It is a large tree (Ezek. 31:8) with flaking bark and hanging flower heads.

Poplar Jacob peeled the bark off twigs of poplar, almond and plane trees and placed them in front of his uncle Laban's sheep and goats thinking this would increase the number of streaked and spotted animals in his herds (Gen. 30:37–43). It is a tall, straight tree often with pale grey bark and leaves that tremble in the wind (2 Sam. 5:23, 24 as 'balsam').

Tamarisk tree Abraham planted one at Beersheba (Gen. 21:33) where there is desert. Tamarisks are small bushy trees with scaly leaves and small white or pink flowers. They are found in dried up stream-beds in the desert.

Terebinth trees These are large trees growing in Bible lands that have been confused with oak trees, and sometimes it is difficult to know which one the Bible really means. It seems that in Hosea 4:13 both are mentioned.

Willows are trees that grow beside streams and rivers, much as poplars do, and the twigs root easily in damp soil. The sad Israelite exiles hung up their harps on the willows that grew beside the rivers of Babylon (Ps. 137:2).

The stone pine is one of the varieties of pine which grows in the Mediterranean area.

A tamarisk tree in bloom.

Fruit-trees

In the Bible lands fruit-trees have always been one of the farmers' most valuable possessions. They were grown, as they are today, either as solitary trees by the house or in orchards, usually called gardens in the Bible, or on the hillsides as groves or vineyards which are described in another part of this book. Moses made a law that their fruit was to be considered as unclean for three years after planting and the fourth year's was for the Lord, which meant that even the trees' owner was not to eat the fruit until the fifth year (Lev. 19:25). As fruit-trees take many years to develop everyone knew how important they were and even warring armies were forbidden to cut them down for siege works (Deut. 20:19).

The following fruit- and nut-trees are mentioned in the Bible.

Almond
A small tree that blooms very early in the year with white or pink flowers, later bearing almond nuts. God proved to the people of Israel that Aaron was his spokesman when Aaron's almond rod miraculously budded, flowered and fruited overnight (Num. 17:1–8).

The blossom and nuts of the almond tree.

Apple
Although the apple-tree is referred to several times in Song of Songs (2:3, 7:8) it is difficult to be sure whether this was really the apple we know nowadays. Some translators have suggested apricot instead of apple.

Carob
This tree grows wild and is also cultivated for the sweet bean pods it produces on its branches. These pods (or husks RSV) were the ones Jesus referred to as the food given to the pigs in his parable of the lost (prodigal) son who also had to eat them because he had wasted his money (Luke 15:16). They are often referred to as 'locust beans' as some believe they were eaten by John the Baptist (Matt. 3:4), but these were more likely to have been the locust insects.

Pods of the carob bean.

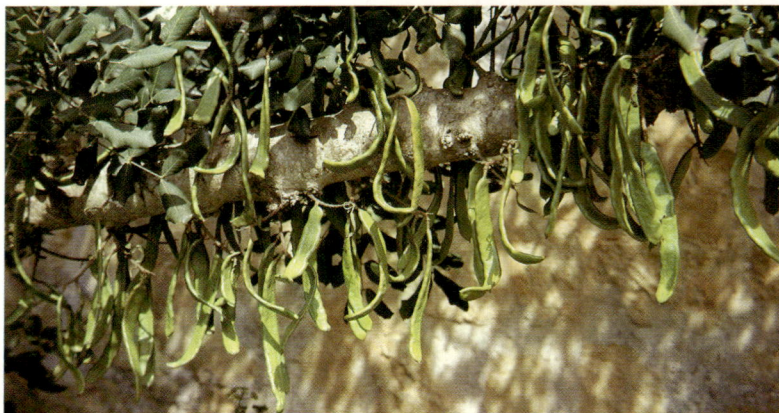

Fig
The fig-tree is one of the most important fruit trees of the Mediterranean region. It is a medium-sized tree that will grow in poor soil; it has large lobed leaves, rough to touch, and Adam and Eve clothed themselves with fig leaves (Gen. 3:7). The sweet, seedy fruits are often mentioned in the Bible, such as the cakes of figs given by Abigail to David (1 Sam. 25:18). The first fruits to ripen were especially delicious and were referred to by Isaiah (28:4), Jeremiah (24:2) and others. Jesus used the fig-trees in several of his parables (Luke 21:29–31).

Fig-leaves and fruit.

Mulberry
A small sturdy tree with blood-red fruits, hence this is the black mulberry (the white mulberry of China is the food of silk worms). Jesus referred to it in connection with believing faith (Luke 17:6 RSV sycamine).

Mulberry fruit.

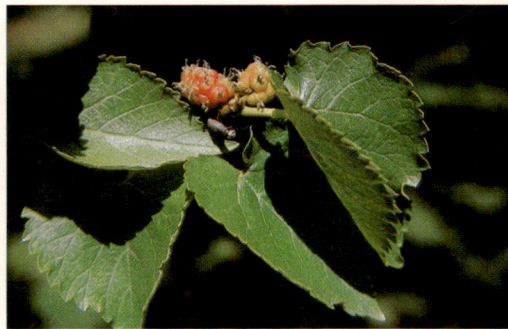

Olive
The olive-tree has long been planted on the hills and terraced fields of the Bible lands where the winters are not very cold and the summers hot and dry. It is a small rounded tree with grey-green leaves that do not drop off in winter. The olive fruits are rounded berries with a hard stone. They are usually pickled in salty water before being eaten or they are crushed and pressed to extract the golden olive-oil that is very important in that region. It was used in

Pomegranate

This usually grows more like a bush with many stems, than a tree. It has numerous bellshaped scarlet flowers and quite large round fruits that are topped by a jagged cup. Inside the fruit there are numerous seeds each surrounded by

The flower and fruit of the pomegranate tree.

refreshing watery pulp. The pomegranate is frequently mentioned in the Bible as it was a popular fruit. Models of the fruit decorated the hem of the high priest's robes (Exod. 28:33) and ornamented the pillars of Solomon's temple (1 Kings 7:20).

Bible times as cooking oil (Elisha helped a widow and her sons by miraculously filling their pots, 2 Kings 4:5), for lamp oil (as carried by the wise and foolish women, Matt. 25:3), and as anointing oil (the Hebrew word Messiah equals the Greek word Christ, meaning 'God's

Olive trees have been known to live for centuries and their gnarled trunk gives an impression of great age.

anointed one'). Samuel poured oil on Saul's head to show he was king, and later, on David (1 Sam. 10:1; 16:1, 13).

Pomegranate designs were popular in Israel at the time of Solomon. Here they decorate the rim of a washstand used for ceremonial washing.

Palm

The palm-tree of the Bible is the date-palm which is a very tall slender unbranched tree topped by a tuft of enormous feathery leaves and bunches of very sweet fruits (dates). Such a beautiful tree was used in Psalm 92:12 as a symbol of elegance and its Hebrew name, Tamar, was given as a girl's name (2 Sam. 13:1). The leaves were a symbol of victory and it is interesting to note that during Jesus' entry into Jerusalem palm leaves (usually referred to as 'branches') were used to welcome him, ready for his victory over death (John 12:13).

Date-palm carved in stone on the ruins of a synagogue at Capernaum, Israel.

Pistachio

The nuts taken to Joseph while he was governor of Egypt (Gen. 43:11) may have been from a kind of pistachio tree that grows wild in Palestine but not in Egypt. It is more likely to have been these small round nuts than the much larger pistachio nuts known today.

Sycomore

The sycomore-tree is a kind of fig that grows in warmer parts of the Bible lands as it cannot stand frost (Ps. 78:47). The prophet Amos looked after sycomores, as well as his herds (Amos 7:14). Sycomore trees branch low down and a tree growing beside the road in Jericho was climbed by Zacchaeus as he was a small man and he wanted to see Jesus (Luke 19:4).

A sycomore fig tree.

Vine

The grape-vine is not a tree but a vigorous climber; nevertheless it is such an important fruit that it fits into this section. The vine has a short trunk that becomes thick with age, and very long branches with tendrils and lobed leaves. The green or

black grapes, borne in clusters, are refreshingly sweet and are also dried for raisins. Wine is made from the fermented grape juice.

The biblical references to the vine and its products are numerous, as well as to vineyards, described in another part of this book. The Promised Land was famous for its grapes and Moses' spies brought back such a large bunch it had to be carried between two men (Num. 13:20–24). The people of God were sometimes pictured as a vine (Ps. 80:8). Jesus spoke of himself as the true vine (John 15:1) and his shed life-blood was like wine (Luke 22:20).

An inviting cluster of grapes.

ANIMAL LIFE

Animals are an important part of the background of Bible times. The Israelites were an agricultural people and used 'beasts of burden', mostly donkeys, to help with their cultivation and carry their goods when they travelled. Much of the land was good for sheep, with the flocks being led from pasture to pasture by the shepherds. Wild animals such as gazelles and goats were used for food and the Old Testament has many words used in hunting and trapping. Other wild animals like bears and lions were once common enough to be a nuisance.

Most of the larger animals are easy enough to recognise in the Bible but we cannot be sure about some of the smaller ones, especially if they are mentioned only once or twice. Some of the large animals have now disappeared from Palestine – such as the lion, bear, deer, oryx and wild ox, and also the ostrich – but we can say that a visitor to the Holy Land today, if he works hard, can see much the same sort or animal life that Abraham and his descendants knew; that is specially true of the reptiles and also the birds, for most of these just pass through twice a year on migration.

An ox driving a water wheel over a well in Egypt.

Working animals

With our tractors and electric power it is rather hard for us to understand how important the 'beasts of burden' were to farmers until even less than 50 years ago. The Israelites depended on their animals, especially their donkeys, for carrying themselves and their goods, and for ploughing and other work in the fields, including threshing corn and probably grinding it too.

The donkey, or the ass as the older versions of the Bible call it, was man's first beast of burden, and this is descended from the Nubian wild ass that can still be seen in a few parts of North East Africa. When Abraham came to Canaan from Mesopotamia, travelling around the edge of the desert, all his possessions were probably carried on donkeys, and the women and children rode on them. Nearly everybody had a donkey, but often only one. All classes of people rode on donkeys, even kings and princes when on a peaceful mission, so it was quite correct for Jesus, hailed as King of the Jews, to ride into Jerusalem on an ordinary donkey (Mark 11:6–11). Except that modern donkeys may be found in several colours, they are very like those that lived in Palestine and like them they have the black cross over the neck and shoulders that they have inherited from the wild ass.

The horse arrived later, having been domesticated from the wild horses living in the grasslands of South West Asia, and it was never important to the ordinary citizen. Only kings, princes and warriors owned horses and they were used just for show or to go to war. God had told the Israelites that they should not trust in horses and chariots, but Solomon and the kings after him took no notice of this and sometimes had several thousand horses, keeping them in huge stables, remains of which can still be seen at Hazor and else-where (1 Kings 4:26).

Although horses are much stronger than donkeys they are not so useful in dry countries because the donkey can manage on much poorer food and go for much longer without water.

The camel is something of a mystery: no one knows just when and where it began to serve men. It first comes on the scene after Abraham had moved into Palestine (Genesis 24:10) and soon became a valuable beast of burden, for the camel is wonderfully fitted for life in the desert. Its lips and tongue can cope with the thorniest twigs. The nostrils close to thin slits and the deep-set eyes have long lashes to keep out the blowing sand. The thick coat protects from cold in the winter and this hair is gathered by the Bedouin to make rough cloth like John the Baptist used to wear (Mark 1:6). Camels' milk is used by their owners and a mother camel may remain in milk for nearly two years. When travelling in the desert the Bedouins even collect the droppings and

The donkey has been used as a beast of burden from earliest times.

The camel's slit nostrils and long eyelashes keep out blowing sand in the desert.

A falconer with his falcon. The art of using birds to catch game goes back several thousand years to the Far East.

dry them in the hot sun to serve as fuel to cook their evening meal.

The camel's feet are big cushions, equally good for walking on sand, pebbles or rocks of the desert. The hump acts as a food store of fat (*not* water) to be drawn on when provisions are short, while it can go for days without water and then fill up again in a few minutes. Perhaps the most important thing of all is that the camel can carry a load of 220 kg for 40 km a day. A special riding camel, often called the Dromedary, can carry a man for as far as 100 km in a day.

There are two kinds of camel. The one found throughout Bible lands, the kind that Abraham used, was the one-humped or Arabian camel. The two-humped or Bactrian camel comes from North Central Asia, but some of these were brought down to Mesopotamia as booty by the kings and their shape can be plainly seen on some old carvings.

In Old Testament times camels were sometimes very numerous; for instance, we read before Job's troubles that he had no less than 3,000, which would have needed very large areas of pasture. As towns became bigger and fewer people lived in the countryside, the camel became less important and it is mentioned only twice by Jesus, each time in a proverb (Matthew 19:24; 23:24).

Camels continued to be used on the main caravan routes, such as the King's Highway that ran from Arabia right up through Petra, and even today some of the Bedouin tribes still use the camel to carry everything when they move camp.

Bullocks work on farms in many parts of the world, sometimes pulling a plough but more often hauling heavy carts filled with various types of produce. Most Israelites were probably too poor to own cattle and many parts of the country are not suitable for them, but wealthy farmers, especially in the north, kept cattle for use in various farm jobs, including threshing corn by trampling it on a special threshing floor, after which the grain was winnowed.

Dried camel dung for use as fuel.

Bullocks threshing corn by trampling it on a threshing floor.

Bedouins still use camels for moving camp.

Pets and care of animals

There are only two direct references to pets in the Bible, one in the Old and one in the New Testament. When Nathan the prophet challenged King David about a very serious wrong that he had done, he told him about a little pet lamb brought up by a shepherd in his home. Today if you go to a part of the country where sheep are kept, you may well find just the same thing. Perhaps a ewe has died in giving birth and the orphan has to be cared for; or a ewe has had triplets and can look after only two of them, so that the other must be taken away. Sometimes the shepherd can persuade another ewe that has lost her baby to look after the little lamb, but if

Dogs

The only pet mentioned in the New Testament is a small dog. Right through the Bible, dogs are described as 'unclean' and the Israelites were not allowed to keep them. This was because they were half-wild, living outside the city walls and acting as scavengers. But it seems that some other nations kept them as pets and when our Lord told a Syro-Phoenician woman that one did not take bread from children to give it to dogs, in her reply she used a special word and said, 'The little pet dogs should have the crumbs that fall off the table' (Mark 7:28).

An Egyptian model of a hunting dog from the Middle Kingdom (2130–1630BC).

'Beware of the dog.' An old Roman mosaic from Pompeii illustrates the role of the watchdog.

Clay watchdogs from Babylonia, 645BC. They were buried under doorsteps to keep away evil. Each dog has a carved inscription such as 'Don't hesitate, bite'.

Dogs have been used by man for hunting from earliest times. Wild dogs, like these from North Africa, live and hunt in packs.

not, it goes home with him and becomes the family pet.

This is a good example of the way in which a shepherd cared for his sheep, but as we look through the long list of rules in the books of Leviticus and Deuteronomy we find something very remarkable. All that time ago – over three thousand years – God told Moses to make rules about kindness to animals and later on, as reported in the Gospels, Jesus reminded people about them (Deuteronomy 22:1–3; Luke 14:5). Here are a few examples. If a cow got lost or stuck in a ditch, whoever saw it had to report the incident and help rescue it, even if it belonged to his enemy (Exodus 23:4). If an animal got lost on the Sabbath, when ordinary work was forbidden, they had to rescue it and see it had food and water. The farmers had to rest their animals on the Sabbath Day. When oxen were threshing the corn by treading on it they were not to be muzzled, giving them a chance to have a bite to eat from time to time. Both cattle and donkeys were used for ploughing but the Israelites were not allowed to use one of each in double harness because they walk differently, and the yokes on their shoulders were certain to hurt.

Finally, there was a rule about bird's-nesting! Wild birds like the dove were important as food. If a farmer found a nest he was allowed to take the eggs or the young birds, but not the mother bird (Deut. 22:6, 7). She had to be given the chance to nest again and bring up some more babies.

A lamb is the only animal mentioned as a pet in the Old Testament.

Food animals

Sheep, goats and cattle are mentioned many more times than all other animals put together and it is clear that they were very important, not only to the Israelites, but in all lands around Palestine. These are all 'clean' animals (that is, allowed for food) because they have cloven hooves and chew the cud; today we call them ruminants, from their strange complicated stomach, which allows them to digest even rough grass.

Sheep There are many Hebrew names for sheep: for old and young, ewes and lambs, and at least one refers to a special breed. We know from ancient carvings and pictures that several breeds had been developed before Jacob's time, including the fat-tailed sheep that is still common in many dry countries. The tail serves the same purpose as the camel's hump: the fat is stored there when grass is plentiful and is used up when food is scarce.

The sheep is a grazing animal, that is, it lives mostly on grass, and in Palestine the shepherd's job was to lead the sheep around from one bit of grazing to another, staying on the edge of the desert with them, protecting them at night in sheepfolds made of rocks and thorn branches and sleeping at the entrance. The usual pattern was for the sheep to follow the shepherd when on the move. He could recognise every one of them and had a name for each (John 10:3). The sheep's ancestor was one of several wild mountain sheep from South West Asia which have now disappeared.

To the Israelite the sheep was most important in the various sacrifices which were offered. Usually, after the sheep or lamb had been killed, only some of the meat was burnt on the altar: much of it was shared between the people and the priests. Few sheep were killed just for eating. The wool was shorn regularly and

the sheep and the goats was not always easy. Sheep have a woolly coat, while ordinary goats have coarse hair, but the most important difference is in their habits, for, while sheep feed mostly on grass, the goat is a browser, feeding mostly on leaves and twigs, even climbing trees to get them. As a result, terrible damage has been done in many dry countries, where goats eat all the shrubs and trees on a hillside. The roots die and when the next storm comes there is nothing to stop the soil from being washed away. In Bible times, goats provided meat, skins, milk and also hair for weaving into coarse cloth. Goats were widely used in sacrifice: in many cases either a sheep or a goat could be offered (Leviticus 1:10). Domestic goats are descended from the wild Greek goat that is still found on a few islands in the East Mediterranean.

Cattle have already been mentioned briefly as working animals, but their main function in ancient Palestine, as all over the world to-day, was to provide milk, meat and leather. They were also used by

Fat-tailed sheep are common in dry countries. Fat is stored in the tail, so the sheep is able to survive longer when food is scarce.

was the commonest material for clothes. It seems that some sheep were kept specially for shearing, and it is recorded that King Mesha of Moab paid tribute of the wool of 100,000 rams each year (2 Kings 3:4).

Goats Although most sheep are pale and white and most goats are dark they sometimes look very alike and separating

A shepherd with his sheep on a hillside in Judea.

the Israelites for certain important sacrifices. Although other cattle breeds like the zebu, with its hump, have since been brought in from India, the cattle of Old Testament times were all descended from the huge wild ox or aurochs, which used to be wrongly translated 'unicorn'. The bull was a very heavy animal and stood 180 cm at the shoulder. The wild ox lived in the forests of West Asia and Europe and the last was killed between 400 and 500 years ago. We shall never know how or why these splendid animals were first domesticated. Some say that it was so that people could have meat available all through the year without hunting. Others that they were wanted to help work the soil. Whatever the reason, it must have been a giant task. The best country for cattle was, and still is, the country sometimes known as the Land of Bashan in the north of Israel, which has always been famous for its bulls.

Domestic fowls were well known in our Lord's time. He spoke of the cock crowing, when he told Peter that he would deny him, and he also taught a lesson from the mother hen and her chicks (Luke 13:34). Centuries earlier, the red jungle fowl had been domesticated in India and had gradually made its way to Palestine, mostly carried in camel caravans, but nobody knows just when it got there. Fatted fowls, probably geese domesticated in Egypt, were among the good things prepared for Solomon's table (1 Kings 4:22, 23). Later on the chicken became important for its meat and eggs.

Below: chicken coop made of mud, dating back to 1200BC.

Right: a goat climbing an olive-tree. Goats often do considerable damage by nibbling trees and shrubs.

Far right: leopards were more numerous in Palestine in Bible times than today.

Wild animals

When the Israelites moved into Palestine they found many kinds of wild animals living there, including lions and bears and members of the deer and antelope family that they hunted for meat. With the spread of farming and a bigger population, most of the larger kinds disappeared from the lands around Palestine but are still well known in other countries.

Lion and bear Towards the end of Old Testament times lions were still found from Greece right across South-West Asia to India, but now the only ones left are in a special game reserve in Western India. David had met lions when looking after his sheep, and he told Saul that he had killed both a lion and a bear (1 Samuel 17:34, 35). This latter would have been a Syrian bear, a rather paler form of the well-known brown bear; the last bear in Palestine was killed near Mount Hermon just after the end of World War II. These bears lived in the forests on the hills and fed mostly on berries, roots, honey and small animals. They slept for part of the winter, and when they woke up in early spring they sometimes came down to the lower ground and it was then that they tried to raid the sheepfolds.

Leopard The well-known proverb about a leopard not being able to change its spots was quoted by Jeremiah (13:23). This smaller cousin of the lion can hide away in patches of forest and in rocky

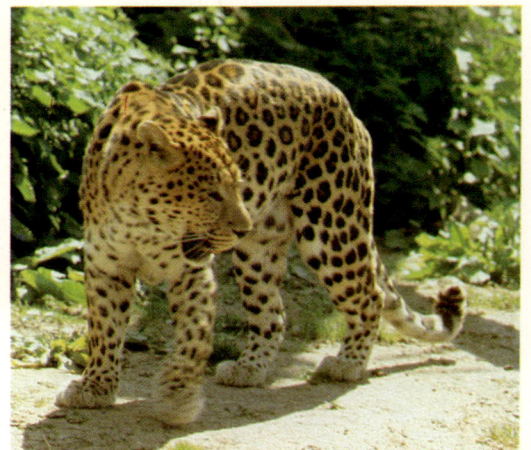

areas and is still found in small numbers in Palestine, though never plentiful enough to be a danger to man or his livestock.

Wolf A few wolves and spotted hyenas still survive in unpopulated areas. Wolves are often mentioned in both Old and New Testament as a danger to sheep, but it is only fair to say they feed mostly on mice and birds, and they probably raided the sheepfolds only when very hungry or when the shepherds were careless and did not protect their flock properly. Palestine wolves are very like the kind, found right through northern Europe and North America, which is the wild ancestor of the dog.

Foxes and jackals are small cousins of the wolf and the Israelites had only one word for them. Foxes are rather solitary creatures, mostly seen in ones and twos, but jackals usually hunt in small packs and are commonest around the edge of the desert. Both catch a lot of mice and voles, but they also eat vegetable matter and fruit, including grapes, as Solomon pointed out when he spoke of the little foxes that spoil the vines (Song of Songs 2:15).

Deer In early times three kinds of deer lived in Palestine: red, fallow, and roe deer. As forests were cleared and cultivation spread, life became difficult for them and they all gradually disappeared from Palestine. They are mentioned as hart, hind and stag, and although these certainly refer to deer, we do not know which kind is meant in each case.

The most striking member of the antelope family is the desert or Arabian oryx, mentioned several times as the antelope. This lives in the true desert, going for weeks without drink, and had few enemies until man could travel across the desert in fast cars, using high-powered rifles, so that now the graceful oryx has almost been wiped out in the wild, though it is being bred in zoos. At one time the little Palestine gazelle, standing only 60 cm at the shoulder, was also in danger, but it is now protected by law and is found not only over much of the Negev Desert but right through Judea and into Galilee. In fact, it is as likely to be seen in farms as anywhere. In older versions it was known as the roe or the roe-deer but the word gazelle appeared as a woman's name in the New Testament. It was Dorcas or Tabitha, the first being Greek and the second Hebrew for gazelle.

Wild goat The Oasis of Engedi, just above the Dead Sea, where David used to shelter, is well known today as the home of the Nubian ibex, a wild goat of which the males have long curved horns. These animals are very much at home on the rocky hillsides, where the kids follow the mothers when they are only a day or two old.

Wild ass One other hoofed animal, named the wild ass in the Bible, lived in and around the desert. This was quite different from the wild ancestors of the donkey, though about the same size, and it should better be called the Persian wild

Bottom left: the Nubian ibex lives on the rocky hillsides of southern Palestine.

Below: a Syrian bear.

Bottom right: this North American timber wolf is very similar to the kind found occasionally in Palestine.

Top row: a fennec fox, a
Palestine gazelle and a
rock hyrax.

Centre: an Egyptian tomb
relief showing two
hippopotami in a river, one
biting a crocodile. Men
standing in a light boat
made of bundles of reeds,
eye them warily. Right: a
spotted hyena.

Bottom: the oryx, referred
to as the antelope several
times in the Bible.

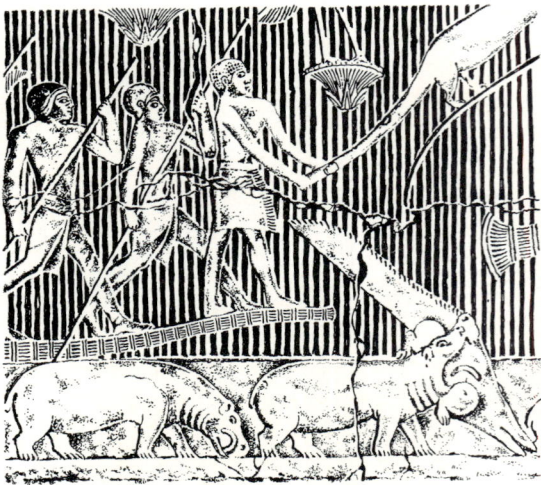

ass or the onager. Although it disappeared from Bible lands many years ago it has been re-introduced into national parks in the Negev Desert.

Coney A much smaller animal can be seen on the rocks at Engedi and in many other parts of Palestine. Called coney for a very long time, it is now known correctly as the rock hyrax. Belonging to a small family on its own, it is about rabbit size and has soft padded feet with which it can climb even steep rocks.

Sea Cow One big animal remained a mystery for a long time. First translated 'badger', its skin was used by the Israelites to make a covering for the Tabernacle in the desert. Now we know that this was the dugong or sea-cow, a marine animal living in the Red Sea and other warm seas, feeding on seaweed and growing to a length of three metres.

Rodents Travellers in the Holy Land reported seeing little heaps of soil such as moles often make on our lawns and fields. In fact these are made by mole rats, which are members of the rodent family and not true moles, which are related to the shrews and hedgehogs. Many kinds of small rodents live there, including rats, mice, gerbils and jerboas, as well as voles, rather like the British field vole, that sometimes do serious damage to corn fields in Galilee. In the book of Kings a serious disease is described that killed many Philistines and was in some way connected with 'mice', a word used for any small rodent. This is now thought to have been bubonic plague, which caused 'the Black Death' and 'the Plague of London', and we now know this is passed on by fleas carried by black rats.

Hippopotamus and Elephant Although hippopotami may not have lived in Palestine, at one time they were found near the mouth of the Nile and it seems likely that this was the fierce animal described by Job (Job 40:15–24). Ivory is often mentioned, and many ornaments and carvings have been dug up. Some ivory came from the Indian elephant, which was once found as near Palestine as Syria, but it was also brought from as far away as India. Probably most was obtained from the African elephant which lived in North Africa and Egypt in ancient times.

Fish

Although we do not know exactly where the Israelites were kept in captivity in Egypt, it must have been close to the River Nile, for the rest of the country was desert. So when they spoke later of the fish they had enjoyed (Numbers 11:5) these must have been some of the many kinds of freshwater fish from the Nile. On their

A Phoenician ivory carving of a mythical winged creature.

Cooking fish for breakfast at the Fishing Harbour, Tiberias.

desert journey they were sometimes close to the Red Sea, where many species of tropical marine fish live, and they may have caught some of those. After they settled in Canaan not many of them lived right on the coast and they probably did little fishing in the Mediterranean where, in any case, fishing is not very good. Certainly they could not have caught the big tuna fish which is so valued to-day. Much of their fishing was probably done in the Lake of Galilee, the River Jordan, and Lake Huleh (or the Waters of Merom as it was then called), which was then still open water and not the big swamp that it became later. The most important fish today, and perhaps also in Bible times, is the *Tilapia,* one of the cichlid family often kept in tropical aquaria, and this is always known as St. Peter's Fish.

Reptiles

Lizards Visitors to the Holy Land to-day, unless there in winter, are certain to see many lizards. Commonest of all is the rainbow lizard, up to 25 cm long, which is always doing 'press-ups' on old buildings and roads. This is among those listed as forbidden food to the Israelites (Leviticus 11:30). In Proverbs 30:28 a lizard is mentioned that lives in kings' palaces and takes hold with its hands. In fact this description fits well a family of lizards called geckos, whose feet have rows of hairs so fine that they can hold on to any surface, including glass, and some kinds live mostly in buildings.

A catch of fish from the Sea of Galilee.

The rainbow lizard is the most common in Palestine.

Birds

Snakes Palestine has at least twelve kinds of snake. They are often mentioned in the Bible, but we should not be surprised that we cannot identify them all, for even today most people just refer to 'snakes' generally and do not bother to distinguish one from another. The largest poisonous one is the Palestine viper which reaches a length of over one metre. This is found almost everywhere except in the true desert and gives more bites than all others put together. As with all true vipers, the female keeps the eggs in her body until all are ready to hatch. When Jesus compared the Pharisees to a brood or generation of vipers he was using just the right word for the group of babies that emerge all together (Matt. 23:33).

Four kinds of viper live in the desert, some in the very driest parts. During the hottest time of the day the ground is so hot that nothing can live on it, so the vipers go underground in holes or in the sand, coming out to hunt for food when it is cooler. One of these vipers is the 'serpent in the wilderness' mentioned in Numbers chapter 4, and the one known today as the carpet viper fits the picture well. Sometimes it can be very common, many hundreds being found over a small area. Unlike most snakes it is very aggressive and also, although it only grows to about 25 cm, its bite is very dangerous, often taking two or three days to kill the victim, so there would be plenty of time for Moses to make the brazen serpent as God commanded him.

Bottom left: the Palestine viper is the largest poisonous snake found in the country.

Below: an eagle.

Bottom right: the white stork passes through Palestine on its annual migration between Europe and Africa.

The Holy Land in spring and autumn is an exciting place for bird watchers because it is on one of the most important migration routes. Millions of birds of nearly 300 kinds pass that way as they travel to and from their breeding grounds in Europe and Asia and their winter haunts in Africa. These annual movements have been going on for thousands of years, and Jeremiah wrote about them in his prophecy, mentioning the **stork, turtle dove, crane** and **swallow** (Jer. 8:7), which are four of the best-known kinds to-day. He pointed out that they knew their seasons, in other words that they went on their regular migrations. All of these pass through Palestine and in April one can sometimes see over a thousand white storks in a single flock, using the thermal currents, as gliders do, to rise to over 1,000 metres and then glide towards the north on motionless wings. Most of the big birds travel this way – pelicans, eagles, vultures and buzzards.

Although vultures are rather rare today, at least two kinds still breed in Palestine: their habit of feeding is described well in

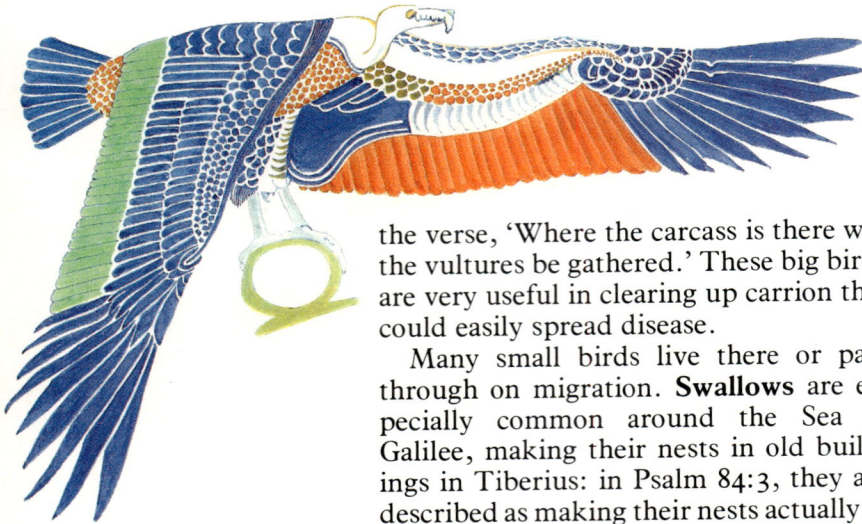

A vulture holding a signet-ring, the symbol of countless years, from an Egyptian tomb painting.

Below: the rock-dove is frequently mentioned in the Bible. In Old Testament times people who were too poor to offer a lamb for sacrifice, could bring a pair of doves.

Right: European swallows gathering ready for migration. Swallows are mentioned several times in the Bible and are common in Palestine.

the verse, 'Where the carcass is there will the vultures be gathered.' These big birds are very useful in clearing up carrion that could easily spread disease.

Many small birds live there or pass through on migration. **Swallows** are especially common around the Sea of Galilee, making their nests in old buildings in Tiberius: in Psalm 84:3, they are described as making their nests actually in the Temple. There are several kinds of **sparrow** but it is likely that the Bible word 'sparrow' refers to almost any kind of small bird: as today, most people then did not distinguish one kind from another. In the same way 'swallow' probably means any swallow or martin and also the three kinds of swift that visit Palestine.

The **ostrich** was well described by Job, in chapter 39. This enormous bird was once found right through Arabia and Palestine but the last one was killed about a century ago and now the ostrich lives only in Africa.

Palestine has eight **owls,** from the tiny Scops owl to the splendid eagle-owls. The Bible mentions them mostly as birds living in deserted places or as kinds that could not be eaten, because they fed on other animals, but, again, they were probably known just as big owls and small owls and never had individual names such as we give them today. This was also true of the day-birds of prey, of which over forty kinds visit Palestine – **eagles, hawks, kites, falcons, harriers** and even the **osprey,** which is glad to stay on the Sea of Galilee for a day or two and catch some fish before flying north.

Two families of birds were important as food to the Israelites. The game bird family (of which our chicken is a member) includes the **rock partridge,** to which David compared himself when he was being chased by Saul. This was hunted by gangs of men armed with sticks and stones which were thrown at the partridge as it flew from one bit of cover to another. The **quail** also belongs to this family. It is a well-known migrant and used to cross the Sinai Desert in huge flocks, just as described in Exodus, when God provided them as food for the Israelites. The other important group was the **dove** or **pigeon** family. Six different kinds live in Palestine or pass through it, and two of these are mentioned more often than any other bird. The pigeon is properly called rock-dove and it still breeds in holes and ledges of rocks in the desert: Jeremiah described it as the dove that nests in the sides of the mouth of the gorge (Jer. 48:28). All of our domestic pigeons are descended from this wild bird. The dove, or turtle-dove, or sometimes just called turtle, is very like the turtle-dove that visits Britain, arriving in May. This was both a wild bird and one that was kept in captivity. These birds were 'clean' and therefore suitable for food and also for use in sacrifices by the poorer people who could bring a pair of doves or young pigeons if they could not afford a lamb (Lev. 12:8).

Insects

Insects find a place in the Bible for two different reasons: either they are useful like the bee, or they are harmful like the clothes moth, locusts and flies.

Bees themselves are not mentioned very often but they have always been a familiar sight in Palestine. This was once called a land flowing with milk and honey, and bee hives can be seen almost everywhere today even in desert oases, big rows and stacks of them, brightly painted in different colours to help the bees find their own hive. Honey was very valuable to the Israelites, for it was almost their only form of sweetening and an important food. The Psalmist spoke of it in Psalm 119:103, and says that God's word is sweeter even than honey. Bee hives such as we know are a fairly modern invention and in Bible times most of the bees were wild and made their homes in holes in rocks or trees. Honey was obtained after driving off the bees, but some people also put up baskets or big pots for swarms to occupy and then the honey was easier to extract.

The **locust** is another unmistakable insect, though in fact three or four different kinds are found in Egypt and Palestine. Locusts are members of the big grasshopper family that have become sociable and fly in huge swarms, sometimes numbering hundreds of millions, and they can do disastrous damage because they eat almost anything that is green. Locusts

An eagle owl.

Beehives by the Sea of Galilee. The Promised Land was described as a land flowing with milk and honey.

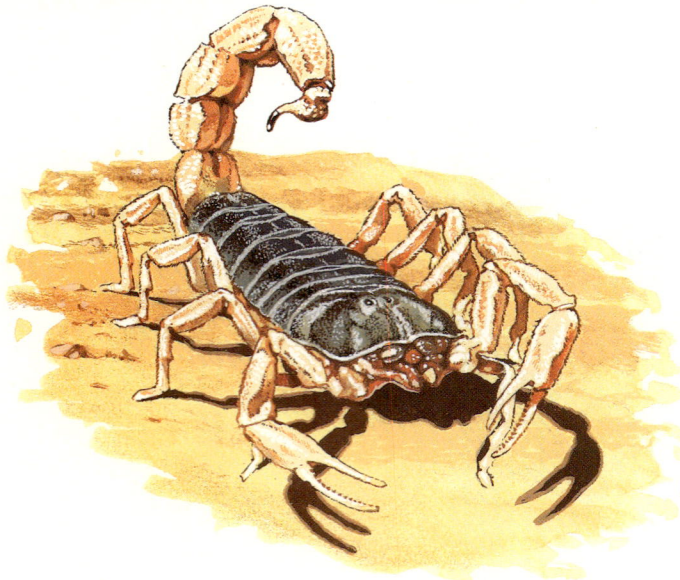

A scorpion.

caused the eighth plague of Egypt (Exodus 10:13–15). They are still a menace in parts of the Middle East and Africa, but by international co-operation the locusts have been controlled and damage has been much reduced. Invaders have often been described as locusts because of the destruction that they cause: one of their five Hebrew names means 'destroyer', and another means 'a cloud that covers the sun'.

Moses prepared lists of the various animals that were allowed as food (Lev. 11) and among these we find the locust, with a strange but quite accurate description – with legs above the feet to leap with. When you look at a grasshopper you will at once recognise the huge legs, like upside-down Vs with which they can make big jumps. In fact, locusts are a useful food in areas where meat is scarce for they contain fat and protein, and it is likely that the Israelites ate them in large numbers when swarms crossed their

Locusts.

A swarm of locusts invade an area, stripping it bare of all vegetation.

desert routes. Locusts formed part of John the Baptist's very simple food when he lived in the desert (Matt. 3:4) and until recent years they were gathered and dried in very large quantities by the desert Arabs, especially in North Africa.

Several other insects can be easily recognised. The **clothes moth** belongs to a small family whose grubs feed on woollen articles. When we see the moth flying the damage has already been done when it was in the caterpillar stage: the moth itself does not feed but it is looking for somewhere to lay its eggs. The **flea** is another nuisance, especially to people living in camps. When King David was being hunted he described himself as a flea which keeps hopping to try to escape (1 Samuel 26:20).

Spiders and **scorpions** belong to a different group from the insects, for they have four pairs of legs and no wings. Both can be identified in the Old Testament. The spider is mentioned in Isaiah 59:5 and also Job 8:14 as making a web. The scorpion is used mostly to illustrate the difficult nature of the desert through which the Israelites passed: several kinds are found there and their sting is very painful, but it is not likely to kill anybody.

GOVERNMENT AND ADMINISTRATION

What was it like to be the king of Israel, or the king of Assyria? How did someone become king? Were kings really necessary? Who led the people before there were kings? All these questions are about government. We could go on to ask how the laws were decided and the punishments for those who broke those laws, who decided how much should be collected in taxes and whether or not the people should go to war, and we would still be asking about government. The way the king's wishes were carried out, the laws enforced, the taxes collected and the army led to war – all this is about administration.

For most of its history Israel has been the name of a people rather than the name of a country. At a decisive point in that history 'all the elders of Israel met and came to Samuel at Ramah and said to him, ". . . appoint us a king to govern us like other nations"' (1 Samuel 8:4–5) Who were these elders? Why did they ask Samuel to appoint a king? What kind of king did other nations have? To answer these questions we must look first at how Israel was controlled before they had a king, then how Israel was controlled by kings and finally other nations and their kings.

In tribal societies rules for government are often decided by the elders of the tribe.

Israel before the monarchy

When Israel settled in the land of Canaan they were twelve tribes linked together in that they recognised the same God, the God of their fathers, who had rescued them from Egypt and brought them through the wilderness to the Promised Land. Their fathers were the patriarchs and the land had been promised to them and their descendants by God many years before.

The Patriarchs

Abraham, Isaac and Jacob are known as the patriarchs because in their time the father (or grandfather) ruled the family. The clan or family group to which a person belonged was far more important than the country in which the clan happened to be living, especially as these clans were often moving from one country to another. These clans were larger than our families. Abraham led 318 fighting men to rescue his nephew Lot (Genesis 14:14). To go to war, or to make peace, was the father's decision. He made agreements with the leaders of other clans over the right to draw water from wells (Gen. 21:25–33). He arranged marriages and his dying words were especially important for sons (Gen. 49). There is an interesting story about Abraham sending his servant to find a wife for Isaac, his son (Gen. 24). When the father died the firstborn son usually received twice the inheritance of any other sons, and the father's authority. Isaac's son, Esau, sold these rights to his brother Jacob for a bowl of soup (Gen. 25:29–34)!

The patriarchs were semi-nomads and on their journeys were seldom far from small cities. Some of these, like Jerusalem and Gerar, had their kings (Gen. 14:18; 20:2). It was from four great kings that Abraham rescued Lot. It seems there were a few powerful rulers who raided far and wide and many lesser kings who were little more than chiefs (Gen. 36:19 RSV).

Israel in Egypt

The account of the patriarchs' wanderings concludes with the story of Joseph who was sold as a slave into Egypt. He became

The Judges

After the death of Joshua, Israel was ruled by judges for about 170 years until the first Israelite king was chosen. Most of these judges were military leaders rather than legal judges and they tried to free Israel from surrounding nations who over-ran them when they rebelled against God. Below are shown an important happening in the life of some of the judges.

EHUD
Delivered Israel from Moabite oppression by killing Eglon, king of Moab. 80 years peace followed. Judges 3:12–30.

DEBORAH
Commissioned Barak to lead Israel to fight the Canaanite oppressors at Mount Tabor. 40 years peace. Judges 4 and 5.

GIDEON
Delivered Israel from Midian rule. Led the people in battle and defeated the Midianites. Peace for 40 years. Judges 6 and 7.

SAMSON
Israel under Philistine rule. Samson born and brought up a Nazirite. He led Israel for 20 years under the Philistines but was finally captured and blinded by them. Judges 13–16.

SAMUEL
Dedicated to God as a baby by his parents, he tried to bring Israel back to worshipping God. At the people's wish he anointed Saul as the first king of Israel. I Samuel 1–10.

manager of the household of Potiphar, the captain of Pharaoh's bodyguard. Later he became the vizier, the highest official in Egypt below Pharaoh. Both of these titles and 'chief of butlers' and 'chief of bakers', whom Joseph met when he was in prison (Gen. 40) have been found in Egyptian inscriptions. As Pharaoh's 'prime minister' Joseph controlled the food supply and, during a famine, all the land of Egypt became Pharaoh's (Gen. 47:14–22). Eventually Joseph's family, including the patriarch, Jacob, or Israel as he was known, joined him in Egypt.

Some years after the deaths of Israel and Joseph a revolution brought a different dynasty of Pharaohs to power. The children of Israel were made slaves, working on great building projects (Exodus 1). From this bitter slavery Moses, an Israelite who had been brought up in Pharaoh's household, was called by God to lead the people out of Egypt. He had to win the support of the elders, probably the heads of families (Exod. 3:16). In the wilderness he appointed elders to help him in the administration of justice (Exod. 18:13–27). At Mt. Sinai the people recognised God as their King and accepted his laws including the Ten Commandments (Exod. 19 and 20).

The Promised Land

Just before his death Moses commissioned Joshua to take his place and lead the people into the Promised Land (Numbers 27:18–23). After successful campaigns against the Canaanites, Joshua called the leaders of the people to renew their loyalty to God at Shechem. The elders were now a different group from the heads of families. There were also separate judges and a group of official writers who kept the records (Joshua 24:1).

After Joshua's death the tribes went their separate ways. Occasionally some of them came together under a particular hero against a particular enemy, but never all twelve tribes at once. These heroes were called judges. Some of them administered justice like our judges (eg Judges 4:5) but others are recorded for one spectacular success (like Ehud, the left-handed assassin, Judg. 3:12–30). The people looked to the priests, and particu-

An Egyptian tomb relief showing an official who has just been given gold chains of honour by King Tutankhamun and is receiving homage from servants. Joseph was similarly honoured by Pharaoh.

larly the High Priest, as their leaders in peace time and not only in religious matters. Some of the regulations in the book of Leviticus show the priest identifying infectious disease (chapter 13) as well as dealing with legal matters (chapter 6:1–7).

Eli was High Priest and judge for forty years and Samuel was judge, priest, prophet and leader into battle. He dealt with legal matters on his annual visits to Bethel, Gilgal and Mizpah, and in his home at Ramah. He offered sacrifices and prayer before the battle of Mizpah (1 Samuel 7). He delivered God's messages (1 Samuel 3:19–21). Why then did the elders ask him for a king? There were two main reasons: firstly, they were not prepared to accept Samuel's sons as judges because they took bribes (1 Samuel 8:1–3), and secondly, the Philistines continually threatened to attack them and made it desirable to have a permanent military leader to whom all the tribes could look for protection.

Slaves making bricks, from an Egyptian tomb painting. The Israelites were forced to work on Pharaoh's building projects.

The monarchy

Monarchy means rule by one man with the title of king. Samuel pointed out to the people of Israel the disadvantages of having a king. He would want an army, personal servants, royal lands and taxes (10 per cent of grain and wine). From one point of view to choose a king could mean rejecting God (1 Samuel 8:4–18) although the king in Israel was never regarded as taking God's place. (Compare this with Pharaoh in Egypt, below.)

In Old Testament times courts in Israel were held at the city gate. Here two men agree a transfer of property in the presence of the elders of the city. It was the custom for the seller to hand over his sandal to the purchaser as a sign of the sale. Ruth 4:7 is an example of such a deal.

An ivory plaque from Megiddo in Israel, showing a king on a throne like King Solomon's, supported by winged beasts.

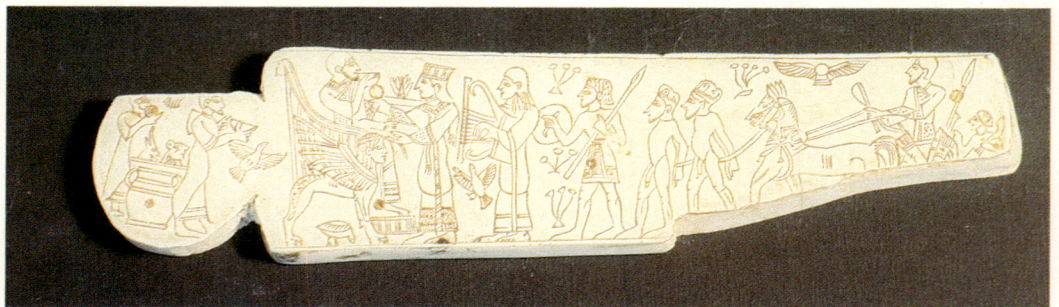

Saul, the first king, was too occupied in military defence, particularly against the Philistines, to develop his royal court. His only officer was his cousin, Abner, who commanded the army. David, the next king, established a kingdom and an empire to hand on to his son Solomon and under these kings government was organised on a large scale.

1. The King. He was the leader in matters of war, peace and justice. He owned the treasures and taxes his officials collected. David captured Jerusalem and Solomon built a new palace and the Temple there, making that city the centre of the nation.

2. Officials. At David's court were: Joab (the army commander), a secretary who kept the records of state, two chief priests, the captain of the royal guard, the supervisor of slave labour, and a royal herald (2 Sam. 8:15–18; 20:23–26).

Solomon added to the court a master of the palace and a supervisor of the twelve provincial governors. He also had 550 supervisors of slave labour working on his building projects (1 Kings 4:1–7; 9:23).

3. Taxes. Conquered peoples paid tribute – usually an annual payment – and customs duties were levied on merchants (1 Kings 10:14–15). The twelve provinces, which did not include Judah, provided food for the royal household, each province providing one month's supply.

4. Justice. People could appeal directly to the king if he had the time to see them. Difficulties over this gave Absalom the opportunity to win popular support against his father David, leading to his rebellion (2 Sam. 15:1–6). Solomon's wisdom was demonstrated as a judge in the case of the two mothers who claimed the same baby (1 Kings 3:16–28).

It was a protest over slave labour which

The Jewish Royal Court

The King

Commander of the army

Secretary for state records

Captain of the royal guard

Chief priest

Chief priest

Slave labour supervisor

Royal herald

Master of the palace

Supervisor of the provincial governors

led to the rebellion of the northern tribes against Rehoboam, Solomon's son, and split the empire into two kingdoms: Israel in the north and Judah in the south (1 Kings 12). The new king of Israel told his people to go to Dan or Bethel as religious centres, instead of Jerusalem. A later king of Israel, Omri, built a new capital city at Samaria. Jerusalem remained the capital of Judah.

Individual prophets, like Nathan, had been advisers to David (2 Sam. 7). They told the king God's messages as Samuel had told Saul. After the division of the kingdom we find some prophets supporting a king's decisions and others criticising the king and the people. King Ahab had about 400 prophets at his court who encouraged him to set out on his last fateful mission while one man, Micaiah, said that it would end in disaster (1 Kings 22). Elijah and Amos, among others, denounced the lack of justice (1 Kings 21; Amos 5:12). The courts of justice were held 'in the gate', that is at the entrance to the city, in the open air. For the peoples' continuing disobedience to God's laws the prophets announced the coming destruction of both kingdoms. In 722BC Samaria was destroyed by the Assyrians and in 597 and 587BC Jerusalem was twice captured by the Babylonians.

A limestone boundary stone with an inscription giving rights and privileges to the warden of a district by Nebuchadnezzar, king of Babylon. Divine emblems are sculptured on the stone.

Other nations and their kings

When the elders asked Samuel for a king like other nations they were probably not thinking of the small city-kings of Canaan or the great imperial kings of Egypt but the kings of the early nation states such as Edom, Moab, Ammon and Aram. The list of the first kings of Edom (Genesis 36:31–39) suggests these kings were chosen by the nation when the previous king died, rather than the son following his father. In the separate kingdoms of Israel and Judah the throne changed hands through violence and revolution in Israel, but in Judah sons followed their fathers.

Egypt

The greatest days of Egypt as an imperial power were over by the time there were kings in Israel but David and Solomon may have borrowed Egyptian ideas about organising an empire. Solomon married an Egyptian princess and as we have seen he divided the land of the northern tribes into twelve provinces. In Egypt the land was also divided into provinces, each with a central city. Pharaoh was the supreme ruler, regarded as one of the gods and surrounded by wise counsellors to assist him. One courtier was described as the King's special adviser and Solomon had a similar official at his court (1 Kings 4:5).

Mesopotamia

To the north-east of Israel was Mesopotamia, the land between the two rivers, Tigris and Euphrates: the land from which the patriarchs had come (Genesis 12). This was later the heart of the mighty Assyrian Empire based on Nineveh in the north. In 612BC Nineveh was destroyed and the Babylonians took control, establishing an empire which itself was overthrown by Cyrus the Persian in 539BC.

In patriarchal times. Before Abraham, a dynasty of kings founded by Ur-Nammu had ruled a large kingdom from Ur in splendid magnificence (see the section on Archaeology). Abraham and his father Terah left Ur for Haran (Gen. 11:31) and this city continued to be an important commercial centre. Later it became an Assyrian provincial capital city. The most famous ruler of patriarchal times was Hammurabi (c. 1792–1750BC) who made Babylon the capital of an empire. He was responsible for one of the earliest known attempts at town planning and a collection of laws known as the Code of Hammurabi. This is similar to some of the later laws of Moses, like the demand that the punishment be equal to the crime. For example, if a house collapsed and killed the owner's son, the builder's son was to be put to death.

The Assyrian Empire. An ancient Assyrian king list describes the first seventeen Assyrian rulers as 'kings who lived in tents'. For centuries the Assyrians were dominated by the kings of the south, like the Babylonians; but in the 13th century

Left: a sculpture of Rameses II, probably the Egyptian Pharaoh who refused to let the Israelites leave Egypt.

Below: King Ashurbanipal of Assyria hunting with his servants, from a 7th century BC relief found in a palace at Nineveh.

Bottom: the panel from the Black Obelisk showing Jehu, king of Israel, bowing before King Shalmaneser of Assyria.

Royal head-dresses. Left to right: Egyptian, Babylonian, Persian, Assyrian.

Five major empires controlled this area around the Mediterranean over a period of 1500 years, each one being overthrown by its successor. Some empires, like the Greek and Roman stretched across a much greater area than others but all of them occupied Syria and Israel.

BC they became independent, and by the 9th century were conquering people as far as the coast of the Mediterranean, over 400 miles (640 km) away. The black obelisk (a stone pillar with four sides, set up as a monument) of Shalmaneser III shows 'Jehu the son of Omri' a king of Israel, bowing before the Assyrian king.

Tiglath-Pileser III (745–727BC) was the first to organise a system of provincial government and by his time the empire was firmly established. Provincial governors were visited by court inspectors and if they were not controlling their pro-

vinces well they were severely punished. Tiglath-Pileser III began the policy of moving rebellious people from their own land to other parts of the empire. Shalmaneser V, his successor, invaded Israel to punish its last king, Hoshea, and the fall of the capital Samaria was followed by the inhabitants being marched away to exile (2 Kings 17:5).

When Hezekiah was king of Judah, the Assyrians under Sennacherib almost captured the city of Jerusalem. Three officials came to demand the city's surrender: the Tartan (army commander), the Rabsaris (chief of slaves) and the Rabshakeh (chief of nobles). Encouraged by the prophet Isaiah, Hezekiah refused to surrender and the city survived (2 Kings 18–19).

The Babylonian/Chaldean Empire. Babylon became the centre of an empire again after the collapse of Assyria at the end of the 7th century BC. Nebuchadnezzar (605–562BC), a Chaldean, rebuilt the city in magnificent style (Daniel 4:30). Life at his court can be glimpsed in the

Assyrian empire
11th-7th century BC

Babylonian empire
6th-5th century BC

Persian empire
5th-3rd century BC

Greek empire
3rd-1st century BC

Roman empire
1st century BC-5th century AD

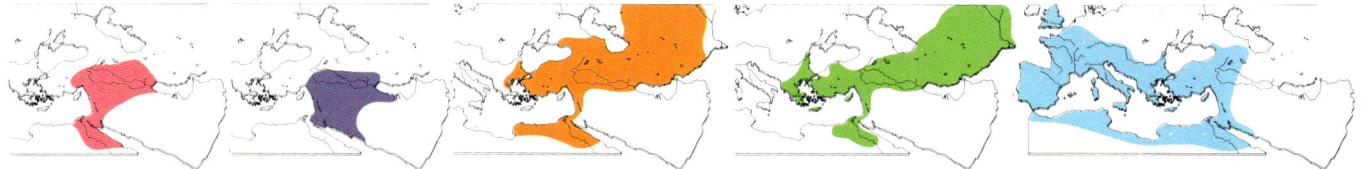

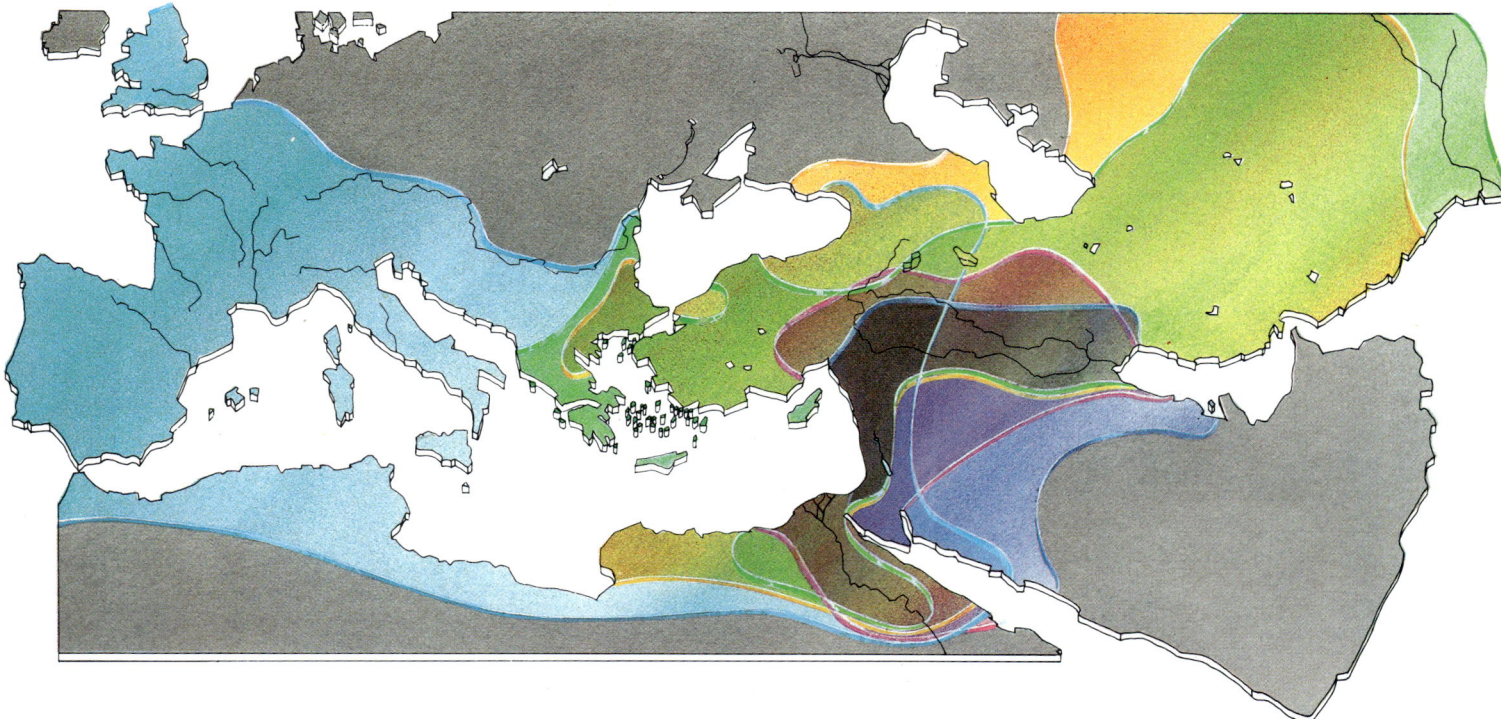

opening chapters of the book of Daniel (1–3). Nebuchadnezzar twice attacked Jerusalem for rebellion and each time he took away some of the people to Babylon (in 597 and 587BC). After the destruction of Jerusalem in 587BC the Babylonians appointed Gedaliah as governor of Judah. He set up his headquarters at Mizpah but was assassinated by Judean guerillas (Jeremiah 40:5–6; 41:1–3). Judah now had no governor of its own but came under the control of the governor of Samaria.

After Nebuchadnezzar's death, King Jehoiachin, who had been taken from Jerusalem in 597BC at the age of eighteen, was set free and treated with honour at the Babylonian court (2 Kings 25:27–30).

The last Babylonian king, Nabonidus, was unpopular and spent the final ten years of his reign away from Babylon leaving his son, Belshazzar, the crown prince, in charge (Dan. 5).

The Persian Empire. Cyrus the Great defeated and destroyed Babylon in 539BC. He issued decrees which allowed people who had been taken into exile to return to their own land and rebuild their temples and cities. In these ways he tried to encourage their loyalty to his empire. His decree for the Jewish exiles is preserved in the original texts of our Bible, in Hebrew, the traditional language of Israel, in Ezra 1:2–4, and in Aramaic, the language of Persian official documents, in Ezra 6:3–5.

Some Jews, led by Sheshbazzar, a 'prince of Judah' (Ezra 1:8) and so a descendant of David, returned to Jerusalem. It was not until 515BC that the

A silver drinking vessel from the time of Nehemiah. It may have come from Persia where Nehemiah was employed as cup-bearer to King Artaxerxes I.

The Ishtar Gate at Babylon – a reconstruction on a smaller scale of the gate through which many Israelite captives may have passed. The glazed blue brick is decorated with bulls and dragons.

Temple was rebuilt. The city took even longer. It was 445BC when Nehemiah, cup-bearer to King Artaxerxes I in the palace at Susa, asked for permission to go to Jerusalem to rebuild its walls (Nehemiah 1–2). He was opposed by San-ballat, governor of Samaria, and Tobiah, governor of the Transjordan; but he armed his men and kept careful guard on the city gates, and eventually the walls were completed (Nehemiah 4; 6; 7:1–3).

The Persian empire by this time was divided into twenty satrapies. Each satrapy was made up of a number of provinces like Samaria and the Transjordan which, with Nehemiah's Jerusalem, were in the satrapy known to the Persian king as Beyond the River (that is, west of the River Euphrates). This organisation of the empire was the work of Darius I (522–486BC) who also introduced one set of coins for all the empire and the first postal system, using excellent roads.

Ezra was another Jew who became an important Persian official, a minister for Jewish affairs. He returned to Jerusalem with the king's authority to make all the Jews who lived in the satrapy Beyond the River obey God's law (Ezra 7:11–26). Ezra brought a copy of the law with him and read it to the people for a week. They accepted again that God was their God and they were his people (Nehemiah 8–9). The wealth and magnificence of Persia was greater than Babylon's and the king's will was law: once a law was issued it could not easily be changed. Both Queen Esther and Daniel nearly lost their lives because of this (Esther 8:8; Daniel 6).

The Persian empire eventually fell to Alexander the Great in 331BC. His Greek empire was divided after his death and Seleucid kings from Antioch fought Ptolemies from Egypt for control of Palestine. The Jews were now led by a council of elders the chief of whom was the High Priest. He collected taxes to pay tribute to either the Seleucids or the Ptolemies.

One Seleucid king, Antiochus Epiphanes (175–163BC) offended the Jews by taking over the Temple in Jerusalem. The wars between rival kings were ended when Pompey conquered Palestine for the Romans in 63BC and brought it into the Roman empire.

Government in New Testament times

The Caesars of Rome

The Caesars were a family of Roman 'noblemen'. That is, they were the most famous men of their day. Because they had won in the civil wars, they became the richest family of Rome and the Romans kept electing them to power. By the time of Christ they had no competitors left at Rome. Each time the ruler died, the Romans turned to another member of the family to take over the main powers of government. At Rome they were called the 'leaders'. They were also army commanders, and the Latin word for this, *imperator*, has given us the English word 'emperor', which we now use to refer to them.

Because the Romans had conquered all the other countries around the Mediterranean Sea, and many of them had been used to being ruled by kings, the subject peoples spoke of the Caesars as 'kings'. That is why, when Pilate said to the Jews, 'Shall I crucify your king?' (referring to Jesus), they said 'We have no king but Caesar' (John 19:15).

The life of everyone in the Roman world of New Testament times was controlled in the end by the Caesars. Jesus was born at Bethlehem (and not Nazareth, where his family lived) because 'a decree went out from Caesar Augustus that all the world should be enrolled' (Luke 2:1). Everyone had to go back to the place of their ancestors for the census. Then they were put on a list for paying tax. The taxes were used to pay for the government and the armies by which Rome kept the world in order.

The following members of the family of the Caesars are referred to in the New Testament (dates give period in supreme power):

Augustus (31BC–AD14)   Luke 2:1

Tiberius (AD14–37)   All other references to Caesar in the gospels

Claudius (AD41–54)   Acts 11:28, 17:7, 18:2

Nero (AD54–68)   All other references to Caesar in the Acts of the Apostles

Below: a Roman coin bearing the head of Tiberius Caesar.

Below left: bronze head of Augustus Caesar, emperor when Jesus was born. It dates from the 1st century BC.

Roman provinces

Because this was mainly a peaceful time for the Roman Empire, many of the provinces did not need a major army. The men appointed as their governors were called 'proconsuls'. They were senior political leaders from Rome, officially equal in rank with the Caesars, and independent of them. They had to report only to the senate in Rome. Examples of this kind of province in the New Testament are:

Macedonia (N. Greece – capital, Thessalonica): no governor mentioned.

Achaia (S. Greece – capital, Corinth): proconsul Gallio (Acts 18:12).

Asia (W. Turkey – capital, Ephesus): proconsuls mentioned (Acts 19:38).

Cyprus (capital, Paphos): proconsul Sergius Paulus (Acts 13:7, 8, 12).

It was in the cities of Achaia, Asia and Macedonia that the churches we know best from the New Testament were founded. They are often grouped and referred to by their Roman provincial names (e.g. Acts 19:21, Revelation 1:4).

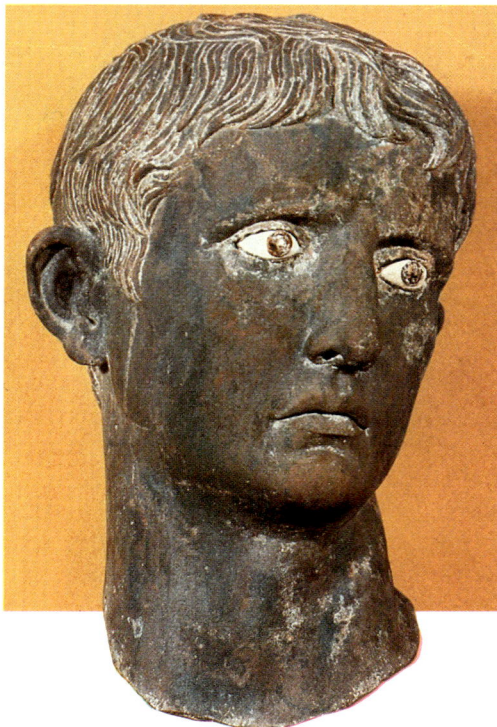

The Roman governors and their provinces

The Romans controlled an Empire which stretched from Britain to Egypt, and from Morocco to the Black Sea. The Empire was divided into 'provinces', each ruled by a governor sent from Rome. The provinces were really army commands, and the main task of the governors was to keep the peace and guard the frontiers. They did not directly run the provinces. This was done by the governments of the various kingdoms and city-states which lay within the boundaries of each province. The Roman governors did however have to settle disputes among the subject states within their provinces, and between the Roman citizens who lived there. The courts of law where these disputes were settled is where we mostly meet them in the New Testament.

A 1st century bronze statuette of the emperor Nero and a bust of the emperor Claudius.

The Jewish coins feature two Roman procurators. Left: Pontius Pilate AD30; right: Antonius Felix

Those provinces which still needed large Roman armies to control or protect them were kept under the direct command of the Caesars. They sent a deputy ('legate') to run them, referred to in the New Testament simply as 'governor'. For example, the province of Syria was governed by Quirinius at the time of Jesus' birth (Luke 2:2). Judea was supervised by the legate of Syria and at times ruled by a 'prefect' or 'procurator', who is also referred to in the New Testament as 'governor'. Those mentioned by name are Pontius Pilate (prefect AD26–36, Luke 3:1),

Felix (procurator AD52–58, Acts 23:24–34), Porcius Festus (procurator, AD58–62, Acts 24:27). These governors held power at times when the country was not ruled by its own kings.

Client kings and tetrarchs

The Romans sometimes liked to keep local kings in power to manage their own countries, especially when the people were hostile to Roman rule. Palestine is a good example of this. When Jesus was born the land was ruled by Herod the Great (Luke 1:5). The Romans officially recognised him as 'king of the Jews', and he was known as the 'friend and ally' of the Romans. Another Roman way of putting it was to call him a 'client'. The legate of Syria appointed him as a prefect, so that he could undertake wars on behalf of the Romans. But the Jews hated Herod because he was not descended from a pure Jewish family, and they favoured those of his sons whose mother came from the old royal house. So Herod had them executed. It was this suspicion of a rival with a better line of descent that no doubt led him to kill the innocent children of Bethlehem when he was told that the Messiah (the 'king of the Jews' promised in the prophets) had been born there (Matt. 2:1–18).

On Herod's death immediately after this, the kingdom was split up among three of his remaining sons. Archelaus took Judea and Samaria (Matt. 2:22), and ruled for ten years until the Jews persuaded the Roman government that direct control by prefects would be better. Galilee was ruled by Herod Antipas for 43 years, and there were two other 'tetrarchs', as these regional princes were called, his brother Philip to the east, and Lysanias to the north (Luke 3:1). It was

Antipas who had the head of John the Baptist cut off (Mark 6:14–28) and who was called in by Pilate to help sort out the charges against Jesus, who came from his tetrarchy of Galilee (Luke 23:6–12).

In AD36 a grandson of Herod the Great, Herod Agrippa, was given as a kingdom the tetrarchy of Philip, to which the Romans added Galilee when they exiled Antipas in AD39. In AD41 Claudius Caesar stopped sending prefects to Judea, and added that also to Agrippa's kingdom. It was this King Herod who cut off the head of James, put Peter in prison, and was struck down on his judgement seat in AD44 for allowing the people to hail him as a god (Acts 12:1–23). Judea and Samaria were then put under a Roman procurator.

The kingdom to the north and east of Galilee was once more entrusted to a king, Agrippa, son of Herod Agrippa. The younger Agrippa was the king whom the procurator Festus asked to help sort out the charges against Paul (Acts 25:13–27).

It was these 'client' kings, propped up by the Romans, who supplied the model we see in Jesus' parable of the gold coins (Luke 19:12–26).

The City-States

Romans and Greeks believed that civilised people should govern themselves, and not be ruled by kings. They tried to arrange for small local republics to take over from the kings. This could only be done if there was a suitable city where the theatre, market, and temples that were necessary could be built. The surrounding countryside was then made subject to the new state.

Galilee and Judea, where Jesus lived and worked, were hemmed in by such states to the north, east and west. Jesus often crossed their frontiers, but he stayed amongst the country people, and did not go into the cities. In the case of Tyre and Sidon (in modern Lebanon), for example, he dealt with the Canaanite woman (Matt. 15:21) who was probably not a member of the Greek city, but one of its subjects. The man from Gerasa, however, out of whom Jesus cast the demons, seems to have come from the city (Luke 8:27, 39). Gerasa and Gadara were both cities which belonged to the 'community of ten' (Decapolis), which reached from Damascus (capital of modern Syria) to Philadelphia, now Amman (capital of modern Jordan).

Jerusalem. Jerusalem was unusual in not being a city of the Greek kind. The revolt of the Maccabees, 150 years before Christ, had put an end to the attempt to make it one. The sects of Jesus' time, especially the Pharisees, stood for various ways of running Jewish community life that avoided going over to the Greek model of civilisation. The council of the Sanhedrin provided an alternative form of government, while keeping the law of Moses was the alternative life-style. It was a religious state, with the chief priests leading it, and the Pharisees setting the tone. Only after the failure of the great revolt against the Romans in AD70 was Jerusalem brought under the normal pattern of city life.

Herod the Great on his throne, from a 13th century Italian mosaic.

The church at Jerusalem was like another of the Jewish sects at first (Acts 24:14). But the gospel was for the Greeks, too. The Jews accused Stephen of having turned against the temple-state (Acts 6:12–14), and the preachers had to flee. Every other place where we know from the New Testament that a church was founded was a city-state of the Greek type. Usually there would be a Jewish synagogue in it, and the preaching would begin there; it often made its first appeal to the Greeks who admired Judaism. Then the believers would be thrown out of the synagogue, and start their own church. The conflict between the synagogue community and the new church was then often taken to the city authorities. The result would often depend on who was closest to the local government, and also on what the city's standing with the Roman governors was.

A law tablet from the Agora, the centre of public life in Athens.

Citizenship. Not everyone was equal in civil rights or status. The typical city would have a limited citizen roll, which would not include the peasants of the surrounding districts. Within it there would be a distinct community of Jews, who would hold the local citizenship, but also keep their own laws. The most wealthy of the citizens, including some of the Jews, would also have Roman citizen-

Colonies

When Paul and his friends were on their missionary journeys they visited several cities that were also Roman colonies.

At Antioch in Pisidia (Central Turkey) the important people were against Paul and Barnabas, and they were quickly put across the border into the territory of the next state (Acts 13:50), even though Antioch was a Roman colony and Paul a Roman citizen.

At Philippi in Macedonia (Northern Greece), also a colony, the trouble was caused by Romans who objected to Paul and Silas as Jews (Acts 16:20, 21). But this time Paul appealed to his Roman citizenship for protection (37–39).

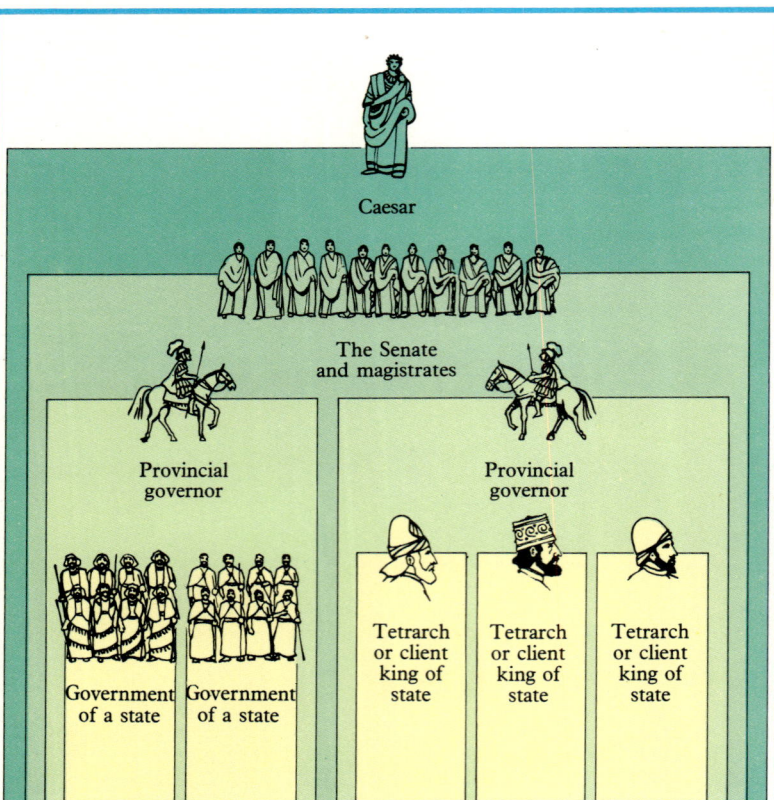

The Roman governing system

Caesar was in overall control of the empire. The line of authority stretched from Caesar at the top through the senate and magistrates to provincial governors, such as Pontius Pilate, and then to the local state government. In some parts of the empire this consisted of an elected group; in others, like Palestine, a client king or tetrarch was appointed by the Roman authorities to rule the state.

ship, even though they would not often go to Rome. Paul himself is a good example of this kind of person, holding rights as a Greek, a Jew and a Roman (Acts 21:39, 22:27, 28). Sometimes the Romans would honour a whole city by raising it to the rank of a Roman colony. A few cities would regularly have a Roman governor visit them, but the smaller ones were more likely to be left alone.

Keeping law and order

The Romans kept the peace in their world largely by leaving the job to the local governments. If the kings, tetrarchs or cities wanted to stay in charge of their own affairs, they had to see that troubles did not get out of hand, or come to the notice of the Roman governor. He, in turn, had an interest in seeing that news of any troubles did not go on to Rome, otherwise

At Thessalonica the city authorities were forced into action against Paul by being accused of disloyalty to Caesar (Acts 17:6–9). They were not a colony, but an independent city, and did not want the Roman governor interfering.

At Athens, the most famous of the independent Greek states, Paul was able to plead his cause directly before the ancient city council of the Areopagus (Acts 17:19). The picture is of the Stoa of Attalus, Athens. This is a reconstruction of the original, built by Attalus in the 2nd century BC, which was a colonnade of shops and statues.

At Corinth, another colony, the dispute was brought by the Jews before the court of the Roman governor of Achaia, who resided there (Acts 18:12).

At Ephesus, where the trouble was brought to the authorities by the Greeks, the town clerk was anxious to avoid the riot being reported to the governor, and wanted the complaint taken straight to him (Acts 19:38–40).

his own position would be called in question by Caesar.

When the people wanted to make Jesus a king, this seemed a threat to the chief priests and council (the Sanhedrin) at Jerusalem, because the Romans could take it as an attempt to go back to the old style of rule by kings which they had stopped. If the council could not keep order, the nation might be put under even more direct Roman control. So, it was argued, Jesus would have to die for the people's sake (John 11:47–50). Pilate, the Roman governor, had to approve the death penalty but he did not really believe the charge that Jesus wanted to be king (John 18:31–37). The chief priests then cast doubt on Pilate's loyalty to Caesar and so made him do as they wanted (John 19:12–16). Many problems among the subject peoples were tidied up by methods like this.

But law and order could also be used to protect the individual, provided he was important enough to start with. A Roman citizen was entitled to special respect (though as Paul's case shows [2 Cor. 11:23–27] he might not always get it) and if he could assert his rights, the whole weight of the Roman army was on his side (Acts 22:23–29, 23:23, 24), and he could even appeal direct to Caesar (25:10–12). Paul's is the first case known to history where this happened.

The riots and violence in which Paul was frequently caught show how risky life could be for ordinary people in the community in spite of the Roman peace. Even the road from Jerusalem to Jericho was not safe. The Roman army did not provide ordinary police services, and travellers had to protect themselves against bandits as best they could (Luke 10:30). Not everyone could count on finding a Good Samaritan!

The Greek voting system

Part of a *kleroterion*, a device used for selecting jurors. Identity cards for jurors were placed in the slots and rows of cards were selected for service in a certain court on any day.

Jurors' ballots and name labels.

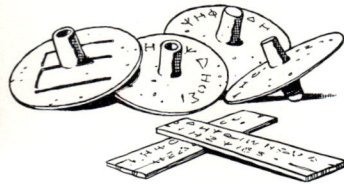

Collecting the taxes

All Jews paid an annual tax for the upkeep of the temple at Jerusalem. Jesus was suspected of not paying it, but he did not claim the exemption he thought one might have argued for (Matt. 17:24–27). Jews abroad also paid this tax. In a similar spirit, Paul collected gifts from the Greek churches for the poor at Jerusalem (Rom. 15:25–27). The Romans still collected the tax even after the destruction of the temple in AD70.

Roman citizens did not have to pay income tax. Instead they raised taxes from the subject peoples to pay for their food and armies. Businessmen undertook the task of collecting these public taxes (and were called 'publicans' as a result). They contracted for a fixed amount, and then raised more to cover their own profit. The publicans employed local people to do the actual collecting. To link oneself in this way with the profits of the occupying power made one particularly hated. Hence 'publicans' were coupled in the popular phrase with 'sinners'.

One of the first disciples, Matthew, was a tax collector who was called to follow

Jesus while sitting in the tax office (Matt. 9:9–12). Jesus then had dinner in his house with many other tax collectors and sinners. When the Pharisees blamed him for this, he said that he had come to cure the sick. So he accepted that there was something wrong with them, but offered a solution at the personal level, rather than attacking the tax system itself.

Another man whom Jesus met was Zacchaeus of Jericho, a 'chief tax collector'. Jesus deliberately called him down from the sycamore tree so that he could stay at his house. The Pharisees were shocked at Jesus being the guest of a sinner. But Zacchaeus gave away half of his property to the poor, and paid back four times over any illegal profits he had made. This was the cure Jesus had for the problem (Luke 19:2–10). The tax collector who recognised his sin was in the right place before God, rather than the Pharisee who did not (Luke 18:9–14).

As for the taxes themselves, Jesus avoided the trap when the Pharisees tried to make him choose between paying tax and honouring God (Matt. 22:15–22). Since Caesar's name and picture were on the coins, it was right to pay him his due, while God was also to have his due.

For or against the government?

Many people, even perhaps one of his own followers (Matt. 26:51), wanted Jesus to lead a revolt against the Romans, who had conquered their land. But he himself rejected violence and was much more critical of the Pharisees and other religious leaders of the Jews than he was of the Romans. His kingship was not based on

force and was not 'of this world' (John 18:36). This meant it could not be the ordinary kind of government. But he insisted that Pilate only enjoyed his power 'from above' (John 19:11), that is, from God. This is no doubt why he had said it was right to pay taxes to Caesar, even though the Pharisees regarded Caesar as the enemy of God for having conquered the Jews.

Paul spelled out what Jesus had meant (Romans 13:1–7). Rulers are given their powers by God, and their duty is to stop wrong-doing. Therefore they have to be obeyed, which includes paying taxes. Peter kept up this view (1 Peter 2:13–17), and applied it to all kinds of authority, even though in the case of slaves he saw that they might be unjustly treated by their masters. They were to remember how Christ too had suffered unjustly (18–24).

But in other places in the New Testament it is clear that government can be misused and turn against God. Paul did not excuse 'the rulers of this age' who 'crucified the Lord of Glory' (1 Cor. 2:8). In the end, he will be the 'only Sovereign, the King of kings and Lord of lords' (1 Tim. 6:15). The Revelation to John is a vision of the final struggle for control of the world between God and satanic powers, who look in many ways like the Roman Caesars. They had killed those who would not worship the image of the ruler (Rev. 13:15). We know from a Roman source (Pliny, *Letters* 10.96) that this was the test used by the governor to sort out the true Christians. Caesar was now demanding the worship that was due to God alone. If forced to choose, 'we must obey God rather than men' (Acts 5:29).

A Jewish tax-collector working for the Roman government.

The Fortress of Antonia was the fortified residence of King Herod the Great in Jerusalem. This is a reconstructed model.

WARFARE

The first wars of Israel as a nation were wars of conquest; they fought to take the land of Palestine which God had promised them. The book of Joshua tells us about those battles. In the times of the Judges and King Saul, Israel was mainly defending what it had won. It was King David who extended Israel's borders. His son, King Solomon, however, ruled during a time of peace, and protected what had been won. When Israel broke into two kingdoms after Solomon's death, they did not live in peace for some fifty years. They fought each other as well as defending their borders from other nations. The northern tribes were eventually conquered by the Assyrians under King Sargon II (721 BC). The southern tribes were weak and eventually fell to the Babylonians under King Nebuchadnezzar (605 BC).

The Jews were controlled by foreign powers for several centuries, even though many returned home to Palestine. Although they had no regular army, they revolted under the leadership of Judas Maccabeus against the Greek kings that ruled them. Eventually the Jews once more gained their national freedom.

A gold model of a chariot from around 500 BC. Part of the Oxus Treasure found in Iran. This collection of precious objects was probably buried around 200 BC and was rediscovered in 1877.

The 'holy war'

Israel was different from other warlike nations that surrounded her. When Israel fought, it was what we could call a 'holy war'; that is, God told Israel when and whom to fight. He is called 'the God of the armies of Israel' (1 Samuel 17:45).

God would fight for Israel, sometimes using the forces of nature against the enemy, and throw the enemy into confusion (Judges 4:15). Before going into battle a sacrifice was offered to the Lord and his advice sought about the fight (Judg. 20:23, 28). Such faith in God gave confidence; the enemy was as good as defeated and fear was removed. Whatever town or city was taken it was to be destroyed, showing that the fruits of victory were God's and not man's. The principles of 'holy war' are seen in Exodus 23:20–33.

All this did not mean that God was cruel. When he commanded Israel to destroy a nation it was because that nation was evil. The Amorites, for example, were spared until their sin became too great. Then God had to punish them (Genesis 15:16). In this way God both punished the wicked nations and gave Israel the land of Canaan, which he had promised them (Deuteronomy 9:4,5). Even Israel was oppressed by other nations when she became unfaithful to God.

The practice of 'holy war' – fighting only when God said – fell away as Israel ceased being faithful to God. After David's reign, war became more of a political affair. Eventually, when the country divided, both the northern and the southern tribes suffered as a result of this unfaithfulness.

We find the practice of 'holy war' reinstated in the time of the Maccabees. Once again the men fast, set themselves aside for war and believe that God is fighting for them (1 Maccabees 4:8–11, see 1 Sam. 7:4–6). However, we do not read that God commanded the fighting or directed it, as he did in the early days.

During their trek across the desert from Egypt to the Promised Land, the Israelites were attacked by the Amalekites, a warlike nomadic tribe of the Sinai area. Joshua led the Israelites in the battle, watched by Moses, Aaron and Hur. As long as Moses held up his hands, the Israelites won. Exodus 17:2–16

Israelite military service

After the Exodus from Egypt, Israel fought unitedly when attacked (Exod. 13:18), although when settling in the land of Canaan they frequently fought as separate tribes (Judg. 1:8–10). At other times the tribes united to fight (Judg. 6:33–35), but there was never an organised army.

The Israelites had various methods of raising an army to face attack. A trumpet (ram's horn) might be blown (Judg. 6:34); messengers might be sent – a gruesome symbol was sent on one occasion (1 Sam. 11:7). When the call to unite was given, a tribe did not have to come, but if a tribe did volunteer, then the whole tribe had to fight: no town or village was excused. Once the war was over, everyone returned to his own home.

Some men were excused from fighting.

There was not a regular, professional army before the reign of King Saul (around 1050–1011BC). In the days of Abraham, about 900 years earlier, all the able-bodied men would unite to fight and protect their tribe. Sometimes tribes would unite against a common enemy. When the danger was past, everyone went home to carry on with his normal work.

The Israelite army

It was David who began a properly organised army. There were three basic parts:

The royal bodyguard
Called the Kerethites and Pelethites, these were mercenaries and separate from the regular army (2 Sam. 8:18). David hired them after conquering the Philistines. They were not free men, but were directly under the King and were 'paid' by being freed from forced labour and from paying taxes (1 Sam. 17:25). They were often given land and tithes.

The professional army
This included at first those who joined David in the desert when he was hiding from Saul. Their numbers grew from four hundred to six hundred (1 Sam. 25:13). It is out of this number that we read of the strongest and bravest men, the 'Thirty' (2 Sam. 23:22) and one of these, Benaiah, commanded David's royal bodyguard. There were also 'Three' whose bravery and skill could not be beaten (2 Sam. 23:17). The entire group was tough, efficient and merciless. Many became skilful leaders and military advisors to David.

As long as battles were fought and won, payment of the soldiers was no trouble: money and rewards could be given. The professional army grew in numbers.

In time, David divided the land of Israel into strategic regions – border areas, for example, needed to be watched. This meant that in times of danger an army could be gathered very quickly. We read of occupation forces under King Rehoboam strategically placed in fortified cities to keep the area under control (2 Chron. 11:11, 12). The professional army was very effective and fought battles without the conscript army (2 Sam. 5:6–10).

The conscript army
This army consisted of all the ordinary men of Israel that were over twenty years of age. We see how it was organised during David's reign in 1 Chronicles 27:1–15. Each tribe would organise as many units of fighting men as possible. For example, in a tribe with ten thousand fighting men, there might be ten units of one thousand men. Each unit had a tribally-selected officer commanding it.

Every month, twenty-four thousand men would be called up, in rotating order. In this way, each tribe would send along a certain number of units to make up the total twenty-four thousand men. A small tribe would send a smaller number of units. Each united group of twenty-four thousand men would complete one month's duty. One of the 'Thirty' commanded them. This meant that a regularly-trained army existed, ready for any emergency. Professional

The Three and their battle exploits are described in 2 Samuel 23 8–12. The Thirties were the core units of David's army and the regiments were built around them. Each of The Thirty had proved himself by feats of valour.

Some were too afraid; or, perhaps, a man had just built a house, or had become engaged to be married. A newly-wed was also excused (Deut. 24:5); so, too, were the Levites, who had their priestly duties to carry out (Numbers 1:47–49).

To go to war, a man had to be at least twenty years of age and he could go on fighting up to any age, as long as he was fit. Payment was in sharing out the spoils (Num. 31:26–30).

Beginnings of the regular army

King Saul saw how important a regular army could be. The old method of raising an army was very haphazard, and so Saul called upon any man he thought to be brave and strong (1 Sam. 14:52) to join his army. These men needed to be paid a

Three of David's bravest soldiers broke through the Philistine lines and brought him water from the well at Bethlehem. David refused to drink it and poured it out before the Lord.

soldiers with special skills such as infantry, slingers, archers and charioteers would go to different regional bases. Some tribes were noted for special skills (1 Chron. 12:2, 8, 32, 33). Such an army would become well-trained and disciplined, yet still remain part-time.

During the reign of King Solomon, no wars were fought. The army, now large and expensive, became patrolmen for the borders. When

recruiting, preference was shown for men experienced with chariots and horses, or for those keen to undergo training for the chariot corps. To be a military soldier was all rather routine.

After the united kingdom split into two nations, it became more difficult for the kings of Israel and Judah, especially for the latter, which was the poorer and less populous nation, to pay the professional troops and so recruiting fell off.

Organisation of the army

The Bible does not tell us very much about army units. We are told that in Moses' day Israel marched in ranks of five and camped and marched in the desert in units of five (Num. 2:2–31). This was how Israel entered Canaan under Joshua.

The people were divided into units of tens, fifties, hundreds and thousands (Exod. 18:21). This would correspond to our section, platoon, company and regiment. These units were

continued by Saul, David, Solomon and later kings. **Foot soldiers** (infantrymen) were the most numerous. It is likely that the army coming out of Egypt at the Exodus was entirely infantry.

Although the sling was used as a weapon of war before Abraham's time, the first mention of **slingers** is found in the days of the Judges (Judg. 20:16). They were also found in David's army (1 Chron. 12:2).

The **archer** has a long history, but it was the

improved bow of David's time that made it an essential weapon.

David probably had only a small **chariot force** whereas Solomon had many. But it was King Ahab who had the most chariots ever found in Israel.

David had a **cavalry corps** which rode mules. (The spur and stirrup were not invented until over one hundred years later.) However, only the most important people rode them (2 Sam. 13:29).

The army continued as an important part of national life in both the Northern and Southern kingdoms until they finally fell to invaders. The northern tribes never recovered. In the south, Jerusalem fell to Nebuchadnezzar, King of Babylonia. The Jews did not have an army again until 168BC. This was not an organised army, as under David, but consisted of guerilla forces led by Judas Maccabeus. The Jews did not have an army in New Testament times. The Roman armies had occupied Judea in 63BC and an uneasy peace had settled.

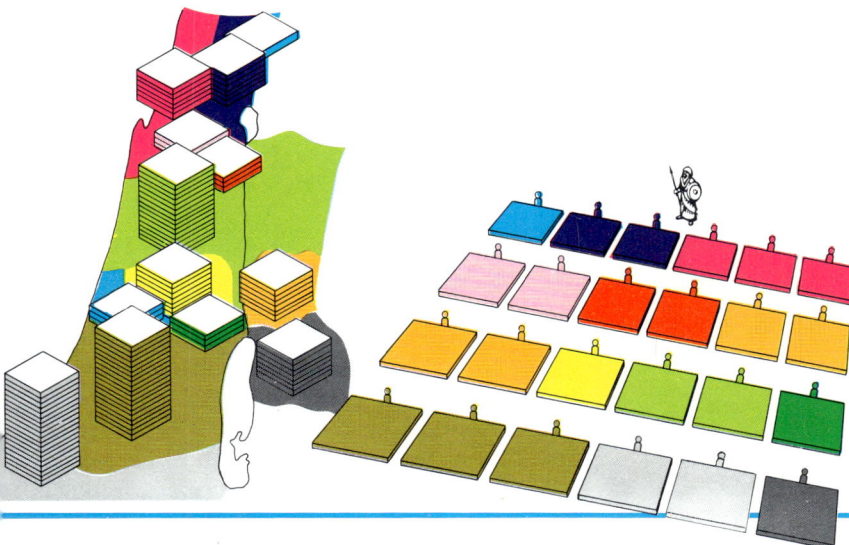

Each month 24,000 men were called to serve in the conscript army under one of the Thirty. Units of 1000 men were sent from each of the twelve tribes to make up the total. The number of units depended on the strength of the tribe.

Each block represents a unit of 1000 men from each tribe.

regular wage, and as Saul's kingdom was not rich, the army had to be quite small. Recruits were given the weapons for fighting and this became the regular practice (2 Chronicles 26:14).

David was a great soldier. When he was in hiding from King Saul, four hundred men joined him in the hills, where they lived by raiding (1 Sam. 27:8–12). Such a life made them tough, well-disciplined and experienced. These men later formed the core of his army when he became king. Under David, the kingdom grew and this meant that borderlands needed protection, both in times of peace and in times of war.

A spring at Engedi in the Judean wilderness. David and his men hid in this area while fleeing from King Saul.

Looking across the plain of Jezreel towards Mt. Tabor. Scene of a resounding victory by 10,000 Israelite foot soldiers, led by Deborah and Barak, over the Canaanite army who had iron chariots.

Israelite battle tactics

This section deals mainly with Israel, although the nations surrounding Israel used similar tactics, as did the Romans.

Against cities and towns

Large towns and cities were often built on a steep, isolated peak. Samaria is a good example. Jerusalem was also built on a hill-top. Walls surrounding a city might be up to six metres thick and nine metres high and provided the first defence against attack. In David's time, city walls were casemated, that is, the wall consisted of a double thickness with enough space between for storage and for housing. This gave plenty of room on the top for ramparts. Towers in the walls held archers and slingers. The city gate was the weakest point, through which enemies could force an entrance by using axes and ramming the doors with beams. (The proper battering-ram came many years after David.) Arrows, fire-brands and boiling water would be showered on attackers. To gain entry, attackers might try to scale the walls with ladders, or dig under the walls, or even through them.

The siege was a common tactic. Cutting off water and food could save the attacker much bloodshed. Cyrus conquered Babylon in 539BC by diverting the water supply. A trick used on occasions was to have the defenders lured from the town. The enemy would then gain entry and open the gates. Gibeah fell in this way (Judg. 20:29–43).

As the entrance gate to a city was always a weak point, Solomon had special gates built at Hazor, Megiddo and Gezer. Anyone entering the city had to pass through three fortified gates manned by sentries.

A moat surrounding a city could be filled with debris to make a bridge on which battering-rams could then be used. Archers and slingers were trained to pick

The conquest of the Promised Land

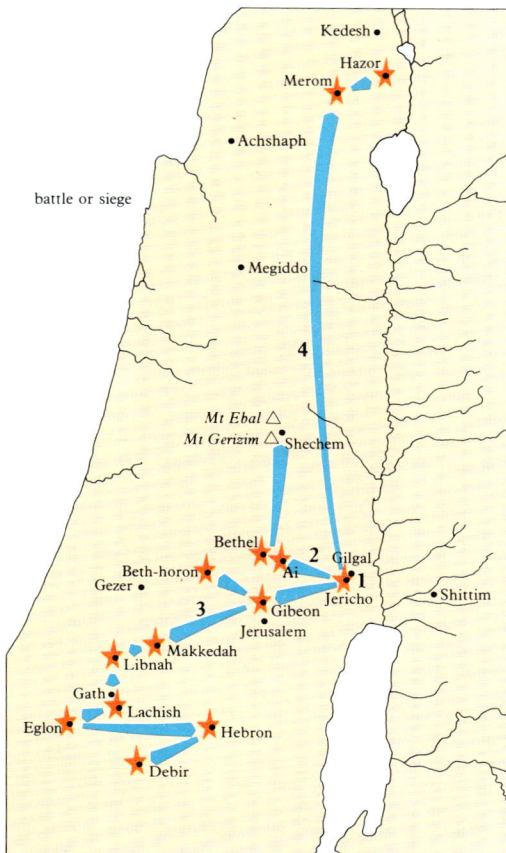

battle or siege

There were four main stages in the conquest. **1** The capture of the important city of Jericho. **2** The taking of Ai – a strategic pattern for later attacks. **3** The southern campaign – a series of battles in quick succession. **4** The northern campaign. The kings of the north united against Israel and were defeated in two main battles.

The Ai campaign
Following a report from spies, Joshua sent only 3,000 men to attack the Canaanite city of Ai. They were defeated. On God's instructions Joshua planned a second attack using different tactics. This time he sent 30,000 men to hide on the far side of the city and posted an ambush force of 5,000 between Bethel and Ai to deal with any reinforcements from Bethel. Joshua led the main body of troops in a 4-stage attack, described in the diagram on the left.

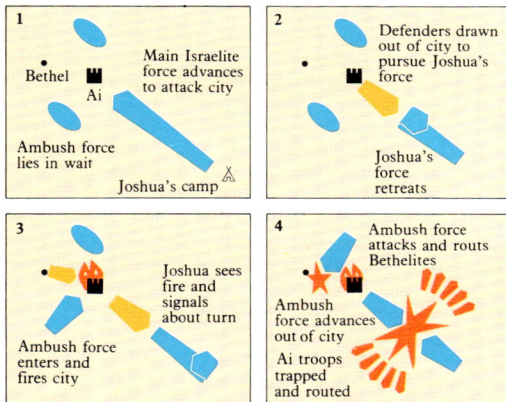

1 Bethel. Ai. Main Israelite force advances to attack city. Ambush force lies in wait. Joshua's camp

2 Defenders drawn out of city to pursue Joshua's force. Joshua's force retreats

3 Joshua sees fire and signals about turn. Ambush force enters and fires city

4 Ambush force attacks and routs Bethelites. Ambush force advances out of city. Ai troops trapped and routed

off defenders. Once the wall or gate was breached, assault troops swarmed in.

In the field
What a commander did with his army often depended on the type of troops and the arms carried. Israel was one of the few nations that rarely relied solely on a pitched battle or head-on assault. They preferred to use spies (Josh. 2:1–6), trick the defenders out of a city (Josh. 8), find a traitor that would let them into a city (Judg. 1:23–25), launch a surprise attack after an all-night march (Josh. 10:9), or use psychological warfare (Josh 6:1–17). Sometimes a handful of men did better than a large force (Exod. 17:9, Judg. 7:1–7).

Other tactics included the ambush, hit-and-run attack after circling around to the rear of an enemy, night attacks, and tricking the enemy into attacking a deserted camp (2 Kings 6:8–10). David, on occasions, let the enemy attack and then divided his force into two, allowing the enemy to run down between the two groups. Then he closed in. On another occasion he used a small force to exert deadly hit-and-run tactics on an advancing column of soldiers. This slowed down the enemy and wore them out. The army usually marched in three or four formations. Each could then be called quickly as the battle advanced.

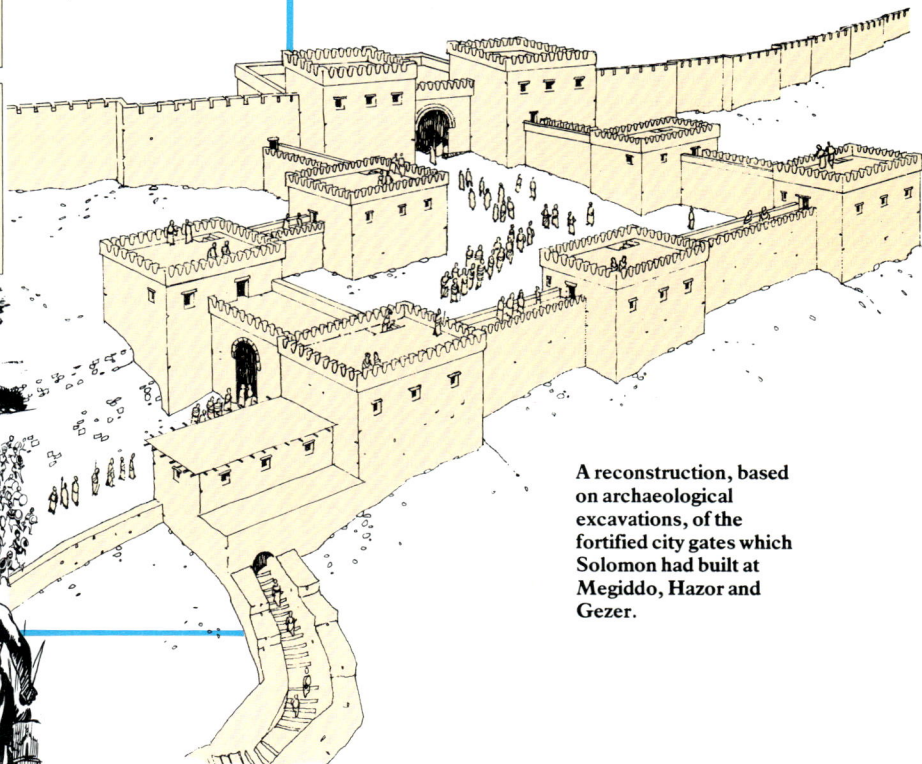

A reconstruction, based on archaeological excavations, of the fortified city gates which Solomon had built at Megiddo, Hazor and Gezer.

Israelite defence tactics usually consisted in standing side by side behind interlocking shields. Spears would point out at the enemy. It was a common defence move and usually kept back an attack. Standing on higher ground was better than a plain, and a ditch or wall in front also helped. Saul was killed in such an attack. When the wall of shields and spears collapsed, the men became afraid and ran.

Camp

The army camped in a square or circle (Num. 2). They slept in tents and the camp was always guarded (Judg. 7:19). During battle a small number stayed behind to protect the camp (1 Sam. 25:13).

On the move

When the army moved through hostile territory it usually marched in four major combat formations. Each formation had three divisions. The HQ and staff marched behind the first division. An advance guard scouted ahead; they would also find a camp site for the night. This general procedure lasted from Moses' day right through the Old Testament period.

David's citadel in Jerusalem. Part of the wall dates back to Crusader times.

Weapons

We do not know exactly what the Israelite weapons looked like. We have some idea of those used by the Egyptians, Philistines and Assyrians, and Israel would probably have used weapons very similar to those of the Philistines. Some weapons would have been of actual Philistine origin.

The Philistines arrived on the west coast of Palestine while Israel was still in Egypt. They knew how to work iron and other metals, so that their weapons were very good and superior to anything Israel had (1 Sam. 13:19–22). King David broke this Philistine monopoly of iron weapons and implements.

Weapons of attack

The sword Before Israel entered Canaan, its army had a sword with only one cutting edge. It was about 50cm long and was used for striking rather than piercing. It was carried in a sheath attached to the waist or around the shoulder, when running. The Philistines had a straight two-edged sword, which was used in hand-to-hand fighting and carried by spearmen, archers and slingers.

Axe and mace The mace was a heavy, roundish object (usually stone) fixed to a wooden handle. It was used to smash an enemy's head. The axe was shaped to pierce a helmet, and was made of metal.

Sling This was a weapon that needed great skill to be used accurately (Judg. 20:16). David was expert with it (1 Sam. 17:50). Even before Abraham's time the sling was in use, and it remained as part of Israel's weaponry throughout her history (2 Chron. 26:14). Stones were used for slinging, but from about 400BC lead balls were often employed. The sling was made of leather strips with a pocket in the middle to hold the stone. Both ends were held in the hand and the loaded sling was whirled around until one end was released, ejecting the stone at high speed. The armies of Egypt, Philistia, Assyria and Babylon also had slingers.

Bow and arrow The early bow was simply a pliable piece of wood held bent by a taut string. It was later strengthened with wood and horn glued together. This was expensive to make. Although other nations used it in war, Israel did not have the bow until David's time, and even then it was not used by very many. When the chariot was used in battle, there was less hand-to-hand fighting, and the bow became essential.

The arrow was made of three parts: a bronze or iron head, a body of wood or reed and a tail of feathers. Different shaped heads served different purposes, such as shooting long distances (up to 550 metres) or piercing armour. Arrows were carried in a quiver, which held about twenty-five.

Chariots From about 1500BC the

Later developments

Battering ram This came into use in the Assyrian army about 900BC. To try to combat this, city walls were made thicker (as much as six metres) and taller (up to twelve metres), and larger stones were used to produce a stable structure.

The earliest battering ram was nothing more than a large beam or tree trunk, persistently swung by a group of soldiers against the wall or door. Later, the ram was suspended like a pendulum within a framework that was on rollers. Once in position, the ram was swung repeatedly against the object of attack. Still later, ropes were used to pull the ram against the door or wall and a domed roof gave some protection to those using the ram.

The Assyrian army was equipped with this last type of battering ram, but the army had another type that prised away the mortar and stones, rather than battered. This second type had a striking end shaped like an axe. The whole structure was on wheels. It was pushed into position, rammed against the wall, and the ram levered from side to side. Great banks of earth and debris were erected against the city wall to form a ramp, and thus enable the battering ram to attack as close as possible to the top of the wall.

Under Judas Maccabaeus
The army had swords, shields, bows and arrows, javelins and spears, which were taken from the Syrians (1 Macc. 6:6, 35, 39) and were probably very similar to the latest developments of those described above. Elephants were used by the Syrians to carry archers. They also used giant catapults (see Roman Army, Catapult).

A reconstruction of the siege of the Israelite city of Lachish by the Assyrian army in 701BC. The city is fortified with double walls but the Assyrian siege ramps and battering rams proved superior. The city was destroyed and many prisoners deported to Assyria.

chariot was a useful weapon of war. Almost every nation had its chariot division. Egypt had chariots in Joseph's time and Pharaoh used them in his attempt to chase Israel at the Exodus (Exod. 15:19). The Philistines had many chariots, but because of the expense involved in making and maintaining them and the cost of buying and keeping horses, David kept his chariot corps deliberately small (2 Samuel 8:4). The chariots were made of wood and were strengthened with bronze or iron armour-plate. A quiver and a holder were fixed to the sides to hold arrows and javelins. Israelite chariots carried three men: a driver, a fighter and a third man. Egyptians had only two: a driver and a fighter. Two horses pulled the chariot and sometimes a third horse was taken along as a reserve.

King Solomon increased the number of Israel's chariots to 1,400 and kept them in Jerusalem and other strategic cities. The chariot was of most use in flat country and could be a handicap in hilly areas. In bad weather the chariot would become bogged down. We read of a chariot in New Testament times in Acts 8:28, but this was probably more like a small, covered wagon than the war chariot used in battle.

Spear This was not just thrown, but would be held and thrust at the enemy in hand-to-hand combat (Num. 25:7, 8). It was about 1½–2 metres in length with a wooden handle and a metal head.

Javelin This was lighter and smaller than the spear (Joshua 8:18), fitted with a wooden handle with a bronze or iron head. The butt was usually weighted to give it a good balance for throwing. A barrage of javelins hurled at an advancing enemy could be devastating.

Weapons of defence

Shield The Israelites used shields only after they settled in Canaan. Shields came

Egyptian warriors with their shields on a relief in the Temple of Hatshepsut.

Warships of Bible times

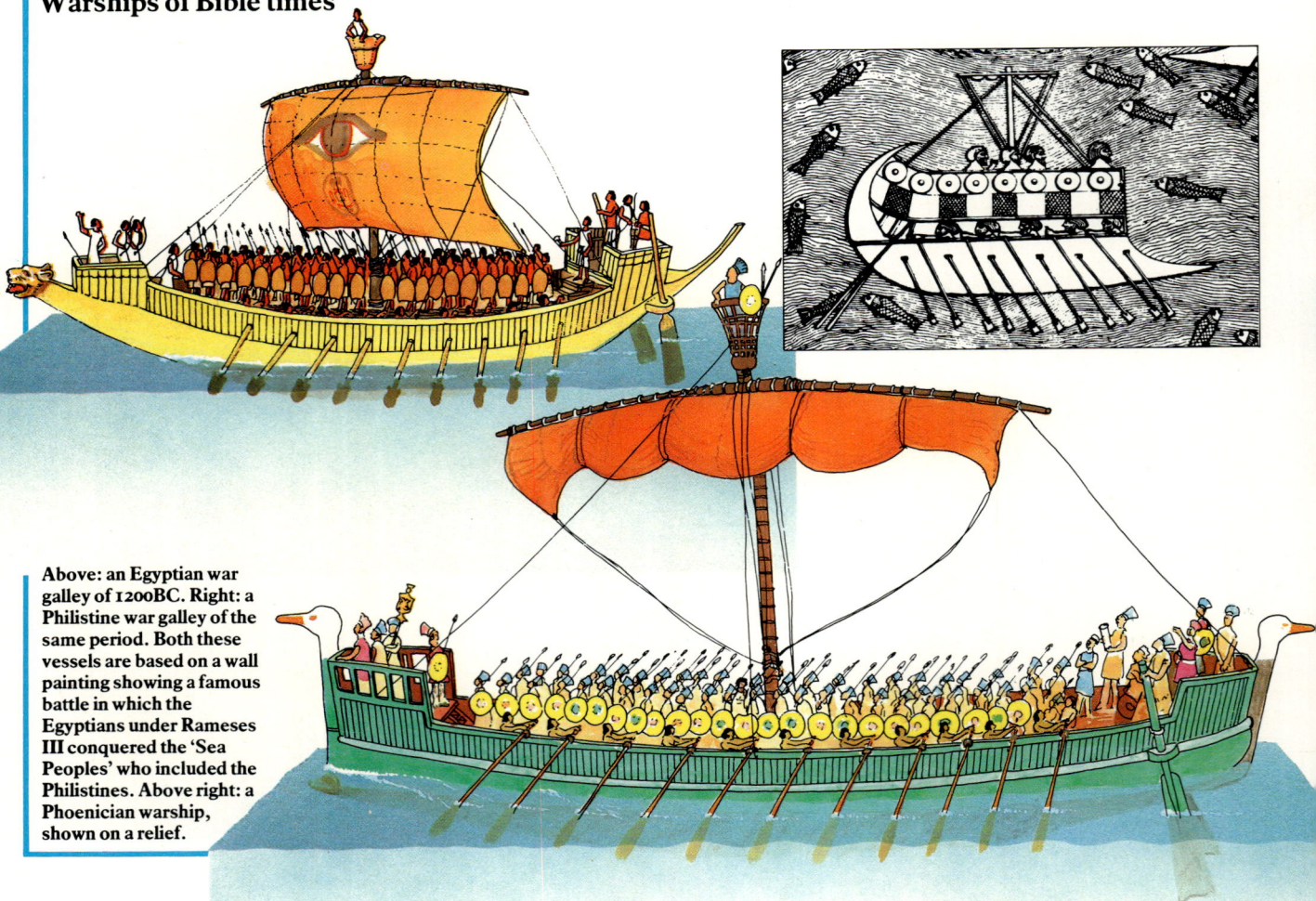

Above: an Egyptian war galley of 1200BC. Right: a Philistine war galley of the same period. Both these vessels are based on a wall painting showing a famous battle in which the Egyptians under Rameses III conquered the 'Sea Peoples' who included the Philistines. Above right: a Phoenician warship, shown on a relief.

Left: a Greek war galley of 500BC. The ship was propelled by fifty oars. The prow had a ram in the shape of a wild boar. The ladder at the stern was apparently used for boarding the boat.

Below: a Roman warship. The ship's eye on the prow was thought to have magic power. The boarding plank with a long spike on the end was dropped on to the deck of an enemy ship, preventing it from getting away. The awning at the stern end protected the officers and the helmsman from the weather.

originally from the Philistines. The swordsmen and spearmen carried shields for protection in the time of David. The Israelite shield was small, round and concave, and was held in the left hand. It was wooden and covered with oiled leather (2 Sam. 1:21) and might be reinforced with metal discs nailed to it. When not in use, it could be carried on the back by a strap. Egyptian shields were a different shape. On royal occasions in Israel, special large shields were made (1 Kings 10:16, 17).

Helmet Israel's helmets were probably similar to those of the Assyrians. They were made of bronze and, to protect the ears, leather or metal straps might be added. The helmet top was sometimes decorated or shaped. This would aid recognition in battle (2 Chron. 26:14).

Armour Before David's time, the Israelite army did not wear armour. The first armour was made of bronze, and later iron, plates of scales linked together. It was standard equipment by about 1000BC and worn by those who did not carry shields. The danger areas were at the joints of the sleeves to the chest, and the stomach (1 Kg. 22:34, 35). The neck was protected with a metal-studded, leather collar. Leg fronts, or greaves, were worn by the Philistines (1 Sam. 17:5, 6).

Coats of chain mail were worn by Greeks and Romans. Horses and chariots could also be protected with armour (Josh. 17:16; Judg. 1:19 – 'iron chariots' were wooden chariots with armour protection).

The Egyptian army

The Egyptian New Kingdom (1560–1085BC) covers the period of the Israelites' Exodus from Egypt.

The New Kingdom saw Egypt rise to the height of her power and prosperity. Egypt was divided into territorial areas and within each territorial boundary the army had an active and a reserve section. Each of these sections was divided into five units and named after an Egyptian god under whose name they fought. These

Israelite weapons from around 1000BC, the time of Saul and David.

Part of a statue of a Greek soldier, showing overlapping plates of armour.

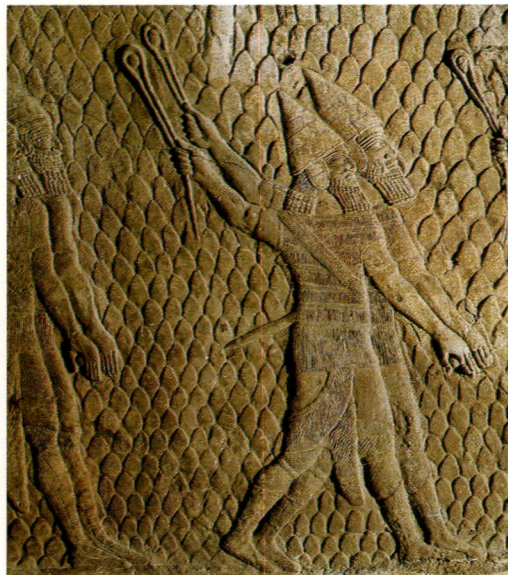

An Assyrian relief showing soldiers with slings.

An Egyptian relief showing prisoners of war before an official. Their long robes and headbands are characteristic of Palestine.

An Egyptian painting showing Rameses II in his conquest of Nubia. The king in his chariot is charging the fleeing Nubians who wear leopard skins and carry bows and arrows.

units, or corps, were made up of 10,000 foot soldiers each, and went into combat preceded, flanked and followed by chariots. The foot soldiers formed battle units of 100 men wide and 100 men deep, and were distributed between two brigades, each made up of five battalions. A special group of soldiers acted as 'shock troops' and could serve on land or sea. At the head of the armies, Pharaoh fought in person from his chariot.

The foot soldier possessed a large shield that protected him in battle, and also acted as a temporary battlement when placed on earth mounds that surrounded an encampment. The archer carried a quiver and used the powerful Asiatic bow, which was made of laminated wood, sinew and animal horn bound together. Armour consisted of tough, leather breast-plates and sometimes a mantle covered with bronze scales. The weapons, made of bronze, were light and strong.

It would have been the sight of such an army that caused the Israelites to be very afraid as they fled from Pharaoh (Exod. 14:5–12).

The Philistine army

We find that Abraham had dealings with the Philistines when he went to live in the southern part of Canaan (Gen. 26:1–Abimelech was a Philistine). But it was in the days of Saul and David that the Philistines became a threat to Israel. Goliath was a Philistine giant that became a symbol of their power. King Saul was killed in battle with the Philistines. During the days of the divided monarchy they were a constant source of trouble. A fierce

A Philistine sword and shield.

and warlike people, they held the control of iron- and metal-working before David took it from them. They had round shields, long, two-edged swords and triangular-shaped daggers. They also used a lance. Their head-dress was of feathers. (See also *Weapons*.)

The Philistine army was noted for its heavily-armed infantry. It was divided into groups of hundreds and thousands (compare Israel – 1 Sam. 29:2). The infantry was its strength, though it had chariots, cavalry, archers and other fighters. It is interesting to note that such a small nation was able to conquer Israel

The Philistines kept their methods of metal-working secret so that the tools and weapons of the Israelites were inferior and they had to rely on Philistine blacksmiths to do their repairs.

again and again. To ensure Israel's continued submission after defeat in battle, the Philistines not only disarmed them and imposed heavy tribute, but also removed all blacksmiths from Israel, thus depriving them of weapons and the manufacture and upkeep of agricultural implements (1 Sam. 13:19–22).

It was probably while David stayed with the Philistines that he learned much about tactics and fighting. In fact, it was David who eventually conquered them. They regained some of their strength after Solomon died, but their old power never returned. We read of them finally in Jeremiah 25:20 and Zechariah 9:5, but they are no longer important.

An Egyptian relief showing Philistine prisoners of war after a battle.

The Assyrian army

The Assyrians were known to the Israelites in the days of Israel's Judges, but they did not take up arms against Israel until the time of Ahab, king of Israel, in 853BC. For some 200 years after this, Assyria continued to cast her shadow over Palestine. The Assyrian warriors were fierce and fanatic fighters. From the river Tigris to the river Nile they eventually swept all before them and their name became associated with terror and destruction.

They built their empire through powerful military rule and defence systems. In time of war the army was recruited from the general population, but when Tiglath-Pileser III (745–727BC) came to the throne he embarked on a series of conquests. Temporary recruitment was no longer sufficient, so he enlisted a permanent army formed around an élite 'royal guard'.

When a new territory was conquered, garrisons were established in the new area. If the conquered people submitted to Assyrian rule, then they lived at peace with their conquerors, even receiving Assyrian help if they were attacked. However, a refusal to pay tribute, or persistent rebellion against their new rulers, led to reprisals. A portion of the population would be systematically deported and foreigners imported. This system of exile was used only as a last resort. It was this refusal to pay tribute, mixed with rebellion, that eventually led to the fall of Samaria and the deportation of its people in 722BC (2 Kings 17:5, 6).

The Assyrian army was ruthless and effective. Its cruelty included burning cities, burning children, impaling victims on stakes, beheading and chopping off hands. The army was organised in units of tens, hundreds and thousands. There were regional and national formations, each with specialised functions in weapons and tactics. Most of their offensive weapons were made of hand-forged iron which, with bronze, was also used to reinforce helmets, shields, leather tunics and the high leather boots worn by cavalry and infantry. The Assyrian foot soldier wore a cone-shaped helmet and a breastplate over an embroidered robe. The heavy infantry was made up of spearmen carrying a two-bladed lance, sword and metal shield, and archers protected by wicker, arrow-deflecting shields. The light infantry also included spearmen and archers, but these did not wear breastplates. For increased mobility and lightness they wore only turbans, loin-cloths and sandals.

The smallest fighting unit in the Assyrian army was a two-man team: an archer and a spearman with a shield, and these were grouped in larger units of ten pairs. The spearman knelt on one knee, protecting himself and his archer with the shield. They moved forward and back as the battle progressed.

The total field strength, with allies, could be as many as 200,000. Not all

Assyrian kings commanded their armies in person; a senior general could assume supreme field command (2 Kings 18:17).

Assyrian soldiers carrying two types of shield.

King Tiglath-Pileser III of Assyria in his chariot, from an Assyrian relief.

174

Assyrian tactics

Not only were the Assyrians excellent in pitched battle, but they were also masters of siege warfare. Having driven the enemy from the field into the enemy city, the Assyrians simply changed tactics. Their siege tactics consisted of four basic aims: first, isolate the city from all external aid (military help, food and water). Second, prepare the area close to a part of the wall selected for ramming, which might mean flattening the earth and building a mound. Water or trenches around the city were crossed by building pontoon bridges, causeways or ramps to get the siege-engines as close as possible to the top of the wall. Third, penetrate the wall. Finally, suppress the enemy with constant arrow-fire from the

archers on the siege-engines and on the ground. Other siege tactics against a city included tunnelling, weakening the foundations of the city walls, and burning the gates and doors in the walls.

Once the rammers had done their job, detachments, first of cavalry, then of infantry, poured in under cover of a hail of arrows from the massed archers.

In the field the light, fast, two-wheeled chariots used to charge massed together, and this was one of the most feared of Assyrian tactics. The Assyrians were the first to make systematic use of cavalry. The rider was an archer and the Assyrians were the first to combine the speed of the horse and the long-range fire-power of

the composite bow. Their vital role was to support the foot soldier, but they were used in reconnaissance, pursuit of a beaten enemy, and hit-and-run attacks.

Although the Assyrian army was skilled in many tactics on various kinds of terrain and changed the history of warfare by their skill and ingenuity, it was their military excess which led to their downfall. Vast areas of land had to be governed, and continual mobilisation gradually exhausted the Assyrian army until eventually, in 612BC, a combined force of Medes and Babylonians destroyed the Assyrians, who were never to rise again.

An Assyrian relief from Nineveh showing the deportation of prisoners after a successful campaign.

The Roman army

The Roman Republic was founded in 510BC and the earliest Roman armies were no more than able-bodied spearmen who turned out in times of national emergency. The soldiers were led into battle by a pair of elected consuls, each man providing his own equipment and weapons. The Roman army continued to develop throughout the fourth century BC.

Ranks

The troops were divided into three types: the **hastati,** the youngest troops, were in the front line; the second line, the **principes,** was the main infantry force, and both lines of men carried javelins. The third line, the **triarii,** consisted of the veterans with thrusting-spears.

The troops were massed in legions of 5,000 men, each legion having 300 cavalry in support. Further fighting in difficult terrain led to the creation of a new and important sub-division of the legion – the

maniple – a company of about 200 men that enabled the legion to operate without losing cohesion. The structure of the early Republican legions was made up of three ranks. The *hastati* had ten companies, or *maniples,* of 120–150 men in each; the *principes* also had ten *maniples* of 120–150 men in each; the *triarii* had ten maniples, but only 60 men in each. Ten squadrons, or **tumae,** of cavalry with 30 horsemen, and skirmishers, or **velites,** completed the legionary troops.

Caius Marius reorganised the Roman army in about 107BC. Any that wished could now join the army; weapons and equipment were provided. The short Spanish stabbing sword became standard equipment and all legionaries carried one light and one heavy **pila,** or javelin. Amongst other changes the legion was strengthened to 6,000 men, composed of ten cohorts each of three maniples. At this time, we find the introduction of auxiliary regiments, composed of non-Romans that spoke their own languages, officered by their own countrymen, and which used the type of weapons with which they had been traditionally trained.

The imperial legion was founded by Augustus and during the first century AD the basic structure of the Roman legion remained unchanged, except that the first cohort was increased from about 480 men, organised in six centuries, to 800 in five centuries. The legion had about 120 cavalry. The legion was commanded by a legate, assisted by six tribunes. The senior centurion commanded the first century of the first cohort. Each century was commanded by a centurion and had its own trumpeter, orderly and standard bearer. The legions were recruited only from Roman citizens and were used for offensive actions, quelling revolts and protecting against invasions. Frontier patrol and garrison work were left to locally recruited auxiliary regiments. These regiments played a vital role in the Roman army and some were given special names (Acts 10:1; 27:1). The regiments were composed of 1,000 men. Each regiment was divided into ten centuries and each century commanded by a centurion.

In New Testament times, there were about 25 legions in existence and out of these, two to four legions were always stationed in Palestine. Pontius Pilate was not a legate, but a prefect, appointed by Emperor Tiberius.

Weapons

The Roman soldier carried three weapons:

The dagger was about 23cm long and might be decorated by the soldier – so, too, the scabbard in which it was carried. It was used for many other purposes than military ones, as a cutting tool.

The sword was two-edged, about 60cm long and was carried in a sheath attached to a shoulder-strap and girdle around the waist.

The javelin was about 210cm long. It had an iron head about 90cm long and it came to a sharp, pyramid-shaped point. It was barbed, to prevent it from falling out of an enemy's shield. The javelin was thrown before hand-to-hand combat began.

There were three types of field weapon:

The catapult hurled small javelins, either singly or, with some catapults, many at the same time. The javelins could be lit with burning tar.

The Ballista hurled heavy stones of up to 300kg and as far as 730 metres.

The Onager hurled lighter stones (about 25kg) and as far as 400 metres.

For defence, the Roman soldier had a shield, helmet and light armour:

The shield was rectangular. It was made of several thin layers of wood glued together and bent into a slight curve. The edges had bronze, or wrought iron,

A Roman army assault on a city. Background: two groups of legionaries in tortoise formation advance under cover of their shields. Left: two soldiers operate a ballista to hurl stones at the walls. Centre: a catapult for hurling javelins is prepared. Right: a centurion gives orders to his men.

Tactics

The Phalanx

This was a huge, rectangular formation of men. It numbered 4,096 men, with sixteen ranks and 256 men in each rank. The advantage of the Phalanx was its irresistible force, but it lacked flexibility. Any instability in the front line, or accident when crossing rough ground could throw it out of order.

The Legion

This developed out of the need to find ease of mobility and manoeuvrability in difficult terrain. The Legion was less powerful than the Phalanx, but it gave the flexibility required. Battle formations could be taken up and altered with the small units, which had rapid and independent movement. For example, the second rank could move up to the first rank and form a solid wall, or single maniples could be deployed to the sides and skirt round the enemy. The maniples could be moved like the pawns on a chess board.

In the field

The attack began with throwing a barrage of javelins. This was the signal for the first infantry wave to charge. If victorious, they moved forward, followed at intervals by the other two lines. If forced to retreat, they fell back to the second line through the spaces provided, while the second line took up the front line of combat. Throughout, the third line knelt, with one knee on the ground, each man holding his shield against the shoulder and his spear tilting forward. Behind this defensive wall, units reassembled and prepared to fight again.

The siege

Around the besieged city, the Roman army placed two circles of entrenchments, just out of range of the enemy's artillery. The inner circle of camps faced the city and the second circle faced away from the besieged city to defend the besiegers from possible attack from the rear by forces coming to aid the city. Between these circles of camps were further encampments that could hold an entire army, if necessary. The city would be bombarded by the Roman catapults in attempts to weaken the wall and weary the enemy.

When the final attack of the city was considered favourable, the Roman army rushed to scale the walls with ladders, or from rolling towers laden with men and pushed up to the wall. The bottom of the ramparts was breached or attacks were made through previously dug tunnels. The defenders threw down rocks, beams, or poured nearly red-hot sand or boiling water. Battering rams were used, some rams being up to thirty metres long and worked by 200 men.

The organisation of a 1st century Roman legion

The legion was commanded by a legate appointed by the emperor. He was assisted by six tribunes. The legion consisted of ten cohorts (divisions) each of which was divided into six centuries. Each century was under the command of a centurion and his deputy. Each century had its own trumpeter, standard bearer and password bearer. The latter was responsible for inventing a daily password as part of the security for the century. The cavalry division was used for scouting and despatch.

Centurion
Optio (second-in-command)
Cornicen (trumpeter)
Signifer (standard bearer)
Tesserarius (password bearer)

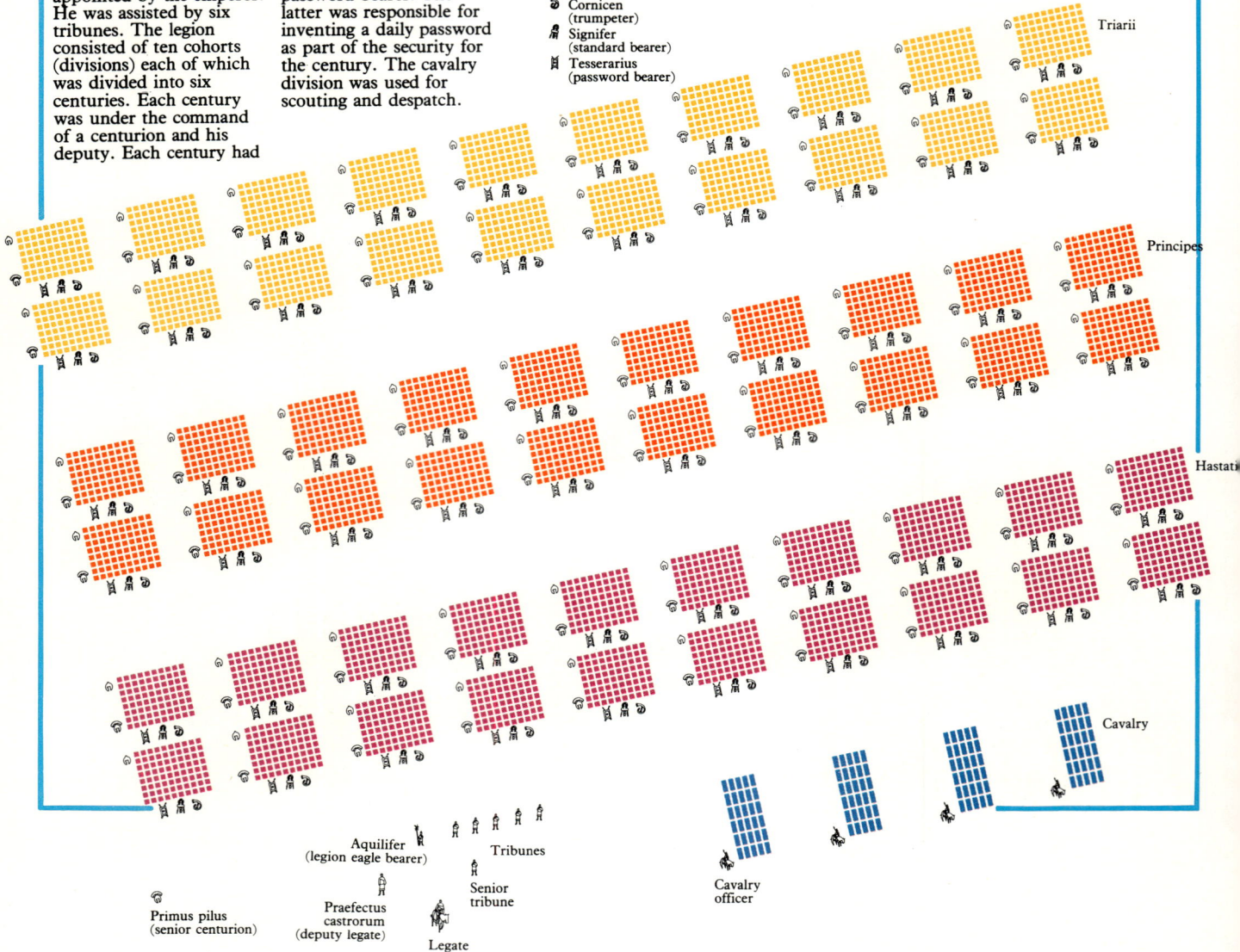

Triarii

Principes

Hastati

Cavalry

Aquilifer (legion eagle bearer)

Tribunes

Senior tribune

Cavalry officer

Primus pilus (senior centurion)

Praefectus castrorum (deputy legate)

Legate

A detail from Trajan's Column, depicting the emperor's Dacian campaign, shows Roman armour of the 1st century AD.

OTHER NATIONS

PERSIANS

The Persian empire spread south as far as Egypt and east to the Indus valley under its most famous kings Cyrus and Darius. The Persian archer and spearman (below) was part of a frieze of glazed tiles representing the Royal Guard from the Palace of Darius at Susa.

GREEKS

Wars were frequent between the Greek city-states. The hoplites, foot-soldiers, were the most powerful part of the army. They fought in close formation so that each man was protected by his own shield and that of his neighbour.

A mounted Greek warrior. This bronze statue dates from 550BC.

A Greek war helmet decorating a vase.

Greek warriors arming, from a 5th century BC painting on a drinking cup. The warrior on the left fits a greave to his leg. The next clasps a cuirass round his body, the next fits on his sword and the last two attend to their helmet and pigtail.

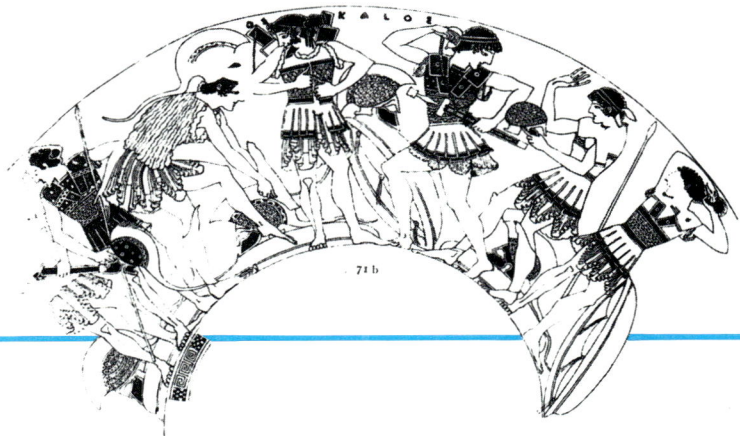

attached. Leather decorated the face. Each shield had the names of the soldier and his centurion on it.

The bronze helmet had an inner plate of iron. The back of the neck was protected by an extension of the helmet, while a ridge in the front helped to shield the face. Hinged cheek-flaps hung at the sides, and the top of the helmet held a plume. This was decorative, but helped for recognition in battle.

The cuirass was a form of armour protecting the upper part of the body. It was a sleeveless, leather jacket with metal strips sewn on. It could also be made of two pieces of metal, front and back, held on with buckles.

Only officers and high-ranking men wore leg armour called greaves. A linen undergarment and a short-sleeved woollen tunic were worn for clothes. The Roman sandal looked like a boot. It was made of several thicknesses of leather for the soles and was studded with shoe nails. Leather thongs were wrapped around and up the leg, to the shins, and tied to keep the shoe on.

The results of war

The results of war were cruel. We find that the Assyrians totally destroyed everything and this was true of many of the wars recorded in the Bible. From the time of the Judges through to the Maccabees we find towns burnt, walls torn down, animals and people killed (Judg. 9:45). Before a town, or camp, was totally destroyed it was stripped of all valuables. So, too, were dead bodies (2 Kings 7:16). No mercy could be expected.

Israel often appeared merciful when compared with other nations (1 Kings 20:31; 2 Kings 6:22). When people were spared, they could be used as forced labour, slaves, or pay tribute. The Assyrians and Babylonians deported whole populations (2 Kings 24:14, 15).

A relief on the Arch of Titus, Rome. Carrying off the Temple treasures after the sacking of Jerusalem in AD70.

TRAVEL AND COMMUNICATION

In the earliest times men travelled on foot or rode on donkeys. Travel was an important part of their way of life. Shepherds travelled from place to place with their flocks to find water. Palestine and the surrounding areas are very dry, and water has always been precious there. Even today the Eastern shepherd follows very old paths. In Palestine he leads his sheep and goats, and pitches his black tents near some of the same wells and springs that Abraham knew nearly four thousand years ago.

More than five thousand years before Abraham's time men had begun to build cities. City life brought many changes. Trade and war became more organised, and this led to improvements in travel.

Some of the first cities were in Mesopotamia (modern Iraq), the land of the great rivers Tigris and Euphrates. There the wheel was used, and the first carts and wagons appeared, drawn by oxen or asses. At first they were small but very heavy, because the four wheels were solid discs of wood. It was hundreds of years later before they were made lighter and faster.

A man on foot or an animal could use any rough path, but the new wheeled carts needed roads. The first roads made travel and trade between cities quicker and easier.

Shepherds travel with their flocks on the Jericho Road to find new pastures.

Animal transport

Abraham's life was largely one of travel. His family came from Ur, one of the great civilised cities of Mesopotamia. But God called him to go to a country where he possessed no land. He moved from place to place in the land which God promised to give to his descendants. He became rich in flocks and animals, but never found a

The camel is particularly useful for travel in desert areas because it can go for days without water.

settled home. We read in the book of Genesis of his travels in the promised land of Palestine, and we can learn how he and his people travelled. Probably most of their journeys were made on foot or riding donkeys. Yet Abraham's servant took camels on his journey to find a wife for

Isaac, and later Joseph provided wagons for his aged father Jacob to bring all his possessions to Egypt.

The camel is an important animal in our story. It was domesticated by desert people from around 2000BC, but was not widely used until several centuries later. It can stay alive many days without water and can carry heavy burdens. It was the only animal on which men could cross deserts. Desert peoples like the Midianites and Amalekites used it for trade and even for war. Joseph was sold by his brothers to Midianite traders who took him to Egypt with their camel caravan.

The horse was another important animal. It was first used for war because it was very strong and fast, and could pull a light cart from which a nobleman could fight. In fact these carts were the first chariots. But the horse was a valuable animal which only the rich could afford. The donkey was still the poor man's beast. Only a few people used the horse for riding: it was at first mainly used for pulling chariots.

Far right: a Greek relief showing a horse-drawn chariot.

Below: the donkey is still used for transporting farm produce.

Right: a wooden-wheeled wagon pulled by asses, shown on the Standard of Ur from Mesopotamia. The function of this box, made of shell, lapis lazuli and bitumen is a mystery.

Israelite trade routes

When the Israelites escaped from slavery in Egypt they lived as semi-nomads until they finally came into the promised land. There they found peoples who appeared to be stronger than themselves. Under Joshua the Israelites conquered a number of Canaanite kings and occupied the rough hill country, but they did not win the richer valleys and coastal plains. The great trade-route which brought wealth into Palestine ran north from Egypt along the Mediterranean sea-shore and the whole way along the flat coastlands, the country of the Philistines. When it reached Galilee in the north, one branch of the route went inland over lower ground towards the great city of Damascus in Syria and eastward to distant Mesopotamia. Another great route, the 'King's Highway' ran north to south over the plateau east of the River Jordan.

Travel developed faster in the great empires and the easy routes between them than in the more remote hill country where the Israelites lived. While Joshua was their leader they had faith in God and even defeated the powerful king Jabin, who had a great army of horses and chariots in the northern lowlands (Joshua 11). Again, later, God gave a great victory over the general Sisera, whose chariots were destroyed by a flooding river (Judges 4–5). But usually they had to fight to hold their hills, and did not reach out to the trade routes and to the sea.

In the hill-country the roads were probably little more than rocky paths. Even the great routes would have seemed very poor roads to us; mostly dirt tracks, where carts could pass only with difficulty. They were sometimes paved at the approach to a city gate.

The modern road to Damascus follows one of the great trade routes of ancient times.

International trade routes were determined by the geography of the land. The map shows the strategic position Israel held in the ancient world.

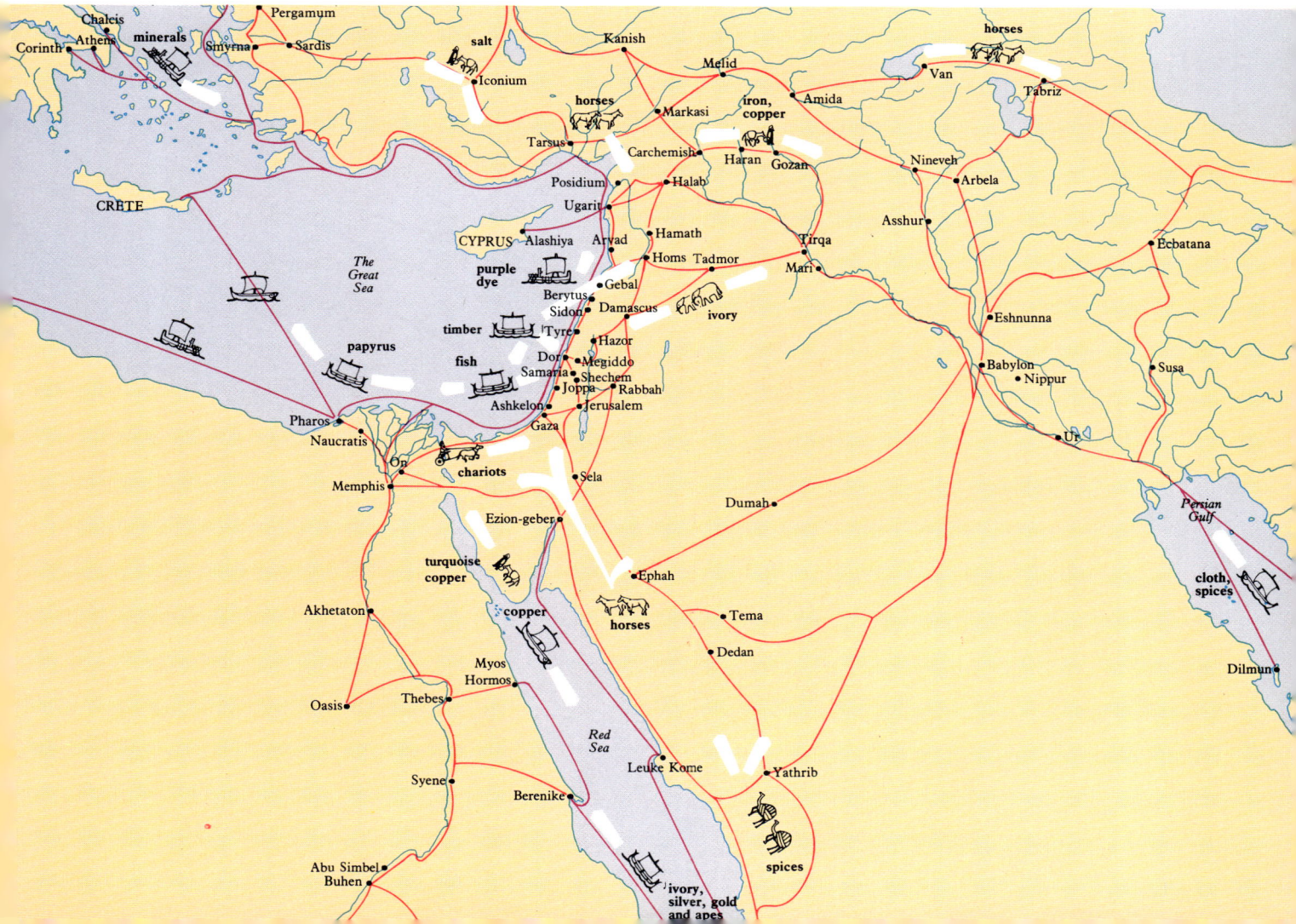

Trade language

Ancient travel was always dangerous, and there were many robbers. The kings tried, when they could, to organize the roads better, for travel was important for the safety of their kingdoms. They sent messengers with official government dispatches, which had to be kept safe. Sometimes they provided rough inns where the messengers could get food and rest and fresh animals for the next stage of their journey.

Private traders used these same roads. Often they must have covered great distances and have done business with people of different languages. This was possible because they had reckoning counters, and writing had been developed. As time went on they agreed on a common language for trade. In fact most of the peoples around Syria and Palestine spoke languages rather like the Hebrew of the Israelites, and one of these languages, Aramaic, became the common trade language of the Near East.

There was never any private postal service; only messengers on official business. If a private citizen wanted to send a letter, he had to find a traveller who would take it. And except on the few main routes there were no inns. The private traveller relied on the custom of the East, where the stranger is received as a guest and given lodging even in the poorest village.

An 8th century BC clay tablet delivery note. The inscription reads, 'gold from Ophir to Beth Horon – 30 shekels'.

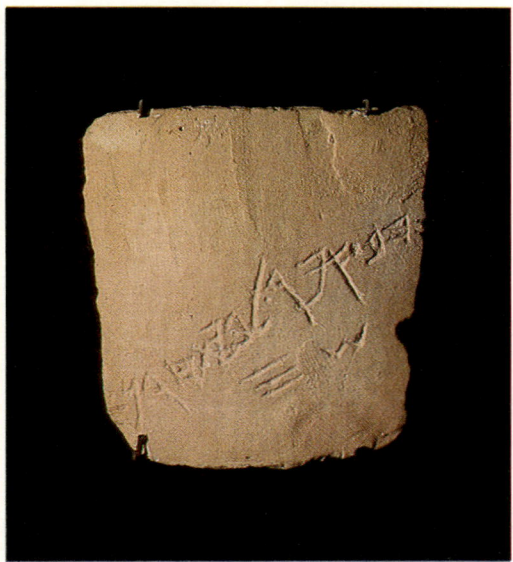

A wall painting showing a 15th century BC Egyptian expedition to the African land of Punt to fetch incense trees, which can be seen being carried on board a cargo ship.

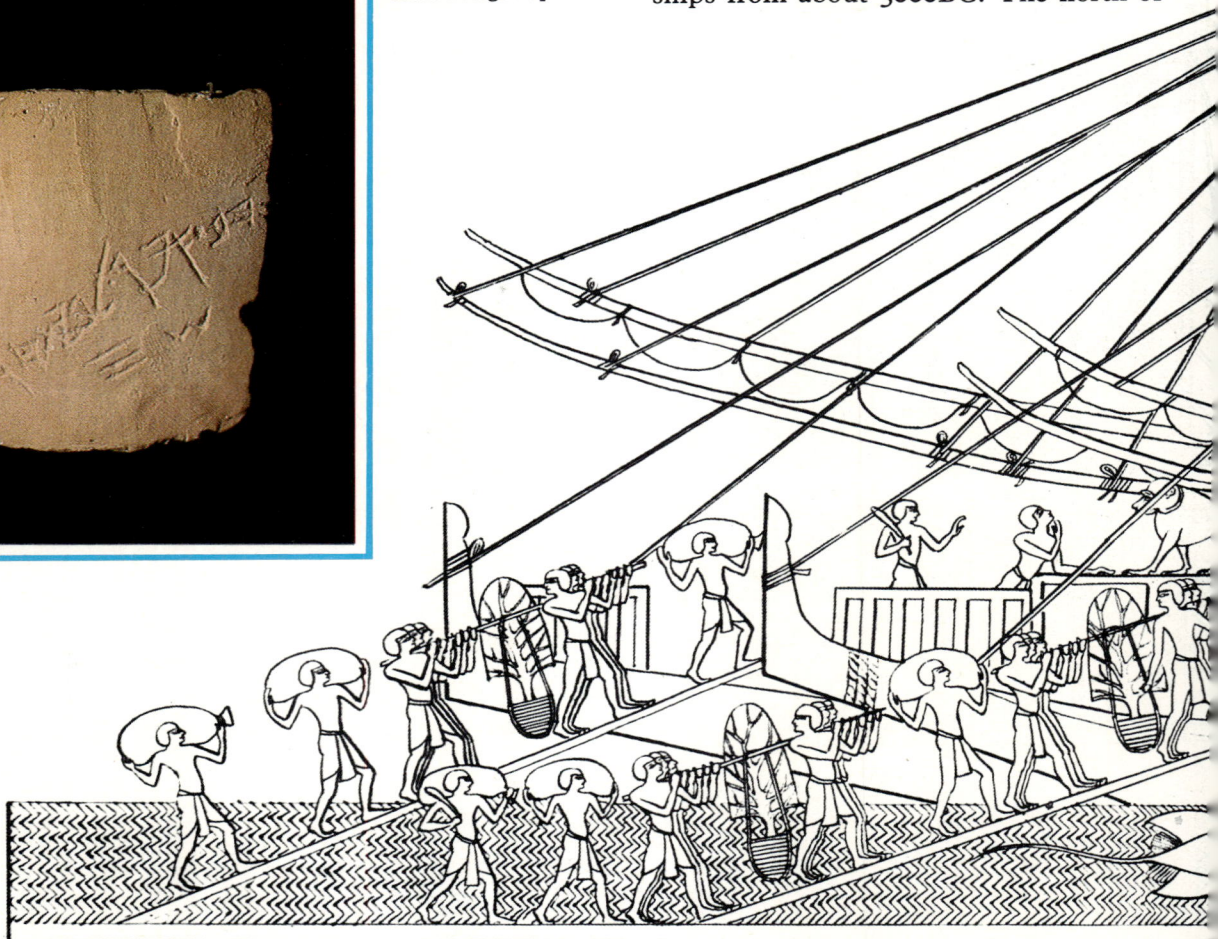

Ships

The Egyptians

There was also travel by water from very early times, as much as six thousand years ago. The first boats were probably made in Egypt. In ancient times, Egypt was a thin strip of rich land along the narrow valley of the great River Nile, between huge deserts. The Nile rises in flood every year, and the low ground was under water until the time for sowing the next season's crops. The towns had to be built on higher places in the valley. Roads would not have been much use in the flooded plain. So the Egyptians learned to sail both up and down the river with the help of the wind, which usually blew north-west and helped them upstream, and the current which helped them downstream.

The Egyptians also built sea-going ships from about 3000BC. The north or north-west winds blow nearly all summer in the Eastern Mediterranean. Sailors could rely on these winds and use them. In winter the weather is changeable and stormy, and very dangerous for sailing ships, so the seas were closed to shipping during the winter. Yet in summer bold voyages were made. The winds made it easier and safer to sail to the east than to the west. Even in modern times a sailing boat might reach Egypt from Italy in a few days, but take weeks to return, creeping from shelter to shelter against north-west winds.

Mesopotamia did not have such helpful winds, and its great rivers were less useful for shipping. Goods were sometimes floated long distances downstream on large rafts.

The Phoenicians

The Phoenicians, who lived on the coast north of Palestine (modern Lebanon) were skilful sailors. They explored and colonised many parts of the Mediterranean in the centuries after 1000BC, braving the dangers of sailing westward. They even made voyages out into the open Atlantic in search of tin, at that time a very important metal for mixing with copper to make bronze for tools and weapons. They found a rich supply of tin in the distant land of Cornwall, at the end of the known world.

They also explored in other directions. The Greek writer Herodotus tells a remarkable story of their boldness in exploring the coast of Africa, about 600BC. Phoenician ships were sent out by the king of Egypt with orders to sail all round Africa. They sailed away down the

A long distance Phoenician ship of 700BC known as a *hippos* (Greek for horse). The prow is shaped like a horse's head and the stern like a fish-tail.

A Roman trade vessel of the 2nd century BC being loaded with grain from Rome. From a tomb painting at Ostia.

Right: a reconstruction of an ancient map showing the world at the time of Herodotus, around 500BC.

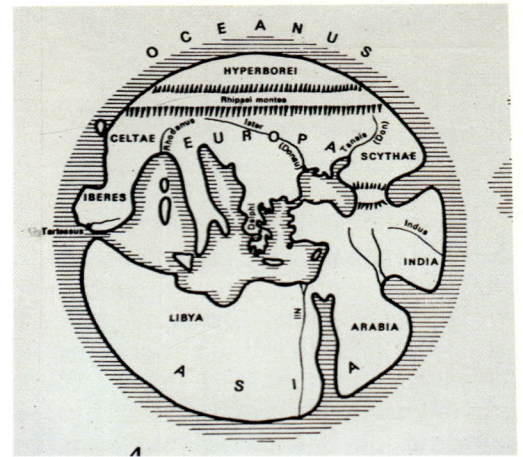

The Samos Straits in the Aegean Sea. The Greeks travelled more by sea than by land.

Red Sea, and three years later they came back to Egypt from the west, along the Mediterranean coast. They had sailed all the way round, stopping on land each year to sow crops and harvest them for food. But they said one thing which Herodotus could not believe: that they had seen the sun cross the sky on the wrong side, to the north. Today we can understand that this must have been perfectly true, for they went south of the equator. When such great discoveries were first being made, there was much which seemed strange, and it was hard to know truth from error.

The Israelites

They differed from their Phoenician neighbours, for they rarely went to sea. Even when the kingdom of David reached as far as the coast they had little interest in it. The straight coastline of Palestine is exposed to the force of the summer winds and has no safe natural harbours. But David and Solomon made alliance with

Hiram, the king of the great Phoenician sea-port of Tyre. Under Solomon (about 970–930BC) Israel became a large kingdom itself: the king built a fleet, and traded with distant parts of Africa and Asia. We read that he had 'ships of Tarshish', which were great sea-going ships like those of the Phoenicians (1 Kings 10:22). Yet using ships is not always a safe and easy way to travel and there is one story in the Old Testament which pictures the perils and terrors of a storm at sea: the story of Jonah, who was thrown overboard by the terrified sailors (Jonah 1).

The Greeks

The Greeks were another remarkable travelling nation. Greece is a hard, rocky land, and there was not enough fertile soil to support its growing population. There were so many mountains that the country became split up into small city-states, which were often at war with each other. The roads between them were bad. Even the few cart-roads were often no more than two lines of ruts cut in the earth or rock, like rails for the wheels.

It was actually easier to travel by sea than by land. There were many mountainous headlands and islands to give shelter from the northerly winds. In fact the islands of the Aegean Sea between Greece and Asia Minor (modern Turkey) provided a way to sail from shelter to shelter from west to east, between Europe and Asia. Many Greeks left their crowded land for new homes overseas, building cities like those they had left in many parts of the Mediterranean. They even moved westward when the Phoenician power grew less. But the Greek colonies in the east were the most important.

Roman sea power

The Romans did much more for travel than build roads. Augustus cleared the seas of pirates, making sea voyages safer than ever before. One army and navy was organised to keep peace throughout the Mediterranean world. This was only possible now that all these lands were under one government, inside secure frontiers. The same currency was used everywhere, and the two languages of the empire, Greek in the east and Latin in the west, were understood nearly everywhere. Now the traveller could cover great distances by land and sea together, following a well-built road to an important seaport, and then crossing the sea to the next port from which another road continued the journey. So a man could travel from Rome to the East by sea, or overland, making short voyages to cross the Adriatic Sea and from Europe to the coast of Asia Minor. Land travel was sometimes tedious, but was safe at all seasons on the excellent roads.

The sea was dangerous in winter, and no ships sailed then unless their business was very urgent. In summer sea travel was faster, especially if the weather was good and the winds favourable. Most of the ships used were not in fact very fast; they were large, heavy merchant vessels. Warships were faster, and used banks of oars for speed, but they were not for ordinary travellers. Even so, it seemed wonderful at the time that ships could sail so safely, and even from east to west. It was possible to get from Rome to Alexandria in ten days; though it sometimes took as long as two months to return against the wind. Many more people travelled than ever before, and for new reasons. They went for study or on health cruises or just on holiday. Rich Romans had country houses by the sea or in the mountains, and often visited them.

Harbours

The Romans also greatly improved harbours. In Paul's time the Emperor Claudius built a great new seaport for Rome at Ostia. There were artificial harbours, made by building great breakwaters or hollowing out basins to give shelter at key places on exposed coasts, such as at Caesarea in Palestine and Troas in Asia Minor. At Ephesus there were great engineering works to keep open a harbour that was slowly choking with mud.

These seaports were all very busy places. There were no fixed sailing times, for the ships had to wait for the right wind and weather. The traveller had to find a ship and book his passage with a captain who would agree to take him. No special arrangements were made for passengers, however, only for cargo; the passenger usually had to bring his own stores of food.

The Roman harbour at Caesarea in Palestine.

Roads

The Persians

Before Alexander conquered the East, the great power there in the 6th to 4th centuries BC was that of Persia. The Persians built an empire which stretched from the heart of Asia to the Greek cities of the Aegean coast. Improved travel was very important for the government of such a huge kingdom. The Persian kings organised a better road system. There was the famous 'Royal Road' from the great city of Sardis near the west coast of Asia Minor to the Persian capital of Susa – a distance of 1,600 miles. It was so good that a traveller could cover the distance in three months. But more than that, the Persians organised posting stations for official business, placing fresh horses and messengers at distances of a day's journey all along the road, so that important messages were handed from messenger to messenger all along the line. Herodotus, the first great Greek travel writer, tells us this system was the fastest thing on earth and went in all weather, even rain and snow, over wild and mountainous country. It was so fast that a message could travel from Sardis to Susa in three weeks. That does not seem so fast today.

The Greeks

The state of the world changed greatly in the last few hundred years before Jesus was born. The Persian empire fell to Alexander the Great, and after Alexander's early death his empire was broken up among several Greek kings. Greek became the language of the civilised world. There was much more trade and travel, and links between Europe and Asia became more important.

There were also wars between the kings, and Palestine became a battle-ground, conquered and reconquered. Many Jews, who were good traders,

became settlers in important cities on the main trade routes all over the Eastern Mediterranean. This scattering of Jews had begun when many of them were taken into captivity in Babylonia in 597BC and in 587BC when Jerusalem was destroyed. Now hundreds of thousands of them made their homes in places like Alexandria in Egypt. These scattered people still looked to Jerusalem as their religious centre, and they often travelled great distances to go to Jerusalem for festivals like the Passover. But as they mixed with other nations in their new homes, many of them came to speak Greek instead of Hebrew, their old religious language, and Aramaic, the everyday language of Palestine.

The spread of the Greeks prepared the way for things that happened hundreds of years later. When the conqueror Alexander the Great (336–323BC) won a huge empire in Asia, he spread the Greek lan-

A statue of Alexander the Great on horseback. His conquests spread the Greek language and culture across Europe, Egypt and Asia.

guage and culture there, and Greek became a common, international language before the time of Jesus. In the second century before Christ the Old Testament was translated from Hebrew into Greek at Alexandria in Egypt, where so many tens of thousands of Jews had settled. This was one of many things which prepared the way for the coming of Jesus. The New Testament was written in Greek, and its message was spread through the known world by roads and communications far better than any that had existed previously.

The Romans

When Jesus was born a new empire had arisen, and ruled what had come to be regarded as the whole known world. The Romans had spread out from their city in central Italy to conquer all the lands around the Mediterranean, from Portugal and, later, Britain in the west to Syria and Arabia in the east. They were superb engineers, and made excellent paved roads on which their armies marched. But in the century before Christ there were bitter civil wars, desperate struggles for power between rival Roman leaders, the most famous of whom was Julius Caesar.

The many nations of the Roman world suffered much from these troubled times. Part of the trouble was that the Romans had tried to rule their huge lands in the same way that they governed a small town. Better leadership was needed and it came with Augustus Caesar, the great-nephew of Julius Caesar, who was the first Roman emperor (27BC–14AD). Augustus was emperor when Jesus was born at Bethlehem and he finally ended the civil wars and brought peace to the whole Mediterranean world. This 'Roman peace' or 'Augustan peace' brought great benefits, some of which lasted for hundreds of years.

One of its greatest successes was in the improvement of communication. Never since then has this huge area of Europe and Asia been united under one government. The new safety of travel seemed like a miracle, for which men were very grateful to Augustus. His work made it possible for men like Paul to carry the Christian message hundreds of miles by land and

Construction of a Roman road, showing the four levels of sand, slabs of stone in cement, crushed stone in cement and, on top, stone blocks. There is a drainage ditch on either side. Left: the Via Sacra in the Forum in Rome is a typical Roman paved road.

A Roman horse-drawn carriage with passengers inside and on top.

sea. It was easier to travel then than at any later stage of history, until the era of modern inventions like steam in place of sail.

The Roman roads are famous. They were very carefully planned, and ran straight for great distances wherever possible, though sometimes in mountainous countries it was necessary to have many bends. They were built on dry foundations, were smoothly paved and well drained, so that they could be used in all weathers. It is remarkable that many modern roads in England still follow the lines of Roman roads.

We get some picture of what travel was like in Roman times from surviving accounts of journeys. Rich people with time to spare could afford to travel in surprising comfort, going safely by road, with their slaves to organise their heavy luggage, their transport and lodging. It was usually necessary to hire vehicles outside the city gate. There were carriages and wagons of many sizes and kinds, to suit the need and pocket of the traveller. Some people were even carried in litters by strong slaves, but the poorest had to walk. The roads were slower, but safer, than the sea.

Inns

If the traveller had friends living on the route, he would probably arrange to stay overnight with them. Otherwise he would go to an inn. The Romans built official inns at regular intervals of a day's journey, with smaller hostels between for slower travellers. These inns were really meant for official use by the imperial post, but they were open equally to private citizens. There were even road-maps showing distances and services available at the various stopping-places.

The typical roadside inn was an oblong

building, with stables, kitchen and dining-room on the ground level, and bedrooms on an upper floor which was built of wood. There would be a courtyard at the side, and a smithy and repair workshop. But there were many other kinds of inns, some very small and poor. In the East there were inns of an old type, a hollow square of building round a central courtyard for the animals. In cities there was a great variety of hostels, restaurants, and even snack-bars, but these places had a bad name, and the visitor who wished to stay more than a day or two hired a private lodging, as Paul did in Rome (Acts 28:30).

We are told little of Paul's manner of travel by land. He probably often went by carriage or wagon with his companions, but probably also knew all the hardships of poverty. The love of the early church was shown in hospitality: the Christian traveller found a welcome among other believers in many towns along the great roads.

A scene outside an inn in Pompeii.

Part of a letter on papyrus from 2000 BC. The letter is from an army commander complaining about a shortfall in provisions for his household.

Spreading the gospel

The early church had good news to tell of Jesus, and we shall see how better travel and communication helped in the task.

Letters

One very important method of communication was the writing of letters. Of course letters had been written for centuries before this, but most of them were official messages, and we know very few private letters. As we come nearer to the time of Jesus, however, thousands of letters are still in existence. Nearly all of them have been found in Egypt. The reason for this is interesting. The kind of paper normally used in the ancient world was made from a sort of reed called papyrus, which grew along the banks of the river Nile in Egypt. So most of the paper was made in Egypt. As trade increased, it was exported to other lands also, but it was naturally much commoner and cheaper in Egypt than anywhere else.

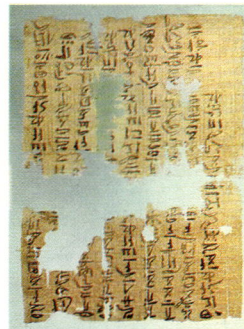

Egypt had another advantage . . . its climate is very dry. As a result, while the papyrus letters written in other lands have rotted away in the damp air, tens of thousands of scraps of papyrus have survived two thousand years in Egypt. Most of them have been found on ancient rubbish heaps, where they were thrown away. The paper is very thin and fragile, but the ink is often not badly faded, and the writing can be read. Many of them are of little value; bills, receipts, notes and scribblings of all kinds. Yet even these tell us about everyday life. Of course these items were thrown away just because they were not meant to be important for the future. Some of them are very interesting indeed because they tell us about ordinary people. There are school exercises, and private letters of many kinds. There is one from a naughty boy to his father, trying to bully him into taking him on a visit to the big city. All these show that many people could read and write in Greek, and that travel and letter-writing were everyday activities.

When Paul was prevented from visiting the Christians of a city in person he wrote to them. Some of his letters are preserved in our Bible, and so have been treasured over more centuries than he could have guessed. The Romans had no public postal system. There was a superb official post, and rich business firms had regular slave-messengers and organised their own posts, using the excellent roads and inns and vehicles. But by the first century so many people could travel safely that Christians too, even if many of them were poor, moved freely along the great roads and sea-routes, bringing letters and encouragement from place to place. There were probably even some of them who belonged to the emperor's own service, and travelled for him between Rome and the East, bringing with them the news of fellow Christians.

Jesus' travels

By the time of Jesus, Palestine had become a part of the enormous Roman empire. Yet Jesus and his disciples lived the lives of poor country people, and they probably travelled in the traditional way,

A Roman inkpot and pen. The apostle John referred to using pen and ink for his letters (2 John 12).

The spread of Christianity. The inset map shows how the influence of the gospel spread out from Jerusalem into Judea and Samaria as Jesus foretold (Acts 1:8). From there it spread across the Roman empire following Paul's missionary journeys and by the end of the first century AD it covered most of the shaded area on the map.

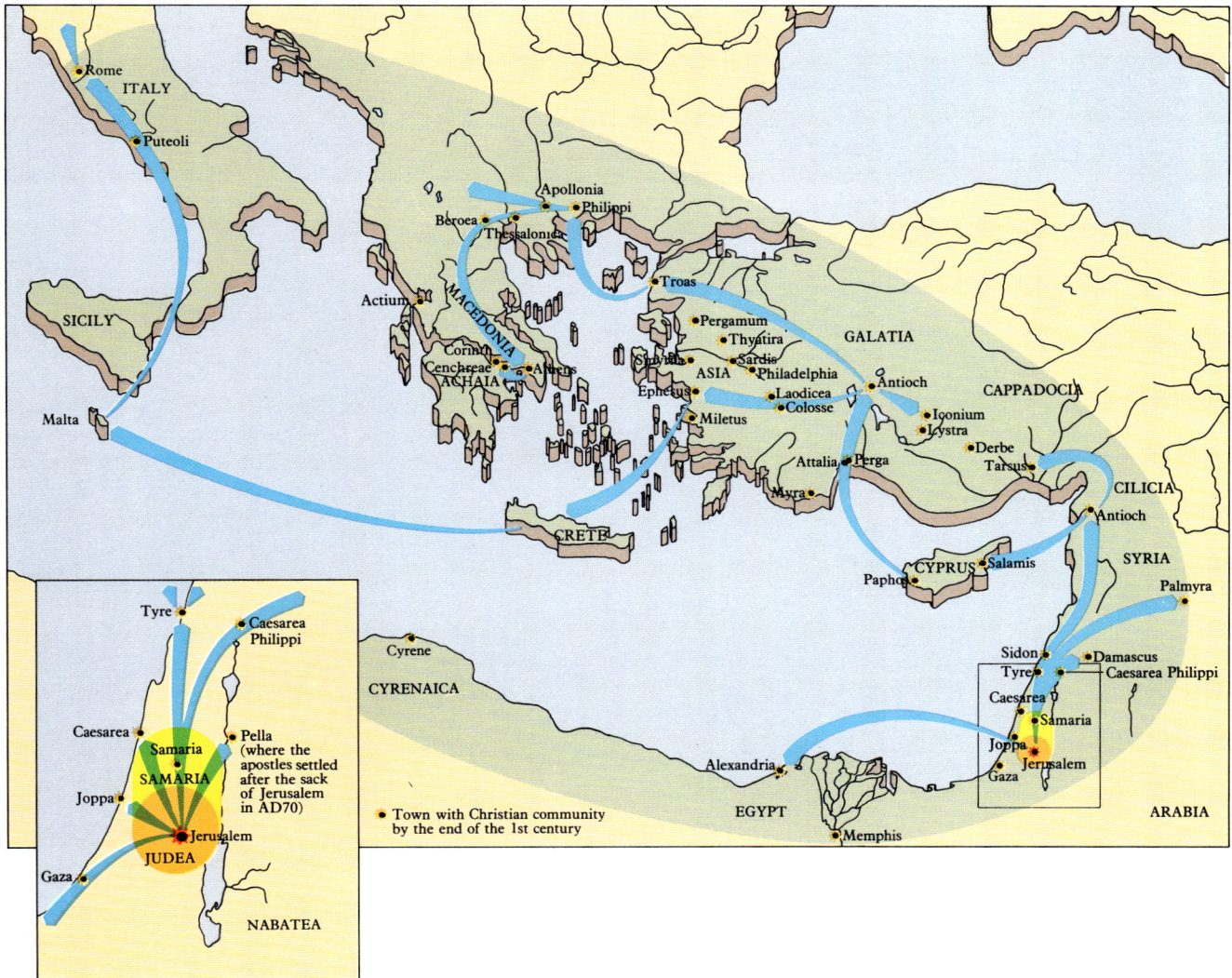

Town with Christian community by the end of the 1st century

Pella (where the apostles settled after the sack of Jerusalem in AD70)

on foot or on donkeys. Although Jesus lived almost all his life in Palestine, he travelled much inside the country. Like other Jews he went up from Galilee to worship in Jerusalem.

Nazareth, where he grew up, was very near the trade routes which crossed Galilee, though the town itself was set in the hills off the road. On one journey between Jerusalem and Galilee, Jesus stopped in the heat of the day by one of the important wells in the dry land, and met there a woman of Samaria. Their conversation is recorded in John 4. He travelled to Jerusalem again at the Passover time, a journey which led to his crucifixion and to his resurrection. At the Passover, and again at Pentecost seven weeks later, the city of Jerusalem was full of Jewish worshippers who had travelled great distances – from countries as far away as Mesopotamia, Asia Minor and Egypt (Acts 2:9–11).

Paul's travels

The book of Acts tells how the good news of Jesus spread. Much of it is a story of travel, an account of how Paul went to many of the most important cities of the Greek world, Athens, Corinth, Ephesus and many more, and finally to Rome. It is a fascinating and exciting story. Paul planned his travels carefully, selecting places where he could stay and teach as many people as possible about Jesus. They were usually great cities at the centre of many routes, or the capital cities of Roman provinces. He went first to the synagogue, the Jewish place of worship. He was seen to be a learned scholar and teacher, and was usually asked to speak to the people who had met for worship.

Right: the town of Nazareth, where Jesus grew up, was near a Galilee trade route.

Far right: a Samaritan village.

The harbour at Neapolis.

Sometimes Paul's careful plans went wrong. This was often because his work made enemies among those who refused to accept what he said, as at Philippi, Thessalonica and Corinth. Sometimes he was arrested or forced to move on before his work was really finished.

We read of one difficult time in Paul's life at the beginning of Acts 16. He planned to go to one place and then another, but was stopped each time. So he found himself in the sea-port of Troas, not quite knowing what to try next. Troas was a place where roads and sea-routes met. Its artificial harbour gave shelter from the northerly winds. It was a place where people often had to wait for a change of wind, and from which they could go direct to many parts of the Roman world. At this time of doubt God called Paul to go to Macedonia, which is a part of northern Greece. We can see it was a very important step to take, for it brought the Christian gospel from Asia to Europe – from its beginning in the East to the West. Paul landed in Europe at Neapolis (modern Kavalla), the sea-port of Philippi. From there a great road, the Egnatian Way, ran westward on its way to Rome itself. Paul may have looked forward even then to going to Rome, the centre of the whole Gentile world.

It was to be another ten years before he got there. He was to face many more sufferings and difficulties in the East before his chance came, and then it happened in a strange way. Meanwhile the work did not depend on one great man. The Christian good news spread through many parts of the Empire which Paul never visited, because many others were

The place where Paul preached in Corinth is marked by an inscription from 2 Corinthians 4:37.

Rome at the time of the emperor Constantine. Some of the buildings, such as the Coliseum, were added after Paul's time.

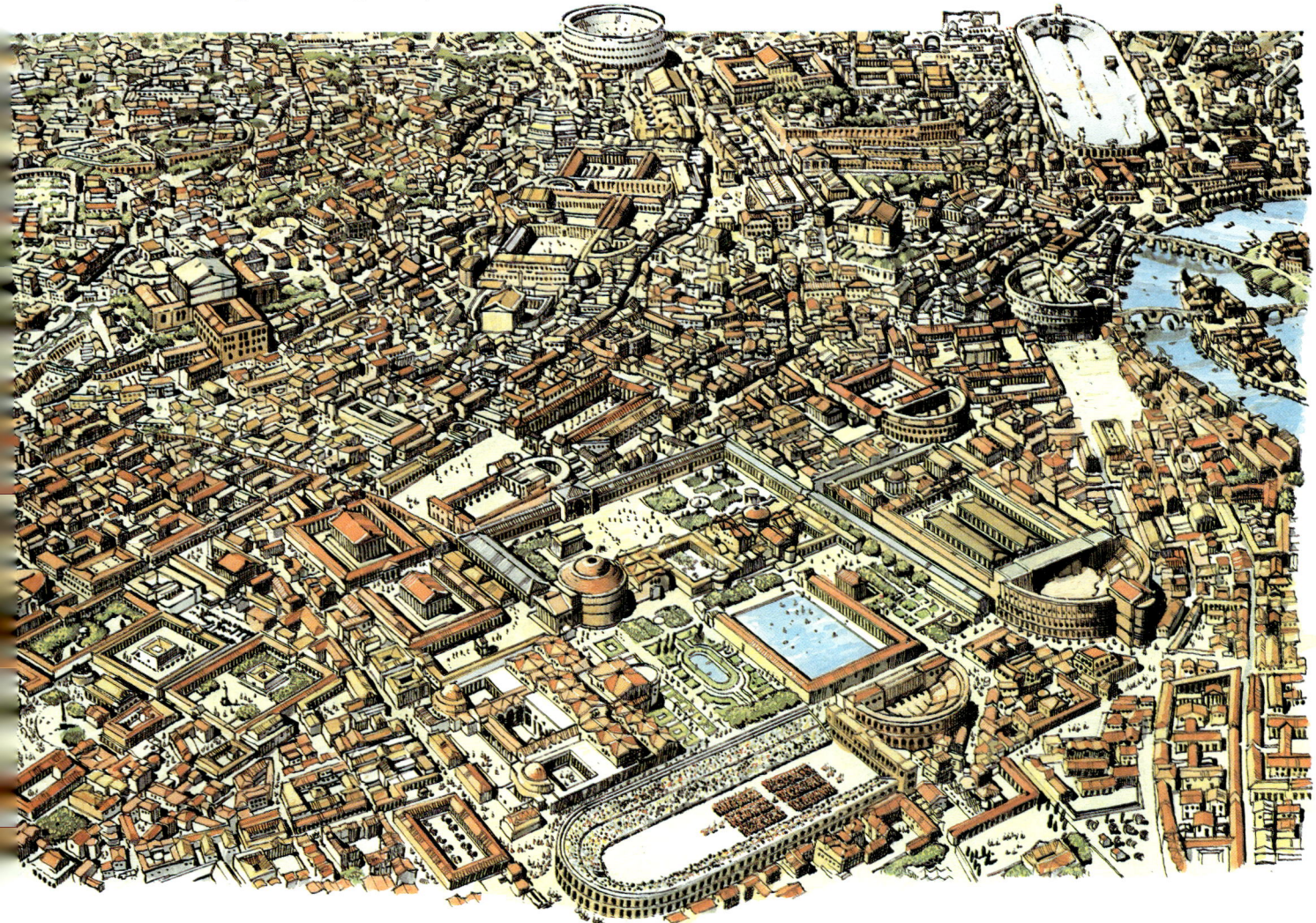

travelling freely and using every opportunity to tell of Jesus.

Paul's last journey was to Rome – as a prisoner on his way to be tried. He was in the charge of a Roman officer Julius, who had official authority to charter a passage for himself and his prisoner. They sailed from Caesarea in Palestine.

At first all went well. The ship coasted along the south shore of Asia Minor with the help of a favouring current. At the port of Myra the party changed ships and boarded one of the corn-ships bound for Italy. It was already late in the summer.

These corn-ships had become famous. They had been organised a few years before by the Emperor Claudius. There were more than a million people to be fed in Rome, and not enough wheat could be grown in Italy. Claudius feared rebellion if there were another famine. So he had corn brought from Egypt by a regular fleet of large merchant-ships based at Alexandria.

When Paul's ship moved away from the shelter of the coast it met strong winds, and it was getting dangerously close to the time of autumn storms. When the ship reached Fair Havens, a small harbour on the south coast of Crete, they knew they would not be able to finish their journey safely before winter. When the weather seemed good for the moment, the captain hoped to take the chance of moving along the coast to a better harbour for the winter. But the wind changed again just when they were out of shelter, and a fierce north-easterly storm swept upon the ship.

They were driven helpless before it. There were hundreds of miles of open sea off Crete, and if the storm went on for days they would probably be driven at last on the dangerous sandbanks and shallows off the African coast.

They managed to get some shelter behind a small island called Cauda. They passed ropes under the ship to strengthen it to meet the battering of the waves, and they fixed the sails so that they might drift further north, away from the danger in Africa. If they could make some leeway northward, they might possibly reach Italy or Sicily before the ship was smashed to pieces.

For days the storm raged. They could see neither sun by day nor stars by night, and could not know where they were. They had to throw the precious cargo of wheat overboard, losing the profits of the voyage for which the crew had suffered so much. Yet the storm went on and there was no sign of land. The sailors themselves gave up hope. The ship would not stand much more, and they must by now have missed the land they had hoped to reach. They were somewhere in the midst of the great Mediterranean in a breaking ship, and there might be no safe landfall in hundreds of miles.

When all seemed lost they found they were nearing land. They dropped a weighted rope over the side and it reached the bottom. And it was getting shallower. It was night, and they could still see nothing. They cast out anchors and waited fearfully for daylight. But the ship struck on rocks and broke up in the surf. At this crisis they were at the edge of a shallow sandy bay. All the crew and the soldiers and prisoners got safely ashore by swimming or by clinging to planks broken from the ship.

The people of the island welcomed them kindly and they found out afterwards that they were on Melita, now Malta. Another corn-ship took the party on to Rome when the seas became safe again in the spring. (The whole exciting story is told in Acts 27 and 28.) So Paul finally came safely to Rome, to be tried before Caesar's court. There he had two years to wait, and, though a prisoner, was free to meet friends and write letters in the centre of the world.

The Via Egnatia. Paul probably travelled along this Roman road between Thessalonica and Philippi.

A Roman grain ship of the type on which Paul travelled from Asia Minor to Rome.

BUSINESS AND TRADE

How big? How many? How much? How far away? These are questions we ask when listening to a story. The Bible constantly gives sizes of objects or people, quantities of food and other things. It is not easy for us to imagine what these sizes are like because we don't use shekels and talents or cubits or seahs today. Goliath, for example, is described as 'six cubits and a span' tall. Was he much taller than an ordinary man? At the court of King Solomon they ate each day 'thirty measures of fine flour and sixty measures of meal'. How much was that? How many would it feed?

An Egyptian tomb painting showing goods traded with equatorial Africa. Left to right: gold, giraffe tails, ebony logs, leopard skin, incense, a baboon and rods, possibly for spears.

Weighing and measuring

Measurement was as important to people living in Bible times as it is to us today. When people bought or sold, they had to know how much they were buying or selling. This was particularly important if they were buying costly items like gold or frankincense or myrrh. They had to be able to measure the amount of their crops, so the tax collector could take his share. Craftsmen, who made objects such as chariots or ploughs – had to be able to measure things exactly so that the parts fitted together. The more complex a society, that is, the more people with special work to do, the more precise measurements had to be.

In Israel and Judah most of the people were farmers living in villages. They were technically backward, agricultural countries, but they were often in contact with more advanced societies in places like Egypt or Babylon or Tyre. From time to time the cities of Israel and Judah almost reached the level of the technologically advanced cities nearby. We know that at these times there were groups of people who set standards for measurements, like the Standards Institutes today (2 Samuel 14:26). It might be the king or the temple or merchant houses. However, even their measurements – cubits and shekels and ephahs – varied from place to place and from century to century. Since Bible times cover about two thousand years, there is likely to be quite a difference between the Old Testament measure and the New Testament measure of the same name.

A 9th century BC Assyrian relief from Nimrud showing tribute being weighed on scales.

In ancient Egypt taxes were gathered in the form of agricultural produce. In this tomb painting an official is seen standing by a field of barley, probably about to assess how much is due to the state.

Units of measurement

Counting

The first accurate measure that people used was counting. The original Bible text uses a decimal system. There are names for numbers one to ten. Eleven is one plus ten, twelve is two plus ten and so on up to twenty. The numbers continue like our system up to ten thousand. There are no words for bigger numbers, but in Daniel 7:10 there is 'a thousand thousand' (our million) and 'ten thousand times ten thousand' (a hundred million). These were extraordinarily large numbers in those days.

Distance

In the old Testament the distances people travelled were not measured. The writers speak only of 'one day's journey', or 'three days' journey'. In the story of Jonah, Nineveh is measured as a city so large that 'it took three days to cross it' (Jonah 3:3). This was probably measured by the distance a donkey caravan would travel in a day, not one person walking. An army on the march might cover 20km a day. The Greek writer, Herodotus, says that people travelled '150 stadia' per day on the Royal road to Persia. The stadion was about 185 metres. So a day's journey would be about 28km. This is pretty good going. On this calculation Nineveh was 60 to 80km across (this must include also the

district and not just the city itself).

The New Testament uses stadia, a Greek measurement (Revelation 21:16 RSV). It also uses the Roman mile (Matthew 5:41 RSV). It is called a 'mile' because it was supposed to be a thousand (Latin *mille*) double paces. A double or military pace is two steps (left-right).

Length

The most important unit of length in the Bible is the cubit. 'Cubit' is an old English word for the forearm, the arm from the elbow to the fingertip.

You may know that your outstretched arms measure, from fingertip to fingertip, about the same as your height. Both are about four cubits. Half a cubit was called a span – the distance between the thumb and little finger in an outspread hand.

We do not have any measuring rods from

Israel or Judah, so we are not sure how long standard cubits were. But some, perhaps most, of the cubits mentioned in the Bible were about 445mm. On this measure Goliath was about 2890mm – nearly three metres (or 9′ 6″) tall.

The largest measure mentioned in the Old Testament is the 'reed' or measuring rod. This was six cubits or a little over three metres, when the larger cubit of 520mm was used (Ezekiel 40:5).

The smallest unit was the 'finger'. The only

reference to a 'finger' (width) is in Jeremiah 52:21 (RSV). The pillars of the temple were made with bronze 'four fingers' thick.

Although there are words for 'half', 'quarter' and so on, they are not used for lengths. Instead, they used '6 cubits and a span' not 6½ cubits. To make things easier, builders tried to make the sides of their buildings an exact number of cubits. Solomon's temple was 60×20×25 cubits. This is about 27×9×11m.

This stadium in Athens is a reconstruction of the original Roman stadium.

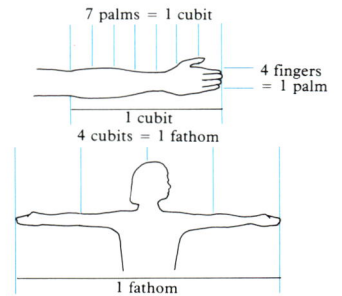

7 palms = 1 cubit
4 fingers = 1 palm
1 cubit
4 cubits = 1 fathom
1 fathom

Ancient Jewish units of measurement were based on parts of the human body.

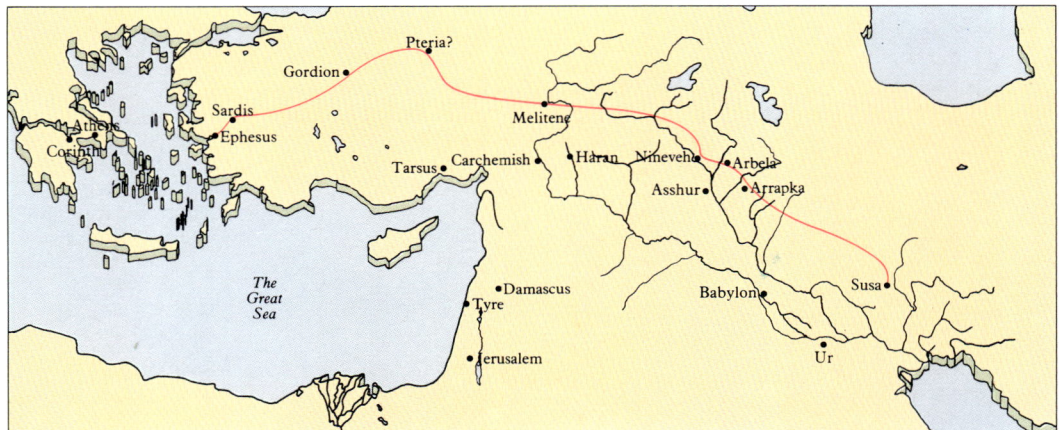

The famous Persian Royal Road led from Ephesus to Susa and provided a communication link across the Persian Empire.

Depth

In Acts 27, we are told the story of the shipwreck of a boat carrying Paul. The sailors measured the depth of the water in 'fathoms'. The sailor measured the depths by dropping a line, with a weight on it, to the bottom of the sea. He then pulled it in, measuring the length of line that had been under the water by his outstretched arms. This distance across his arms is a fathom.

Standard Greek measurement for a fathom from the 5th century AD.

Area and capacity

There is no idea of square or cubic measure in the mathematics of the Bible. Sometimes an area might be said to be square or round, and the length of the sides or outside given. The bronze tank for Solomon's temple was circular, with a diameter of 10 cubits (1 Kings 7:23). The volume is given as two thousand 'baths'. This is a Hebrew word – not a bath tub of course. The New International Version of the Bible says that a bath was 22 litres.

A unit of about the same size as the *bath*, called an *ephah*, was used for measuring wheat. The ephah became so much the standard measure that we find people speaking of 'one sixth of an ephah' and 'one tenth of an ephah' instead of the smaller units. There was also a homer (10 ephahs or 220 litres) and a cor (about the same).

We cannot do much more than guess about

An Egyptian frieze showing slaves towing large wine jars. The waterpots in Jesus' miracle at Cana may have been about this size.

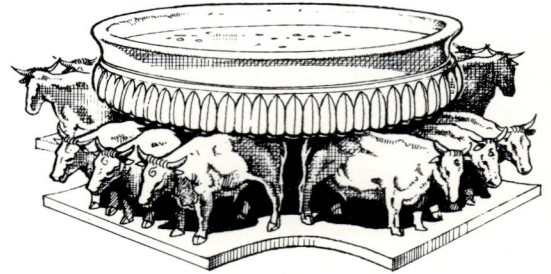

some of the units of quantity mentioned in the Old Testament. When ordinary people bought wheat or flour, they did so in small amounts. The most important measure before the exile was the seah, translated 'measure'. It may have been one-third of an

ephah (about 7 litres). We are also told of the existence of an omer, equal to one-tenth ephah (2.2 litres), which is also called simply a 'tenth'.

In the New Testament the old measures are used at times. In the parable of the unjust steward the oil is measured in baths (Luke 16(RV)). The Jewish historian Josephus gives a Greek equivalent which comes out to about 40 litres. The bushel measure mentioned in Mark 4:21 was a Roman measure of about 9 litres. This is quite big enough to cover an oil lamp. In the story in John 2:6 where Jesus turned water into wine at a wedding, the waterpots contained 'two or three' metreles. A metrele may have been about 40 litres, the same as a bath. If so, Jesus provided them with as much as 700 litres of wine for the wedding feast. Unlike our weddings, the feast lasted for up to seven days.

The huge bronze water container for the courtyard of Solomon's temple was about 4.5 metres in diameter and held 44,000 litres of water. It rested on the backs of twelve bronze bulls.

Land Area

Farming land was measured in two ways. Firstly, by how long it would take to plough it. The unit was the amount two oxen could plough in a day. The Romans introduced units of square feet. The old

British unit of an 'acre' (two-fifths of a hectare) was also originally 'as much as a yoke of oxen could plough in a day'. Land might also be measured by the amount of seed needed to sow it (Leviticus 27:16).

Farmers ploughing with a yoke of oxen in Egypt. Farm land was measured by the amount two oxen could plough in a day.

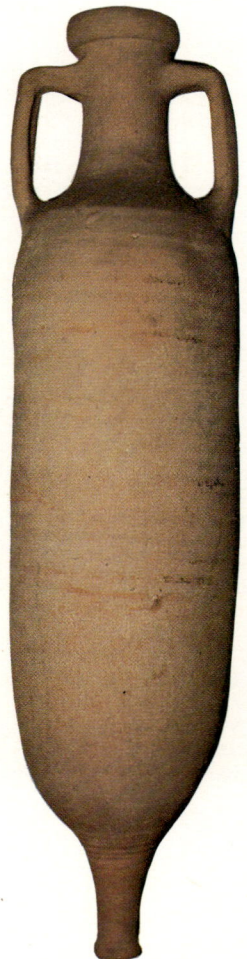

A Roman wine amphora.

Weight

It is harder to weigh things than to measure their size or quantity. It takes a lot of practice to be able to 'guess' weights, as there is no obvious 'natural' standard like the 'foot' or 'cubit'. Weights are usually artificial: and weighing must be done on scales. Weighing can, however, be more precise than other measurements of quantity. In the Bible only precious things were weighed. In the story of Mary anointing the feet of Jesus we are told that she used a 'pound' (or 300g) of costly ointment (John 12:3 RSV).

In Jerusalem today the fellahin (peasant) women weigh grapes or figs or green almonds with a primitive balance. In the Bible food is not weighed except during famine.

As the weights were made out of stone, many have survived until today, whereas no cubic measures have survived. It was difficult for the people to make weights accurately and the stones became worn away with use. Different countries had different weights. In Babylon there were two shekels, one lighter and one heavier than in Israel or Judah. The unit of weight also varied over the centuries and depending on the people using it, or authorising its use (king, temple or merchant houses).

Talent

The largest unit of weight was the talent, which was probably about 30kg. It would be used most often for copper or bronze. Gold was measured in talents when large amounts were involved, such as the state income or tribute paid to conquering kings. Hezekiah had to pay 300 talents of silver and 30 talents of gold to Sennacherib, king of Assyria (2 Kings 18:14 RSV).

Shekel

If we examine the weights which have been found, the weight of a shekel varies considerably, but a figure of about 11.5 grams would seem to be reasonable.

Some biblical writers use fractions of a shekel –

half-shekel, one-third, quarter (1 Sam. 9:8 RSV). The earlier writers used special names for smaller weights. The half shekel was called a beka. This is the poll-tax that every man had to pay. It is the tax that Peter paid for himself and Jesus (Matt. 17:27). A stone weight labelled 'beka' has been found which weighs 5.9g. This would make the shekel nearer 12g than 11g. All fractional weights are heavier than we would expect from the size of the shekel. This may be because they couldn't make small weights accurately.

In New Testament times the shekel was 8g, or even 7g. We have a weight from the time of King Herod, 9BC, which is labelled in Greek, 3 minas and weighs 1233g. In AD41 a mina weighed only 365g.

It is almost impossible to calculate the equivalent value of a shekel of silver in modern money because the economic systems are so different and because money values change so frequently. In the time of the kings of Israel (9th–6th centuries BC) a shekel was probably equivalent to about £2 today.

An Egyptian weighing scene from around 2500BC. The men are using a balance hung from a wooden frame.

Roman weights found in excavations at Pompeii.

Sometimes weights were made in unexpected shapes. These lion weights are from Assyria.

Exchange, money and banking

The standard of value in the Old Testament is a weight of silver. The only word for money is 'silver'. By New Testament times, when coins were common, there are other words.

Even before the invention of coins there appears to have been silver 'money'. Many hoards of silver pieces have been found. The bits and pieces of silver are of all different shapes. Many may be scraps of broken jewellery, or pieces left over from making jewellery or drinking vessels. We do not read in the Bible about bronze or gold being used strictly as money before the introduction of coins. The value of various items is given in terms of the weight of bronze or gold in them.

We are sure that people continued to exchange goods, rather than buy or sell. But we don't often hear of this in the Bible. Taxes and tribute were often paid in goods, such as the provisions for Solomon: 'the barley and straw for the horses and draught animals', the 'gold vessels, silver vessels, robes, armour, spices, horses and mules', or the presents of the Queen of Sheba – 'camels laden with spices, great quantities of gold, and precious stones' (1 Kings 10:2, 14, 25). Solomon exchanged wheat and olive oil for the cedar and pine wood used to build the temple (1 Kings 5:10, 11).

As there was no fixed size for the pieces of silver, the amount of money needed to

Before goods were handed over, the purchaser's money had to be weighed in the days before standard coins.

buy anything had to be weighed out. The shopkeeper or trader owned a balance and a bag of weights. The purchaser had no way to check that the weights were accurate, or the balance true. It was also possible for the shopkeeper to make his measuring utensils (jars, cups) too small. A poor person buying his/her food was at the mercy of unscrupulous traders. Many biblical writers warned shopkeepers how to behave (Deuteronomy 25:13–16; Amos 8:5).

Coins

Coins are believed to have originated in eastern Turkey. They were a combination of earlier ideas of pieces of metal and stone weights. If each piece of metal is stamped with the weight, there is no need to weigh it every time. This idea was eagerly adopted by the Greeks, who for centuries made the best silver coins.

Symbols were stamped on the coins to show where they came from. Athens put an owl on its coins, and this was copied by a lot of people who didn't live in Athens.

King Darius I, king of Persia, made

gold coins which were named after him: darics (Neh. 7:70, 71 RSV). The Persian kings didn't allow any country they conquered to make gold coins, but they allowed silver ones to be made in important cities like Tyre. There may have been bronze coins also.

To make a coin a circular piece of metal was cut out to the right size. This was then placed on a die, a piece of metal with the design cut into it. A punch, a rod of hard metal with the design on the other side, was placed on top of the metal blank. The punch was then hit with a hammer and the design would be embossed on both sides of the metal. Often the maker missed, and the design was positioned crookedly on the coin.

In all parts of the Roman Empire, Roman coins were the official currency. They had to be used for tribute. So when Jesus was asked about tribute (taxes to the Roman emperor) he asked for a denarius (Mark 12:15 RSV). This was a silver coin, weighing about 3.9g. The denarius had the head of the Roman emperor on it. At this time it would have been Tiberius. In

A mould used for making coins and some metal blanks which have been cast. These would then be stamped and cut into separate coins.

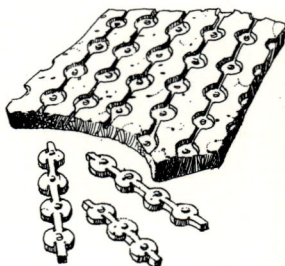

A panel from the Black Obelisk showing subjects bringing tribute to the Assyrian King Shalmaneser III.

This Jewish coin from shortly before the birth of Christ shows a Menorah (seven-branched candlestick). From the shape of the coin it may have been made in a mould like that seen above.

Jewish shekels photographed in the state in which they were dug up, before cleaning.

the parable of the workers in the vineyard, the denarius was the daily wage for a casual agricultural labourer (Matt. 20:1–16).

The Greek coin almost equivalent to the denarius was the drachma (3.5g). The 'lost coin' in Jesus' parable was a drachma (Luke 15:8).

The silver stater was also called a tetra-drachma (four drachmas), and weighed about 14g. So when Peter found a 'stater' in the fish's mouth, this was enough to pay his tax and for Jesus too. These coins were almost pure silver.

The thirty silver coins given to Judas for betraying Jesus were probably tetra-drachmas. The talent of Matthew 25:15 (the parable of the talents) was 6,000 drachmas (about £3,000). The 'pound' (mina) of Luke 19:12–27 was 100 drachmas.

Banks

We do not know of any private banking firms in Jerusalem in Old Testament times. In Babylon private banking began about the year 650BC. But in Judah the older practices continued.

For an ordinary person the safest place to hide money was in a hole in the ground. This is why so many 'hoards' of silver or coins have been found. Achan, when he stole the ingot of gold and the pieces of silver from Jericho, hid them 'in the

This double daric of Babylon, showing the king with sceptre and bow, dates from around 325BC.

A Roman denarius bearing the head of Tiberius. Jesus referred to a denarius when questioned about paying tribute to the Romans.

A hoard of silver coins found buried in a clay jug. They date from the 4th century BC and were found in excavations in Israel.

A silver tetradrachm of Philip II, the founder of the Greek city of Philippi in 356BC.

An Athenian coin with an owl symbol.

ground inside my tent' (Joshua 7:21). Pieces of silver were often put in pottery jars. In Matthew 13:44, the owner of the hoard hidden in a field must have died, as someone else found it, and it became his when he bought the field. If someone went on a journey, he might give his money to a neighbour to look after, or to his servants (Exod. 22:7). In the parable of the talents, the man who went abroad gave all his property to his servants. One of them hid his share in the ground, the safest place (Matt. 25:25).

In Judah and Israel the temple was always a store-house for money. The king might have his own separate treasury, but the king of Judah often used the temple in Jerusalem as his treasury. The wealth of the king – or temple – was wealth in the shape of gold shields. He stored them in the room called the 'Hall of the Forest of Lebanon', so called because of its many wooden pillars made of tree trunks from Lebanon. All the household goods in the temple – tables, lamp-stands, knives, bowls – were of gold. And much of the woodwork was coated with gold, including the statues. All this wealth had to be paid to Pharaoh, Shishak of Egypt, when he conquered King Rehoboam (1 Kings 14:25–28). Shishak didn't take everything, because Rehoboam's grandson King Asa 'took the remaining silver and gold from the treasuries of the Temple of the Lord and the royal palace' to bribe the king of Syria to attack Israel (1 Kings 15:18).

Pontius Pilate acted in the same way when he used money from the temple treasury to build an aqueduct to supply Jerusalem with water. (This is not mentioned in the Bible.) The people felt this was sacrilegious. The writer of the book of Maccabees also felt that the temple funds were sacred and should not be touched by any king (2 Maccabees 3). But in the 2nd century BC the temple was being used as a bank. Both very rich people and the less rich deposited their money in the temple, trusting 'in the sanctity of the place and the inviolable majesty of a Temple venerated throughout the entire world' (2 Macc. 3:12). Herod the Great used some of the money from the treasury to rebuild the temple.

A money-changer at work. Jews from abroad coming to the Temple in Jerusalem had to change their foreign currency into Jewish shekels required for the Temple. Rates of exchange were often excessive.

Moneylenders

There was very little use for money in the villages of early Israel or Judah. People worked their farms to get food and clothing. They had to sell some of their produce to buy bronze or iron for their tools. But as more people became labourers they became more dependent on money. In hard times it became necessary to borrow money.

The laws of the Old Testament are based on the idea that a man who has money which he is not using should lend it to someone in need. In the simple economy of the Old Testament there was no use of 'capital'. So Exodus 22:25 says, 'You must not play the usurer with him: you must not demand interest from him.' The man had to give back the money which he had been lent but he was not to be charged for using it. This was reasonable in that economy – the money was not being used by the owner, so to lend it to a needy person was the same as hiding it in the ground. To charge interest was merely exploiting the poor man's need. Deuteronomy 23:20 says people were allowed to charge interest to foreigners, but not to Israelites.

Interest was charged in Jerusalem. While this was acceptable in a developed economy like Babylon, in Jerusalem it just exploited the poor. The rate of interest was about 20 per cent. That is, a debt would double in five years. It is clear from the parable of the talents in the New Testament that lending at interest was common (Matt. 25:14–30).

The worst part of lending money was the penalty placed on those who did not pay back. People could be sold into slavery for debt. In 2 Kings 4:1–7 the widow of a prophet was going to lose her two children to a creditor.

Another practice involved the use of pledges as a reminder of what was owed. Exodus 22:26–27 states that if a poor man pledges his cloak, the lender (of money or food) must let him have it back at night when he needs it for a blanket. It was common practice to take pledges and use them until the money was repaid. In this way there was no need to charge interest, because you got the benefit of the pledge.

Trade and commerce

Israel and Judah were always agricultural producers. There were also local craftsmen who made goods out of metal, pottery, wood, cloth, leather and stone. They did not export handmade goods, and even for use within the country they had to compete with skilled workmen abroad. Israel and Judah were typically underdeveloped countries. Perhaps in the short times of great influence such as the time of Solomon, or Jeroboam II in Israel, industries and prosperity also flourished. But mostly the two countries exported agricultural products, and imported metals and manufactured items.

We can see this easily in Ezekiel 27, which lists the imports of Tyre from Judah and Israel as wheat, honey, olive-oil and spices (v. 17). The hatred for Tyre shown in this chapter is partly due to the economic exploitation of other countries. Israel and Judah made Tyre rich, and got little in return. The exports from Tyre are not named, but we can guess that they were mostly manufactured goods.

There was considerable trade between Egypt and various parts of Africa from early times. This tomb painting from 1400BC shows gold ingots and gold chains from Nubia. This raw material was then worked into precious objects by Egyptian craftsmen.

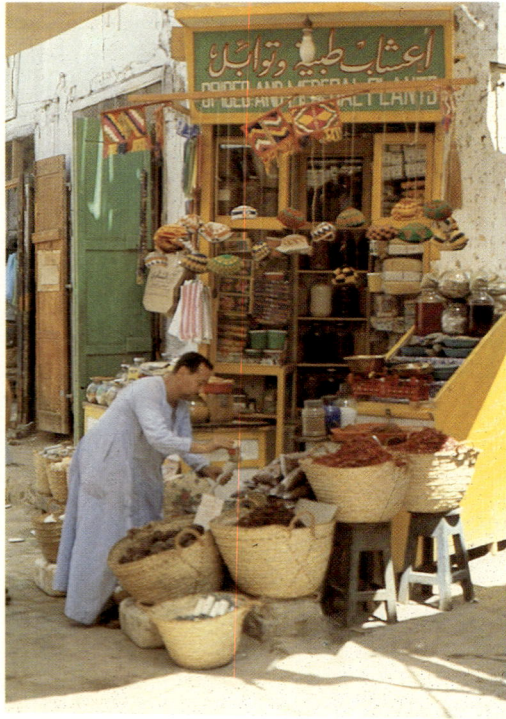

The shops in an Eastern suk have changed little since Bible times, except in some of the articles for sale! The goods on sale at this shop include hats and saffron.

able army machine. The kings of the Hittites and the kings of Aram (Syria) obtained their chariots in the same way. Some think Solomon sold chariots to these kings, but this is unlikely.

In the time of Nehemiah, traders from Tyre lived in Jerusalem. They sold dried fish, and all kinds of manufactured goods. These goods would include gold and silver vessels and clothing dyed with Tyrian purple.

Merchants

The great commercial centres of Old Testament times were Babylon and Tyre and the men who controlled the international trade became very rich. Neither Judah nor Israel was ever an important trading nation. The capitals – Jerusalem and Samaria – were inland and on mountains. No important roads went there. No highway on which raw materials or luxury goods travelled went near them. Even bitumen and salt from the Dead Sea did not pass through Jerusalem.

When a king fought wars, killed people and captured other countries, he was able to build an empire. If it was the king of Jerusalem or Samaria he could control trade from the south. It was then that some people became very rich (Amos 6:1–7). But we do not know if there were many merchants even then and it is thought that much of the international

Solomon had to import gold, silver, copper, myrrh, frankincense, horses, chariots – probably also all iron goods including ploughs. He was able to export only wheat and oil. He could build his wealth only by military force – tribute from conquered countries and taxes on merchants.

Solomon employed merchants to buy horses from Cilicia and chariots from Egypt. In this way he built up a formid-

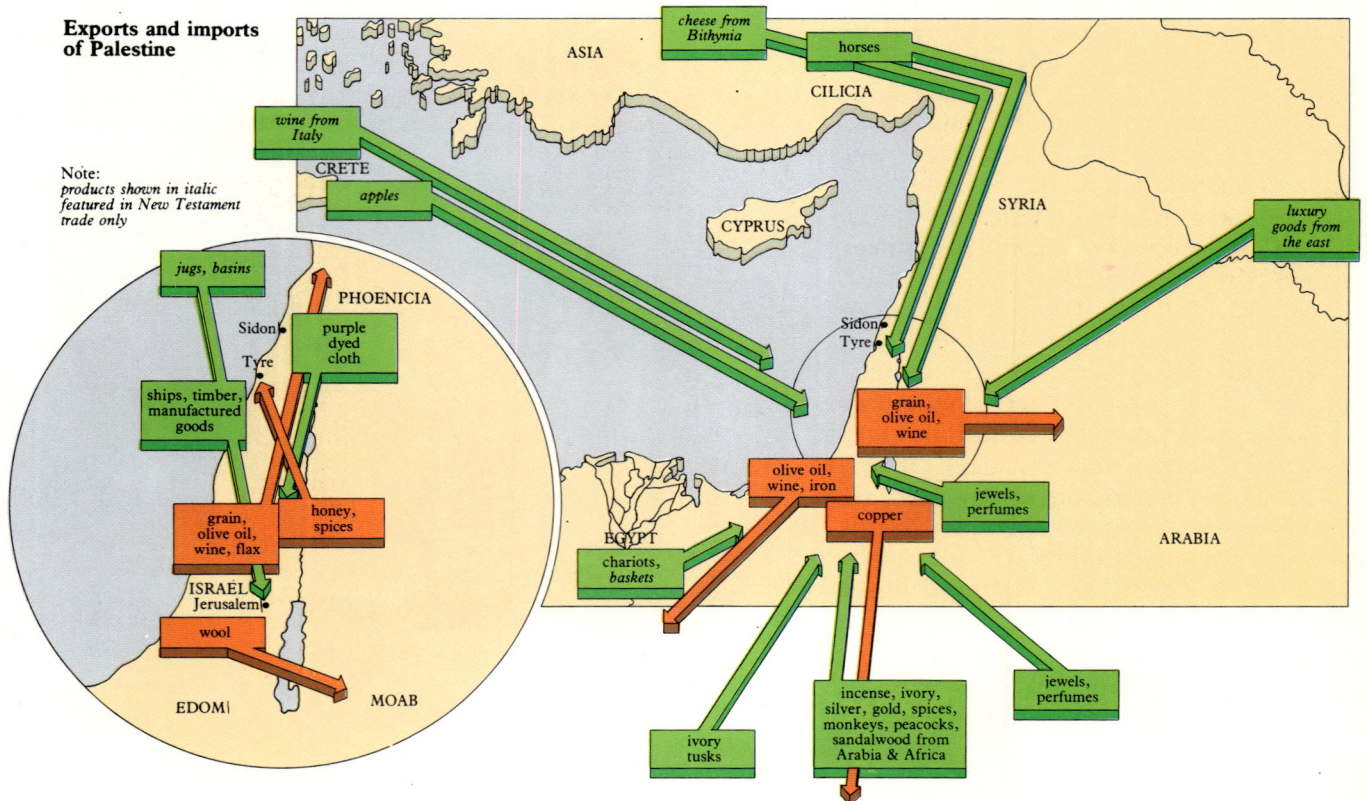

Exports and imports of Palestine

Note: products shown in italic featured in New Testament trade only

trade was controlled by the king. Ben Hadad I had traders in Samaria, and after winning a war Ahab, king of Israel, was able to put his traders into Damascus (1 Kings 20:34). It was a time, the prophets tell us, of great differences between rich and poor. The rich made life impossible for the poor. There was a great deal of bitter resentment. The resentment against Tyre was almost entirely due to its riches (Isaiah 23).

By New Testament times Rome had become the commercial as well as the political centre of the Empire. In Revelation Rome is referred to as 'Babylon'. 'There will be weeping and distress over her among all the traders of the earth when there is nobody left to buy their cargoes of goods; their stocks of gold and silver, jewels and pearls, linen and purple and silks and scarlet; all the sandalwood, every piece of ivory or fine wood, in bronze or iron or marble; the cinnamon and spices, the myrrh and ointment and incense [so far, luxury goods]; wine, oil, flour and corn [basic necessities]; their stocks of cattle, sheep, horses and chariots, their slaves, their human cargo' (Rev. 18:11–13 JB). The big businessmen were probably Roman citizens, though we hear of 'traders who had made a fortune out of' Rome. Jews who lived in Rome or Alexandria may have become merchants. The 'merchants' of the gospels are not very important men. They are rich by contrast only with the many poor in Judah and Galilee. The pearl merchant in the parable has to sell everything to buy one special pearl (Matt. 13:45, 46).

Local traders

There were no shopkeepers until New Testament times, though there were almost certainly stall-holders in a market. We know very little about the way goods were sold. Perhaps people went to the workshops to buy goods straight from the makers. Food was brought for sale into the city from the farms. They 'took sheaves of wheat and loaded them on donkeys, with wine, grapes, figs and every kind of load' (Nehemiah 13:15). The people who grew the food would sell it. The owner of large estates would have men to sell the food in the towns.

Phoenician ivory carvings were exported throughout the ancient world and were much in demand. This delicately carved panel showing a lioness holding an African by the neck was found in Assyria.

The goods were sold in the town square inside the entrance gate. Probably the traders who brought goods from distant places also sold their goods there. The square probably looked much like a bazaar or suq of modern times.

Some of the things sold were oil, wine, grapes and figs, fish, animals, pottery and clothing.

There are no special market days mentioned in the Bible. Nehemiah reprimands the Jewish leaders for turning the sabbath day into a market day. The sabbath is the day of the Lord: and is the one day goods must not be sold (Neh. 13:15–22).

Jesus found a market in the Temple grounds with people selling cattle and sheep and pigeons. He ordered the stall holders: 'Stop turning my Father's house into a market' (John 2:16).

A shop reconstructed at Pompeii. Holes in the counter held the containers of produce for sale.

A customer inspecting poultry in a Roman shop. The Romans had a low opinion of shopkeepers who were mostly slaves.

Craftsmen

For some reason the rich of Israel and Judah do not seem to have encouraged the development of art. They appear to have appreciated literature – hence the superb literature of the Old Testament. But while at times foreigners were brought in to produce works of art, most art produced in Israel and Judah was of poor quality. There were, however, skilled craftsmen who produced good honest work. This is especially true of ordinary household pottery.

Some craftsmen were travellers. The Kenites were a Midianite tribe of smiths. They were something like tinkers and they made and repaired copper and bronze tools or vessels. A painting found in Egypt gives us some idea of what they looked like. One of the donkeys carries bellows for blowing the fire.

Most craftsmen lived in the towns because only there were there enough people who could afford to buy their goods. Some craftsmen were part of large households and lived as part of the 'family'. They were given food and clothing and perhaps a wage. The king had craftsmen in his palace, and the temple also employed craftsmen. For example, men made 'his weapons of war and the gear for his chariots'. Women would be 'perfumers, cooks and bakers' (1 Sam. 8:12, 13). When Solomon used craftsmen from Tyre, he paid the king of Tyre, not the craftsmen.

The different types of craftsmen lived together. Sometimes the whole of a small town would be involved in one type of industry, such as dyeing or weaving. In larger towns whole streets or areas were occupied by one type of craftsmen which made it easier for those who brought the raw materials. This is the way it still is in many towns in the Near East.

Traders also had their own section of Jerusalem. This made it easier for buyers to compare prices and quality of goods and it also meant that it was easier to control conditions and competition. Each craftsman would be 'kept in line' by the others. They could also deal with the public or with government as a group. As a result, we find guilds were formed. These were officially recognised groups of craftsmen. Nehemiah 3 speaks of the guilds of goldsmiths and perfumers.

In New Testament times members of the guilds were able to become employers of labour. Such people could react violently if their wealth or position was threatened. In Ephesus there was a flourishing trade in religious knick-knacks – including silver models of the Temple of Diana. One of the guildsmen convinced the others that Paul was going to destroy this trade by encouraging people to believe in God rather than pagan gods. He therefore 'called a general meeting of his own men, with others in the same trade'. He was able to inflame these people to start a riot (Acts 19:23–41).

In the Roman Empire the guilds had considerable power over the crafts. This power could be used against those who were different in some way. Christians who would not join in the religious ceremonies conducted by the guilds would find themselves out of a job.

The Kenites, a travelling Midianite tribe of smiths, shown in an Egyptian painting.

The crafts

Metal working

Among the craftsmen it was the metal workers who had the highest status. When King Nebuchadnezzar captured Jerusalem in 598BC he took away to Babylonia everybody of social importance: King Jehoiachin, the king's mother, his officials and the leading men of Judah . . . all the important men, seven thousand in all, and one thousand skilled workers, including the blacksmiths (2 Kings 24:15, 16). These were the men who worked iron, copper, silver, gold and probably also lead.

The most technologically advanced machine used by the people of Israel and Judah was the chariot. Probably Israel was never advanced enough to make chariots. We hear only of men making the 'equipment for chariots' (1 Sam. 8:12). Chariots needed very many skilled craftsmen to keep them going, just as modern aircraft need mechanics, electricians and so on, in the ground crew. There would be need for different kinds of workers in wood, iron, bronze and leather for the different parts of the chariot.

In the early days of Israel and Judah, many of the things later made of iron such as the blades for ploughs, knives, arrows and special bowls were made of stone.

The first metals in use were silver and gold. Only very rich people could afford to have things made of these metals. A goldsmith would make rings, goblets and bowls out of pure gold. He would also plate things with gold. Statues could be made of iron or wood, and then covered with a thin layer of gold by the goldsmith (Jer. 10:3, 4).

Gold was made into leaf and also into

This painting of Belshazzar's Feast by Rembrandt van Rijn depicts the Babylonian king using the gold and silver vessels which he had plundered from the Temple in Jerusalem.

Assyrian sculptures for their royal palaces often included gigantic carvings such as this human-headed winged bull from Nimrud.

A princess' head dress of precious metals from Egypt, dating from the 16th century BC.

Stonemasons at work in the Holy Sepulchre church, Jerusalem.

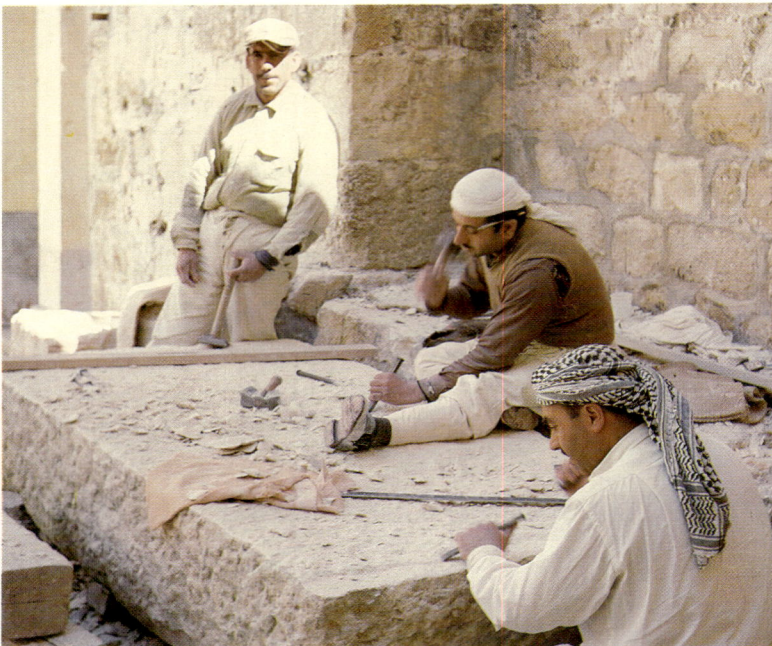

thread, to be woven into expensive cloth. 'They hammered out sheets of gold and cut them into thin strips to be worked into the fine linen and into the blue, purple and red wool' (Exodus 39:3). Gold might be melted and poured into a mould or beaten out.

In Isaiah 44:12 there is a vivid picture of the blacksmith at work: 'The blacksmith works on it over the fire and beats it into shape with a hammer. He works on it with his strong arm till he is hungry and tired.' Strength wasn't enough of course. He had to be a kind of metallurgist to produce a knife that could be sharpened, a plough-share (blade) that would not break when it hit a stone. The kind of iron obtained from the ore was not very tough. A blacksmith had to be very skilled in order to produce something rather like steel. This can be done by heating, hammering and cooling. This is why they were the most important craftsmen.

Bronze continued to be used for body armour. As bronze was quite expensive, only rich people could afford armour. Bronze was, as today, used for decoration by people who could not afford gold. When King Solomon's gold shields in the temple were stolen by King Shishak of Egypt, Rehoboam made new ones out of bronze (1 Kings 14:27). (Ordinary shields would be made of leather or basket work and leather.)

Stone

Another important group of craftsmen were those who worked with stone. Quarried blocks were cut into regular shapes and used like bricks. Only at certain times was this done in Israel and Judah since expert skill was needed. At other times people often wrecked old buildings and used the nicely shaped stones in their much rougher walls and houses. We are not sure whether there ever were good masons in Israel or Judah. Most of the good work done, whether for Solomon or Ahab or Herod the Great, was done by foreign craftsmen, usually Phoenician. We do not know who was in charge of the work of building Solomon's temple. The repair in about 623BC (2 Kings 22:3–7) was in the charge of 'the masters of the works', possibly the head of the guilds of carpenters, builders and masons.

It was the stone masons who built the important buildings – with the help, of course, of builders' labourers. In 1 Kings 6:1–10 King Solomon is said to have built the temple of stone, meaning of course that the men he employed built it. Stone was used much more frequently in Jerusalem than elsewhere.

Wood

Wood was a very useful material. Israel and Judah soon became very short of good wood, and it had to be imported from abroad (Lebanon, Nubia): cedar and pine in particular. Olive wood was generally used for sacred objects, though in Exodus 25, acacia wood is used for the Tabernacle furniture.

Boats were not made by the people of Israel and Judah. The Phoenicians were the boat builders, and probably built the fleet for Solomon at Eilat (1 Kings 9:26). Pine was used for the planking, a cedar trunk for the mast, and oak for oars (Ezek. 27:5–6).

Carpenters were needed for making many other things from chariots to buildings. The carpenter would not have much to do in ordinary homes other than to make doors and some simple furniture. The roof was made of wood, but probably did not need a skilled carpenter. It was spanned with large branches of trees, then laced with smaller branches down to twigs. This was then plastered over with clay.

Important buildings gave more scope to the carpenter. We see this in the description of Solomon's temple, where beams of wood were used between courses of stone (1 Kings 6:10–36). But most importantly the stone was completely covered by wood – cedar on the walls, pine on the floor.

An even more specialised form of woodwork was carving, used to decorate buildings, or to make statues. The walls of the temple were decorated with 'carved figures of cherubs, palm trees and rosettes' (1 Kings 6:29).

In Isaiah 44:13 there is a clear description of the wood carver's trade. 'The carpenter measures the wood. He outlines a figure with chalk, carves it out with his tools and makes it in the form of a man.'

Clay

Many different objects were made from clay. In Mesopotamia, where metal and stone were scarce, sickles for reaping wheat and barley were made of baked clay.

All house builders used clay somewhere in their construction. Most houses were made of clay bricks dried in the sun. Some clays would crack unless they were 'tempered'. One of the things used to temper the clay was straw. The Israelites in Egypt were using straw for their bricks (Exod. 5:6–14). When the archaeologists rebuilt the gateway of the Judaean city of Beersheba they mixed straw with the clay to

This wall made of mud and straw bricks was reconstructed among excavations at Beersheba.

Jesus would have seen carpenters' tools like these in Joseph's workshop. On the wall (left to right) hang a saw, chisel, set square, hammer and plumb-line. On the bench are an adze, drill, pincers, plane, and awl.

Art: Ivory and Gems

Besides goldsmiths, there were those skilled in 'cutting stones to be set'. Some of the Jewels are mentioned in Exodus 39:10, 'Ruby, topaz, garnet, emerald, sapphire, diamond, turquoise, agate, amethyst, beryl, carnelian, jasper'. We read in Ezekiel of jewels such as these being imported from Edom and Arabia (Ezek. 27:16). The queen of Sheba brought jewels with her when she visited King Solomon (1 Kings 10:2).

Ivory engraving was also a special craft. King Solomon's throne was made of ivory (1 Kings 10:18). The houses of the rich, especially palaces, were decorated with ivory (1 Kings 22:39). The best ivory workers lived in Tyre and Sidon. They imported elephant tusks.

The artists of Israel and Judah seem to have produced rather poor work. What art there was was meant for religious use. Ezekiel speaks of 'paintings of Chaldaeans coloured vermilion' (Ezek. 23:15).

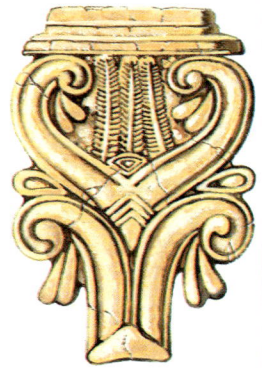

Many pieces of ivory were discovered in excavations at Megiddo, Israel. This panel with a palm design may have been an inset for a piece of furniture.

This Egyptian tomb painting from around 1400BC shows jewellers at work. One man in the upper register is polishing beads on a wooden block; another in the lower register assembles an elaborate collar. Some examples of their work are seen on the right.

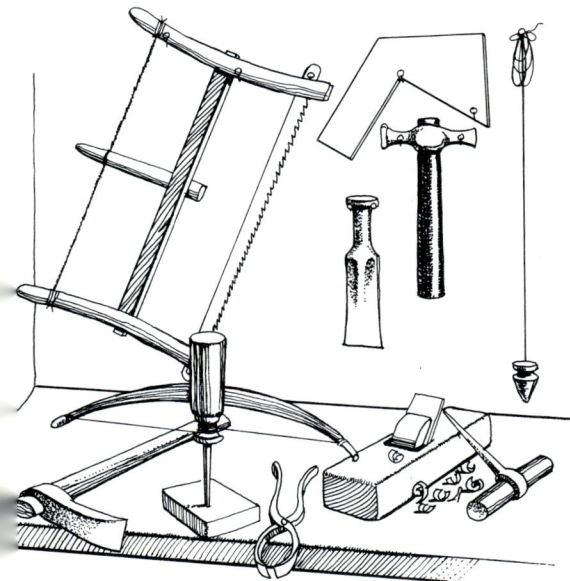

make it look right.

Builders were employed to set the clay bricks into position. The bricks were 'cemented' with more clay. The wall might be the wall of a house – or a huge wall to defend a city. Where the rock was very soft a thick clay wall would be stronger than a rock wall. Tobiah was being rude when he said about the Jews who were rebuilding the wall of Jerusalem, 'What kind of wall could they ever build? Even a fox could knock it down!' (Neh. 4:3). This could easily happen if the stones were rough and the builders inexperienced. Unless a plumb-line (a piece of string with something heavy like a lead weight on the end) was used, the wall would not be straight, and could fall (Amos 7:7). Ordinary houses may not have been made by craftsmen, but by the owner and his neighbours.

Clay was used also by potters. Jeremiah describes a potter working at his wheel (Jer. 18:1–6). The potter first had to pound all the air out of the clay with his feet. Before Jeremiah's time potters probably shaped the clay by hand. If the clay is thrown on a wheel, it must have no stones or chaff in it. So a craftsman must know a lot more about clay to use a fast wheel. That does not mean the pots will be more beautiful. Some of the pots made with poor clay in the early days, before Israel and Judah became states, are very beautiful indeed.

The pottery from the time of the kings of Israel and Judah is very attractive, even though it comprises ordinary things like storage jars, jugs, bowls, platters and cooking pots. We cannot say this of the little figures of people and horses that were made. They are really quite ugly. These were probably made in moulds. Both the pots and the figurines were baked in pottery ovens (kilns) to make them hard.

An Egyptian potter shaping a pot on his wheel.

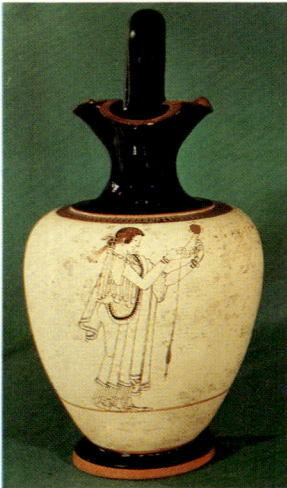
A Greek jug from around 500BC with a detailed decoration showing a woman spinning thread.

A painted Israelite pot from around 1000BC, the time of David and Solomon.

Those in financial difficulty sometimes had to sell their children as slaves. Here a Jewish slave girl meets her new Roman master.

Slavery

If a person could not survive any other way he might be reduced first to selling his children as slaves, and then to selling himself. If a man borrowed money he couldn't repay, and he owned nothing else valuable enough, he would become a slave. He was supposed to be a slave for six years only and then be released.

There was no such regulation for foreign slaves – people captured in war or bought from slave traders. Girls were sold into slavery to become wives. They carried water, looked after the sheep or worked for the woman of the house until they were grown up. They were then married to the master of the house or his son or his slaves. Exodus 21:11 states that if they do not marry the girl, she must be set free. If a temporary slave married her and then was released, he couldn't take his wife or children with him. The only way he could stay with his wife and children was to renounce all rights to freedom.

A slave might have some little money of his own. In certain circumstances a slave could buy his own freedom or be released (Lev. 25:47–53). He became a 'member of the family' and it was possible for affection to develop between the slave and the owner of the house.

FARMING AND FISHING

Imagine what would happen if all the shops and supermarkets closed down; if you couldn't buy tinned or frozen vegetables. Would you know how to grow your own food? Would you know how to catch fish?

Most people today wouldn't know where to begin. Yet in Bible times, nearly everybody was involved in some sort of farming or fishing. This is why we find so many references to these ways of life in the Bible, and why Jesus used scenes from them in his teaching.

Harvesting in Israel using simple implements.

Nomads

Nomads did not settle in towns and farm the surrounding land as other people did. They preferred to wander from place to place, looking for pasture and water for their cattle, sheep and goats. They had a recognised territory, visiting different parts of it according to the seasons, and travelling with all their possessions packed on donkeys.

This sort of life meant that they had to live in tents rather than houses. Their tents were made from the skins or hair of their goats, and everything inside the tent had to be easily carried when they moved.

People of many tribes lived in this way, but some nomads lived a more settled life than others. They planted crops, and left their settlement only if absolutely necessary.

God's people

Abraham, the founder of the Israelite nation, was a city-dweller who became a nomad. He and his family moved from the great city of Ur in Mesopotamia to the land of Canaan (Genesis 12:1–9). When famine came to the land, they went south to Egypt to find better pasture (Gen. 12:10).

This nomadic way of life was continued by Abraham's descendants, Isaac and Jacob, in Canaan until another famine drove the family to Egypt again (Gen.

46:1–7). Here they became a settled people for four hundred years, growing into a nation and enjoying peace and prosperity for much of the time. When they returned to a nomadic way of life under Moses (to escape the life of slavery which a new king had imposed upon them) they found it very difficult. After centuries of living in the fertile Nile basin, they had forgotten how to live the nomadic life and could no longer cope with its hardships (Numbers 20:2–5).

The true nomadic way of life amongst God's people came to an end when they finally settled in the Promised Land. The land was divided between the twelve tribes, and each family was given its own land to farm. However, God's people never forgot that their ancestors had been wandering nomads (Deuteronomy 26:5). Many felt that this had been the best time of their nation's life, for a lack of permanent home and land had made them depend on God and not on their possessions.

As the nomads settled down in the land of Canaan, they continued to rear cattle, goats and sheep, but they also began to grow crops.

Modern nomads with their possessions laden on camels.

A Bedouin tent provides very little protection from the weather and contains only the bare necessities for living.

The shepherd

The life of a shepherd could be very hard and lonely, as Jacob discovered (Gen. 31:40–41). Out on the hills in all kinds of weather, he watched over his sheep, leading them to good pasture, rescuing them from dangerous places, and protecting them from wild animals. Without their shepherd, the sheep were helpless. A good shepherd took his work very seriously; he would risk his life for the sheep if necessary (John 10:11), and would search for even one missing sheep until he found it (Luke 15:4–6).

The shepherd's only protection from the sun, wind and rain was his camel-hair cloak, woven by his wife, and a simple head veil. While in the fields he lived on a diet of cheese, bread, dates, olives and dried raisins, which he carried in his shepherd's bag. King David would have lived in this way when, as a boy, he looked after his father's sheep on the hills around Bethlehem.

The shepherd's tools

Like any worker, the shepherd had his special 'tools'. Some of these are men-tioned in Psalm 23. The shepherd's **rod** was a club, about a metre long, which was used for driving off wild animals. It was made from the root or branch of an oak tree and had pieces of flint or, in later times, nails driven into the end. The shepherd's **staff** was about two metres long with a curved end, like a bishop's crook. The shepherd used this to guide the sheep, pull them back, or lift them out of dangerous spots. He always carried a **horn** filled with olive oil to put on any scratches or wounds which the sheep might get. He also had his **sling,** made of leather or plaited hair, for hurling stones at animals which threatened the sheep. The sling was whirled quickly around the head and when the shepherd let go of one end, the stone inside it would be thrown at great speed towards its target. Shepherds could be very accurate with a sling, as the story of David and Goliath reminds us (1 Samuel 17:34–51).

Sheep and goats

Sheep and goats were often kept together in the same flock and were separated only when necessary, for example when the goats were milked. Although sheep and goats sometimes looked alike, the shepherd never found it difficult to know which was which, and he could separate them easily. Jesus used this picture of separating the sheep and goats to show how God would divide people on Judgement Day (Matthew 25:31–46).

Sheep were kept for their wool, rather

A shepherd with his flock on a Judean hillside.

Agriculture

than their meat, and sheep-shearing took place in spring after the lambs were born. The shepherd kept his sheep for a long time and so got to know each one by name, and they learned to recognise his voice (John 10:3–5). Some sheep were used for food, and the fat tails of one breed were enjoyed as a delicacy. Lambs from the flock were used for sacrifices in worship.

Goats were used to provide milk (and from this, butter and cheese). Goats' hair was made into tent-cloth and rough clothes, and their skins were used to make wine-bottles.

(See the Animal Life section for more information on sheep and goats.)

The sheepfold

The sheepfold was very important in a country where wild animals, including wolves and lions, took as much interest in the flock as the shepherd himself did. Therefore, to protect the sheep at night, an enclosure known as a sheepfold was built, using dry stone walls. These were built as high as possible, and thorn branches were put around the top. There was no door to the sheepfold but the shepherd himself acted as the 'door', by lying across the entrance. Shepherds would sometimes share a sheepfold and would take it in turns to be on duty at night.

The Bible often uses this familiar picture of the shepherd caring for his sheep to show how God cares for his people (eg, Psalm 23, Isaiah 40:11, Ezekiel 34:7–31). Jesus used the same picture of himself in the parable of the Good Shepherd (John 10:1–16).

When the Israelites finally settled in Palestine, after many years of living as nomads and exiles, they settled amongst a people who had cultivated the earth for centuries. It was quite natural, therefore, that they should become a nation of farmers, as well as animal-breeders.

On arriving in Canaan, each family was given its own plot of land, which was to be handed down from one generation to another. Sometimes a poor man found it necessary to sell his land to a richer farmer, but God's law did not allow it to be sold on a permanent basis. Every fiftieth year it was to return to its original owner or his descendants (Leviticus 25:8–10, 23). A man's land was so important that not even the King had the right to make his subjects sell him land. Naboth was within his rights to refuse to sell his vineyard to King Ahab (1 Kings 21).

While some parts of the land were very fertile, like the Jordan Valley and the Plain of Jezreel, others needed hard work to produce crops. Even after all his hard work, the farmer was still completely dependent on God to send rain at the right time and to protect the crops from plague and disease.

(There is more information about the cereals and vegetables which the farmer grew in the Plant Life section.)

This farming scene on a Greek drinking-cup dating from the 6th century BC shows a ploughman driving two oxen pulling a plough and behind him a man broadcasting seed.

The farmer's work and implements

The farming year began in the late autumn. For six months the sun had scorched the earth dry and made it rock-hard. No seed could be planted until the rains began to fall in October. These 'former rains', as they were called, were vital to the farmer. Only when the rain had softened the earth could his hard work begin.

Sowing As a general custom in Egypt, and frequently in Palestine, sowing was the first task to be done, usually in the early morning or late afternoon when it was cooler (Ecclesiastes 11:6). The Babylonians invented a seed-planter to do this work, but the Palestinian farmer sowed his seed by 'broadcasting': carrying the seed in either a basket or in a fold of his coat, the sower walked up and down the field, scattering handfuls of seed as he walked. With this type of sowing, some seed was inevitably lost, falling on the paths between the strips of land or where the soil was not deep enough for it to grow. Of the seed which did grow, some would be choked by weeds, for the farmer rarely weeded his field. He simply burned down the weeds or cut off the tops, which left the roots to grow again. Jesus used this familiar picture of the farmer's work in a parable about men's response to his teaching (Matt. 13:1–9, 18–23).

Ploughing The next job was ploughing. The farmer did this after he had sown his seed in order to push the seed into the ground where it would germinate away from the dangers of birds or ants or the heat of the sun. If the ground was rough and stony, it was ploughed both before and after sowing.

The plough had been a major invention in the farming world, enabling the farmer to work much faster. The plough of Bible times was very different from the plough we know in the western world today. It was both very simple and very light, so it was easy to use and easy to lift over any rocks that might be in the way. It was little more than a wooden stake with a curved wooden cutting edge. This was attached to a long pole, fastened at one end to the yoke linking the oxen, and held at the other end by the farmer. With one hand he directed the plough; in the other hand, he held a long stick to prod and guide the oxen. By the time of King David (10th century BC) when iron was readily available, a metal tip for the plough was being used. Where the plough could not be used, for example around trees, the farmer used a **mattock** instead. This was a hand-held implement with a long handle and a triangular head for breaking up the soil.

Waiting After the sowing and ploughing was completed, the farmer had to wait for his crops to grow. Of course, there was always work to be done, such as hoeing the fields to loosen the soil or scrape up weeds. Once again, during this growing season the farmer depended completely on God sending rain. The main rains came from December through to February. Then, in March and April, came the 'latter rains'. These heavy showers were vital, for without them the grain did not swell in the ear. Only when these rains had done their work could harvesting begin.

Harvesting The harvest was a busy time for the farmer and he needed as much help as he could get. Sometimes labourers were hired, and often the whole family helped, leaving their home and living out in the fields until the harvest was gathered. Flax and barley were the first crops ready to be harvested, in April and May. Wheat was ready about a month later.

Harvesting had to be done completely by hand, using a **sickle.** This had a short handle, with a semi-circular cutting blade. In early times the blade was made of pieces of flint set in wood. Later, an iron blade was used. The farmer took hold of the grain in one hand and cut it with his sickle in the other. The bundles were then tied together into sheaves and loaded on to donkeys or carts to be taken away for threshing. The donkey, or ass, was the main working animal on the farm.

A Judean farmer ploughing with a simple wooden ploughshare.

Farming in Mesopotamia and Egypt

While farmers in Palestine were completely dependent on the rains for crops to grow, those in Mesopotamia and Egypt were not. Great rivers passed through these lands (the Tigris and Euphrates in Mesopotamia, and the Nile in Egypt), and so they were able to practise 'irrigation farming'. In this type of farming, water is brought to the crops from the nearby river along man-made canals and ditches.

An Assyrian relief from Nineveh showing water being raised by a water-sweep in the 7th century BC.

Moses stressed the contrast between this 'irrigation farming' and 'natural farming' to God's people before they entered the Promised Land (Deut. 11:10–12).

Sowing took place after the rivers had flooded their banks and then subsided. The flood waters softened the rock-hard soil and left rich mud on the fields. This acted like a fertiliser in which the seed could be sown.

As the crops grew in the coming months, water was brought to them along the irrigation ditches. In Egypt this was often done by using a '**shaduf**': a water bucket on a long pole. At one end

of the pole there was a leather bucket, and at the other a heavy weight held the pole in balance on the two stakes to which it was fastened. The bucket was dipped into the river and then swung round to be emptied into the field or irrigation ditch. Fields were divided into squares by little channels with mud walls. When the farmer wanted to water a square, he blocked up the channel and kicked a hole in the mud wall, allowing the water to run out. When the field had been watered, the blockage was removed, the mud wall remade, and the water allowed to pass on to other fields.

Although irrigation

farming meant a lot more work for the farmer (breaking and mending the mud walls, keeping the channels clear, using the shaduf), it also meant he did not have to worry about whether the rains would come, as the Palestinian farmer did.

Both in Mesopotamia and Egypt many crops were grown in this way from very early times –

An Egyptian papyrus showing agricultural scenes. On the top row flax and corn are being harvested. In the centre row are ploughing scenes.

cereals, flax, dates, figs, olives and many garden vegetables. Egypt was well known for her grain, and there was a great corn market at Alexandria.

An Egyptian painting showing a shaduf in use.

A wooden model of an Egyptian granary. Models of everyday objects like this were put into tombs in the belief that they would be useful to the dead person in the after-life.

Ploughing with oxen on the bank of the River Nile, Egypt.

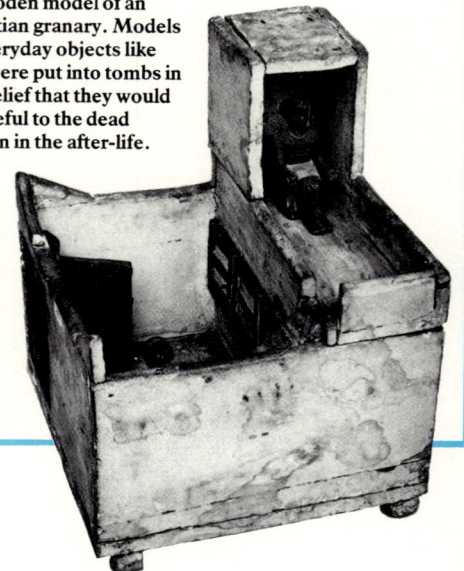

Farming and God's law

Many of the laws God gave to Moses were designed to help the life of the farmer. For example, concerning the keeping of animals, God's law said that all men had a responsibility to catch any animal found running loose and to help any animal in need (Deut. 22:1–4). Special concern was to be shown to animals at work (Deut. 22:10), and an owner was held responsible for his animals and their actions (Exod. 21:28–36).

The growing of crops was also controlled by God's law. A man who started a fire in his field to burn off the weeds was held responsible if the fire spread to the next field, and a man whose animals destroyed another man's crops had to pay for the damage (Exod. 22:5–6); at harvest time, the farmer must leave some crops for the poor to glean (Deut. 24:19–22); fruit could not be eaten from a new tree until the fifth year after planting in order to let it get established (Lev. 19:23–25).

Tithing and giving

The practice of tithing (giving one-tenth of your income to God) was originally related to farming life. To remind the farmer that the land and the flocks were not his, but that they really belonged to God, he had to dedicate to God each year one-tenth of the produce of his land (both fruit and crops), and one-tenth of the new additions to his flock and herd (Lev. 27:30–32; Deut. 14:22–29).

As well as the tithe, the farmer had the opportunity of giving thank-offerings to God at the great festivals of the year, for example at the Harvest Festival, or Feast of Weeks, in the summer (Deut. 16:9–12), and at the Festival of Shelters, or Feast or Tabernacles in the autumn (Deut. 16:13–17). These were joyful times in the farmer's life, when he was glad to bring a gift to God because of God's blessings to him.

The Sabbatical and Jubilee Years

God's law said that every seventh year (**the Sabbatical Year**) was to be a year of rest for the land when it was to lie fallow (Lev. 25:1–7). This made good sense in the days before fertilisers were known, for this year of rest allowed all the goodness of the soil to be restored.

The people were told not to worry about what they would eat that year. God promised to provide a bumper harvest in the sixth year which would provide food until the crops of the eighth year were ready (Lev.

Donkeys pulling a heavy load.

25:20–22). Any crops which did grow during the seventh year were to be left for the use of the poor and the animals (Exod. 23:10–11).

Every fiftieth year was called **Jubilee Year**, when once again the fields had to be left fallow and the farmer could neither sow nor reap. This meant, of course, that the land would be left fallow for two years running, for a Sabbatical Year would always precede a Jubilee Year.

As well as leaving the land fallow in Jubilee

Year, all land was to be restored to its original owner, slaves were to be set free, and debts cancelled. To the Israelite farmers and people, this was a reminder that not only the land, but everything that they owned, belonged to the Lord God Almighty. Sadly, this Law does not seem to have been generally obeyed during the period of the kings.

The Farming Year in Palestine

The centre of the diagram shows how our Roman calendar relates to the Jewish months. The next circle shows the timing of ploughing, sowing, growth and harvesting of the grain crops. The cycle of blossom, fruit and harvest of the main fruit crops and the rainy and dry seasons are shown in the two outer rings. The dates of the main Jewish feasts are also shown.

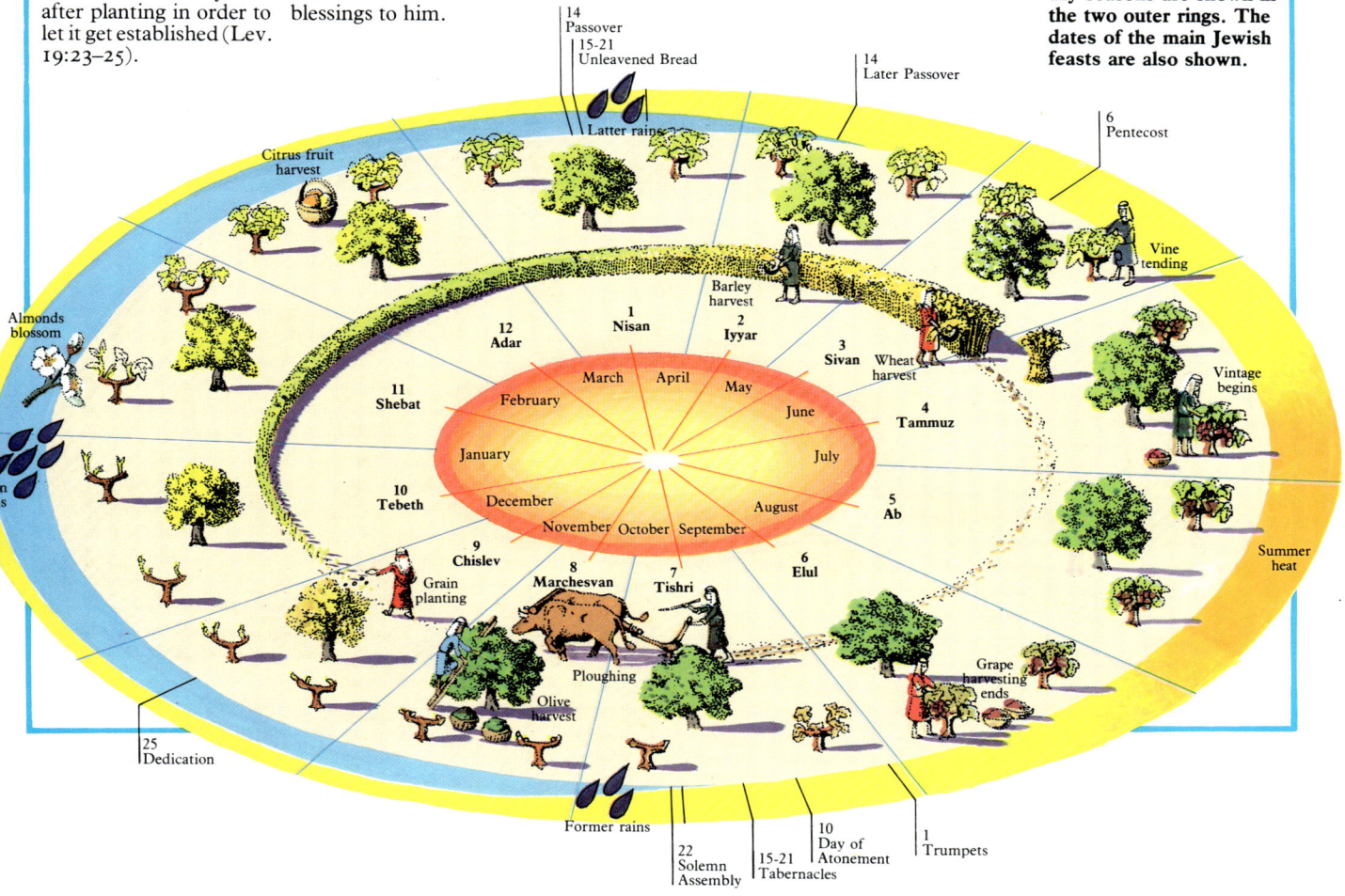

Gleaning After harvesting was over, the gleaners came into the fields. These were poor people who had little means of supporting themselves. God's law said that everything dropped on the ground during the harvest or left growing in the fields was not to be gathered up, but was to be left for the poor to take (Deut. 24:19–22). The story of Ruth is the most well-known example of this (Ruth 2).

Threshing When the crops had been harvested and tied into bundles, they were taken away to be threshed to separate the grain from the stalks. This was done on a threshing-floor which would often belong to the whole village. It was a circular patch of hard ground on which the sheaves were scattered, about 30 cm deep. The sheaves were then beaten with sticks or trampled by an ox. Sometimes a **threshing-sledge** was used. This was a flat wooden board, turned up at the front, with pieces of stone or iron fixed to the bottom. It was dragged over the sheaves by oxen to break up the grain from the stalks.

Winnowing Even after threshing, the precious grain was still mixed with chaff – husks and pieces of straw. The farmer separated this chaff from the grain with a **winnowing fork**. The winnowing fork had a long wooden handle with a wooden fork or shovel fixed to the end. With this, the farmer tossed the grain into the air. The grain, because it was heavy, fell back on to the threshing floor, ready to be gathered; the chaff, because it was light, was blown away by the breeze. It was not wasted however; it was gathered up and kept either for fuel or for winter fodder for the animals.

John the Baptist used this picture of the farmer winnowing when he spoke of the work that Jesus would do, not with grain, but with people, in separating the good from the bad (Matt. 3:11–12).

Storing Once the grain had been win-

Threshing in the Yemen. The farmer is standing on a threshing board which is pulled over the grain by two donkeys.

Harvest time at Nazareth.

Winnowing. The grain is tossed into the air on a winnowing fork to separate it from the chaff.

Fruit crops

A grain mill operated by a donkey. The grain, put in by the farmer at the top, was ground between the rotating outer stone and the ribbed inner stone.

Grapes ripening on a vine.

A threshing board used for separating grain from stalks.

nowed, it was sieved before being put into sacks to be stored. As long as it was dry, grain would keep for a number of years. Joseph stored grain carefully when he was Governor of Egypt in order to prepare for the years of famine which God had told him were to come (Gen. 41). When the grain was needed, it was taken and ground into a coarse flour by the housewife on a small **hand-mill**. The hand-mill consisted of two flat circular stones. The bottom one was very heavy and had a wooden pivot fixed to the centre. The top stone was slotted on to this through a hole. Grain was poured down the hole with one hand, and a handle on the top stone was turned with the other, trapping the grain between the stones and grinding it as they turned. Some mills were much bigger (Judges 16:21), and by New Testament times large millstones were being operated by donkeys.

Caring for his crops meant a very busy and hard life for the farmer all the year round, from the time the rains came in the autumn of one year to the time when they fell again the following year, when his work began all over again.

Although many types of fruit were grown in Palestine, the three most important were the vine, the olive and the fig. In this section, we shall look at how the farmer cared for them. (For information about other fruits see the Plant Life section.)

The Vine

The vine was one of the most important of all the fruit crops. Vines grew plentifully in Palestine and when Moses sent spies to explore the land, they came back with a branch so full of grapes that it took two men to carry it (Num. 13:23).

The vine was pruned to a short main stem but with long side branches. It was either left to grow freely on the ground, with the branch held up by a forked stick as the grapes grew, or was planted singly among other trees and allowed to trail on them. Most were grown in well-kept vineyards.

The vineyard A vineyard was very carefully prepared, as we can see from the parables told in Isaiah 5:1–2 and Mark 12:1. The site was first cleared of stones and dug over. A wall, or a fence of prickly shrubs, was put all around it to keep animals out, especially foxes which had a great liking for fresh grapes. Then the vines were planted in rows, about two and a half metres apart, which gave the grapes plenty of room to grow and the farmer room to clear away any weeds. In hilly areas, the vines were planted in terraced vineyards. A terrace is a flat step cut into the hillside.

Some vineyards were owned by rich foreigners who lived abroad or in the great cities. They would either leave a steward, or manager, in charge of the work on their behalf, or let the vineyard to tenants. Tenants would pay an agreed rent each year at harvest time. Jesus based one of his parables on this practice (Mark 12:1–12).

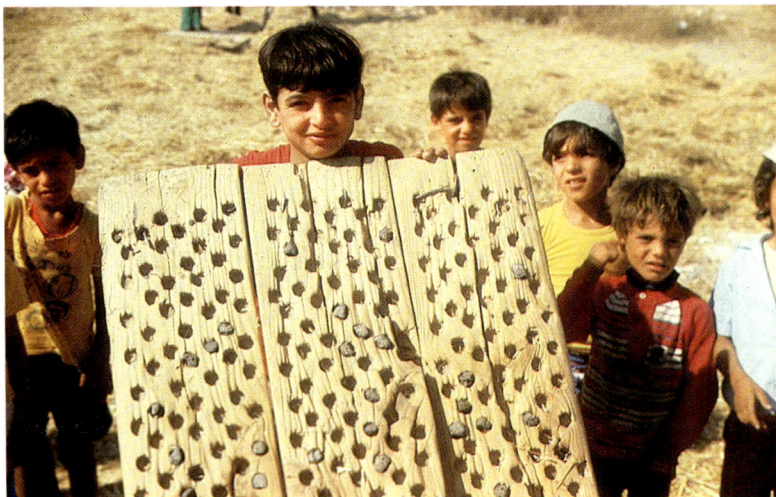

The watchtower Each vineyard had its watchtower. The poor man could only afford to make a simple shelter of branches. Here, in the shade, the man on watch-duty would sit, keeping a look-out for thieves and foxes. Some vineyards had a much more elaborate watchtower made of stone, with a storeroom on the ground floor. A simple outer staircase led to the roof from where the lookout kept watch, again under a roof of branches to protect him from the sun. Whitewashed stone 'scarecrows' were also built to ward off foxes.

The Year's Work Each spring, the vines were pruned with a small pruning-hook (Joel 3:10). Pruning was one of the most important jobs if the farmer wanted a good crop of grapes. Without pruning, there would be little fruit. Jesus talked about pruning in the parable of the vine (John 15:1–17).

The grapes began to ripen in July, but they were not ready to be harvested until August and September. Once the harvest had begun, the labourers had to work very quickly, for the grapes had to be gathered before they rotted or were ruined by the

Grapes spread out to dry in the sun to make raisins.

A stone watchtower in a vineyard.

This drawing of wine-making, adapted from an Egyptian frieze shows the sequence of events from grape harvest to treading the grapes, offering the first fruits to the gods and storing the wine in jars.

coming autumn rains. The whole family often went out to the vineyard to help with the work and sometimes lived there during the harvest in simple shelters. The rich farmer would hire extra labourers for the harvest period. Jesus' parable in Matthew 20:1–16 shows just how urgent the farmer considered the work of harvesting the grapes to be.

The grapes were gathered into baskets by the workers and then carried away. Some were dried in the sun to make raisins. Others were boiled to make 'grape honey', a thick golden sweetener. But the majority of grapes were turned into wine.

Wine-making We have a wide choice of drinks these days, but in Bible times the choice was far more limited – milk, vinegar thinned with water, drinks made from various fruits, water and wine. By far the favourite drink was wine, and so most of the harvested grapes were taken to the **winepress.** The winepress was often cut out of the solid rock and measured about two metres by three metres. Sometimes it would be built of limestone above the ground, or a pit would be dug in the soil and lined with stones and mortar.

When they had been brought from the vineyard, the grapes were put into the winepress. They were trampled by barefooted helpers who held on to ropes above their heads and sang and shouted as they worked (Jeremiah 25:30). As the juice was squeezed out of the grapes, it flowed out at the bottom of the press into another smaller vat. This liquid was then allowed to ferment undisturbed for six weeks. During this time, the stalks and skins would sink to the bottom and form a sort of sludge, known as 'lees'. Then the wine was drawn off and strained, and stored in large pottery wine jars or in goatskins.

Vineyards on a terraced hillside near Hebron.

A 4th century mosaic showing grapes being harvested and trodden.

220

An olive press in Judea.

Olive gathering, depicted on a Greek storage-jar from around 520 BC. The boy in the tree and the two men are beating the branches to make the olives fall. They are gathered into a basket by another boy.

The goatskins had to be new ones, because wine gives off gas as it ferments, and only a new skin is strong and supple enough to expand. Jesus used this picture to show that his message was like new wine which could not go in the old 'skins' or structures of the Jewish religion (Matt. 9:17).

The importance of the vine The importance of the vine to God's people is seen by the fact that there are so many references to vine-growing in the Bible. Even the Law had special regulations about it (eg, Exod. 23:11; Lev. 19:10; Deut. 22:9).

The vine became a symbol of peace and prosperity in Israel, and Israel herself was often seen as a special vine that God himself had planted and was caring for (Ps. 80:8; Isa. 5:1–5). Jesus based no less than five parables on vine-growing. He also described himself as the True Vine without which we, the branches, would shrivel up and die (John 15:5–7).

The olive-tree

The olive-tree was just as important as the vine, for olives had many uses. As a food, they were eaten fresh or pickled. Oil from the olives was used in cooking, as fuel for lamps, as an ointment and as a dressing for the head. The wood of the olive-tree was used for making special things, such as parts of the Temple furniture (1 Kings 6:23). With all these different uses, it is easy to see why the olive-tree was valued so much.

The olive-tree can grow to about six metres high. It is very slow in growing, taking up to fifteen years to reach its full yield. Once established, it provides a good crop even when there is little rain; and it can produce fruit for several hundred years.

The olive grove While some olive-trees were grown singly, it was common to grow them together in groves or orchards. Bethlehem was just one of the many towns famous for its wealth of olive groves. The Mount of Olives, just to the east of Jerusalem, was rich in olives in the time of Jesus. One of his favourite places on the Mount was a garden called Gethsemane, which means 'an oil press'.

The olive harvest The olive harvest came last in the farming year (October to November). The olives were removed either by shaking the branches or beating them with a long pole so that they fell to the ground. They were then put into baskets and taken away on the back of a donkey.

The olive-press While some of the olives were kept to be eaten, fresh or pickled, most of the crop was turned into oil. This could be done in two ways, either by trampling them in vats (as with grapes), or by putting them into an olive-press. The press was very simple, but very effective. A wooden beam was fitted into a hole in a wall or rock. Weights were fastened to the other end of the beam to pull it down and crush the olives which were placed underneath. Oil that was going to be used in the Temple was prepared more carefully by hand, using a pestle and mortar.

After being pressed, the oil was allowed to stand in vats until all the skins had sunk to the bottom. The oil was then poured off into skins, jars, or rock cisterns, where it was stored until needed.

The fig-tree

The fig-tree was also a very important fruit-tree. It was often grown singly by the side of a house. Like the olive-tree, the fig-tree was tall, sometimes ten metres high, although it was often pruned and kept short so that fruit could be picked more easily. It was slow-growing and long-living, and could produce a fine crop, even in stony soil, and needed little care from the farmer.

Because it is a slow-growing tree, the fig can bear fruit for about ten months each year. 'First-ripe figs' were ready in June, and these were particularly enjoyed for their freshness and flavour. The main crop, called late or autumn figs, was ready from August onwards. A third crop of green or winter figs could be found in spring.

Figs were normally harvested for immediate use, for they were a part of everyday diet. Some were preserved in 'pressed cakes', which were wrapped up in fig-leaves.

Like the vine, the fig was so common that it was frequently used as a 'visual aid' by the prophets and by Jesus (Jer. 24:1–10; Luke 21:29–31).

Bees and Honey

The many references to honey in the Bible, and God's description to Moses of the Promised Land as 'a land flowing with milk and honey', make it clear that honey was a favourite food of people in Bible times.

The climate and the many varied flowers of Palestine were ideal for bees. Much honey was made by wild bees nesting in rocky holes or hollow trees. When Jonathan was hungry during a battle, he found wild honey in a tree (1 Sam. 14:24–30). Samson found a hive in a lion's carcass (Judg. 14:8–9). John the Baptist found enough honey to live on, together with locusts, in the desert of Judea (Matt. 3:4).

While farmers did not keep bees as the modern bee-keeper does, using special man-made hives, they encouraged bees to make hives in baskets or pots so that they could collect their honey more easily.

From earliest times honey was an acceptable gift and a valuable item for trade. It was among the specially-chosen gifts sent by Jacob to the Governor of Egypt (Gen. 43:11).

An Egyptian tomb painting shows how honey was extracted and processed. Here we see the honey combs being removed from the hives once the bees have been smoked out. A lamp bowl with three wicks was used for this and it seems to have dealt with all the bees save one!

This relief of picture-writing from Karnak, Egypt shows a clear representation of a bee.

The ancient Egyptians trained baboons to pick figs.

Fishing

Fish which were caught on a land line in the Sea of Galilee.

The Israelites knew very little about fishing in Old Testament times. This is shown by the fact that they had only one word in their language for 'fish', from the tiniest tiddler to the great fish that swallowed Jonah. They were a people of the land rather than the sea. Occasional references in the Old Testament to fishing and to the types of fish that could be eaten, show that a small amount of fishing was done, but certainly not to the extent that other peoples practised it, such as the Phoenicians and the Egyptians.

The Phoenicians (known in the Old Testament as Canaanites) were a great seafaring nation. They used boats not just for fishing on the Great Sea (the Mediterranean), but also for trading. Tyre was their main port, and fish from that city was often sold in Jerusalem (eg, Nehemiah 13:16).

The Egyptians were also good fishermen, and the Nile was a good source of fish. The loss of the fish in the first great plague would have been a disaster (Exod.

7:20–21). The Egyptians also practised fishing as a sport, and large social parties would often go out on fishing trips.

By New Testament times, fishing had become more important to the Israelites too, and fish had become a vital food. No fish could live in the Dead Sea, because it was too salty, but a thriving fishing industry had grown up on the Sea of Galilee where fourteen different kinds of fish could be found. Fish from Galilee became famous. It was not only sold in Jerusalem's fish market, but was salted and then exported as far away as Rome and Spain.

The fisherman's life

The life of a fisherman was hard and his work tiring. Often, the fishing lasted all night (Luke 5:5; John 21:3), and the cleaning, sorting and selling of the fish, followed by the cleaning and repairing of the nets, were all done the next morning. Not only was the work hard, but it could also be dangerous. Sudden storms often blew up on Lake Galilee, which could make even skilled and experienced fishermen afraid (Luke 8:23–24).

The boats used by fishermen were quite small and were propelled by oars or a single sail. They normally held about six men. Fishermen often joined together to buy a boat and nets and then worked together as partners (Luke 5:7, 10). When the catch had been sold, the money was

An Egyptian relief showing fishing with a clasp net.

divided between them.

When Jesus chose his twelve disciples, at least half of the men chosen were fishermen (Matt. 4:18, 21; John 21:2), and he often used examples from the life of the fisherman in his teaching.

Fishing methods
Four ways of catching fish are mentioned in the Bible.

1. Spearing (Job 41:7). This was often done at night. A light would be held over the edge of the boat to attract the fish, and then the fisherman speared them with a harpoon. In Old Testament times, Egyptians did this as a sport.

2. Casting a line and hook (Isa. 19:8; Matt. 17:27). This was done by fastening a hook of bone or iron to a line and casting it into the water. The fisherman did this by hand, not with a rod like the modern fisherman.

3. Cast-net (Matt. 4:18). This was a small circular net which was thrown into the water by hand. The fisherman stood on the shore or waded into the water, whirled the net around over his head and cast it into the water. Weights on the edge of the net made it sink. As it sank, the fish were taken by surprise and caught in it. The fisherman then pulled the net to the shore.

4. Drag-net (Matt. 13:47–50). This was a much larger net, up to five hundred metres long. The net was drawn out, either between two boats on the lake, or between a boat on the lake and men on the shore. It was then lowered into the water. Floats at the top of the net and weights at the bottom made a net-wall in the water

An Egyptian tomb painting showing fishing.

which was closed around the fish to trap them. By pulling hard on the ropes, the net was drawn to land or into the boat.

After the catch
When the fisherman had completed his work, the fish were sorted. Weeds, driftwood and unwanted fish were all thrown back. The good fish were put into baskets ready to be taken to market. They were normally salted to stop them going bad. Finally, the nets were hung up to dry, and any damaged parts repaired.

Fishing on the Sea of Galilee.

A fisherman mending his nets.

SPORT AND LEISURE

People in Israel believed that life was a gift from God and should be taken seriously. Therefore the games they played had a serious purpose: they were to strengthen the body and make people fit for work and war, or sharpen the mind so that they could think better.

Other nations took sport seriously. The Greeks thought it was just as important to be fit and healthy as to be well educated. The Romans loved shows and spectacles of all kinds; the more bloodthirsty the better.

In the visual arts, the Israelites did not produce any paintings, sculpture or pottery as good as those of the Egyptians, Assyrians or Greeks. Music and literature, however, played a more important part in the Israelite culture. Their main aim was the praise of God. Life was not dull or gloomy for the Jewish people. Every month there was a festival of some kind and there are many references to celebrations in the Bible. Both in their family feasts and their national festivals they have always had a great ability to enjoy themselves.

A Greek jug of the 5th century BC shows small boys playing with a toy cart.

Games

Most houses in Bible times were dark, with small windows to keep out the sun, so children played outside. They played in the market place (Matthew 11:16) and the streets (Zechariah 8:5). They must also have played on the shore and out in the fields and hills. Hide-and-seek and blindman's buff were played. A wall-carving from ancient Egypt shows boys playing tug of war.

Children played 'pretend' games of funerals and weddings (Matt. 11:16). Probably they copied other adult activities, too, and played at shops, farming and fishing. Girls in Israel never played with dolls because God commanded in Exodus 20:4 that images must not be made of anything in heaven or earth. A doll would have been regarded as an image. But children probably played with whistles, rattles, hoops and spinning tops.

Ball games

There were no bats or racquets. Nobody played football, baseball or cricket. But leather-covered balls have been found, and Isaiah talks of throwing a ball (Isaiah 22:18).

The Romans used at least five different sorts of ball. In one game children stood in a circle and quickly threw small balls to each other. On one side of the circle a slave stood with a silver tray for the dropped balls, while on the other side there was a slave with a bag of spare balls. The game ended when all the balls were used up and the winner was the player who had dropped the least number.

Games with pebbles and stones

On the paving stones of Pilate's fortress in Jerusalem lines have been found drawn for hopscotch.

In the same place is a circle drawn on the ground. This was for a game (described by the Roman writer Plutarch) played with four knucklebones or jacks. On each side of the jacks were letters and numbers, and players threw the jacks and moved pieces of wood to different positions in the circle. Some of the moves were named: there was a King's Move, for example. There is an outline of a crown on the ground, and also the first letter of the Greek word for King. Some people suggest that when Jesus was on trial before Pilate in this courtyard and the soldiers jeered at him and dressed him up, they were perhaps playing this game, using Jesus as a live playing-piece.

In another game a trench was dug, and the players had to see how many stones or pieces of bone they could throw into it.

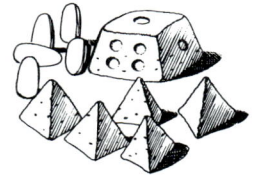

Dice and gaming pieces from Old Testament times, discovered in excavations in Israel.

Toys from ancient Greece. Two animals on wheels and a baby's rattle.

An Egyptian drawing on papyrus shows two animals playing chess.

Knucklebones (which we sometimes call jacks, or fives) was also played, using small pieces of stone, and in Egypt children played with marbles.

Riddles

Riddles were sometimes taken very seriously, and prizes were offered, just as on television quiz games today. An example is given in Judges 14:10–20 when Samson asked riddles at his wedding feast.

When the queen of Sheba visited Solomon, the Bible says she tested him by asking him riddles (1 Kings 10:1–4). The Jewish people remembered these and later wrote them down. Many are ordinary

Children in ancient Greece enjoyed playing with dolls as much as today's children.

questions about the Bible, but one real riddle the queen is supposed to have asked is: 'Without movement while living, it moves when its head is cut off, what is it?' The answer is 'a tree', which, when its top is cut, can be made into a ship.

Board games

These have been found throughout the ancient world, with quite a few at places in Israel. Jews were not forbidden to play these games, but neither were they encouraged, as their teachers felt such trivial pastimes were a waste of time, especially for men. Board games are never mentioned in the Bible.

At Mizpah in Israel squares have been scratched into the smooth rock floor. These may have been for a game like draughts, with pebbles for draughtsmen. Draughts, played on rectangular boards with twenty or thirty squares, seems to have been quite a common game. Often dice were used.

Chess was played in ancient Babylon and it is quite likely that it was played in Israel.

A Greek relief showing youths playing a ball game with curved sticks.

Stones from The Pavement, where Christ was on trial before Pilate, show games scratched on the ground.

A relief from Carchemish, Assyria, showing women playing knucklebones.

Boards were made from wood, clay, stone and even ivory. A board found at Megiddo is shaped like a violin, and has fifty-eight holes: presumably for little pegs. Some boards are very ornate. Among the treasures in the royal graves at Ur in Mesopotamia, where Abraham came from, there was a beautiful wooden board, 5,000 years old. The squares are made of shell, and it is decorated with precious stones and red limestone. The people at Ur thought the king would play with it in his new life after death.

The playing pieces are often made of ivory. In one Egyptian game there are ten pieces, five in the shape of a jackal's head and five in the shape of a dog's head.

Dice

Some dice have been found with six sides, like ours today. Others have only two sides. Some, called teetotum, look like pyramids with the top cut off. One has from one to four holes pierced in its sides. A teetotum often has letters on the sides and a rod through its centre. The player spins the teetotum on the rod. When it stops spinning the letter or number on top is the one needed for the next move.

Gambling

In the Bible the only reference to gambling is when Jesus was on the cross and the soldiers 'cast lots' for his clothes (Matt. 27:35). Probably they used dice which they carried in their belts.

The Mishnah, a Jewish law book written after Jesus died, refers to gambling with dice and betting on pigeons. The Jewish teachers disapproved and said that no one who took part in these activities could be a witness in a court of law.

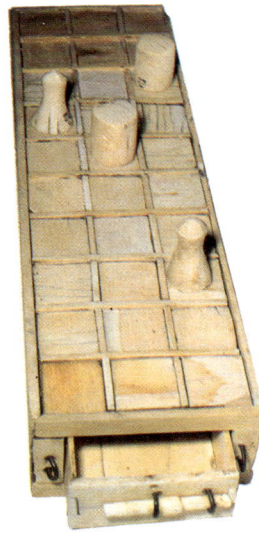

An ivory gaming board and box marked out for senet, an ancient Egyptian game.

A gaming board and counters from 3000BC, found in the royal graves at Ur, Mesopotamia.

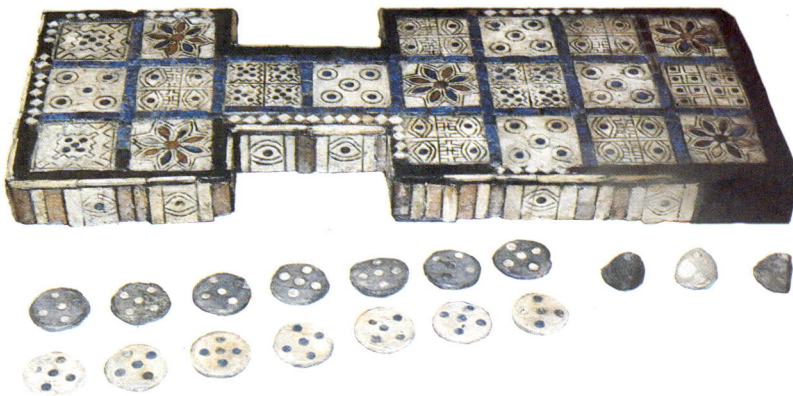

Jewish sports

Wrestling

From ancient times young men took part in wrestling matches. They wore special belts and took hold of the belt in different ways to make the throws.

A wrestling match is described in Genesis 32:24–26. When Jacob's opponent could not beat him, he gave him a nasty blow at the top of his leg. The Hebrew expression 'gird up your loins' (Luke 12:35; Eph. 6:14 AV) is a wrestling term. It means, get ready for action by putting on your belt.

Archery

In 1 Samuel 20:20 Jonathan mentions target shooting with arrows, and there is another reference in Lamentations 3:12. There was also 'long distance shooting'. Bows and arrows were used in war, so this game had a very serious purpose.

Sometimes the bow had two curves, and sometimes only one. It was made from wood or horn, and the string was gut taken from the intestine of an ox.

Slings and stones

Another weapon used for sport as well as war was the sling. Judges 20:16 says that 700 men were so accurate with the sling that they could even hit a strand of hair. When David was a boy he played with his

References to sports in the New Testament

The Gospels do not mention sport. However, Paul, who grew up in a Roman colony and wrote to Christians throughout the Roman empire, used examples from Greek athletics.

In Galatians 2:2(RSV) and 5:7(RSV) and in Philippians 2:16(RSV) he compares the Christian life to the Greek foot races while he probably refers to chariot racing in Philippians 3:13(RSV).

sling and used it to frighten wild animals away from the sheep. He became so deadly accurate that he was able to kill Goliath (1 Sam. 17:40–51).

This skill must have come from many hours of practice in childhood and there were probably many friendly contests between young people. (See also the section on Warfare.)

Sports days

We are told that Asahel ran as fast as a wild deer (2 Sam. 2:18) and Jeremiah mentioned running races (Jeremiah 12:5). So there must have been sporting events when boys and men raced and perhaps jumped.

Below: This Greek cup shows young men wrestling at a gymnasium. Such activities were frowned on by the Jews, who disapproved of nudity.

The Greek Games go back to 750BC. This statue of a discus thrower stands in the Athens Stadium.

Greek games

In Greek cities boys trained in running, long jumping, chariot racing, horse racing, boxing, wrestling, discus and javelin. The training was long and hard (1 Corinthians 9:25,26). The games had strict rules, and anyone who broke a rule was beaten. No one could be a full citizen of his town and vote in elections until he had completed this training.

The Greek Games were held in the important cities and small towns sent teams, just as towns today compete in football matches. Winners were given crowns of olive, pine or laurel leaves and were greatly honoured, like Olympic medallists today.

The sports were also religious ceremonies so at the opening of the Games there were sacrifices to the gods.

Another difference between the games then and now is that then everybody who took part was naked. Competitors were proud of their bodies and felt that they could compete much more effectively if they were not burdened with clothes.

Greek boxing

This is mentioned by Paul in 1 Corinthians 9:26, 27. There was no grading according to weight, no boxing ring and no rounds. The fight ended when one boxer was knocked out or gave in. There were no boxing gloves. Fingers were left free so that the fist could be clenched, but the palms and arms were wrapped in strips of leather. This strengthened the arms so that punches were harder. If a fight went on and on and spectators got bored, the judges ordered a 'climax'. Then the soft leather straps were replaced by hard ox leather, sometimes with metal attached. Each boxer took it in turns to slash out at his opponent, and no one was allowed to defend himself. This was dangerous and boxers were often killed.

Weights like these were used by long-jumpers to give them added thrust.

A drawing from a Greek water jar showing competitors in the pentathlon: wrestlers, javelin-throwers, a discus-thrower and runners, with an official.

This relief shows the names of the Games and the wreaths given to the winners.

An oil jar and strigil. Athletes rubbed their skin with oil and scraped it clean afterwards.

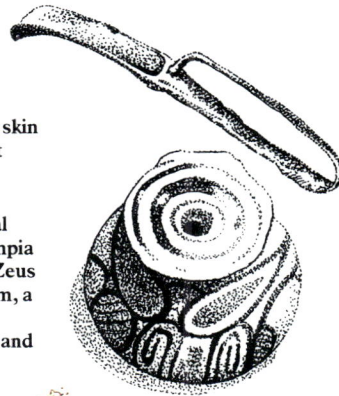

The site of the original Greek Games at Olympia included a temple to Zeus as well as a gymnasium, a running track and courtyards for discus and javelin-throwing.

Greek sports in Israel before Christ

About 300 years before Jesus was born, the Greeks became conquerors of Palestine. Greek ideas and customs spread throughout the country and some of the wealthy Jews took part in Greek sports. The first Greek gymnasium was built at Jerusalem in 170BC and for a time athletics were very popular. But the strict Jews were horrified because the games were in honour of heathen gods and because participants wore no clothes. They refused to take part, and after a few years all Greek sports were forbidden. This lasted till Herod the Great came into power in 37BC.

Roman games

In 63BC the Romans took control of Palestine, and many of the wealthy Jews began to follow Roman ideas.

Chariot racing

Chariots were light, two-wheeled vehicles, made of wood bound with brass, and pulled by four horses. An average race was seven laps of the stadium, or six miles. Crashes were frequent as the chariots careered round the bends. Each driver wore a crash helmet and tied the reins round his body. He had a knife to free himself if he got trapped.

The Roman chariot drivers were slaves or people from the lower classes. Chariots were bought by companies for whom the game was big business. As in horse racing today, there was heavy betting and racing cards were sold giving the names of horses and drivers. Between races the audience was entertained by acrobats, rope dancers and jugglers.

Gladiatorial shows

Gladiators were slaves, criminals or poor people owned by wealthy men who trained them to kill and then hired them out for shows.

There were many sorts of gladiator: some specialised in fighting with nets; some fought blindfold, on horseback; others in one-to-one combat with swords. A gladiator armed with a shield and sword might be set against a slave with a trident and a net; or rival teams of perhaps eighty-five men would attack each other. At the end of a fight like this there would be only one or two men left alive to get a laurel crown or a bag of gold or their freedom.

In a day's entertainment there were many different fights, and sand was strewn on the ground to hide the blood.

Fights with animals, called venatio, were also very popular. Sometimes beautiful and perhaps rare animals were set loose in the ring and slaves driven in to kill them. At other times there were fights between maddened animals, or single

This frieze, found in Turkey, shows men fighting with bears and bulls.

A Roman relief of a chariot race. The chariot is just reaching the turning point.

combats between wild animals and armed or unarmed men; or unarmed war prisoners were released in the ring and a pack of starving animals driven out to devour them.

Both men and women went to enjoy these shows, and boys too, if accompanied by an adult.

Athletics

Herod the Great, who reigned over Palestine from 37–4BC brought back Greek and Roman Games. The Jewish historian, Josephus, says that Herod 'appointed solemn games to be celebrated every fifth year in honour of Caesar'.

Herod built a gymnasium in Jerusalem where athletes could train, a magnificent sports stadium for running, and a hippodrome for horse and chariot racing. This he decorated with gold, silver and precious stones. He also built a huge amphitheatre on the outskirts of Jerusalem to which gladiators came from all over the world. This amphitheatre con-

sisted of a large oval space surrounded on all sides by rows of seats in tiers. Amphitheatres were also built in other Jewish towns, such as Jericho, Tiberias and Caesarea.

Some of the Jewish teachers supported athletics because they were good physical exercise for the young men, and good discipline. Some Jews even became gladiators, and were bought for large sums of money. But most of the Jews still strongly disapproved, and after AD70, when there was a rebellion against the Romans, the people stopped the Games.

Part of a Roman mosaic showing fights with animals for public entertainment.

This Roman coin shows men in combat with wild animals.

A mosaic from the floor of a Roman villa showing gladiators and their trainer.

The arts

The theatre

One of the favourite Greek pastimes was theatre-going. Even today we can enjoy the plays of the famous Greek dramatists, like Euripides and Sophocles, who wrote tragedies, or comedy writers like Aristophanes.

The open air theatres were important social centres. That is why, when there was a riot in Ephesus, everyone rushed to the theatre for the demonstration (Acts 19:29).

In Palestine in Greek and Roman times theatres were built in some of the larger towns and touring companies performed variety shows and plays. However, all the plays were written by non-Jews. We know of only one Jewish playwright, a man called Ezekiel, who lived in Alexandria in the first century before Christ. He wrote tragedies for the theatre based on biblical stories and these were performed in Egypt.

There were a few Jewish actors. When Nero was Emperor, one, called Alcturus, was a favourite of the Emperor. And in Rome there is the tomb of a Jewish actress.

All Jewish teachers disapproved of the theatre, and devout Jews never watched plays.

The storyteller

Instead of the theatre the Jews had the storyteller and travelling teacher. Round the evening camp fires in the desert, on the rooftops in towns and villages, families listened to stories told by a village elder, or travelling stranger. By the river bank, on the mountain side, in the deserted place, crowds of people went to hear the prophet or teacher.

All the stories were about the great deeds of their ancestors, about God's love for his people and about the Bible. The speakers used poetry, proverbs and vivid short stories.

The best example is Jesus himself, seen in his stories in the gospels.

Books

All the Jews' books taught them about God. Their only purpose in reading books or in listening to books being read, was to learn how God had guided people in the past, and how he wanted them to live.

Many of the books now form our Old Testament. They include poetry, adventure, war stories, wise advice, love stories, history books and laws.

A Greek relief showing actors, holding their masks, before the god Dionysus. Greek drama originated at religious festivals.

This theatre at Philippi dates from the 4th century BC. The best seats in the front rows were made of marble.

Reconstruction of part of the Library at Ephesus.

Four or five hundred years before Jesus was born, Jewish teachers began to compose commentaries on books in the Old Testament. These commentaries, called the Mishnah and the Midrash, were originally passed on by word of mouth and memorised, but were eventually written down. They include many hundreds of laws to help the Jewish people understand exactly how God wanted them to live.

In the Old Testament there are references to some very old books which we have now lost. For example, Numbers 21:14 refers to the *Book of the Wars of the Lord,* and Joshua 10:12, 13 mentions the *Book of Jashar.* These probably described great Hebrew battles.

In ancient Israel most of the people who wrote down these acts of God were not interested in a beautiful writing style. But later on, about 300 to 200BC, the vocabulary became richer and the style more interesting.

After Jesus died the early Christians told each other the deeds and sayings of Jesus. Eventually they wrote everything down, and read aloud what they had written. They also read to each other the letters of Paul, James, John and Peter, and made careful copies.

In those days probably nobody ever picked up a scroll and read silently. All reading was done aloud.

Libraries

In Israel copies of the Old Testament were kept by scribes and teachers in private libraries. Probably they were stored in earthenware pottery jars, like the scrolls that were found near the Dead Sea a little over thirty years ago.

There were no public lending libraries in Palestine. In Egypt, however, the first public lending library in the world was built at Alexandria, about 300BC. It contained 600,000 scrolls. All the great works of Greek literature were there, as well as the new writings of Alexandrian authors. In Rome in the time of Jesus, there were public reference libraries, where one could sit and read the scrolls, though they could not be taken away. Wealthy citizens also made up their own private libraries. One rich Roman is said to have had 62,000 scrolls.

Art, painting and sculpture

The people of Israel respected artists. They believed that anyone who could draw, design, paint or model had God's spirit in him (Exodus 35:31). Yet they produced no works of visual art of any kind – no great paintings or sculptures or engravings, no wall murals as in Assyria, or tomb paintings as in Egypt.

One reason for this was the command in Deuteronomy 5:8. The Jewish teachers said this command meant that no one was to paint or make a model of any living creature. They could draw only flowers, trees, plants, and one or two objects used in the Temple worship, like the seven branched candlestick and the scrolls.

A statuette of a harpist from Keros, dating back to 2000BC, looks surprisingly modern.

An intricate mosaic floor from a Roman villa.

A wall painting found in a house at Pompeii shows a man reading.

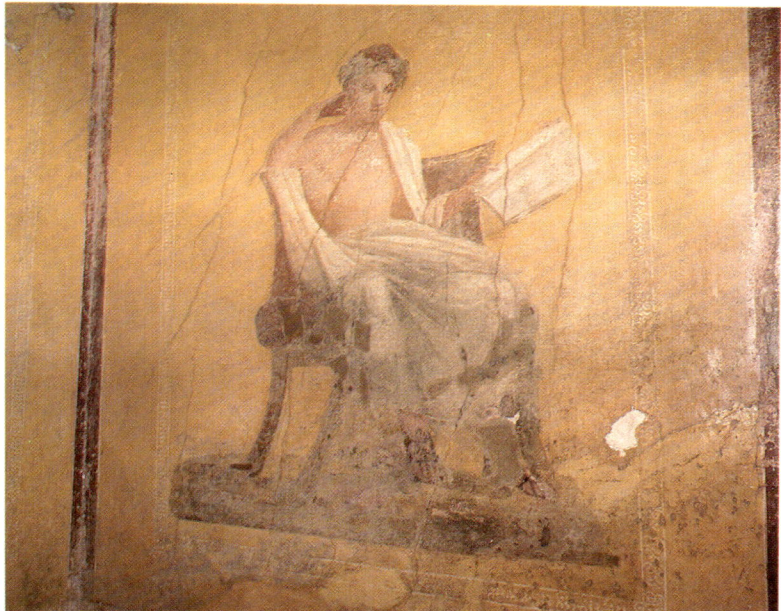

234

The Jews do not seem to have had much skill at drawing or modelling, and had little sense of colour. On one special occasion, when God told the Israelites in the wilderness to build the tabernacle, he gave some of the men artistic skills to do the work (Exod. 31:2–6). But the people did not develop these skills. In later centuries, whenever art did do well, and craftsmen were needed, as at the time of King Solomon and King Herod who both rebuilt the Temple and did much other building, foreign craftsmen and artists were used (I Kings 5:6; 7:13–15). Solomon employed

A pottery hedgehog from ancient Egypt.

Phoenician workmen; Herod employed Roman workmen.

In other countries artists decorated pots, vases and kitchen utensils with fine pictures and designs. But in Israel even the pots were copies of those made elsewhere and they were decorated with only a few zigzag and wavy lines.

Painting is not even mentioned in the Bible. It is certain that no one painted for pleasure or made models to pass the time away. However, the people may have amused themselves by carving in wood or ivory. This was a very ancient skill and is mentioned in the Bible (Exod. 35:33).

Poetry and music

You cannot separate Hebrew poetry and Hebrew music, for all Hebrew poems were made to be sung, or chanted, with musical instruments.

Music-makers were important people in ancient Israel. The writer of Genesis divided mankind into three groups, and placed musicians in the second group (Gen. 4:20–22).

Although the Canaanite people were the best musicians in the ancient world, and all early Israelite music copied Canaanite music, the later Israelites became famous as skilled musicians and song-writers. When an enemy, King Sennacherib of Assyria, attacked Jerusalem and demanded gifts from King Hezekiah, one of the gifts he asked for was Hezekiah's 'male

A statue of the Greek goddess Athena from 330BC.

Carved statues of an Egyptian court official and his wife from the 14th century BC.

This Egyptian tomb painting shows the Egyptians' love of colour and detail in their paintings.

and female musicians'. Later he boasted about these players in his court records.

Most books in the Old Testament refer to singing, dancing and music. People turned to poetry and song whenever they wanted to express their feelings. One of the best examples is David. He wrote poems when he was sorry (Psalm 51), afraid (Psalm 31), grateful (Psalm 34), and to express many other feelings.

There were funeral laments when people died and merry dancing songs at weddings (Psalm 45 is a song for the King's wedding), at all family parties, feasts and banquets, and victory celebrations. There were drinking songs and love songs, court music and music when the king was enthroned. Heroes were greeted with triumphant music and ordinary people sang rhythmic songs as they worked (well digging: Numbers 21:17; planting grapes: Isa. 16:10).

Battle music threatened the enemy and signalled to the people or soldiers (Numbers 10:35 is a marching chant). Above all, music was used to worship God in the Temple. The book of Psalms is the Temple hymn book. (See the section on Religion.)

The singers and musicians

In the very earliest days women played most of the music. There were choruses of dancing women who sang and chanted, often quite wildly, as they banged their timbrels (Exod. 15:20, 21). They celebrated all the great battles and important events in the country. Later some of the priests in the Temple were trained to play musical instruments and sing. Then they scorned the dance instruments which the women played and would not allow them to be used in the worship of God in the Temple.

When the Hebrew people came back from Exile, the professional Temple singers and musicians lived in small villages near Jerusalem (Neh. 12:28). They were respected people in the community and were excused from paying taxes (Ezra 7:24).

The tunes

Today one person usually composes a piece of music and other people play and

sing it. But in Bible times every singer sang his own songs.

There were only a few tunes, which were traditional folk tunes, and the singer made up his own variation on the tunes rather as jazz musicians do today with well-known tunes. When several musicians played together, they all played the same tune and there were no harmonies as there are today. When people sang

A Mesopotamian lyre, based on a lyre of 2500BC found at Ur.

A decorative initial showing David and musicians from the 13th century Ormesby Psalter.

This Egyptian wall painting shows girls playing harps. From evidence like this, a similar harp has been reconstructed.

together, it was normally antiphonal singing, that is, one group or one singer sang one line, and a 'chorus' or the congregation replied with the next. This was not just in religious services, but whenever people sang together. An example is when David returned from killing his Philistine enemies: one group of women sang, 'Saul has slain his thousands'; the second group replied, 'And David his ten thousands' (1 Sam. 18:7 AV).

Only in the Temple is there evidence of new music being composed. Josephus, a Jewish historian who lived not long after Jesus, wrote that the Levites in the Temple studied the text and music of 'new hymns'. Nevertheless, even here we think there was not much variety.

The instruments

The people who wrote the Bible took it for granted that everyone knew the musical instruments. It never occurred to them to describe their instruments, any more than it would occur to us to describe a guitar or drum. We generally have to guess what their instruments sounded and looked like by comparing old pictures on wall paintings or sculpture and by studying the different ways the instruments were used.

WIND INSTRUMENTS

Flute The Hebrew name for flute is *masroqita* which comes from a word meaning 'whistle' or 'hiss'. It was a shepherd's instrument made of cane, wood or bone (Judg. 5:16). It was like a recorder, but it did not sound very musical, and was not fit for use in the Temple.

Pipe or, in Hebrew, *halil*, from a word meaning to drill a hole. This was a primitive clarinet or shawm, and was the most popular wind instrument. Jeremiah (Jer. 48:36) talks of 'moaning like a *halil*' so the pipe must have had a sad wailing tone. It was probably not used for Temple worship, but was played to express sorrow, for example at funerals (Matt. 9:23) or joy, as at weddings and feasts (Isa. 30:29).

Horn (Hebrew *qeren*). Originally an animal's horn, the *qeren* was later also made from wood or metal. It was most popular in the very early days before Joshua. Joshua's priests played the *qeren* as well as the trumpet when they were marching round the walls of Jericho (Joshua 6:5).

Trumpet People in the Bible had several different kinds of trumpet. The *hasosera* was the priests' trumpet. It was made of silver, bronze, copper or gold, was about two feet long, and gave out a high, shrill noise. Normally two were used together, but on one very special occasion 120 were blown (2 Chronicles 5:12). The *shophar* is the most frequently named instrument in the Bible and is still blown in Jewish synagogues today. It is made of ram's horn, and, unlike the *hasosera*, which was straight, the *shophar* turns up at the end. It produces only two notes and its function was not to make music but to signal to the people. In war it terrified the enemy and warned of approaching danger. When the Temple was destroyed by the Romans in AD70 the Jews banished all musical instruments except the *shophar* which indicates that they did not think of it as a musical instrument.

STRING INSTRUMENTS

Lyre, or, in Hebrew, *kinnor*. (Sometimes this has been called a zither and in the King James' version of the Bible it is translated 'harp'.) This

A Canaanite girl playing a lute from a reconstructed statuette.

was the most respected of all the instruments, for it was David's instrument. The aristocracy played the *kinnor* and it was used by the Levites in Temple worship. It was quite small, made of wood, often very expensive wood, like almug (1 Kings 10:12) and decorated with silver and ivory. The number of strings seems to have varied between three and twelve. Probably it was played with the fingers and a plectrum.

Harp (sometimes translated psaltery and lute). The Hebrew word, *nebel*, means a skin bottle or jar, so the sound box may have been round and fat like a water bottle. It was often made of precious woods and metals. We have pictures of Egyptian harps and if the *nebel* was the same instrument, it could have been over two metres tall, and have had ten to twenty strings, played without the plectrum. Like the lyre, the harp was an instrument for the priests and nobles, not for the women, and was normally used only in

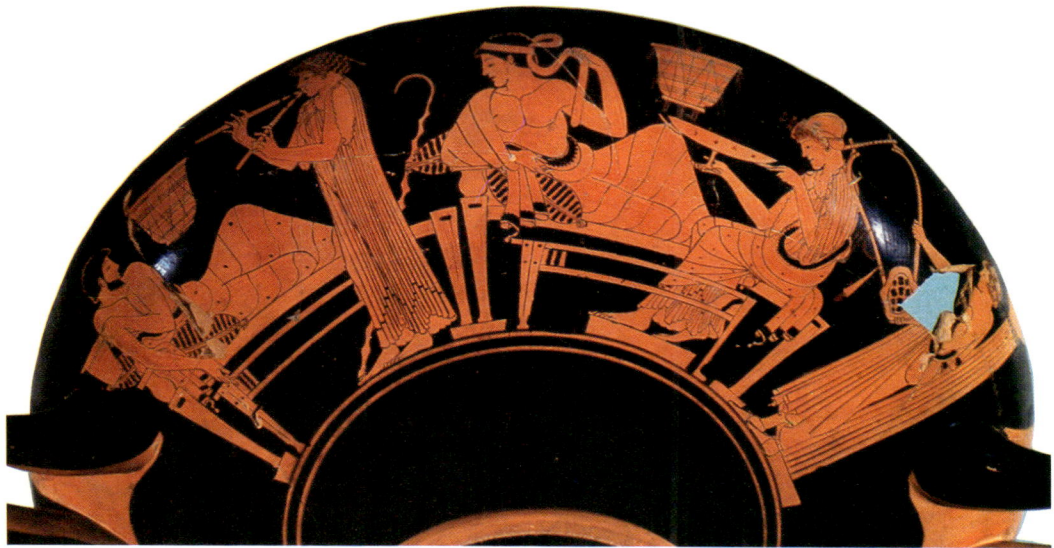

This Roman wall painting from Herculaneum shows a music lesson in the 1st century AD.

A party scene shown on a Greek vase of 490BC includes a girl playing the double pipes.

Temple worship, probably as the bass. It is often pictured as providing the music in heaven (Revelation 14:2–3).

Lute (Hebrew *shelishim*). This is from the Hebrew word for three, which could refer to three strings or to a three-cornered shape. Usually played by women, it was never used for Temple worship.

Trigon (*sabbeka*). This appears only in Daniel 3 and was a Babylonian instrument in Nebuchadnezzar's orchestra. It was like a harp, but was played only by low class musicians.

Reconstructions of early Jewish instruments, based on reliefs and excavations. A lyre from the 7th century BC.

PERCUSSION INSTRUMENTS

Timbrel (also called tambourine and tabret). The Hebrew word is *top*. This was a small hand-held drum, made from two skins stretched over a wooden hoop. It probably sounded like a tom-tom. It was played by women as they sang and danced, at feasts or in processions (Exod. 15:20) and whenever people wanted to celebrate and enjoy themselves, but was not allowed in Temple worship.

Cymbals The Hebrew words are *meziltaim* and *selselim*, both words coming from a Hebrew word meaning whirr or quiver. There were two types in ancient Israel. The 'loud cymbals' which gave out a harsh jangling noise were thin metal plates. One was held in each hand and they were crashed together. The other, the 'high sounding cymbals', were like hollow metal cups and made a ringing sound. One was held still and the other banged down on top of it. As far as we can tell from the Bible, cymbals were used only in Temple worship.

Castanets (also translated sistrum and rattle). The Hebrew word is *menaaim*. The only time this instrument is mentioned in the Bible is 2 Samuel 6:5. It was used by wailing women at funerals, and at celebrations. We are not sure what it looked like, but if it was similar to an Egyptian instrument found at Ur, it did not look at all like our castanets. It may have been like a hollow table-tennis bat with loose metal wires stretched across it which jangled when shaken. The wires may have been threaded with metal discs which rattled up and down.

A reconstruction of a statuette of a girl with a

THE BANDS

In 1 Chronicles 15:16–24 the writer talks of an orchestra of lyres, harps and tambourines which David organised for the Temple. And in 2 Samuel 6 we read of a band of lyres, harps, tambourines, castanets and cymbals. Normally the instruments were played separately or in small groups of two or three to accompany singing.

timbrel from around 900BC.

Large cymbals of unknown date.

Metal cymbals with wooden handles from the 8th century BC.

238

A Greek pipe player shown on a Greek vase.

Two Greek statuettes showing a woman playing a lyre and another woman dancing.

Dancing at the Rejoicing of the Law ceremony at the Western Wall, Jerusalem.

Dancing

Dancing for fun The people in Israel loved to dance. The Bible talks of children dancing (Job 21:11; Luke 7:32). Moses found the people dancing when he came down from the mountain (Exod. 32:19). And David was greeted by dancing women when he returned from his battles (1 Sam. 18:6). The guests at the Prodigal Son's party all danced (Luke 15:25).

At these dances the men and women danced separately.

Dancing in worship People often danced at their religious festivals to show their delight in God and to thank him, perhaps, for a good harvest (Judg. 21:19) or for a great victory (Exod. 15:20). In the early days of the Old Testament the women danced by themselves, whirling and twisting their bodies, banging and shaking their timbrels. On one occasion, however, King David himself danced. He jumped and leapt before God as he led the procession carrying the ark into Jerusalem.

In Greek and Roman times Later on, in New Testament times, the Greeks and Romans employed professional women dancers to entertain them at banquets and celebrations. We know that some Jewish women took part in these dances because Salome, Herodias' daughter, danced at Herod's birthday feast (Mark 6:22).

Recreation

Gardens and gardening

The king's palace in Jerusalem had a garden attached to it (Jer. 39:4), but generally in towns there were no gardens because the houses were too close together. At most there may have been some flowering plants in a courtyard. The gardens were on the flat ground outside the city walls, or on the slopes of nearby hills, like the Garden of Gethsemane on the Mount of Olives. Only in the villages were there gardens next to the houses.

Generally gardens were either orchards, with olives and vines, sycamores, almonds and pomegranates (Song of Songs 6:11), or kitchen gardens watered from a spring or pool (Isa. 58:11). King Ahab wanted Naboth's vineyard so that he could make a vegetable garden (1 Kings 21:2). Herbs were also grown (Song of Songs 5:13). Where there were flowers, they were grown among the vegetables and used to decorate the tables. Violets and roses were liked, but the range of flowers was small.

The hillside gardens were surrounded by a wall of rocks to keep the soil from washing away in the occasional heavy rains. There was sometimes a thorn hedge to keep out wild animals. Orchards may have had a small watch tower, and a vine and olive press.

What gardens were for In Bible times people did not garden for pleasure. They had gardens because they wanted fresh

This painting from a Roman villa in Pompeii shows a garden by the sea.

A relief showing servants preparing food and drink for a feast.

240

The Garden of Gethsemane on the Mount of Olives, Jerusalem.

herbs and vegetables to eat, or quiet shady places to walk and relax (compare Gen. 3:8). Jesus occasionally went to the Garden of Gethsemane to be quiet and pray. There was sometimes a summer-house for resting in, and a pool for bathing. Banquets and parties were held in gardens, and the family tomb was sometimes there (John 19:41).

Far Eastern and Roman gardens From Persia and Babylon came the idea of ornate pleasure gardens. In the book of Esther, King Ahasuerus had a fine garden where he entertained his guests (Esther 7:8).

Roman gardens were like these Eastern gardens. There were beautiful flower beds (often in terraces like the hanging gardens of Babylon) avenues of trees, and evergreen hedges clipped into interesting shapes.

Very wealthy people in Palestine copied the Romans. The ruins of a beautiful garden belonging to Herod the Great have been found in Jericho. There were many terraces with pools and fountains, flowering trees, bushes and flowers.

Public holidays

Nowadays most people take their main annual holiday at different times and go away to the country or seaside with their family. In Bible times everybody had their holidays at the same time, like our Bank Holidays and Christmas and Easter holidays. These were not just family holidays, for all the people in a village celebrated together. Every month there was a festival of some kind.

Lesser feasts

Victory days
One of the happiest holidays was called just 'yom tom' – 'the good day'. It was the Feast of Purim, which was in memory of a victory against the Jews' enemies (Esther 8:17; 9:22). Everybody celebrated it by feasting and drinking, playing games, dressing up in fancy dress, and giving presents. This was one of the few general holidays which was not also a religious festival.

Feast of Nicanor
This celebrated a victory over a Syrian General, Nicanor. A great fire was lit and runners carried burning torches to every part of the land.

Shearing Festival
This was held at the beginning of summer when the sheep were shorn. And there was a feast when the flocks were blessed.

Family festivals
Parents might want to thank God for his goodness, perhaps because their baby had been born safely, or someone in the family had recovered from a serious illness. All the relatives and friends would pack a picnic, take a lamb or sheep or just a couple of pigeons for a sacrifice and, in Old Testament times, would climb to their local high place where there was an altar and a priest. In New Testament times they would go to the Temple in Jerusalem. After the animal had been sacrificed, the priest roasted it, and everyone sat down in the open air to eat. Then, as the day ended, they sang and danced, 'rejoicing before the Lord'.

Sabbath
Every Saturday was a festival, as God had commanded (Deuteronomy 5:12–15). No work was done at all, not even cooking. Everyone worshipped God, and relaxed.

(For *The Great Feasts* see the section on Religion.)

The Feast of Purim is celebrated by processions in fancy dress.

EDUCATION AND TRAINING

Education is about schools and teachers, classrooms and libraries, writing and arithmetic. It is also about learning how to live, how to work and how to make a home of one's own.

This section describes what is known about education in Bible times not only among the Israelites but also in those countries which came into Israel's story at various times in history: Mesopotamia, Egypt, Greece and Rome. It is interesting to see how the arrangements made for the education of boys differed from those made for girls: it has not always been thought a good idea to have education for everyone!

A Greek school scene shown on a vase. The pupil is seen reciting Homer, writing with a stylus and learning to play musical instruments. He is escorted and observed by the family slave, seen seated on the right.

Learning in Mesopotamia

Mesopotamia, the land between the two great rivers Tigris and Euphrates, was the land that God told Abraham to leave when he set out for the country which became the Promised Land. Abraham sent his servant back there to find a wife for Isaac, and Isaac's son Jacob travelled back to Mesopotamia to find himself a wife. Many years later it was from Mesopotamia that the Assyrian armies came to destroy Israel, and the Babylonians later still to capture Jerusalem and take prisoners into exile to that same region.

Sumerian schools

Long before Abraham, from sunrise to sunset the sons of wealthy families attended schools for scribes in ancient Sumer. A scribe was a professional writer but these boys, and possibly a few girls, learned drawing, reading, counting and biology as well as writing. This writing was made by a stylus, a piece of bone or reed, which was pressed into damp clay. The stylus was shaped like a triangle at the end and was held at an angle. Writing like this is called cuneiform meaning wedge-shaped. When the writing was finished the clay tablet was baked in the sun.

Archaeologists have found thousands of Sumerian clay tablets. One of them includes the following lines:

Schoolboy, where did you go from earliest days?
I went to school.
What did you do in school?
I read my tablet, ate my lunch,
prepared my tablet, wrote it, finished it . . .

The school was called the Tablet House. The pupils learned to write by copying lists of names and words and great stories of their people. Sometimes they made mistakes and their teachers' corrections

Pupils in Sumerian schools wrote on clay tablets with a stylus. The boy on the left is smoothing over the clay so that he can use it again. A basket containing fresh balls of clay stands ready, covered with a damp cloth. Some boys have brought their lunch with them.

can still be seen on tablets which have been found. There was a headteacher and a deputy head called 'Father of the Tablet House'. The teachers were called 'tablet writers' and they prepared work for the pupils each day. They were very strict; there are a number of references to the cane. After success in the Tablet House the clever students went on to the House of Wisdom for more advanced studies in mathematics and literature.

Further north on the River Euphrates the remains of two classrooms from about Abraham's time have been found in the palace at Mari. Here the pupils sat on stone benches and had desks made of clay. Small shells found scattered on the floor may have been used as counters.

Babylonian schools

A little later than Abraham, in Hammurabi's Babylon, schools were usually connected with the temple. Again, clay tablets found on the floor of one of these schools have helped archaeologists to picture what school was like. The pupil collected a soft ball of clay which he rolled out on a wooden tray. He then practised writing, smoothing out the clay with a flat piece of wood or stone if he made a mistake and starting again. One of these tablets has this saying on it: 'He who shall excel in tablet-writing shall shine like the sun.'

Assyrian scholars

A thousand years later the Assyrians were not only fierce warriors who dealt with prisoners with great cruelty, they were also writers and scholars. Ashurbanipal, the grandson of the great Sennacherib who terrified King Hezekiah of Judah, collected a library of thousands of clay tablets at Nineveh. Most of these are now in the British Museum. They show that the Assyrians studied botany, geology, chemistry, astronomy, medicine, mathematics and law as well as many ancient religious stories and practices. Nineveh was destroyed by the Babylonians in 612BC.

One of the Jews taken into exile in Babylon by Nebuchadnezzar in 605BC was Daniel. The first chapter of the book of Daniel describes how he and his friends were educated at the royal court. They learned to read and write the Babylonian language and studied all that was necessary to become a royal adviser. Evidently this training also included a special diet to make them healthy, although Daniel and his friends refused this special food. They were taught by the king's chief official. We have some idea of the texts that Daniel and his friends studied from archaeological finds at Babylon. In addition to the many items found in the library at Nineveh there were collections of wise sayings, grammars and dictionaries, magic texts, history and the calendar.

An Assyrian letter in cuneiform script in its original clay envelope. The letter is written to an official and the writer complains of the lack of a reply to three previous letters.

Scribes are depicted in the centre of this Assyrian relief. They are recording those killed and captured in battle.

244

Education in Egypt

Egyptian scribes making notes on writing boards. In the tomb painting, right, scribes are making a cattle census.

This relief from 2345BC shows a scribe seated at his desk.

Abraham visited Egypt but the most important links between the Bible and Egypt were during the time of Joseph and, later, the years just before the Exodus.

In early Egypt schools were attached to temples and education was controlled by the priests. The remains of writing boards show that pupils worked at counting, writing, geography and science. Much of their writing was copying stories, wise sayings, songs, laws, history, prayers and hymns. They sometimes chanted these aloud. In one text an old school friend is called 'one with whom you once did *sing* the writings'. If they were going to be priests they

studied religion and medicine. Only the privileged few learned the difficult tasks of the scribe.

Little is known about Egypt under the rule of the foreign Hyksos kings which was probably at the time of Joseph. When the Egyptians drove the Hyksos out they destroyed everything which would have reminded them of those hated kings.

Court education

By the time the Israelites escaped from Egypt under Moses' leadership, Egypt had become an empire. Moses was educated at Pharaoh's court and according to

one later Jewish writer he was skilled at arithmetic, geometry, poetry, music, philosophy, astrology and all branches of learning.

He was probably educated with the children of the court by an official called 'Teacher of the king's children'. He may have learned the twenty letters of the early Canaanite alphabet as well as the more complicated hieroglyphic script. Since Egypt was an empire, in contact with other nations, other languages were taught. He studied law, perhaps the famous law code of Hammurabi, religion and the wise sayings of the past. Older princes were given a tutor to themselves. These tutors were either high court officials or retired army officers.

Schools

There were schools for boys who intended to become scribes or priests. At the age of five pupils went to the School of the Book where they learned to read and write until they were sixteen or seventeen. From the age of thirteen onwards they also had practical training as apprentices to a scribe or priest. At seventeen those learning to be priests went on to the Temple School. There is an interesting reference to the House of Life which may have been a college where the main study was how to survive death, a major interest of the Egyptians.

The beginner who was learning to write used cheap surfaces like limestone or pieces of broken pottery. After some progress they advanced to writing boards and then to papyrus. Most 'books' were made of papyrus sheets gummed together. Teachers corrected their pupils' work in red ink. Mathematics was of the practical kind which could be used in surveying a field, counting taxes or measuring corn in store-houses. The most brilliant students went on to advanced studies of medicine, astrology (including the calendar), magic and teaching.

The advantages of being a scribe were avoiding the heavy labour of the builder or gardener, the blacksmith and the cobbler and being one's own boss. 'Behold there is no profession free of a boss – except for the scribe: he is the boss' as one classroom exercise put it.

An Egyptian child had to learn the hieroglyphic script at school. These hieroglyphs appear on the Tomb of Nakht from the 15th century BC.

Hebrew and Jewish education

God's chosen people are called by different names in the Bible. Earlier on they are the children of Israel or the Hebrews. Only from the time of the Exile in Babylon are they called the Jews.

In the family

Among the Hebrews the home has always been the centre of life, faith and education. Until the children were three years old their mother was their teacher and she continued to be responsible for the education of the girls. She would tell her children the great stories of what God had done for his people long ago, people like Abraham, Isaac and Jacob. Was it because the Egyptian princess had unknowingly employed his own mother to look after him when he was a baby that Moses knew about God when he first met him (Exodus 2:7–9; 3:4–6)? The father took a special interest in the education of his son. One of the first lessons a Jewish boy learns today is to recite the Shema which is found in the book of Deuteronomy (6:4–9): 'Israel, remember this! The Lord – and the Lord alone – is our God. Love the Lord your God with all your heart, and with all your soul, and with all your strength. Never forget these commands that I am giving you today. Teach them to your children. Repeat them when you are at home and when you are away, when you are resting and when you are working. Tie them on your arms and wear them on your foreheads as a reminder. Write them on the door-posts of your house and on your gates.'

This shows the importance of the home, the many different ways the father could use to teach his son and that when he grew up he would have to teach his children too. The idea of the father teaching his son was so important that the words 'father' and 'son' were used for a teacher and his pupil.

Learning about the faith

The father had to teach God's Law. The word translated 'law' is 'Torah' which means 'instruction'. In other words the father was teaching his son what God had first taught the Hebrew people. This included stories of God's dealings with his people in the past, especially the story of the Great Escape (the Exodus) from slavery in Egypt, the wilderness journey with Moses, the giving of the Law at Mount Sinai and the conquest of the Promised Land led by Joshua. Children were encouraged to ask questions such as, 'Why did the Lord our God command us to obey all these laws?' to which the answer was the story of the Great Escape (Deut. 6:20–25). At the Passover meal every year when the Hebrews celebrated the Great Escape the son would ask, 'What does this mean?' (Exod. 12:26) and the father replied by re-telling the story. The menu of the meal itself reminded them of parts of the story. For example, the bitter herbs spoke of the bitter slavery and the unleavened bread (cooked without yeast) of the haste with which the journey to freedom began (Exod. 12:39). When the book of Joshua was written it was still possible to see the stones he had ordered to be set up at the place where the Israelites had crossed the River Jordan to enter the Promised Land. Joshua's men had put them there to make children ask what they meant (Joshua 4:5–9).

The father also taught his son about right and wrong and practical matters like how to pray and how to get on with people and keep out of trouble. Examples of this kind of teaching can be found in the Ten Commandments (Exod. 20:1–17 and Deut. 5:1–21) and in the book of Proverbs, a moral code for life. This teaching always encouraged the children to put God first (Proverbs 1:7) and to remember what their parents had taught them (Prov. 1:8; 6:20). The parents were also instructed to punish their children with a good spanking, if they really loved them (Prov. 13:24; 22:15)!

Training for girls

What the Israelites believed affected their daily lives in many other ways. Part of the mother's teaching to her daughters was how to prepare meals according to the Law. This included, for example, not cooking meat dishes and milk together and using special dishes for Passover. The mother would also teach the girls all they needed to know to become good wives and mothers themselves. So they learned to grind corn and make bread, to look after clothes, washing and mending them when necessary, making new ones by spinning and weaving, and to take care of the children. Some girls looked after the family's flocks (Genesis 29:6) and helped with the harvest (Ruth 2:8). The capable wife, described in Proverbs 31:10–29, not only makes the clothes, shops and cooks the meals, she also buys land and plants a vineyard. There were some professions for which a girl could train, for example she could be a midwife (Exod. 1:21) or a singer at court (Ecclesiastes 2:8). A prophetess like Deborah or Huldah would have had a good education to know the story of Israel's history and draw lessons

A girl spinning. She draws the yarn from the spinning bowl behind her. The weighted spindle attached to the other end of the yarn causes it to twist into thread which is then wound on to the spindle.

A Jewish boy wearing the tefillin on his forehead and arms. These small leather boxes contain Bible verses from the Law.

At the Jewish Passover meal the youngest child traditionally asks the father questions about the meaning of the ceremony.

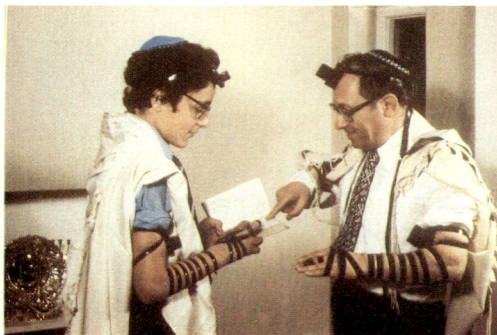

from it for the time in which they lived.

Probably most girls in Israel learned just what was needed for each to look after her husband and children and she learned this by copying the way her mother lived.

Training for boys

Boys learned to mind the family's sheep from a fairly young age. When Samuel arrived at Bethlehem to meet Jesse's family it was David the youngest who was left with the flock (1 Samuel 16:11). He had evidently also learned to play the harp and played well enough to get the job of court musician for a while (1 Sam. 16:14–23). Usually the father taught his son his own trade. This led, after the settlement in Canaan, to some villages where all the men practised the same trade like linen-weaving or pottery (1 Chronicles 4:21–23). The list in Genesis 4:20–22 suggests the occupations of herdsman, musician and toolmaker had been passed down many generations. Many years later a Rabbi said, 'He who does not teach his son a useful trade is bringing him up to be a thief.' Jesus was known as 'the carpenter's son' (Matthew 13:55) and also as 'the carpenter' (Mark 6:3).

Some trades were taught by a master craftsman like Bezalel or his companion Oholiab (Exod. 35:30–35). Paul probably learned his craft of weaving goats' hair cloth to make tents and cloaks from his father (Acts 18:3).

After David had established an Israelite empire some boys probably trained to be professional soldiers. Before David's time, everyone had to learn to fight (Judges 3:2). They would have learned to use the sling, the bow, the spear and the sword.

Occasionally, a boy was sent away from home to learn his future occupation. Samuel, for example, was taken at a very early age to the high priest Eli at Shiloh to be trained as a priest (1 Sam. 1:24–28). It is interesting that Eli was given the job of training Samuel but was criticised for failing to bring up his own sons properly (1 Sam. 2:12–17; 3:12–13)

The education of kings and princes

As with other boys the mother of a prince was his first teacher and if her son became king she could be a very important person. This is why Bathsheba worked hard to make sure her son Solomon would follow David (1 Kings 1:5–53).

All young princes received the same

In Bible times a Jewish girl received all her education from her mother. Today the mother still plays the dominant role in the upbringing and education of the children.

In the synagogue the Jewish child learns about his faith when the Torah is read. The Torah scrolls in this synagogue in Jerusalem are kept behind the ornate curtains.

Jewish girls of 12 years take part in a special ceremony after completing a religious study course. Women have an equal but different status to men in Judaism.

Jewish mothers come to pray for their children at Rachel's Tomb in Bethlehem.

Young boys still help to mind the family sheep as David did.

weapons and drive a chariot as well as plan the battle as a whole. The art of government included dealing with messengers from other kings, knowing something about geography and trade and perhaps speaking Aramaic, an international language from the 8th century onwards. It also included knowing how to organise the kingdom. When King Uzziah caught a dreaded skin disease his son Jotham was able to take over all his duties (2 Kings 15:5). Solomon and Amaziah made important decisions as judges and must have been well taught the Law of Moses (1 Kings 3:16–28; 2 Kings 14:6). Solomon built and dedicated the Temple and Joash and Josiah carried out important repairs. When the book of the Law was discovered and read to Josiah he knew and understood what the people had to do. One important teacher in the life of Joash was the priest Jehoiada (2 Kings 12:2).

Priests and prophets

The duties of the priests included teaching adult Israelites the Law (Torah) of God (Leviticus 10:11). They would do this when the people came to worship and celebrate the religious festivals at Jerusalem or another sacred place. The priests were obviously experts in all that was involved in worshipping God. Every seven years at the Festival of Shelters they were to read God's Law as Moses had written it, to men, women, children and foreigners who gathered at Jerusalem (Deut. 31:9–13). King Jehoshaphat sent priests on a tour of the cities of Judah to remind the people what was in the Book of the Law (2 Chron. 17:8, 9).

To carry out these teaching duties and all the detailed actions involved in offering sacrifices required a long training. They also had to know how to tell if someone had the dreaded skin disease leprosy and when it was healed and about other diseases too. They also looked after the collection of money in the Temple (2 Kings 12:9–16). No wonder their preparation to be a priest lasted until they were thirty years old (Numbers 4:3).

In theory the priests were to teach without charging for their services. The prophet Micah criticised the priests and prophets of his day for teaching only for

education, for if they did not become king themselves they could expect to be advisers or governors of important cities. David arranged for his sons to be taught by his uncle Jonathan and another man called Jehiel (1 Chron. 27:32), and Ahab's seventy sons were in the care of certain 'guardians' who failed in their task of protecting the princes (2 Kings 10:1–7). No doubt the king also took a fatherly interest in the education of his sons.

There were three main parts to the education of a prince: the art of warfare, the art of government and religious duties. Most kings led their armies into battle and therefore had to be able to use their

money (3:11). It is interesting here to see priests and prophets grouped together as teachers. The usual picture is of a prophet like Micah attacking the priests and their many sacrifices (6:6–8). The prophet's job was to declare God's message and some of them, like Amos, were on their own. Others had disciples (eg, Isaiah 8:16) who learned and then taught others what their master had said. It is probably due to disciples, often unknown, that we have the words of many of the prophets in the Old Testament.

Wise men and women

In every society some men and women are recognised as being wiser than the rest and other people come to them for advice. Joseph was such an adviser to Pharaoh (Genesis 45:8). Joab sent for a wise woman from Tekoa (2 Sam. 14:2 RSV). Daniel and his friends were trained to be wise men at the court of Nebuchadnezzar (Daniel 1). From the time of King Solomon there was a group of wise men at the court of Israelite kings. They advised on practical matters of state and daily living and their advice was copied and passed on by their successors (Prov. 25:1). By the time of Jeremiah, however, they were leading the people astray. He accused them along with the priests and prophets (Jeremiah 8:8–10).

Scribes

There were people who could write from early times in Israel's history. Moses wrote down the laws God gave him (Exod. 34:27). The young man whom Gideon captured wrote down seventy-seven names for him (Judg. 8:14). One interesting archaeological find, known as the Gezer Calendar, is possible evidence of a boy's writing lessons. A twelve-year-old could hold it easily and the writing is a rhyme about the months of the year, something like 'Thirty days hath September . . .' Probably those who could write taught their sons, and the skill of professional writing was at first and for many years a family business (1 Chron. 2:55). The family of Shaphan held the position of king's scribe from the time of Josiah to the Exile (2 Kings 22:3).

The scribe's first lesson was to master

the Canaanite alphabet. It looks as if Isaiah is referring to such early learning in 28:9–13 where he refers to letter by letter, line by line, lesson by lesson. The next step would have been copying short texts like the Gezer Calendar. Then he would progress to writing letters and official

This illuminated manuscript features the Israelite kingly line descending from Jesse the father of David (bottom) to Christ (top).

The Hebrew Calendar from Gezer, scratched on stone by a schoolboy in the 10th century BC, appears to be a rhyme listing agricultural tasks for the year.

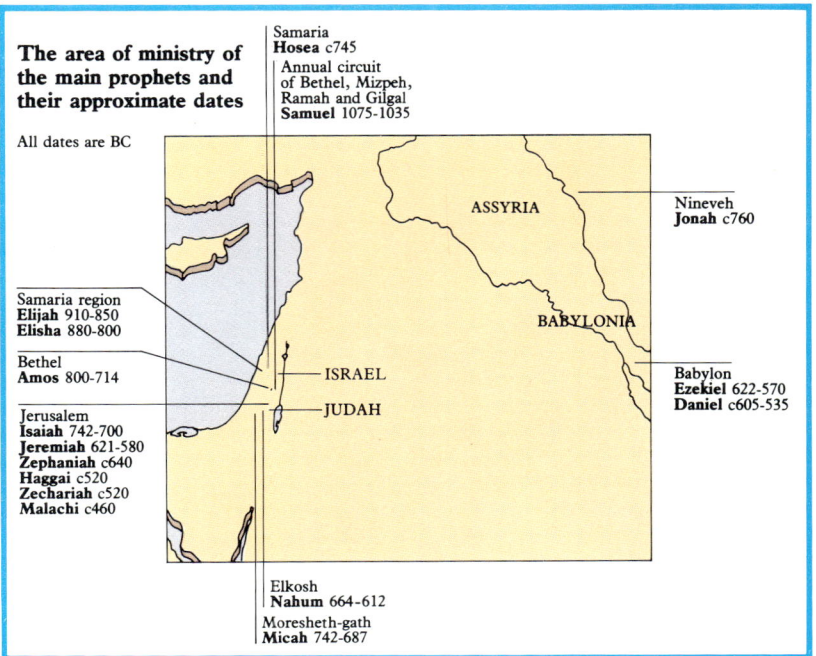

The area of ministry of the main prophets and their approximate dates

All dates are BC

Samaria
Hosea c745
Annual circuit of Bethel, Mizpeh, Ramah and Gilgal
Samuel 1075-1035

ASSYRIA

Nineveh
Jonah c760

Samaria region
Elijah 910-850
Elisha 880-800

Bethel
Amos 800-714

ISRAEL

JUDAH

BABYLONIA

Babylon
Ezekiel 622-570
Daniel c605-535

Jerusalem
Isaiah 742-700
Jeremiah 621-580
Zephaniah c640
Haggai c520
Zechariah c520
Malachi c460

Elkosh
Nahum 664-612

Moresheth-gath
Micah 742-687

forms and all the documents which go with legal matters like marriage and the sale of land. The king's scribes would have to learn languages like Aramaic (2 Kings 18:26), Assyrian and Egyptian. They would be experts in international law and probably knew practical mathematics, enough astronomy to work out the calendar and were able to draw maps and diagrams.

The Exile began for thousands of Jews in 597BC, and ten years later Nebuchadnezzar destroyed Jerusalem and took more captives to Babylon. Here, many miles from their ruined Temple and sacrifices which had been so important to them but were now impossible, they kept their faith alive by stressing those parts of it they could still practise. They kept the sabbath day as a day of rest. They studied the Scriptures and the Law they contained. The most important writing work for scribes now was copying the Scriptures. As some of the priests became scribes it was natural for them to combine their work of teaching with writing. Nobody else knew and understood the Scriptures as well as these scribes, so they

The scribes became highly respected as teachers of the Law. This painting by Mazzolino shows the young Jesus in the Temple questioning the doctors of the Law.

became highly respected as teachers of the Law.

During the Exile the Scriptures grew to include not only the Law, the Torah (now understood to be the first five books of our Bible) and the Prophets, but also the writings of wise men and poets. Some of these wise men joined the scribes and added to their reputation as teachers. They also memorised and taught their disciples a large amount of unwritten law usually in the form of explanations of the Scriptures by famous teachers.

Schools

It is possible that there were schools at the royal palaces in Samaria and Jerusalem before the Exile to train boys to become government officials but there is, as yet, no evidence for them like the evidence found at Sumer, Mari or in Egypt. Schools were required, following the work begun by Ezra and continued by his successors.

The words 'house of study' are found first in the last chapter of the book of Ecclesiasticus in the Apocrypha (51:23). It is part of the wise man's invitation to join his disciples. 'Your share of instruction may cost you a large sum of silver, but it will bring you a large return in gold' (51:28 NEB). This suggests that it was an expensive business but profitable to those who became teachers in their turn. Such schools for the training of future scribes were found in Jerusalem and also in Babylon where many of the Jews had stayed. The teaching method was the spoken word which was learned by heart and recited by the students. Nothing was written down. There were several ways of helping the students remember what they had to learn: frequent repetition, sometimes beginning each sentence or line with the next letter of the alphabet, telling stories and putting some teaching in poetic form.

Some of these schools became famous and had famous teachers. There is the story of Hillel who had been a beggar and day-labourer in Babylon. He came to Jerusalem to complete his education but could not afford the fee. He was found outside the classroom window listening, covered with snow. He became a well-known teacher himself.

Synagogue schools

Ezra and his successors are known in Jewish tradition as 'men of the great synagogue' but the origins of the buildings known as synagogues and found all over the Roman world in the pages of the New Testament are obscure. It may have been during the Exile that gatherings to hear a prophet like Ezekiel, or one of the scribes, became regular meetings to hear the Law read and for prayer. The earliest evidence of the existence of a synagogue is an inscription found near Alexandria in Egypt and dating from the 3rd century BC. Whatever the truth about their beginnings the synagogue became not only a place of worship but also a means of education. Scripture readings were given four times a week: twice on the sabbath at morning and evening services, and also on Mondays and Thursday mornings. These days were market days when people came to the towns from the countryside. Further readings were given on fast days and festivals and on the first day of each month.

It took another crisis to make the Jews take synagogue school for boys from the age of six seriously. That crisis was the attempt of King Antiochus IV to impose Greek learning on the Jews. He had persuaded the high priest Jason to set up a Greek school in Jerusalem in 175BC not far from the Temple and many wealthy Jews sent their sons there to learn the basic skills of reading, writing, counting and wrestling before moving on to military training, Greek literature, music and sport. While this was accepted by most of the priests of the Temple, the scribes and their followers thought it was a threat to the Jewish faith. When King Antiochus was defeated in 164BC the scribes and Pharisees, as they were now called, led by Simeon ben Shetah, taught that all boys should attend the 'House of the Book' for a thorough Jewish education. The first of these schools was in Jerusalem but the idea soon spread to other towns and cities and by New Testament times such schools were found throughout the Roman empire.

Teachers and lessons

The teacher was a synagogue official paid for now by the men of the synagogue and not allowed to accept fees from pupils in case he should favour the rich. For every

Ezra the scribe

Nothing so clearly shows the importance of education in the Jewish state after the return from Babylon as the great gathering to which Ezra read the Law (Nehemiah 8).

Ezra was a priest and scribe who had returned to Jerusalem with authority given him by the Persian emperor to teach the Law of God to those who did not know it and to punish those who would not obey it. (You can read the Persian emperor's decree in Ezra 7:12–26.) He had brought a Book of the Law with him and all the people 'men, women and the children who were old enough to understand' (Neh. 8:2) listened carefully as he read to them, standing on a wooden platform built for the occasion. The reading lasted from dawn to midday and the impact was tremendous (Neh. 8:5, 6). Then the Levites explained the Law to different groups of people in the crowd and they were moved to tears.

The next chapter of Nehemiah describes another three-hour reading from the Law and in the chapter after that the people made a solemn agreement to live according to God's Law (10:28, 29). Such a programme made a system of education for everybody a necessity.

twenty-five pupils a teacher had to be appointed and if his class reached forty an assistant teacher would help him. As in the schools for scribes the method of teaching was to get the pupils to repeat the scriptures until they knew them by heart. They began with four basic texts: the Shema, the command to love God (Deut. 6:4–9 quoted above), the Hallel, a psalm of praise (like Psalm 135) used at festivals such as the Passover, the story of Creation and the laws about offerings and sacrifices. In Palestine the language used was Aramaic but in other countries the people learned a Greek translation of the scriptures. Teachers probably tried to find ways of making lessons interesting but the hours were long and the holidays few. The teachers were highly respected men. They had to be married and of very good character. They had to be patient and kind, punishing only when necessary and then not too harshly. For too much punishment a teacher could lose his job.

Although most boys were taught by their fathers and at synagogue school it was not until AD63–65 that school was compulsory for all boys. Apparently some boys had run away from school when the teacher had become angry with them, and other boys had no fathers, so the High Priest, Joshua ben Gamala ordered that 'in every province and in every town there should be teachers appointed, to whom the children should be brought at the age of six or seven years'.

Learning to be an adult

The boys also learned about farming and trade, but not at school. Astronomy (needed by farmers to work out the seasons) and practical mathematics were learned on the job when boys were working under a farmer or carpenter or merchant, whichever occupation they were to follow. This was his 'secondary' education after the boy was thirteen. That birthday was important for when it arrived the boy was taken to a special service in the synagogue at which he was recognised as 'bar mitzvah' – a son of the Law, now an adult and responsible for his own faith.

Girls were not admitted to synagogue schools. The education the girl received was, as in Israel's earliest days, what her mother taught her. Since she was usually married by the age of sixteen she needed to know how to be a good housewife and mother. She also learned her faith through the customs and ceremonies of the weekly sabbath and festivals. Women were allowed to attend services in the synagogue where they heard the scriptures read, but they sat apart from the men and took no active part in the services.

Rabbis

The teachers at synagogue schools were the scribes who were usually called 'Rabbi', which meant 'Teacher'. They had continued their education after the age of thirteen at the House of Study. It was in such a group that Mary and Joseph found Jesus when he was left behind in Jerusalem when he was twelve (Luke 2:41–52). At these advanced schools the

On his thirteenth birthday a Jewish boy attends a 'bar mitzvah' ceremony and is now recognised as an adult. These boys are carrying the Torah scrolls at a bar mitzvah ceremony in Jerusalem.

In most synagogues women sit apart from men, often upstairs in a gallery.

subject was the unwritten teaching which was passed on by word of mouth to each new generation. This teaching was mainly comments and explanations of the written Torah from famous Rabbis in the past, discussing how it was to be obeyed in daily life. The method of learning was by argument. Most of these advanced schools belonged to the Pharisees but even they were divided into parties: a strict group which followed the teaching of Rabbi Shammai and a more lenient group who taught the sayings of Rabbi Hillel. Rabbis taught not only the children but the adults too, reading and explaining the scriptures every sabbath.

Jesus and Paul

Jesus was called 'Rabbi' (John 3:2) and there is an interesting description of him teaching in the synagogue at Nazareth, his home town (Luke 4:16–30). Notice how he stood to read but sat down to teach as the Rabbis did. This lesson ended in the teacher nearly losing his life. The people recognised that his teaching was different from the regular Rabbis (Matt. 7:28–29). He used parables and poetry (eg, Matt. 5:3–10) as they did but he did not quote other teachers except to disagree with them (Matt. 5:21–22).

Paul had been brought up and educated as a Pharisee (Acts 26:5). He had come from Tarsus where he was born, to Jerusalem to sit 'at the feet of Gamaliel' (Acts 22:3 RSV). This reminds us of the way students sat on the ground in front of their teachers. This kind of school was sometimes called 'the vineyard', because the rows of students were so neat that they looked like vines in a vineyard or flower-beds in a garden. Rabbi Gamaliel was the grandson and follower of the great Rabbi Hillel and we can see him in action in the story in Acts 5:17–42, where he advises the Council not to prevent Peter and the other apostles from preaching. Paul may have studied some Greek literature and ways of argument too, but scribes were not encouraged to learn foreign languages. Josephus, the Jewish historian, wrote that he had taken great trouble to learn Greek and still could not pronounce it correctly for 'our nation does not encourage those who learn the languages of many nations. It looks upon this sort of accomplishment as common'. True wisdom for the Jews was only to be found in the study of the Jewish Law.

Greek education

About 200 years after the return of the Jews from Exile, Alexander the Great began his conquests of the Middle East, spreading Greek ideas and culture. Greek ideas of education aimed at producing the perfect man, educated in body, mind and soul. He would be a man of outstanding physical strength and courage, skilful with weapons and musical instruments, knowing all about the world and man and clever in speaking. To him athletics, dancing and the theatre were as important as history and philosophy.

Primary education

Until a Greek boy was seven his mother was his teacher and his sister had no further education outside her home. After that, because his mother knew too little and his father was too busy being a citizen, the Greek boy was sent to school. The amount of time he spent there depended on how wealthy or poor his parents were, although some schools were cheaper than others; but then some schools were worse than others. In some families a slave called a paidogogos was ordered to look after the boy and take him to school, carry his books and lyre (a seven-stringed harp), and take him home again. He had to see that the boy behaved himself well. At this primary school where he stayed until he was fifteen (if his parents could afford it), he studied three groups of subjects: basic skills, music and physical fitness. The basic skills were reading, writing and counting. Music included poetry and dancing as well as learning to play an instrument. Physical training included wrestling, boxing, running, jumping and throwing the javelin and discus.

Further education

At the age of sixteen he went to the 'gymnasium', a school built and owned by the

A humorous painting of a Greek pedagogue – described as a new-style lecturer of the cult of reason.

Greek terracotta figures showing a boy being taught to read, probably by his father.

A music lesson is shown on this Greek water jar from the 5th century BC. In the centre a pupil is learning to play the lyre while others wait their turn.

A reconstruction of part of the Greek gymnasium at Sardis in modern Turkey.

Greek education included the art of speechmaking. Speeches in court were strictly timed by a water clock. When the speech began, the plug at the base of the top vessel was removed and the water began running into the lower vessel. When the top vessel was empty, time had literally run out for the speaker.

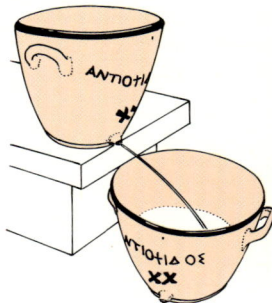

Roman education

State. Here he continued to improve his physical fitness and music but added literature, politics and philosophy to his subjects. The gymnasium was like a social club for adults too, and students could join in public debates about topics in the news. In the days when the Greek states were powerful it was important for every educated adult to be able to speak in public and to have military training. After Rome came to dominate the world the art of public speaking continued to be important for the professional speaker (orator) but the military side of Greek education disappeared. In a world without radio, television or a daily paper the orator was the man to whom people listened for news and comment on current events. He was as well known as news readers are today. His education included how to make a speech, how to arrange words and ideas to impress or persuade an audience, how to give a good performance. He would have left the gymnasium at eighteen and travelled to one of the famous cities of learning like Athens, Alexandria in Egypt or Paul's home city of Tarsus. Here he could complete his education arguing and debating with the leading philosophers of the day. There is an example of what this was like in the New Testament when Paul visited Athens (Acts 17:16–34). In his speech Paul quotes two Greek poets (verse 28) and the Epicurean and Stoic philosophers did not really understand him (verses 18 and 32). At Alexandria it was possible to study literature and public speaking too. Apollos, one of the early Christian missionaries who was a clever speaker, was born in that city (Acts 18:24). It was also possible to study many other subjects at Alexandria. There were zoological and botanical gardens, a library with a million 'books' in scroll form and students of engineering and medicine. Steam power was discovered but not developed in that city. Students of medicine practised cutting up human bodies, some of them still alive!

What was true of Alexandria under the Greeks was the same under the Romans, for although the Romans had conquered the Greeks they learned and used the Greek language for trade and read Greek books in Roman schools.

The main difference between the Greek and Roman attitudes to education was that the Romans did not respect teachers. Most of their teachers were slaves or men who had been slaves and they were badly paid. In early Roman times the father had been responsible for his son's education. Schools then were regarded as second best but useful in the days of the empire when many fathers were away from home on military campaigns.

School

The paidogogos (see above) still took the children to school unless the family was too poor to afford one. The school was sometimes a converted shop with only a sheet of tent cloth to shut it off from the

street. The one teacher sat in an armchair and faced his pupils on their stools or benches. There were no desks. The writing tablets were held on the pupils' knees. These tablets were like shallow boxes with the bottom filled with wax which could be written on with a stylus, smoothed over and used again. It was the same idea as the Sumerians, with their clay two thousand years before. School began before dawn, without breakfast and went on until the afternoon without much change. The

A Roman school scene. Two pupils with scrolls are seated either side of the teacher. On the right, a latecomer makes his excuse.

A wooden tablet and stylus from Roman times.

youngest children sang their alphabet before learning to write, with the teacher's hand guiding their own over a pattern already traced on the wax. Older pupils copied letters or words or sentences. They learned to count on an abacus, a board marked out in lines with pebbles placed on them. They had to recite poetry and proverbs by heart and those who did not please the teacher were beaten. Primary school lasted from the age of seven to twelve and many Roman writers describe those years as a time of boredom and fear.

Teaching methods

Sons of the wealthy went to secondary school, sometimes having to travel away from home to do so. If girls were taught after the age of twelve it was by a private tutor. The secondary school classroom could still be a shop but decorated with statues of famous writers and perhaps a map or two on the walls. The teaching was still boring, with students repeating what they had been told and learning to recite long passages from books by Greek and Roman authors with a special emphasis on poetry. Some Romans suggested that music, mathematics and gymnastics should be studied, not for their own sake, but because they would produce students who could speak well and knew how to live.

Respect for an orator was something the Romans had taken over from the Greeks. The one reference to a school in the Bible is to a lecture hall which Paul used in Ephesus (Acts 19:9). It looks from the margin of the Good News Bible as if Paul used it during the hottest part of the day while Tyrannus lectured at the more normal times of morning and evening to teach public speaking. This was the most fashionable form of higher education.

Other occupations were learned in their own special schools (shorthand) or by becoming an apprentice and learning on the job (doctor, lawyer, builder, architect, engineer, etc.). Romans tended to look down on practical occupations because there were large numbers of slaves to do these. Many doctors were slaves. Many slaves had at least a primary education and could read an inscription, understand weights and measures and add simple sums.

Christianity was born in the Roman world with its many ideas taken from the Greeks but in education the Jewish influence was the most important (2 Timothy 1:5; 3:14–17).

A frieze on a Roman sarcophagus showing the development of a child from infant to schoolboy.

RELIGION

What people believe is very important because it affects the way that they live. In the Old Testament we have the account of how God taught his own people, the Jews, about himself, and about the sort of behaviour he expected from them. It took them a long time to learn this, especially as the other nations around worshipped very different gods. This is one of the reasons why God taught them not only in words that they could hear and read, but also in things that they could do. Their religion included special services, feasts and buildings; in fact, it affected everything they did – the food they ate and the clothes they wore, as well as their work.

Jesus and his first followers were Jews, and they taught that this same God, the God of the Old Testament, had sent his Son into the world to tell people about himself. They claimed that the experiences of God's people in those early days had prepared the way for the coming of Jesus. This is why so many of the ideas and promises in the Old Testament are taken up in the New. In this way, although there are sixty-six separate books in our Bible, it is really only one book, because it tells us how to believe in and obey the one true God.

The city of Jerusalem is holy to Christians, Jews and Moslems.

Jewish religion

The Tabernacle

God made the Jews his very own people when he helped them to escape from slavery in Egypt. Under Moses' leadership they went to Mount Sinai where God made a special agreement, called a covenant, with them. He would be their God and would care for them: they would be his people and obey him.

God told Moses that he wanted to be worshipped in a tent, or Tabernacle, which could be taken down like their own tents every time they moved camp to a new site (Exodus 25–27). In this way God showed the people that he would go with them to guide and protect them.

The tent was made of blue, purple and scarlet cloth with beautiful patterns worked on it by the Israelite women. It was set up rather like our modern frame tents, although the frame was of hard wood fitted together with silver sockets. Because the roof had to keep the rain out, it was made of two coverings, one of rams' skins dyed red, and the other of porpoise or sealskin. All the curtains of the tent were held together with golden clasps.

The tent had two sections. In the inner section behind a curtain was the Ark of the Covenant or Covenant Box. This was a wooden box into which Moses put the Ten Commandments, written on two stone slabs. The box had poles which passed through rings fitted at the sides so that the priests could carry it to the next stopping-place. This part of the tent was called 'the Holy of Holies', and was particularly set aside for God. The ordinary people never went in there; only the High Priest once a year on the Day of Atonement. Over the box was a slab of pure gold called the Mercy Seat.

In the other section, 'the Holy Place', there was an altar covered with gold plate on which the priests burned sweet-smelling incense. There was a table as well, also covered with gold, on which they put a gift of loaves each day. Besides this there was a golden lampstand with seven arms and seven lights. All these things were set apart for God. No one touched them, except the priests and the Levites.

Around the tent was an open space surrounded by linen hangings on poles. Inside this enclosure, in front of the tent door, was another altar covered with copper on which the priests burned the sacrifices. There was also a copper bowl where they washed their hands.

The people came to the tent when they wanted to pray, and when they wanted to bring their gifts and sacrifices, but only the priests were allowed to take the services. In this way God taught them that he was great and holy, separate from anything sinful, and that they needed their sins forgiven if they were going to please him.

For forty years the people of Israel wandered around the wilderness between Egypt and Palestine taking the Tabernacle

A horned altar found at Beersheba in Israel.

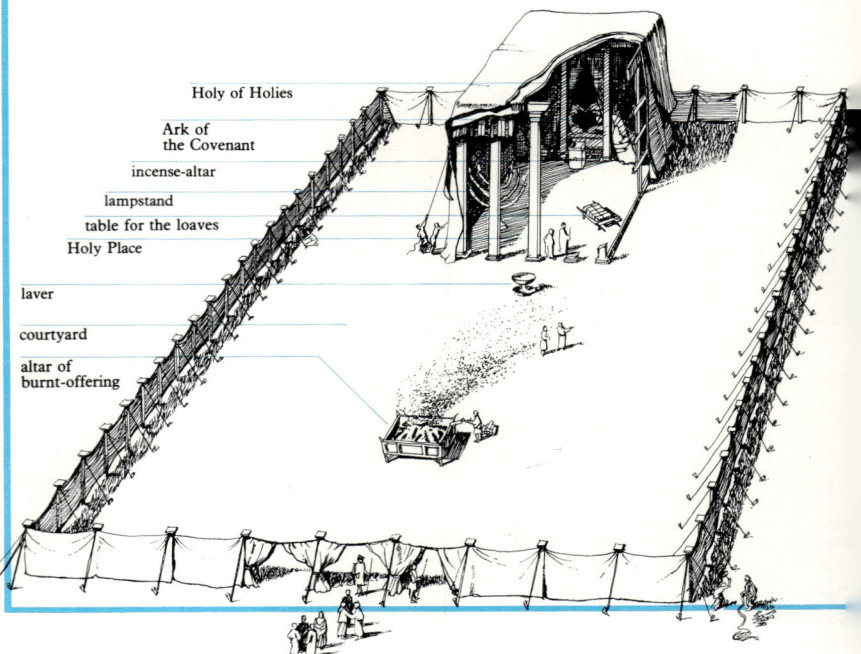

The Tabernacle — completed around 1260BC

The tent and its furnishings were made by the Israelites during their wilderness wanderings. The Tabernacle served as a place of worship throughout this 40-year period and on into the early years of settlement in Canaan.

Holy of Holies
Ark of the Covenant
incense-altar
lampstand
table for the loaves
Holy Place
laver
courtyard
altar of burnt-offering

with them. When at last they entered the land of Canaan which God gave them, they set up the tent in a more permanent location, and the people came there when they wanted to worship. Once they even took the Covenant Box out into battle against the Philistines, and it was captured when they were defeated. There is a very wonderful story about how the Lord got it back for them (1 Samuel 4–6). In the end, King David brought the Tabernacle to Jerusalem, and it stayed there until his son, King Solomon, built the Temple to replace it.

The Temple

King Solomon built the first Temple in Jerusalem. Inside, it was the same shape as the Tabernacle, but on a much bigger scale, while outside there were court-yards, pillars and storerooms. It was a beautiful building with walls panelled in wood overlaid with gold, rich carvings and

A model of the golden lampstand in the Tabernacle.

This painting by the 17th century French artist Bourdon, depicts the Covenant Box being returned to the Israelites by the Philistines who had captured it in battle.

A model of the Covenant Box.

Solomon's Temple — completed 950BC

Solomon's Temple in Jerusalem was divided into the same rooms as the Tabernacle. Some of the furniture was also the same. The building was much larger, though, and richly decorated. The rooms were panelled with cedar wood, carved by Phoenician craftsmen with flowers, palm trees and cherubim, overlaid with gold.

Holy of Holies

Holy Place

store-rooms

laver

altar

Court of the Israelites

Court of the Women

porch

altar of sacrifice

onze ng bowl

Herod's Temple — built 19BC-60AD

This Temple, built of cream-coloured stone with gold decorations, was a magnificent building. It was the last Temple ever built in Jerusalem. There were strict rules about access to the various courts of the building.

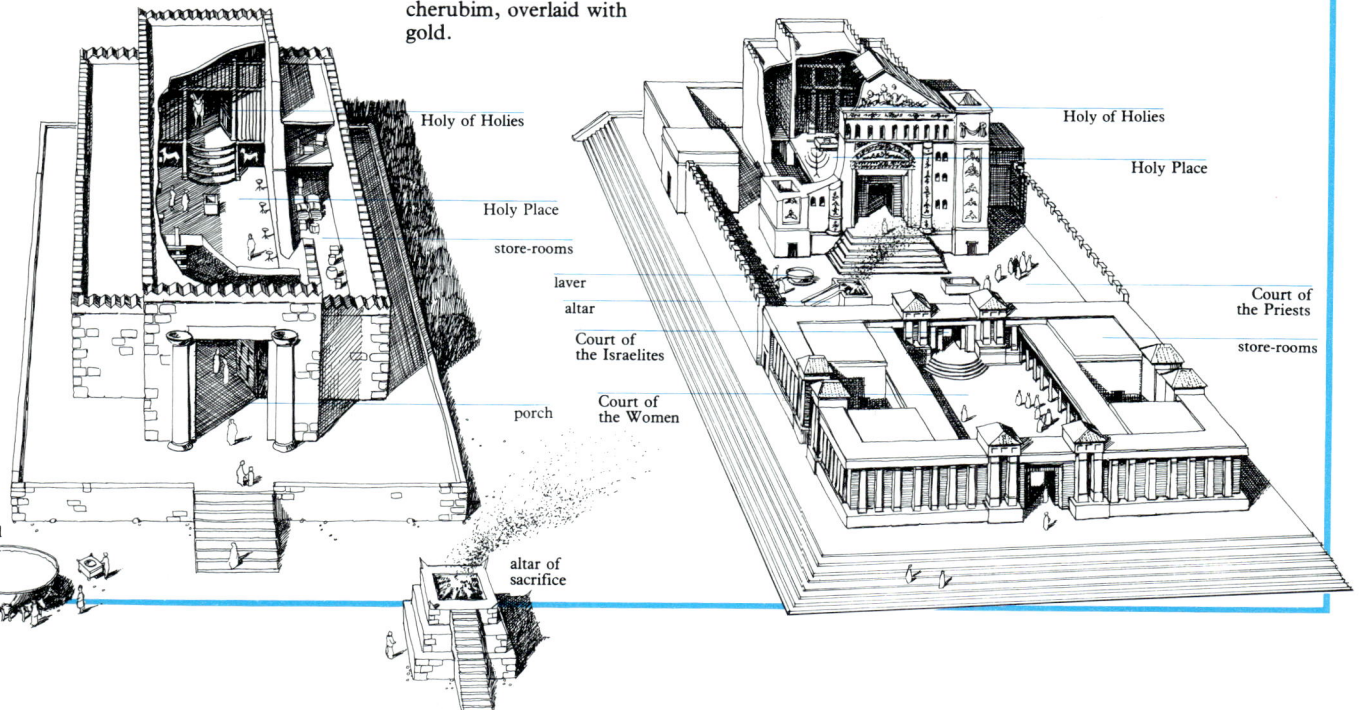

Holy of Holies

Holy Place

Court of the Priests

store-rooms

A synagogue service. The parchment scrolls of the Law are kept behind the curtain facing in the direction of Jerusalem.

The Levites carried the Covenant Box and other Tabernacle furniture when the Israelites moved camp. They also provided the music for worship.

those who were buying, selling and money-changing (John 2:13–22). People who were not Jews could go into this outer courtyard, women were allowed into the next one, and Jewish men into the third. Beyond the men's court was the court of the priests, containing the great altar for burnt offerings. Only priests and Levites could enter this court and the Temple itself.

Jesus' disciples could hardly believe him when he foretold that one day this marvellous building would be destroyed, but it was so only about forty years after his death. In AD70 the Roman army carried off the Temple treasures and burned the building. The Jews never built another Temple.

The Synagogue

When King Solomon's Temple was destroyed, there was nowhere for God's people to worship. This, of course, always had been so for those Jews who did not live in the land of Israel. Some had been taken away as prisoners and others went for work or because it was not safe at home.

To make up for their loss they began to construct simple buildings called synagogues where they could meet, pray and hear God's Law taught. Inside, opposite the entrance by the far wall was a wooden box in which they kept the Old Testament scrolls. They called this the Ark, like the box in the Tabernacle. Sometimes, in special services, they would carry it around in procession. The leaders of the synagogue sat on the 'chief' or special seats in front of the Ark, while the rest of the people sat on wooden benches. There was usually also a reading-stand where the scrolls could be read aloud.

Ten men at least were needed for a synagogue service. The women and children could only watch and listen, and they sat by themselves, sometimes in a screened gallery. Although each synagogue had its leaders, any man, and that included boys over thirteen, could be asked to read or take the prayers. Jesus did this in his home town of Nazareth, and startled those who knew him by what he said (Luke 4:16–30). Special visitors might be asked to preach, and this is how

tall folding doors. All the Israelites were expected to come to Jerusalem to visit the Temple for the great feasts.

To begin with, Solomon made sure that the Temple and its services were the best for God, but other kings came after him who let it fall into disrepair. At times their enemies even made them take the gold from the Temple to pay them to go away. In the end, King Nebuchadnezzar's troops from Babylon fought their way into Jerusalem, and burned the Temple down (2 Kings 25).

For a long time the Temple lay in ruins until a later Persian king, Cyrus, allowed some of the Jews to return to Jerusalem. They rebuilt the Temple, but it was poor by comparison with Solomon's wonderful structure.

It was King Herod who built the Temple that Jesus and his friends knew. It was the most wonderful of the three Temples. It took over eighty years to finish. It was made of costly white stone, overlaid in places with gold. There were wide courtyards surrounded by colonnades of pillars where people could meet out of the cold and wet in winter. Jesus taught the crowds there when he was in Jerusalem. It was from the outer courtyard that he chased

we find Paul and his friends speaking in synagogues about Jesus (Acts 13:13–43).

The synagogue was also a school where the boys learned to read the ancient Hebrew scrolls. This was difficult in countries where they did not speak Hebrew any more, and when they read from the Old Testament, someone would translate it into their own language, usually Aramaic in Palestine and Iraq, and Greek elsewhere.

The synagogue teacher also had the job of punishing those who had done wrong. If the leaders so judged, the culprit could be beaten with a rod, or even stopped from coming to the synagogue services. The blind man Jesus healed was put out of the synagogue because he annoyed the leaders by saying that Jesus was sent by God (John 9). The apostle Paul upset the Jews so much by preaching the Gospel that he was beaten at least five times!

Synagogues were very popular and were built everywhere, including Palestine. Even after the Temple was rebuilt by Herod, the people enjoyed synagogue worship so much that they kept on going there, and there were a good number in Jerusalem itself in the time of Jesus.

The Priests

These were all descendants of Aaron, Moses' brother. Aaron himself was called the High Priest, sometimes known as the Chief Priest. When the High Priest died, his eldest son took over the post.

Priests had the important task of praying and offering sacrifices, not only for themselves, but for all God's people. They had special clothes made for them, and they had to do everything in the Tabernacle – and later in the Temple – exactly as required by God's Law. They were also supposed to teach the people about God and about the sort of lives he wanted them to live.

Unfortunately it did not always work out like this as some of the priests in the Bible story neglected their duties and lived wicked lives themselves. They forgot that good behaviour was just as important as taking the Temple services correctly.

In the New Testament Jesus is called our great High Priest. He did not come from Aaron's family, but his death on the cross was the great final sacrifice so that we might be forgiven and get right with God.

Mount Gerizim, near Samaria, is regarded as a holy mountain by the Samaritans. They still sacrifice the Passover Lambs there once a year.

A Jew in his prayer shawl at the Western Wall, Jerusalem.

The Levites

All the members of the tribe of Levi were Levites. Apart from Aaron's family, they could not act as priests, but they did have the job of helping the priests both in the Tabernacle and later in the Temple. It was the Levites who packed up and carried the tent and its furniture from one camp site to the next. In the Temple their duties included being doorkeepers and porters, while some made up choirs and an orchestra – although with very different instruments from ours. The book of Psalms contains some of the hymns and songs they used to sing.

Sacrifices

In both the Tabernacle and the Temple, the main duties of the priests were to offer sacrifices and pray. The people would bring their animals to be presented to God as part of their worship. Special instructions about this are given in the book of Leviticus. They had to be the very best animals, and they could be offered in several different ways. The animal was killed, and then either parts or all of it were burned on the altar. Sometimes the priests were allowed to have some of the meat for themselves, and with some of the sacrifices, the people also took part in a meal. When a person was too poor to bring a goat or a lamb, he gave a gift of fine flour or oil.

Sacrifices took place every day, but the most important was offered once a year on the Day of Atonement in the autumn. Atonement means getting right with God by having our sins forgiven. This is why on that day the High Priest confessed the sins of all the people and asked for God's forgiveness. Then he took two goats, one of which was chased off into the desert as though it was carrying the people's sins away, while the other was killed. He then took some of the blood, went into the Holy of Holies, and sprinkled it on the Mercy Seat above the Covenant Box (Leviticus 16).

Offering sacrifices was partly a way of thanking God for all his goodness, just as we might give a gift to a friend who has been kind to us. But God was teaching the Jews something else as well. He wanted to let them know that worshipping him was

The Great Feasts

Although God's people remembered him every week on the Sabbath, three times a year they stopped work and came together for feasts where they celebrated and thanked him for his goodness (Deuteronomy 16:16–17).

At the **Feast of the Passover,** which takes place at our Easter-time, they remembered how God had brought them out of Egypt (Exod. 12, 13). They acted out that great night all over again, each family killing a lamb and putting some of the blood on the doorposts. Then they had a meal together, dressed as though they were going on a journey, and told their children about the time when they had escaped from Pharaoh, king of Egypt, across the Red Sea. Because they ate bread made without yeast which tasted rather like dry biscuits, this feast is sometimes known as the

The Feast of the Passover starts with a family meal.

Feast of Unleavened Bread. It was probably this meal which Jesus turned into the Last Supper with his disciples, which has become our Communion Service today (Matthew 26:17–30).

The Feast of Weeks, which came to be known later on as Pentecost, came fifty days after the beginning of the Passover Feast. Christians know it today as Whitsun, for it was at this time that the Holy Spirit came upon the Church at Jerusalem (Acts 2). For the Jews it was the beginning of their harvest, when they offered the first of their crops to God.

The third feast was their Harvest Festival. It took place in the autumn and was called the **Feast of Ingathering** or **Tabernacles.** This was because the people reminded themselves that they had once lived in tents in the desert by camping out for a week in shelters made from branches.

Later in their history, the Jews added two more feasts to their calendar. At **Purim** they remembered how God had saved them from destruction through Queen Esther. The **Feast of Dedication,** which happens around Christmas-time, recalls a time before the birth of Jesus when their enemies, who had taken over the Temple, were defeated and thrown out.

(For *Lesser Feasts*, see the section on Sport and Leisure.)

The Festival of Tabernacles is a joyful harvest thanksgiving celebration. Temporary huts roofed with leaves and decorated with fruit and vegetables are erected on rooftops or balconies.

The blowing of the shofar, the ram's horn, announces the beginning of a Jewish festival.

The lighting of the candles and the blessing of the bread accompany the start of the Jewish sabbath at dusk on Friday evening.

Celebration of the Hanuka in Israel.

costly, and that wrong-doing grieved him. Instead of punishing them for breaking his rules, God accepted the sacrifice of an animal. The person bringing the sacrifice realised that it was being killed instead of him. When Jesus died on the cross, he did so as a perfect sacrifice in our place and for our sins. This is why we do not need any more sacrifices today.

Clean and unclean food

One of the ways in which God's people were to be different from other nations was that there were certain kinds of meat that they were forbidden to eat. These included some animals, fish, birds, insects and reptiles. They were called unclean, and they could not use them in their meals or in their sacrifices.

This may seem strange to us, but we know now that some animals carry diseases, and that it is dangerous to eat them. For example, they were told not to eat pork, and we know today that it is only safe to eat if it is thoroughly cooked.

All this made it rather difficult in the early church when both Jews and non-Jews – or Gentiles as they were called – became Christians. The latter thought they could eat any kind of meat. They had to learn not to offend Jewish Christians by what they ate, while at the same time Jewish Christians had to learn that rules about food were a thing of the past.

The Sabbath

One day in seven, on the Sabbath, which is our Saturday, the Jews were told to rest and remember God. Because they counted days somewhat differently from us, this Sabbath began on Friday evening at sunset and lasted until Saturday evening. During this time no one did any work at all, not even the servants or the animals.

God commanded them to do this because he had rested on the seventh day when he made the world, and because they had once been slaves in Egypt when they never rested. Later on, this welcome break became a time of strict rules. Jesus even upset the Jews because he healed people on the Sabbath. They thought that was work. He had to remind them that the Sabbath was made for people to enjoy, not to be a day filled with restrictions.

264

A drawing representing the Jewish Council – the Sanhedrin – from the Stackhouse Bible of 1733.

Excavations at Megiddo, Israel, uncovered this Canaanite altar of sacrifice.

The message of the prophets

ISAIAH lived in Jerusalem in the 8th century BC. He saw a vision of God commissioning him to warn the nation of punishment unless they trusted in God. He also foretold the coming of the Messiah.

EZEKIEL was a Jewish exile in Babylon. His vision of a valley of dry bones coming to life foretold the return of the Jewish exiles to a new life in their homeland.

DANIEL, a Jewish captive, became a minister of state in Babylon. God saved him from death in a den of lions. He interpreted dreams for the kings of Babylon and foretold the rise and fall of several empires.

Other prophets including **Amos**, **Hosea** and **Micah** spoke out against oppression of the poor by the rich and against dishonesty in business. They warned of God's judgement on the nation for worshipping other gods.

JOHN wrote the book of Revelation at a time of persecution by the Romans. He foretells the ultimate triumph of Christ over Satan and the creation of a new heaven and earth.

The Jews still observe the Sabbath and go to synagogue on Saturday, but the Christian Church replaced it with Sunday, the day when Jesus rose from the dead.

The prophets

These were men and women through whom God used to speak to his people. By his Spirit, he gave them his words, sometimes to encourage the people, but more often to warn them because they had done wrong. We see this in the story of the prophet Elijah who told the wicked King Ahab that unless he put things right by stopping the worship of the Canaanite god Baal, there would be no rain. The drought, which lasted three years, ended in a contest between Elijah and the prophets of Baal, when God showed that he was God alone by sending down fire from heaven (1 Kings 17–18).

In the later history of Israel, some of the prophets wrote down their messages, and we have these in the Old Testament books from Isaiah to Malachi.

One of the problems with prophecy is that all kinds of people could say that they were speaking God's words, so we are told in the Bible about false prophets as well as true ones (1 Kings 22). Many of these false prophets led the people astray into the Canaanite religions which did so much harm.

Because God knows things before they happen, he sometimes gave his people an insight into the future through his prophets. Sometimes it was a warning of what he would do if they did not put him first. At other times he gave wonderful promises. When the people were taken away from their land, he assured them that one day he would bring them home again. He also promised that he would send them a king who would rule them wisely and well. This is why the Jews were

expecting the Messiah – God's anointed and chosen One.

When Jesus came, both he and his disciples claimed that these old sayings were coming true. He was the One who was to come, and his death and resurrection, as well as his reign, had been seen and foretold by the prophets.

There were also prophets in the young Christian church whose job was to tell people what God wanted, and to encourage them to go on with the Christian life, especially when things got difficult (1 Corinthians 14:29–32). The apostle John also wrote down a long prophecy about the end of the world, and we have it in our Bibles as the book of Revelation.

The Pharisees

These were people who spent a great deal of time studying God's Law, and who tried hard to keep every detail of it. Unfortunately they often did it in a way that made it very hard for them and for others. They were very strict about their praying, fasting and giving, even down to things like how much mint they ought to give God from their gardens. Some were sincere, godly men, but others became proud of themselves, thinking that God must be pleased with their efforts.

Jesus was often angry with the Pharisees because he saw that much of what they did was a sham, put on to make out that they were very religious. But they did not practise what they preached (Matt. 23). When one of them, Nicodemus, came to ask Jesus questions, he was puzzled when Jesus told him that he had to make a completely new start, like being born again (John 3:1–15).

Although some of the Pharisees thought that Jesus was a good man, many of them became jealous, especially when so many people followed him and listened to him instead of listening to them. This is why they had a hand, with the other Jewish leaders, in planning his death. Paul the apostle was a Pharisee before the risen Jesus met him on the road to Damascus and made him his servant instead (Acts 9).

The Sadducees

The Sadducees were a group of wealthy and powerful people living around Jerusalem. The chief priestly families, including the High Priest, were usually Sadducees, but the group also included businessmen and landowners. They were not as strict as the Pharisees about religious matters, confining themselves to the first five books of the Old Testament, Genesis to Deuteronomy. Unlike the Pharisees, they did not believe in an afterlife or resurrection.

They enjoyed the peace and security of a comfortable life, and got on quite well with the Romans. If there was political trouble, they had a great deal to lose, and they were keen to get rid of Jesus because they thought he was a troublemaker. Although they were not usually on good terms with the Pharisees, they agreed with them that Jesus had to die.

The Zealots

The Zealots were freedom-fighters who disliked their country being run by the Romans, and because of this they were always stirring up trouble. The Romans called them 'dagger-men', because they carried daggers and were ready to use them. Sometimes they went by their Aramaic name of Canaaneans. One of Jesus' disciples was Simon the Zealot, and many of Jesus' followers would have liked Jesus to become their leader in ridding Palestine of the Romans. They did not understand that he had come to set up a different kind of kingdom, in people's hearts, which would make them live different, better lives.

The Zealots eventually did rebel against the Romans, but without success. They were defeated and Jerusalem was captured. It was then, in AD 70, that Herod's beautiful and costly Temple was burned to the ground.

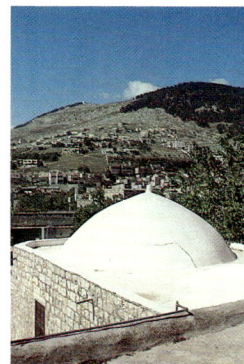

The white-domed roof of Joseph's tomb with Mount Gerizim in the background. Jesus accused the teachers of the law of being like whitewashed tombs which look beautiful on the outside only.

Masada, once a splendid palace fortress of Herod the Great was captured by the Zealots and was the scene of their last stand against the Romans. It was taken in AD73 after a year's blockade but the Zealots had committed suicide rather than surrender.

Jewish and Christian beliefs

About God

Unlike the other nations, the Jews believed that there is only one God who was their Lord. They did so, not because they had thought it out themselves, but because God had made himself known to them, choosing Abraham and his family to be his own people (Genesis 12:1–3). He showed them that he was the Creator, the one who made the world and who keeps it going, and that he was great and all-powerful. Because he was spirit, they could not see him – though they

Hebrew Menorah on the Rock of Inscription in central Sinai, where camel caravans camped. The Rock is covered with ancient graffiti.

could see what he did in the same way that we can see what the wind does, even though we cannot see the wind itself. They were strictly forbidden to make idols or pictures of him (Exod. 20:4–5).

The Old Covenant

Although God cares for all people, he loved Israel in a special way. From the beginning it was his plan that his only Son should come into the world as a Jew, and he was preparing the world for that time long before it happened. Because of this he made a special agreement with the Jews which we call the Old Covenant. He promised

that he would be their God and look after them, and for their part, they had to obey him if they were to be his people (Deut. 7:6–11).

The Law

God showed the Jews that he was holy and separate from anything evil. For this reason, if they were going to be his people, they had to be careful how they lived. To help them to do this, God gave them his Law, or his rules for daily behaviour in every part of their lives. We find the most important in the Ten Commandments (Exod. 20:1–17). Jesus summed up the Law as loving God and loving others (Matt. 22:34–40).

A fish symbol scratched on a wall of a church in Rome recalls the use of a fish as a secret sign among the Christians in times of Roman persecution.

Bread, salt and wine, the symbols of the Jewish sabbath. The two loaves of bread recall the double portion of manna collected each week before the sabbath by the Israelites in the wilderness.

Sin

The Jews, like us, found it hard to live good lives. They were always breaking the Law, which God calls sinning. God promised to forgive their sins if they were sorry, and if they brought the required animal sacrifice to the priest. Jesus was the only person who never sinned, and his death was accepted by God as the perfect sacrifice for all sins. Because of this God promises to forgive our sins when we confess them to him.

The New Covenant

One of the promises which God gave his people in the Old Testament was that one day the old arrangement that he had made with them would come to an

Bread and wine, the symbols of the body and blood of Christ, used in the Christian communion service.

end. He would then make a new agreement with them, what we call the New Covenant (Jeremiah 31:31–34).

This is what Jesus said was happening when he came to die for men and women (Mark 14:24). From then on, a closer relationship between God and man was possible. As part of this new arrangement, God sent his Holy Spirit who gives us the strength we need to live lives which please God, and to make us like Jesus in our behaviour.

The Messiah

When God made a covenant with his people, he also promised them a land of their own if they were prepared to worship and obey him. This is how Canaan became the Promised Land, although the Israelites had to fight those who were already there before they could settle in it.

In time, God also gave them a king. The greatest king, though not the first, was King David, and God promised that all true kings of Israel would come from his family in the future. This

included the great king whom God would send one day to reign for ever, not only over the Jews, but over the whole world. Because they appointed their kings by anointing them, that is by pouring sweet-smelling oil over their heads, he came to be known as the Anointed One. This is what 'Messiah' or 'Christ' means.

At the beginning of Matthew's Gospel, which tells us that Jesus was the

Christ, his family tree goes right back to David. This is also why the crowds welcomed him to Jerusalem as 'Son of David', that is, a man of David's family who was coming as their king (Matt. 21:1–11). Jesus had come to be their king, but not quite in the way that they expected. He wanted to reign in their hearts and lives.

After he had been crucified and had risen from the dead, his followers went everywhere telling people that he was the Messiah, that they could have their sins forgiven and their lives changed. Jesus also promised that one day he would come back, not as a peasant this time, but as God's king, reigning over those who love and obey him.

A Christian catacomb painting from the 3rd century AD showing loaves of bread and a fish, significant Christian symbols.

An early Christian church built into a natural cone of volcanic rock in Cappadocia, Turkey. Paul visited this area on his missionary journeys.

Other nations and their religions

Amun, one of the chief Egyptian gods.

An Egyptian priest with shaven head, carrying a small shrine.

Egyptian beliefs

The ancient Egyptians believed in a variety of different gods and goddesses, including Re or Atun, the sun-god. One of the most popular was Osiris who had a wife, Isis, and son, Horus. The king, or Pharaoh, was supposed to represent Osiris who was god of vegetation – very important when their crops depended on the river Nile – and lord of the dead.

Gods and goddesses were worshipped in temples by priests who treated their images just like earthly kings, 'wakening' them in the morning with a hymn, washing, dressing, and presenting them with

An Egyptian king making offerings to the gods.

Sphinx with Pyramid of Cheops, near Cairo. The Egyptian kings built the pyramids as magnificent tombs and many of their treasures were buried with them.

offerings. The ordinary people joined in the worship in times of religious festivals.

The Egyptians had a strong belief in life after death, and when they buried their dead, they not only preserved the bodies with spices, they also often buried all that they would need in the next life. Many of these tombs have been found, and they show us what life was like in those days.

Canaanite religion

The Canaanites, who were already living in the land God had promised to the Jews, had a very different religion from them. Instead of worshipping one God, they had a number of gods and goddesses. We find some of them like El and Dagon, Baal, Astarte and Anath mentioned in the Old Testament. They made idols which were supposed to look like these gods, and prayed to them in their temples and on hills called high places. They thought that just as people marry and have children, these gods and goddesses married and produced the crops if they were worship-

These metal figurines found on an excavation site in Israel were probably linked with idol worship.

Gold Canaanite jewellery. The pendant may have been a symbol of the goddess Astarte.

The ziggurat of Ur was built around 2000BC by the king. It was dominated by a temple to the moon god.

A clay model of a sheep's liver from Babylonia inscribed as a guide to diviners.

The sun-god tablet showing a king of Babylon about 870BC worshipping in the shrine of the sun-god.

ped in the right way. If not, there would be bad harvests, drought and even famine.

Their worship was often cruel and immoral. Sometimes they would even sacrifice their own children to their gods, and their religion became so horrible that God punished them by allowing his people to take over their land. Unfortunately the Israelites never really got rid of these other religions. They were always trying to mix them up with worshipping the Lord. There were even some kings – and queens, like Jezebel – who encouraged this, something which caused great difficulties for those who wanted to worship the Lord as God. It became such a problem that in the end, God punished them too by letting *their* enemies conquer them and take them captive to Assyria and Babylonia.

Religion in Babylon and Assyria

The Babylonians worshipped a large number of gods and goddesses in many elaborate temples. Some had special tasks to perform. Adad was the god of storms, Sin the moon god, Nergal the god of plagues and diseases, while Ishtar was the goddess of love, and so on.

They believed that the king represented a god, while at the same time being chief priest, but they had many other priests and priestesses to help conduct their services and festivals.

The Assyrians borrowed a great deal of their religion from Babylon, although the names of the gods and goddesses were often different. The king represented the chief god, Ashur, but there were many others as well.

Roman and Greek religions

The Romans and Greeks shared a number of gods and goddesses, like Mars the god of war and Venus the goddess of love, although they were often worshipped

The ruins of the Temple of Apollo at Didyma in Turkey show clearly the impressive size of these ancient places of worship.

270

A sculptured head of the Greek god Zeus, believed to be the ruler of the gods on Mount Olympus.

A Roman house shrine. Most households had their own gods who, they believed, watched over the family.

A Roman relief showing a procession to sacrifice to the gods.

The Parthenon in Athens, a temple to the Greek gods, built in the 5th century BC.

A statue of the Greek goddess Artemis at Ephesus, where Paul's preaching let to a riot by her followers.

under different names. However, by the time the New Testament was written, many of these older religions had lost their popularity, although they were still practised in places. At Lystra, because they healed a lame man, Barnabas was thought to be Zeus, the chief god, and Paul was thought to be Hermes, his messenger (Acts 14:8–18). At Ephesus the worshippers of Artemis strongly objected to the apostles' preaching (Acts 19:23–41). Many of the people had gone over to newer religions, some with secret services and mysterious worship. The emperor himself also expected to be worshipped, which was impossible for Jews or Christians who believed that there was only one God.

One of the problems which early Christians faced was the fact that almost every social activity involved worshipping pagan gods. If a friend invited you to dinner, you had to eat meat sacrificed to idols. If you joined a club, you had to go through pagan ceremonies.

The Romans did not really mind how many gods people worshipped, but not all religions were officially allowed. Christianity was not a permitted religion. At first this did not matter as the authorities did not distinguish Christians from Jews, who were allowed to worship in their own way. However, as more and more non-Jews joined the church, Christianity was seen as a new religion, and because Christians would not worship the emperor, a dangerous one. It took the Romans nearly 300 years to see that the Christian faith was not a political threat, and in the meantime many Christians were imprisoned and put to death.

HEALTH AND SANITATION

Disease was widespread in the ancient world, and people suffered from illnesses that are well known to us today. Sometimes the sicknesses are hard to recognise, due to difficulties in translating or understanding the original languages, but many others can be diagnosed quite readily from the descriptions supplied in the Bible.

Because of the widespread nature of disease, health was valued greatly, and it was often thought of as the most important of all earthly blessings. Health does not just mean that there is no disease present, but that the various parts of the body are working together in harmony to produce an active and vigorous person who can lead a creative and enjoyable life.

Sanitation, from the Latin word *sanitas*, meaning 'health', is a word used to describe ways by which health can be safeguarded and sickness prevented. For example, a serious disease known as typhus, which can spread more easily among people in overcrowded places that are dirty and have little fresh air, can disappear completely when people live in clean, roomy houses. Sanitation also involves the careful control of human waste, so as to prevent water and food from becoming contaminated and dangerous to health. Good sanitation is an important form of preventive medicine.

Crowded housing in the Kidron Valley, Jerusalem.

Illnesses

Eye infections

Eye infections were very common in Bible lands, with infants being frequent victims. Flies would land on their faces and discharge infection into the eyes to produce an irritating condition known as ophthalmia. Often this developed to the point where the child became either partly or completely blind. Another infectious eye disease known as trachoma may even have afflicted the Apostle Paul for a short time (Acts 9:8, 18). When the germs invade the eyes they cause a thick crust to form over the edges of the eyelids, which are usually already badly inflamed, making them stick together. In the case of Paul, after the hard crust had fallen off, he still had some difficulty in seeing, probably

Modern missionaries often work in co-operation with the government to offer health care. This patient in Bhutan is receiving eye treatment.

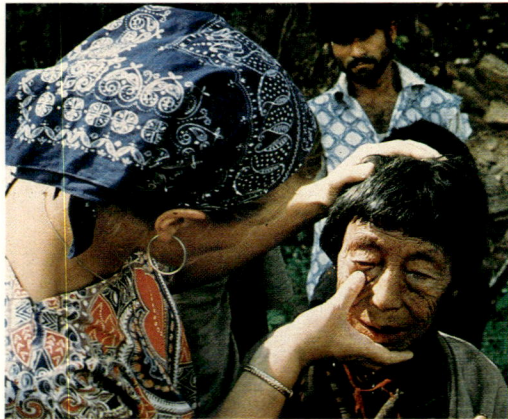

because the corneas had been scarred. After that time he wrote his letters to the Christian churches in large script (Galatians 6:11).

There is also a form of blindness that can spread like an epidemic: it is caused by a gonorrhoea germ that results in a severe blinding inflammation of the eyes. This may have been the cause of the blindness that overtook the Syrian forces in the days of Elisha (2 Kings 6:18).

A relief showing a blind harpist, from an Egyptian tomb of the time of King Tutankhamun.

Worms

Worms in the intestines caused much illness among the people of eastern countries in Bible times, as they do today. One of the most common worms producing such ailments is the roundworm, which can grow as long as sixteen inches inside the bowels. If it interlocks with others, it can result in a serious blockage of the intestines which may cause the patient to vomit some of the worms. Perhaps Herod Agrippa I died from some such ailment (Acts 12:21–23). Tapeworms also resulted sometimes, when people ate poorly cooked meat containing the infecting organisms.

Drinking water containing dirt and other forms of pollution was another way in which people could become ill. For example, if while drinking water, one swallowed a tiny worm about 5mm long, it could cause swellings to arise in such places as the lungs, liver, heart and brain, often causing death. Another disease caused by a worm is called bilharziasis. It is still found in some countries and it affects the abdominal organs, causing swellings and sharp pains. Walking

barefoot could result in a hookworm infection of the small intestine. The organism would enter the body through cracks or sores on the feet and produce an illness marked by tiredness and a shortage of iron in the blood.

Since all these worms live in the soft tissues of the body, there is no means of proving their existence in the past just by examining ancient skeletons. But because the conditions under which they flourished have existed for many centuries, the diseases themselves would be of early origin also. This is also true of such sicknesses as malaria, cholera, typhoid fever, hepatitis, and dysentery, to name just a few.

Bubonic plague

There is an excellent description in 1 Samuel 5:9 of an outbreak of bubonic plague, the dreaded 'black death' of the Middle Ages. This fearsome disease is carried by the rat flea, which bites human beings. Painful glandular swellings arise in the armpits and groin, and the patient can die with a fever in 24 hours. The disease spreads quickly from one inhabited place to another, and was one of the terrors of the ancient world.

Skin diseases

Another dreaded disease was leprosy, of which there are now two main varieties. The Biblical form was possibly lepromatous leprosy, in which patches of skin lose their feeling, ulcers arise on the legs, and a pale patch appears in various places on the bodies of sufferers. The priest confirmed the ailment (Leviticus 13:3), and the victims were compelled to live by themselves in deserted places, so as not to spread the infection. They survived by begging food from travellers, and in the time of Christ some of them moved to the outskirts of cities to beg (Luke 17:12).

Diseases that are actually quite different sometimes look alike in the early stages, and when the priest was examining a suspected leprosy patient, he had to be certain that he was not dealing with some other less serious skin disease such as ringworm, psoriasis, impetigo, or eczema, which existed in ancient times but which did not require the patient to be isolated.

Leprosy sufferers come for treatment to an open air clinic in Bhutan.

Source of the River Jordan. River water may look clean but it can contain pollution and is usually not safe for drinking.

An illustration from a French 14th century manuscript depicting Christ raising the dead, making the lame walk and the blind see.

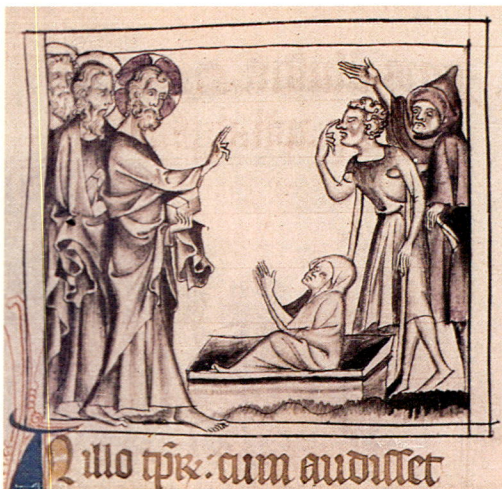

The Babylonian god Marduk: from a cylinder seal votive offering. Like other pagan nations, they trusted in offerings to the gods to cure sickness.

Boils were apparently a common infection, and King Hezekiah suffered so badly from one that he almost died. The painful swelling was relieved when the prophet Isaiah told him to apply a poultice made of figs to the boil (2 Kings 20:7). Some writers have suggested that Job's boils were actually smallpox, a virus disease resulting in a rash and blister-like swellings covering the entire body. The sufferer feels very ill, and untreated cases can die rapidly. Vaccination has now brought this disease under control, but in Bible days it was a very serious affliction indeed.

Other diseases

Social diseases such as syphilis were present in the East some two thousand years before Christ was born. Syphilis, an infectious disease which is spread through sexual contact, may have been the 'botch of Egypt' mentioned in Deuteronomy 28:27, while gonorrhoea, another disease of the reproductive organs, may have been the 'issue' of Leviticus 22:4. Syphilis sometimes became epidemic, and a probable instance of this is recorded in Numbers 25:9.

Cases of spinal tuberculosis can be seen in the hunchbacks of Leviticus 21:20, while tuberculosis of the lungs would probably result from under-nourishment among those who lived in large cities when food supplies were cut off by enemy forces (see Jeremiah 21:6–9). It seems possible that the fever affecting Peter's mother-in-law (Mark 1:30) was malaria, while the unusually heavy bleeding of the woman in Luke 8:43–44 was no doubt the result of a tumour of her womb. What is sometimes described in the Old Testament as 'consumption' was apparently a disease that brought with it a loss of weight and a general wasting-away of the body. Several illnesses could be covered by this one term, and this was no doubt the case in ancient Israel. Diseases spoken of in this way would include tuberculosis, malaria, typhoid fever, dysentery, and cholera.

It is very difficult to say if cancer in any of its forms was present in the ancient world. The only real way of knowing would be to discover a cancerous growth in old bones, unless one happened to be examining soft tissues that had been preserved in mummies. Even so, it has not been possible to discover the presence of cancer either in bones or mummy-tissues. It is possible, of course, that the disease is referred to by special terms in ancient languages, and because we still do not know the meaning of many medical words used by ancient peoples, we may have thought that they were describing some other ailment. Perhaps, therefore, we shall only be able to recognise the presence of cancer in ancient life when our knowledge of ancient Near Eastern languages improves.

Mental illness

Mental illness was a dreaded affliction in ancient times because of the very common opinion that it was caused by the presence of demons in the body. Thus when King David pretended to be mad during his stay at the court of the Philistine ruler Achish (1 Samuel 21:12–15), he was allowed to escape, since it was thought that, if he were killed there, his madness would come upon those who did the deed. In the book of Daniel, King Nebuchadnezzar of Babylon was overtaken by a rare mental disease which made him imagine he was a bull, and he lived on grass as best he could, finding his food away from the city. In the New Testament, demons are often said to possess people and bring about physical and mental diseases such as blindness (Matthew 12:22), insanity (Luke 8:26–36), dumbness (Matthew 9:32–33) and suicide attempts (Mark 9:22).

Medical treatment

As we now understand it, medical treatment by means of drugs and operations was not widely practised amongst the ancient Hebrews, perhaps because God was believed to be the one great Healer as well as the person who could send disease (see Exodus 15:26; Deuteronomy 28:60). Outside Israel, the ancient Sumerians had discovered the healing powers of many plants, including the ability of the leaves and bark of the willow tree to act as a primitive form of aspirin; resinous gums for various kinds of ointments, and the castor oil plant as a laxative. Later the Babylonians used these and other remedies, while the Egyptians developed mixtures of animal and vegetable substances in the treatment of diseases. All pagan nations in the ancient world relied heavily on magical spells and chants to make these medicines work.

Because of the difficulties in translating ancient medical documents, we do not know as much as we might about the herbal treatment given to sick people. No doubt the Hebrews used folk-remedies

also, since in the days of King Asa of Judah (911–869BC) 'physicians' were mentioned (2 Chronicles 16:12). One instance of the use of folk-medicine can be seen in the application of the fig poultice to King Hezekiah's boil, a practice familiar to the Canaanites also.

Surgery
The Hebrews did not practise surgery, although some other nations did. The Babylonians were good at setting fractures and performing various operations which included the removal of cataracts from eyes. The Egyptians also treated fractures and other conditions, and some of these cases are recorded in a very old papyrus case-book, probably written about

Aesculapius the Greek god of medicine, treating a patient while another waits his turn.

A Greek relief showing a physician treating a patient.

A plaque showing cupping vessels, forceps and other instruments from a Roman relief in a catacomb, Malta.

2700BC. Egyptian priest-physicians were the first to discover the way to put a dislocated jaw back into place: the same method is still used today. Aside from the treatment of small surface wounds, there is no indication that the Hebrews ever attempted to set fractures or reduce dislocations.

Dentistry

Dentistry was first mentioned as a profession by the Greek historian Herodotus, about 500BC, but we know that before that time some attempts had been made to treat decayed teeth or replace missing ones. There is evidence that the Mesopotamian priest-physicians used aromatic resins as fillings for cavities in teeth, and the Egyptians probably attempted some forms of dental work also, since they were worshipping a god of dentistry as far back as 2700BC. When the teeth of royal mummies were examined, it was discovered that artificial ivory or wooden teeth had been placed in position between healthy ones to fill gaps in the mouths of some people. Some writers have even stated that the Egyptians used gold for filling decayed teeth, but this is not really true since the gold used was actually gold leaf, and was meant for decorating the surface of the teeth, not for filling cavities. The practice of dentistry began properly with the Greeks, and continued among the Romans.

The people of Bible lands left no records describing dentistry, and probably the most that they did was to knock out aching teeth with a hammer or the end of a spear-shaft, or to cut and drain infected areas with a bronze knife or a sharp flint. Toothache from a broken tooth is mentioned in Proverbs (25:19RSV), while the 'skin' of the tooth to which Job referred (Job 19:20RSV) is the very thin layer of enamel that covers the hard dentine surrounding the pulp cavity of the tooth, and is not a true skin.

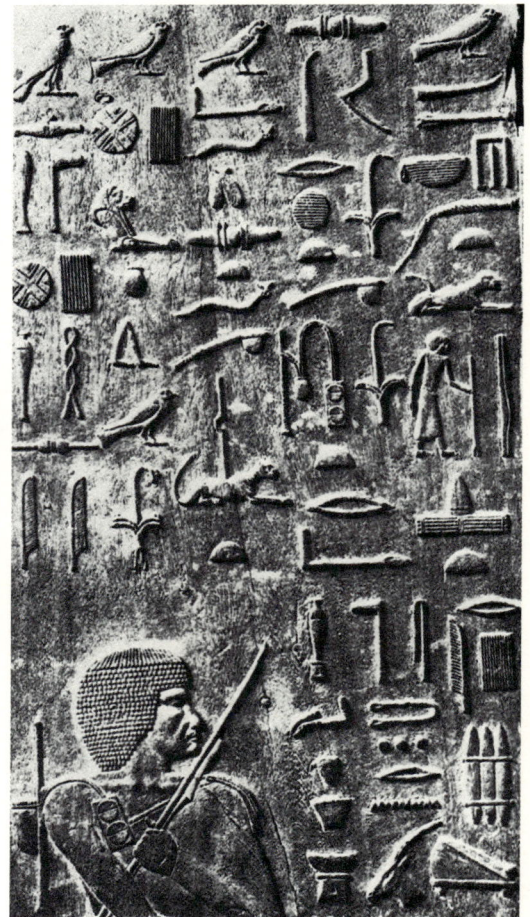

An Egyptian relief from 3000BC entitled 'Chief of the Toothers (Dentist) and the Physicians' advertises the services of a medical specialist.

Sanitation

Babylonia

Sewage systems consisting of drains and underground septic tanks were already well known to the Sumerians when Abraham was young. Archaeologists who dug at his birthplace, Ur of the Chaldees, uncovered the remains of houses going back to about 2500BC with indoor toilets connected to underground cesspools by means of pottery drains. Baths sunk into the floor were also in use at this period, and they too were connected by drains to an underground sewage system. When a royal palace in north-western Mesopotamia was unearthed in 1935, a bathroom was found containing two terra-cotta bathtubs, beside which were some simple toilets. The pottery drains that went deep down beneath the palace foundations were in excellent working condition some 3,500 years after being installed. All these sanitary systems worked on the same principle as the modern septic tank, with its central container and the various pipes leading from it providing a means of breaking down and getting rid of the waste.

Israel

Sanitation of this kind existed only in cities in Babylonia, while people who lived in tents were compelled to follow more primitive ways of disposing of human residue. The trouble was that if it was left exposed to insects, it could spread serious illnesses like poliomyelitis. This is why the Mosaic law instructed people that such residue should be buried by country-dwellers at all times (Deut. 23:13). The Israelites followed this practice during the wilderness wanderings as part of the community practice of cleanliness.

When, however, they arrived in the Promised Land and began to live in cities, they discovered that the Canaanites did not have the sanitary arrangements that some earlier Mesopotamian people had enjoyed. Cities like Jerusalem, built on solid rock, did not lend themselves to good indoor sanitation because it was too difficult to dig through the rock to install septic tanks. As a result, the city-dwellers had to throw their garbage and night-soil into the streets. Nearby ravines such as the Valley of the Sons of Hinnom in Jerusalem also served as places where rubbish, garbage and dead animals were dumped. Cities were thus serious sources of infection, especially in the heat of summer, and those who lived there normally moved out to the nearby countryside during the summer months to escape the overpowering smell of decaying material and to avoid infection.

When, by the time of Amos (about 750BC), the cities of Israel and Judah became overcrowded, sanitary problems were very serious indeed. Royal palaces

A bronze hip-bath from Ur, Assyria, dating from the 6th century BC.

Aqueducts were used in Assyria by the time of the Israelite exile. One can be seen on this relief from Nineveh.

seem to have had some form of indoor sanitation (Judges 3:24), but even by the time of Christ the outdoor lavatory was the most common means of relieving natural processes.

Baths

Public baths apparently originated in Greece among the Lacedaemonians, who are said to have invented a hot-air bath. Later, the Athenians had public baths as well as private ones, but by far the largest and most elaborate public baths were those built by the Romans. When aqueducts were built to carry water to Rome, a succession of emperors built huge public baths called *thermae*. The walls were resistant to moisture, and con-

Excavations of ancient Corinth have revealed both private and public baths.

tained flues through which hot air could travel to warm the cold water. A visitor could thus swim in cold or warm water, rest for a while in a heated room, or perspire in a vapour bath. Attendants were on hand to rub oils and ointments into the skins of the bathers.

The bodily exposure involved aroused opposition amongst the Jews of the first two centuries before Christ, for even though some were in favour of introducing Greek customs into Palestine, they associated nudity with immorality, as well as with the thefts and low conversation that took place in the Greek and Roman public baths.

The shortage of water in Palestine made public bathing in a building almost im-

possible unless there was a stream or a river at hand. King Herod (37–4BC) had a palace at Masada near the Dead Sea that contained a heated bath-house and an outdoor pool, and these were probably used by the last Jews to occupy the site between AD65 and AD72. At nearby Qumran, where the Dead Sea scrolls were found, there were several reservoirs which were probably used for public washings or baptisms, but only by the Essenes, the small religious sect that lived there. Public baths belonged to the age of the Greeks and Romans, and were found chiefly in the countries of these people, being unsuited to the hotter and drier climates of other Bible lands because of poor water supplies and evaporation problems.

Washing

Washing of the body by soaking in water, or by having water poured over the head and limbs, was more popular in Mesopotamia, Syria, Palestine and Egypt. Even so, washing of this kind did not take place with any regularity, especially among the poorer people and the desert nomads. Scents and ointments were often applied instead to the body when water was scarce, and to this day rose-water is used among Bedouin women for this purpose. Quite probably there were times in Israelite life when the High Priest had only one full bath each year, this being required by the Law before the ceremonies of the Day of Atonement were observed (Lev. 16:4).

Houses that had luxurious private baths were not normally part of the Israelite way of life, being reserved for royal palaces and the residences of high state officials, if they were found at all. As was the case with most other people of Bible lands, the Israelites did not carry water over long distances for purposes of washing, preferring instead to live close to where water was available. Only when the Romans occupied Palestine was water brought from a distance by aqueducts.

Where there was a stream or river nearby, the people would occasionally bathe in the waters, or else stand waist-deep and have water poured over them from a pottery jar. In general the ancient Hebrews preferred running water to that in a bath or pool, since the running stream or the water poured on their bodies carried away the dirt from the skin instead of allowing it to settle, as would have happened in a small enclosed pool. In addition, it was not necessary for the water to be absolutely pure to guarantee cleanliness as long as it was running from some source, since this movement would help to filter the water and prevent it from becoming stagnant, thus reducing the risk of infection through breaks in the skin.

In general, the hands and face were washed before being anointed, and the washing of the hands before meals in our Lord's time was regarded as an outward observance of the Jewish Law (Matt. 15:2). Hospitality demanded that there should be a supply of water for washing guests' feet (Genesis 18:4), a task normally undertaken by a servant (1 Sam. 25:41) and therefore a mark of humility when performed by Jesus (John 13:9–10). In Old Testament times it was a sign of mourning to leave the face and clothing unwashed (2 Sam. 12:20), but Jesus did not like this custom being carried over into the religious fasts that took place in his day. Instead, he ordered his followers to look neat and tidy during fast periods (Matt. 6:17), and to turn away in their hearts from evil thoughts and actions.

At shearing-time, lambs were washed to remove impurities from their wool (Song of Solomon 4:2), and at birth babies were washed before being given to the mother

This Greek water jar carries a scene showing women at a fountain house. The water can be seen gushing out of fountain heads into similar jars.

for feeding (Ezekiel 16:4). When a person died, the body was washed before the burial. Even though the body was normally buried soon after death, there would be less probability of infection occurring from a washed body than from a dirty one.

Shallow pottery basins used for washing parts of the body have been found at various places in Palestine by archaeologists. At Er-Zib, a pottery figurine showing a woman taking a bath in a large shallow bowl has been discovered. The object was made around 800BC, some fifty years before the time of the prophet Amos.

Ceremonial

Certain ceremonies related to health were part of the laws given by God to the Israelites. When a person felt cured of leprosy, he went to the priest to be examined, and if the disease had really disappeared he was ordered to offer sacrifices, wash his clothes, shave himself, and have a bath (Lev. 14:7–8). Then he had to live outside his tent for a week, after which he had to shave again and wash his clothes and his body before being accepted as clean. Whenever men or women had bodily discharges they were considered unclean, and they also made unclean whatever persons or things they touched. A ceremony of washing had to be followed before the unclean could be considered clean once more (Lev. 15:1–30).

The High Priest and his sons were washed with water before the great consecration ceremony (Lev. 8:6) to show that they had to be pure to work in the Lord's house. Parts of the burnt offering were also washed before being sacrificed by fire to God (Lev. 1:9, 13), since they too, were holy. Hebrew priests always washed their hands and feet before entering the sanctuary, to keep that place holy (Exod. 30:19–21). In Christ's time it was the custom to wash the hands before eating (Mark 7:3, 4), and this is now recognised as an excellent means of stopping various kinds of infection from spreading.

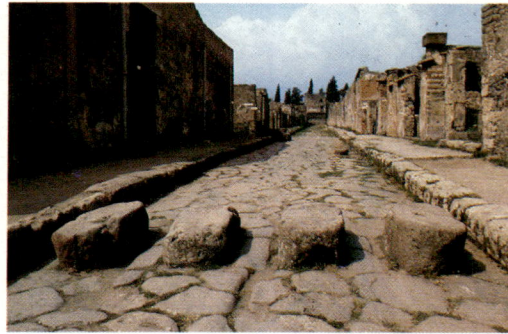

This street in Pompeii has stepping stones to enable pedestrians to avoid walking in the drainage. The spaces between the stones allowed wheels to pass.

This drawing showing Roman aqueducts testifies to the skill of their engineers and builders.

Prevention of disease

In the Old Testament the Hebrews were encouraged to prevent disease rather than treat it, so a good deal was said about personal and social cleanliness. Sources of infection, such as leprosy sufferers, were to be kept far away from other people so that they would not spread the disease, and similarly the Hebrews were forbidden to touch dead animals. The priests enforced laws of cleanliness, and were always consulted when such dreaded diseases as leprosy were suspected. Whenever the Hebrews had been in contact with any form of uncleanness, they were required to wash before being allowed to mix with people again. A very important law ordered the regular observance of the sabbath, or day of rest, so that the Israelites would worship God each seventh day, and by not doing any work at that time would give their bodies a chance to rest and regain energy.

Food laws

One way of preventing illness is to eat nourishing food, and the Law of Moses contained a list of rules which told the Israelites the foods that were fit to eat ('clean') and those that were not ('unclean'). Fruits and vegetables could be eaten readily, except the fruit of newly-planted trees. Animals that lived on vegetation were also suitable for food: animals that chewed the cud and had a parted hoof (Lev. 11:3–8).

All other animals were to be considered 'unclean' because they fed on dead flesh, on garbage, or on other things that could bring infection to the eater. They might also contain worms. The 'clean' animals had to be killed and drained of blood before being eaten. Any animal that had died naturally or had been killed by other animals was not to be eaten. The Hebrews were not allowed to eat fat, because it also could carry disease. Whenever fat was needed for cooking, olive oil was used instead of animal fat.

Just as there were 'unclean' animals, so there were 'unclean' birds also. These were the sort that fed on decaying flesh, or obtained their food from polluted rivers or lakes. 'Clean' birds, like 'clean' animals, were completely vegetarian in their diet. All fish that had fins and scales could be eaten, but a fish that had only one of these two requirements was regarded as 'unclean'. The only insect that could be eaten was the locust: this formed part of the wilderness diet of John the Baptist (Mark 1:6). Chocolate-covered locusts with their wings removed can still be bought in Arab bazaars in various parts of the Near East.

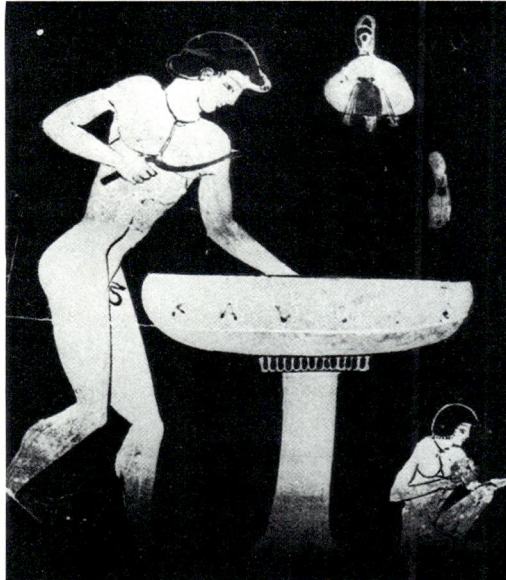

A Greek athlete washing. After scraping the oil and dust off his skin with the strigil in his right hand, he splashes himself with cold water.

The Greek Hippocrates who laid the foundations of modern medical teaching.

An ancient Egyptian ointment-box.

THE WORLD OF THE BIBLE

Part of the Middle East, seen from the Apollo spacecraft. Egypt and the Nile can be seen in the foreground, the Red Sea and the Sinai peninsula dominate the centre of the picture and the coastline of Palestine curves up north to the left. The Dead Sea can be seen and the Sea of Galilee to the north-west.

From earliest Bible times this area has been significant. Abraham travelled to Egypt from Canaan several times. His grandson, Jacob, and his sons resettled in Egypt because of famine in their homeland. Some 400 years later their descendants, now a whole nation, escaped from slavery under the Pharaohs. Led by Moses they left Egypt and journeyed on foot across the Sinai Peninsula. During their forty years wandering in this harsh, arid area they were given the Law at Mount Sinai. Eventually they travelled north into Canaan, crossing the River Jordan from the east. Throughout Old and New Testament times Palestine was the homeland of the nation of Israel and the centre of Bible events.

The holy city

Growth of the city

- Extent of Zion (the City of David)
- Extended under the Kings (1000—600BC)
- Extended after the Exile (500—400BC)
- Extended under Herod the Great (30BC—AD4)
- Added by Agrippa I (AD41—54)
- Pool

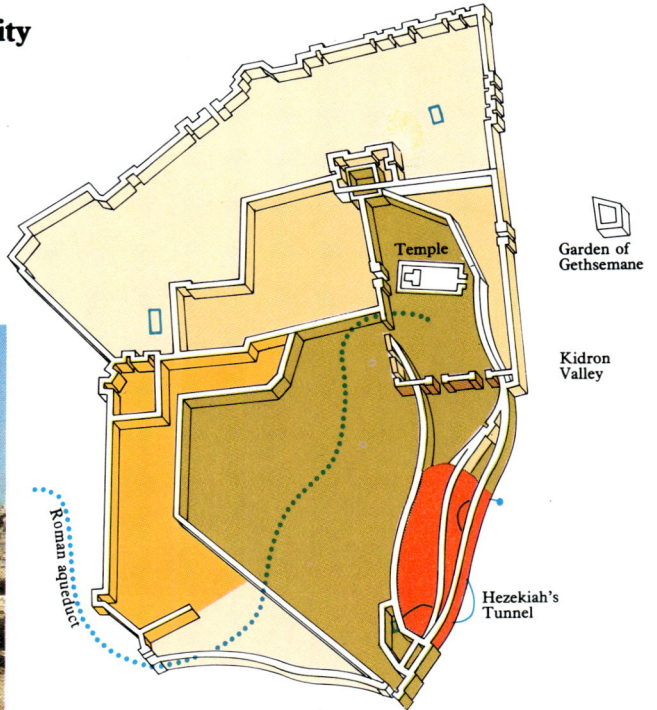

Temple

Garden of Gethsemane

Kidron Valley

Roman aqueduct

Hezekiah's Tunnel

A view of the modern city of Jerusalem.

Herod's Palace

?Calvary

Fortress of Antonia

Temple

Garden of Gethsemane

High Priest's house

?Upper Room

Jerusalem has been in existence since 3000BC at least. Its position on top of a hill made it a natural fortress. When the Israelites entered Canaan they did not take the city and it remained in the hands of a local tribe, the Jebusites, until the time of King David. He saw that it would be valuable as a capital and he and his men captured it by a surprise attack using a water shaft to gain access.

David and Solomon improved the city's fortifications and the Temple was built there during Solomon's reign. After his death, the kingdom was divided and the city became capital of Judah only.

Jerusalem was destroyed by the Assyrians in 587BC and the people carried into exile to Babylon. Seventy years later the Jews were allowed to return to their city and they rebuilt the Temple and, later, the city walls. The city was again invaded in the 2nd century BC by the Greeks and by the Romans in the 1st century BC. The Temple and fortifications were destroyed by the Romans in AD70.

Jerusalem has since been captured by various nations over the centuries and today is regarded as a sacred city by Jews, Christians and Muslims.

Jerusalem at the time of Jesus

The red line shows Jesus' movements from the Last Supper via the Garden of Gethsemane to his trial and crucifixion.

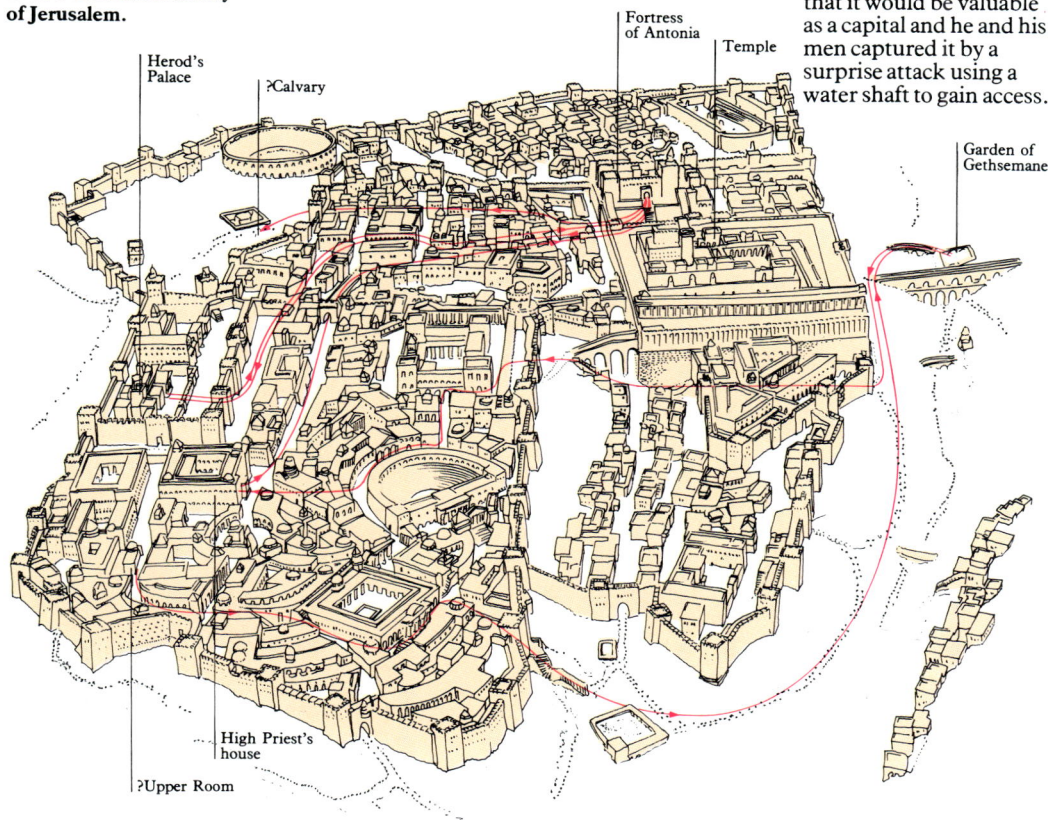

Timeline (top band, BC dates):

2700 2600 2500 2400 2300 2200 2100 2000 1900 1800 1700 1600 1500 1400 1300 1

Pyramids built

• Ur ziggurat built

• Isaac

Period of the Patriarchs

• Abraham leaves Ur for Canaan

• Jacob

• Joseph

• Jacob and family settle in Egypt

• King Hammurabi of Babylon's law code

• Pharaoh Rameses II

• Pharaoh Tutankhamun

The Exodus

Israelite conquest of Palestine

Period of the Judges

• Moses

• Joshua

• Israelites become slaves in Egypt

• Israelites enter the Promised Land

Gideon •

Samson

San

• Troy burned by the Greeks

— 1s of

Timeline (lower band, AD dates):

10 BC   0   10   20   30   40   50   60

• Birth of John the Baptist

• Death of Herod

• Birth of Jesus

The life of Jesus

• Baptism of Jesus

• Conversion of Paul

• Crucifixion and resurrection

• Paul's 1st missionary journey

• Paul's 2nd missionary journey

• Paul's 3rd missionary journey

Paul's imprisonment in Rome

Emperor Claudius

Emperor Nero

• Fall of Jerusalem

• Mas falls Rom

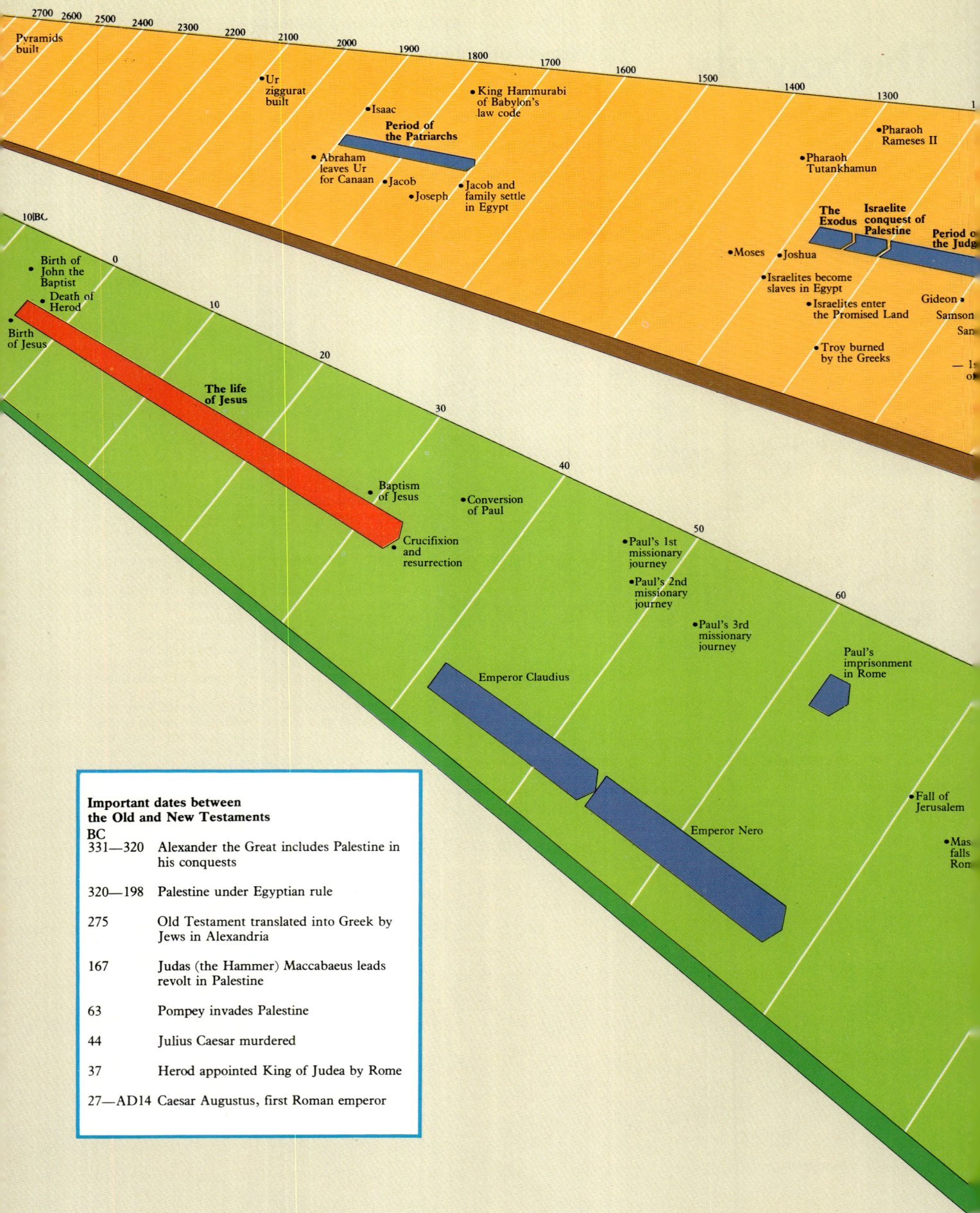

Important dates between the Old and New Testaments

BC

331—320 Alexander the Great includes Palestine in his conquests

320—198 Palestine under Egyptian rule

275 Old Testament translated into Greek by Jews in Alexandria

167 Judas (the Hammer) Maccabaeus leads revolt in Palestine

63 Pompey invades Palestine

44 Julius Caesar murdered

37 Herod appointed King of Judea by Rome

27—AD14 Caesar Augustus, first Roman emperor

Bible time chart

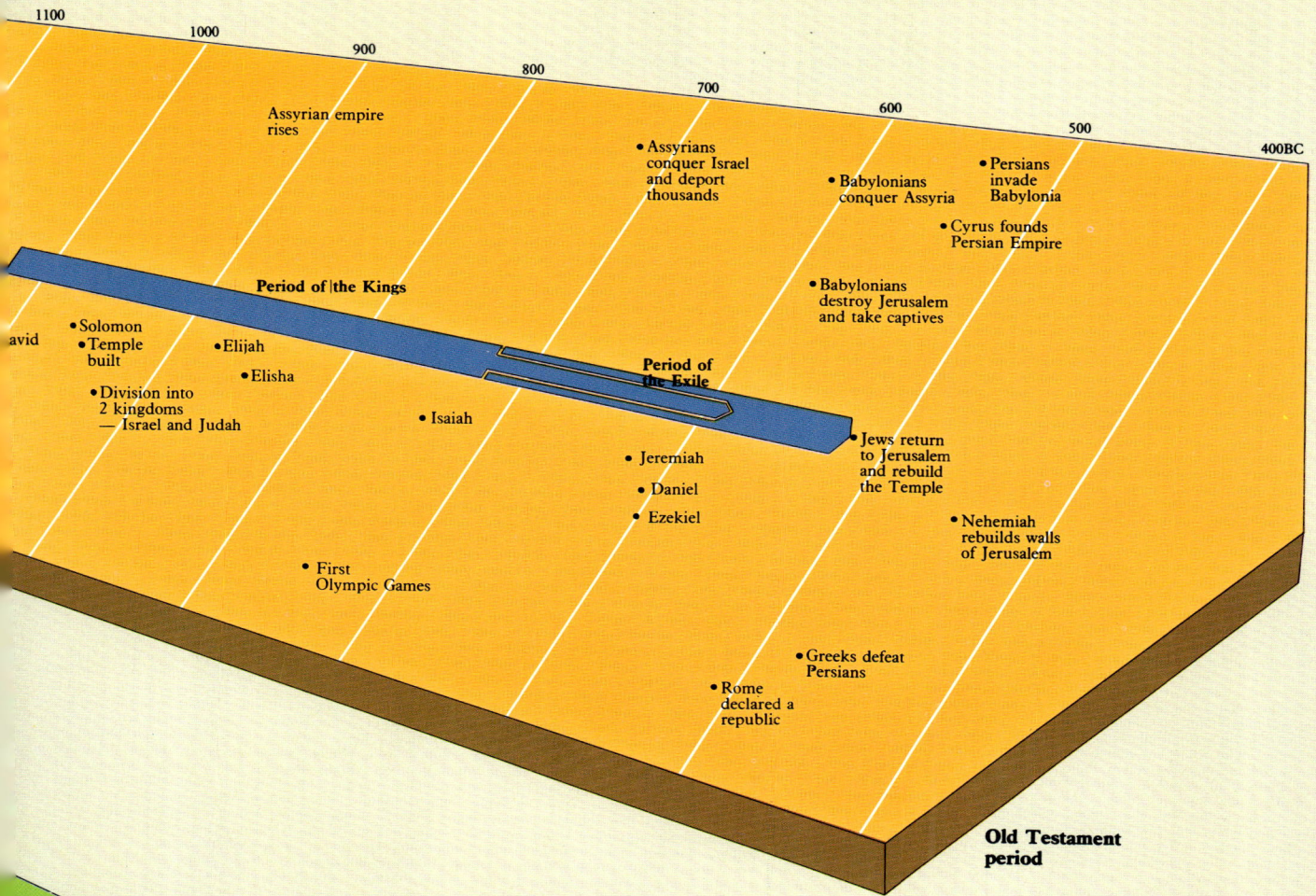

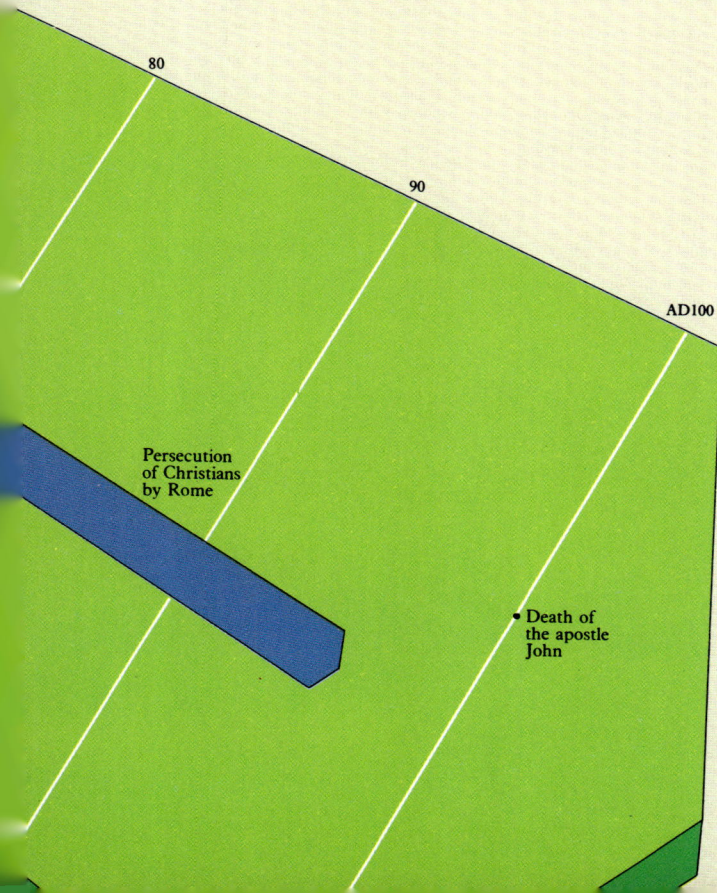

1100   1000   900   800   700   600   500   400BC

Assyrian empire rises

- Assyrians conquer Israel and deport thousands
- Babylonians conquer Assyria
- Persians invade Babylonia
- Cyrus founds Persian Empire
- Babylonians destroy Jerusalem and take captives

Period of the Kings

avid
- Solomon
- Temple built
- Elijah
- Elisha
- Division into 2 kingdoms — Israel and Judah
- Isaiah

Period of the Exile

- Jews return to Jerusalem and rebuild the Temple
- Jeremiah
- Daniel
- Ezekiel
- Nehemiah rebuilds walls of Jerusalem

- First Olympic Games

- Greeks defeat Persians
- Rome declared a republic

Old Testament period

80   90   AD100

New Testament period

Persecution of Christians by Rome

- Death of the apostle John

Israel in the Old Testament

Tyre
Dan
PHOENICIA
Merom • Hazor
Sea of Chinnereth
△ Mt Carmel
R. Kishon
Beth-shemesh
Plain of Megiddo
Endor
Dor
Shunem
Valley of Jezreel
Megiddo
Jezreel
△ Mt Gilboa
• Ramoth-gilead
Dothan
Jabesh-gilead
Tishbe
Br. Cherith
ISRAEL
Samaria
Tirzah
Zarethan
R. Jabbok
△ Mt Ebal
Succoth
Mahanaim
△ Shechem
△ Mt Gerizim
R. Jordan
The Arabah
Shiloh
Joppa
Bethel
Michmash
Plain of Sharon
Ai
Gilgal
Rabbah
The Great Sea
Gath
Gibeon
Jericho
AMMON
Gezer
Gibeah
Jerusalem
Mt Pisgah △ △
Heshbon
PHILISTIA
Ekron
Br. Kidron
Mt Nebo
Ashdod
Bethlehem
Ashkelon
JUDAH
Wilderness of Judah
Salt Sea
Gaza
Lachish
Hebron
En-gedi
R. Arnon
• City of Moab
Gath
MOAB
Beer-sheba
• Kir-hareseth

Israel in the Promised Land

Allocation of tribal areas after the conquest

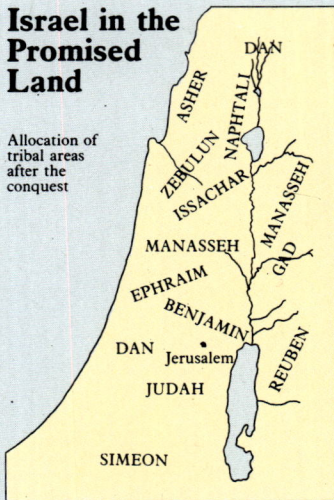

DAN
ASHER
NAPHTALI
ZEBULUN
ISSACHAR
MANASSEH
MANASSEH
EPHRAIM
GAD
BENJAMIN
DAN
Jerusalem
REUBEN
JUDAH
SIMEON

The divided kingdom

The nation of Israel divided into two after the death of King Solomon

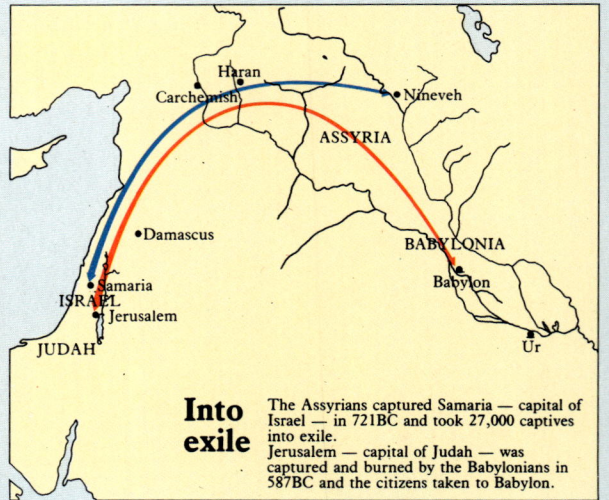

SYRIA
SIDONIA
BASHAN
GILEAD
ISRAEL
Samaria
AMMON
Jerusalem
PHILISTIA
JUDAH
MOAB
EDOM

Haran
Carchemish
• Nineveh
ASSYRIA
• Damascus
BABYLONIA
ISRAEL
Samaria
Babylon
Jerusalem
JUDAH
Ur

Into exile

The Assyrians captured Samaria — capital of Israel — in 721BC and took 27,000 captives into exile.
Jerusalem — capital of Judah — was captured and burned by the Babylonians in 587BC and the citizens taken to Babylon.

Palestine in New Testament times

Sidon

Tyre

PHOENICIA

Mt Hermon

Where Peter openly stated his belief that Jesus was God

Traditional site of transfiguration

Caesarea Philippi

Wedding at Cana. Jesus' first miracle

- ◉ Cities of the Decapolis
- ▣ Fortresses
- ⋯ Political boundaries

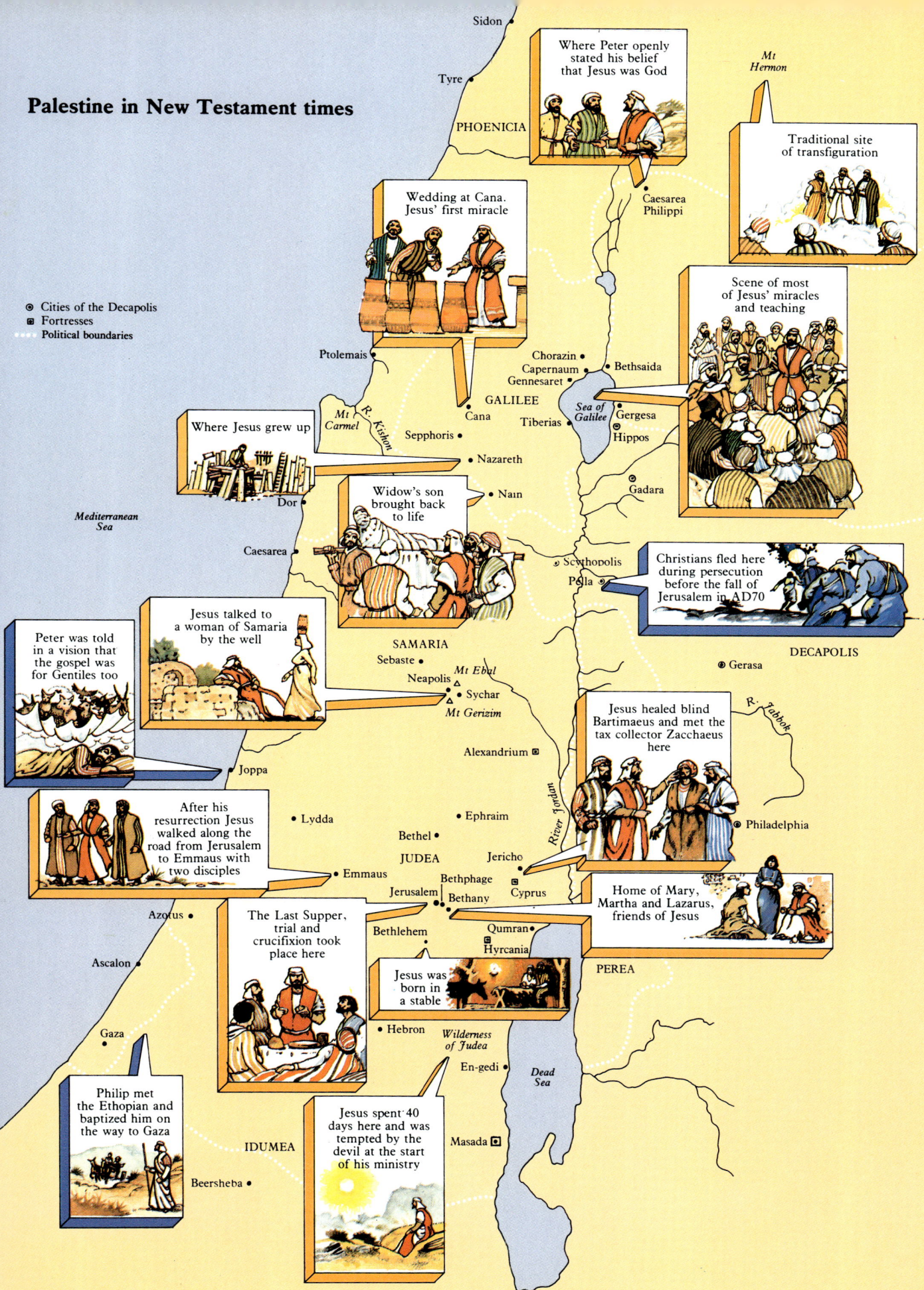

Scene of most of Jesus' miracles and teaching

Ptolemais

Chorazin
Capernaum • Bethsaida
Gennesaret

GALILEE

Cana

Sea of Galilee

Mt Carmel

R. Kishon

Sepphoris

Tiberias • Gergesa
Hippos ◉

Where Jesus grew up

Nazareth

Dor

Nain

Gadara ◉

Widow's son brought back to life

Mediterranean Sea

Caesarea

Scythopolis ◉
Pella ◉

Christians fled here during persecution before the fall of Jerusalem in AD70

DECAPOLIS

Peter was told in a vision that the gospel was for Gentiles too

Jesus talked to a woman of Samaria by the well

SAMARIA

Sebaste •

Gerasa ◉

Neapolis • *Mt Ebal* △
△ Sychar
Mt Gerizim △

R. Jabbok

Jesus healed blind Bartimaeus and met the tax collector Zacchaeus here

Alexandrium ▣

Joppa

After his resurrection Jesus walked along the road from Jerusalem to Emmaus with two disciples

Lydda •

Ephraim •

Bethel •

Philadelphia ◉

JUDEA

Jericho

River Jordan

Emmaus •

Bethphage

Azotus •

Jerusalem •• Bethany

Cyprus

Home of Mary, Martha and Lazarus, friends of Jesus

The Last Supper, trial and crucifixion took place here

Bethlehem

Qumran •
Hyrcania ▣

Ascalon •

Jesus was born in a stable

PEREA

Gaza •

Hebron •

Wilderness of Judea

En-gedi •

Dead Sea

Philip met the Ethopian and baptized him on the way to Gaza

IDUMEA

Jesus spent 40 days here and was tempted by the devil at the start of his ministry

Masada ▣

Beersheba •

The world of the New Testament

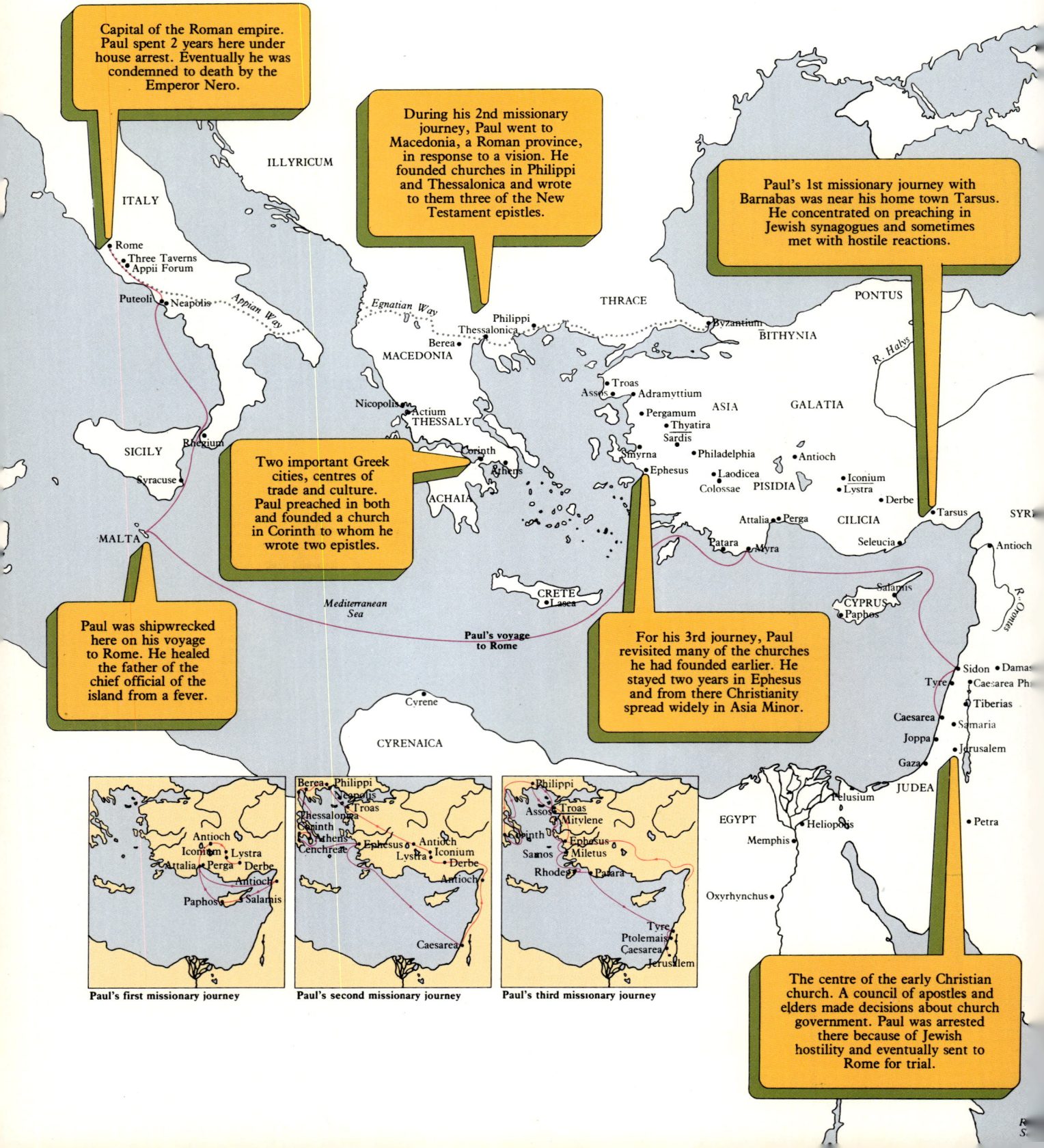

Capital of the Roman empire. Paul spent 2 years here under house arrest. Eventually he was condemned to death by the Emperor Nero.

During his 2nd missionary journey, Paul went to Macedonia, a Roman province, in response to a vision. He founded churches in Philippi and Thessalonica and wrote to them three of the New Testament epistles.

Paul's 1st missionary journey with Barnabas was near his home town Tarsus. He concentrated on preaching in Jewish synagogues and sometimes met with hostile reactions.

Two important Greek cities, centres of trade and culture. Paul preached in both and founded a church in Corinth to whom he wrote two epistles.

Paul was shipwrecked here on his voyage to Rome. He healed the father of the chief official of the island from a fever.

For his 3rd journey, Paul revisited many of the churches he had founded earlier. He stayed two years in Ephesus and from there Christianity spread widely in Asia Minor.

The centre of the early Christian church. A council of apostles and elders made decisions about church government. Paul was arrested there because of Jewish hostility and eventually sent to Rome for trial.

ILLYRICUM

ITALY

Rome
Three Taverns
Appii Forum
Puteoli   Neapolis
Appian Way
Egnatian Way

THRACE

PONTUS

BITHYNIA
R. Halys

Philippi
Thessalonica
Berea
MACEDONIA

Byzantium

Troas
Assos   Adramyttium
Pergamum
Thyatira
Sardis
Smyrna

ASIA

GALATIA

Antioch
Philadelphia
Laodicea
Colossae   PISIDIA
Ephesus

Iconium
Lystra
Derbe

Nicopolis
Actium
THESSALY

Corinth
Athens

ACHAIA

Attalia   Perga
Patara   Myra

CILICIA

Tarsus   SYR

Seleucia

Antioch

SICILY
Rhegium
Syracuse

MALTA

Mediterranean
Sea

CRETE
Lasea

Paul's voyage
to Rome

Salamis
CYPRUS
Paphos

R. Orontes

Sidon   Damas
Tyre   Caesarea Ph
Tiberias
Caesarea   Samaria
Joppa
Gaza   Jerusalem

JUDEA

Cyrene

CYRENAICA

Pelusium
EGYPT   Heliopolis
Memphis

Oxyrhynchus

Petra

Paul's first missionary journey

Antioch
Iconium   Lystra   Derbe
Attalia   Perga
Antioch
Paphos   Salamis

Paul's second missionary journey

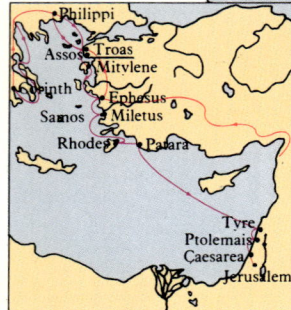

Berea   Philippi
Neapolis
Troas
Thessalonica
Corinth   Athens   Ephesus   Antioch
Cenchreae   Lystra   Iconium   Derbe
Antioch
Caesarea

Paul's third missionary journey

Philippi
Assos   Troas
Mitylene
Corinth   Ephesus
Samos   Miletus
Rhodes   Patara
Tyre
Ptolemais
Caesarea
Jerusalem

R
S

Index

Page numbers in **bold type** refer to pages with pictures of the subject. Numbers in *italic type* refer to maps.

Acknowledgments

The photographs in this
book are reproduced by
kind permission of the
following:
Barbara Anderson 106 bottom, 210
bottom, 265 centre.
Ashmolean Museum 196 centre
left.
Michael Baughen 50,63 top left and
bottom right.
BBC Hulton Picture Library 177
bottom right.
Bible Scene 156 centre right.
Bible Society 4, 14 top and centre,
31 top left.
Bodleian Library 24 bottom, 27
top, 28 bottom left, 30 both, 31 top
right, 235 bottom, 249 centre right, 274
top.
British Museum 7 left, 9 right and
bottom, 10 top left, 13, 16, 18, 21,
22, 33, 44 all, 46 top, 61 centre right,
63 bottom left, 66 left, 68 bottom left,
74 top right, 76 bottom, 82, 84 top
centre and right, 90 right, 91 centre
right, 92 bottom left, 133 centre
group except mosaic, 139 centre, 149,
150 centre left and bottom, 152 left,
153 left, 154 right and left, 160, 167,
170/171 centre bottom, 174, 177
centre right and left, 180
bottom right, 188 centre, 193, 194
both, 198 centre and bottom left, 199
top right, 201, 207 bottom right, 208
centre left, 212, 214 top and bottom
right, centre left, 220 bottom left, 221
bottom, 223 top right, 224, 225
centre, 229 top left, 230 bottom, 234
top, 236, 237 top, 238 top all, 243
bottom, 244 right, 254 top right and
centre, 269 centre both, 275 bottom
left, 277 both, 279.
British Library 28 right, 31 bottom.
George Cansdale 136 centre, 140
right, 141 bottom left.
J. Allan Cash 15, 56 (left), 83 top
left, 137 right.
Peter Clayton 172, 196 bottom left
and right, 199 centre right, 202, 203
top, 204/205, 206 (centre), 207 top
left, 214 centre, 207 top left, 214
centre right, 215, 217 centre, 221
right, 222 bottom, 227 centre, 231
right, 243 top, 244 left and bottom,
245, 256 top.
Council of Christians and Jews 72
top, 240 bottom right, 246 both, 247
top, 248 top centre, 252 right, 260,
261 bottom, 262 both, 263 top, 266
bottom left.
Tony Deane 132 bottom, 133 bottom
138 centre right and left, 141
bottom right, 142 bottom right, 143
left.
C. M. Dixon 68 centre left, 231
bottom.
Elisabeth Photo Library 115 top,
209.
Gordon Gray title page, 1, 6, 7 right,
11 all except top left, 12, 19 bottom
left, 20, 23 both, 24 top and centre, 25
top, 36, 41 right, 43 bottom — 3, 45
left, 46 bottom right, 47 both, 48
both, 49, 52 bottom, 54 bottom, 56
right, 57 centre right, 58 centre right
and bottom, 59 centre left, 60 top, 61
bottom left, 62 left, 63 centre left, 67,
74 centre, 83 top right, 88, 103 left,
107 top right and centre left, 108
bottom right, 111, 112, 114 right,
116, 117 all, 122 top, 129 top left and
bottom, 134, 136 right, 140 left, 141
centre, 142 bottom left, 143 right,
145, 159, 164 top, 166, 179, 180
centre right, 181, 190 centre both, 210
centre, 218 centre, 219 top right, 222
left, 223 bottom right, 226 left, 230
centre, 231 top, 240 top, 248 bottom
left, 252 left, 254 centre, 257, 263
centre, 265 bottom, 266 centre left,
266/267 centre, 269 bottom, 271, 273
bottom, 276 top left both. **British
Museum** 46 centre, 75 all, 79 all, 80
all, 83 centre right, 84 bottom left and
centre, 89 centre right, 91 all except
centre right, 92 all except bottom left,
93 all, 94 both, 96 all except bottom
left, 268 bottom left, 269 top centre,
281 bottom. **Ephesus Museum** 270
top right and bottom left.
Hannibal, Greece 233 top right,
234 centre.
David Harris 199 left.
Nigel Hepper 9 centre, 10 below left,

11 top left, 26 right, 27 bottom, 40, 42
bottom, 45 right, 46 bottom left, 59
top right, 77, 103 right, 104 centre,
118 bottom left and right, 119-121 all,
122 bottom, 123-124 all, 126-128 all,
129 right top and centre, 130, 132
right both, 157 bottom right, 184
bottom, 206 bottom, 216 centre both,
217 bottom left, 220 top left, 232
bottom.
Michael Holford 177 top.
Elrose Hunter 26 left, 58 centre left,
191, 218 right.
Alan Hutchison Library 54 top, 64,
65, 76 centre, 87, 89 left, 90 left, 102,
107 bottom, 131 bottom, 268 bottom
right.
Iraq Cultural Centre 99, 152
bottom, 206 top, 269 top right.
Leprosy Mission 272 left, 273 top.
Mansell Collection 29 both, 32
bottom, 118 centre right, 150 centre
right, 154 centre, 155, 182/183, 184
top left, 187 bottom right, 188 left,
241, 254 top left, 255, 256 bottom,
264.
Paul Marsh 216 bottom.
**Medical Illustration Support
Services Ltd** 275 centre right, 281
centre right.
Metropolitan Museum, New York
214 bottom left.
NASA 282.
The National Gallery, London 205
right, 250, 259 left.
National Museum, Athens 226
centre right.
Adrian Neilson 60 bottom right, 106
top, 107 top left, 108 all except
bottom right, 140 bottom, 131 top and
centre, 135 both, 136 left, 137 left,
139 right, 144 bottom, 148, 164
bottom, 180 bottom left, 185, 207
right, 211, 213 both, 261 top, 265 top,
268 centre. **Haifa Maritime
Museum** 168, 184 top right. **Haifa
Music Museum** 237 bottom all.
Megiddo Museum 170 top, 208
bottom. **The Negev Museum,
Beersheba** 89 bottom right, 258. **Tel
Aviv H'Aretz Museum** 153 right,
182 left.
Palestine Exploration Fund 249
centre right.
Canon J.C. Phillips 38.
David Porter 28 top left.
David Rennie 8, 10 bottom right, 52
centre, 61 bottom right, 100 top, 104
bottom, 169, 234 bottom left, 283.
Gill Rennie 2, 5, 19 left both, 25
bottom, 42 top, 43 bottom — 1, 2, 4,
5, 52 top, 57 left, 58 top right, 59
centre right, 60 centre and bottom
left, 66 right, 72 bottom, 78, 84
bottom right, 101 all, 105, 109 all,
113 both, 114 left, 115 bottom, 133
centre top right, 156 left, 157 centre
and bottom left, 170 centre left, 180
centre left, 198 bottom right, 203
centre, 228 centre, 232 centre, 233
bottom, 247 bottom, 248 top left, 266
centre right, 269 top left, 270 bottom
right, 278 both, 280 centre. **Agora
Museum** 158. **Isthmia Museum,
Corinth** 229 right, 233 centre.
**Museum of Roman Civilisation,
Rome** 96 bottom, 147, 239 right, 270
centre both. **National
Archaeological Museum, Athens**
177 centre bottom, 225 top, 232 top.
**Rijksmuseum Van Oudheden,
Leiden** 147 top right, 170/171 centre,
234 bottom right, 272 right.
J. Ruffle 147 bottom right.
Scala 219 bottom, 267 top right.
Science Museum 197 centre left.
Shell Photographic Library 144
bottom left.
Ronald Sheridan 9 top left, 14
bottom, 17, 19 right both, 35, 41
centre, 43 top both, 62 right, 71, 170
centre, 174 top right, 178, 238
bottom, 239 left, 240 bottom left, 263
bottom.
Jamie Simson endpapers, 73
bottom, 100 bottom, 267 bottom
right.
Swiss National Tourist Office 34.
Tap Service (Greece) 200 top left.
Margaret Wallace 156 bottom
right, 157 top, 186.
**Wellcome Institute for the History
of Medicine** 274 bottom, 275 bottom
right, 276 bottom right, 280 bottom,
281 centre left.
Werner Forman Archive 68 right,
top and bottom.
P. Widdison 259 centre and right.
Roger Wood 57 bottom right, 110.
Wycliffe Bible Translators 39.